AF344603

HARVARD ECONOMIC STUDIES
VOLUME XC

Federal Control of Entry into Air Transportation

LUCILE SHEPPARD KEYES

HARVARD UNIVERSITY PRESS

Cambridge, Massachusetts

1951

To

Morris Sheppard

Acknowledgments

The author is deeply indebted to Professor Edward H. Chamberlin, under whose direction the present work was originally prepared as a doctoral dissertation, and to whose criticisms and suggestions must be attributed a very large part of whatever value this study may possess. Thanks are also due to Professor George P. Baker, whose suggestions have been of particular help in connection with immediate problems of national policy in the air-transport field.

CONTENTS

INTRODUCTION

THE PURPOSE of this study is to analyze and evaluate the policies of the Federal Government toward the entry and exit of firms engaged in the air-transportation business. The analysis will be in terms of economic performance: an attempt will be made to evaluate these policies from the point of view of their effect on the functioning of the controlled markets. Political and ethical considerations will be largely ignored; therefore, the study cannot and is not intended to provide final answers to the questions of policy that are involved. However, in so far as economic performance is regarded as one element to be considered in the formulation or evaluation of policy, this aspect of policy must be examined on its own terms as a necessary preliminary to policy determination, so as to avoid fruitless confusion.

Although the present inquiry is concerned with a limited field of economic activity, the same general problems of market performance arise throughout the economic collectivity, and the tools of analysis found useful here should be capable of much more general use. This inquiry may therefore serve to suggest a pattern for investigations in other fields.

Since this study is concerned with the analysis and evaluation of policies in terms of economic performance, it is to theoretical economics that we must look to provide us with the necessary analytical apparatus. This apparatus, we find, has been greatly altered and refined in recent years, so that the models generally used in market analyses have been demonstrated to be defective. It will be useful, therefore, to review the major features of the recent progress in economic theory, the policy recommendations that have been based on analysis by the tools at hand being pointed out at each stage. This review (Part I of this study) is intended to serve two main purposes: (1) to explain why the impact of regulation on the economic performance of the affected markets is not here analyzed in terms of market categories such as "monopoly" and "pure competition" and (2) to clarify the nature and origins of the concepts that will be used in the present study.

PART I

THEORETICAL GROUNDWORK

CHAPTER I

PARTICULAR EQUILIBRIUM THEORY

TRADITIONAL THEORY

BEFORE THE DEVELOPMENT of the theory of monopolistic competition, market analysis was largely limited to the classification of industries by means of two rigidly distinct categories: an industry was said to be either monopolistic or competitive. The first category was usually employed where the industry was composed of one or a few firms; the second, where many firms were included. Relations among firms in the same industry were thus in general reduced to one of two standard patterns, and relations among firms in different industries were ignored. The industry itself, although its real significance lay in the implication of perfect substitutability among the products of the included firms, was usually vaguely defined in terms of a "common-sense" criterion of technological or even terminological similarity of product.

It was demonstrated that, under conditions of pure competition, and with perfectly free entry and exit, not only would investment in the industry be adjusted to the optimum level, but also each industry's output would be produced at maximum "technological" efficiency. That is, investment equilibrium would be such that demand price would be just equal to supply price for the amount of the commodity that this investment would produce, and each firm within the industry would be producing an output corresponding to the minimum point on its long-run average-cost curve.[1]

---

[1] This statement should be, and sometimes was, qualified to take into account the fact that a perfect achievement of the optimum might be made impossible by cost conditions such that the number of firms could not be perfectly adjusted to demand.

It was argued that, if factors are perfectly free to move into and out of any particular use, equilibrium will exist only when demand price is exactly equal to supply price. A further argument was needed to show why, under conditions of pure competition, this equilibrium should necessarily involve the achievement of maximum "technological" efficiency. The key to this result lies in the fact that pure competition implies an infinitely elastic sales curve for each individual firm. When equilibrium has been attained on the factor market, it is necessary that the average-cost curve of each firm be tangent to its average-revenue curve. (This is true not only of the "marginal firm" but of all the firms in the industry, since pure competition on the factor market will iron out cost differences among individual firms.) Further, since this point must also be consistent with the conditions of the equilibrium of the firm (i.e., maximization of net revenue), the average-cost curve must be above the average-revenue curve on each side of the point of tangency. In conjunction with the requirement that the average-revenue curve be horizontal, it is immediately evident that the tangency condition requires that each firm be producing an output corresponding to a minimum point on its average-cost curve. Since it is also generally postulated that the average-cost curve of each firm has a unique minimum point, it follows that at equilibrium each firm must be producing at maximum "technological" efficiency. (It should be emphasized that this condition of tangency between the average-cost curve and the average-revenue curve does not rule out "rents" to the factors in the sense of returns in excess of those available to the factors in the next best alternative *use*. The tangency condition, although compatible with the receipt by factors of rents from the point of view of the industry, is not compatible with the receipt of rents from the point of view of the firm.)

Under conditions of pure competition, then, the best public policy was said to be to limit intervention to the elimination of all possible obstacles to free entry and exit and, apart from this, to let nature take its course.

In monopolistic industries, on the other hand, it was demonstrated that the uncontrolled maximization of returns by factor owners would probably not result in an optimum level of investment, and at any rate production would be carried on at less than maximum technological efficiency. Here a distinction was made between so-called "natural" and "artificial" monopoly. In the latter case, the fewness of the firms, with its attendant control by each firm of an appreciable part of the supply of the product, was attributed not to basic technological conditions but (usually) to conscious limitation of the number of competitors on the part of existing firms; it was thought that the best policy would be the elimination of the artificial barriers and the establishment of competition. In the "natural" monopoly case, the fewness of the firms was attributed to technological conditions making the most efficient size of firm so large relative to the market that the establishment of many firms would be uneconomic. This was not to say that the number of firms actually established would always conform to the number required by maximum efficiency, but only to rule out the possibility of pure competition.

In the first place, it was seen to be probable that entry into a naturally monopolistic industry would not be perfectly free, so that in most cases there would be underinvestment, giving rise to "excess returns" to certain factors in the form of rents from the point of view of the firm. In the second place, it was seen that even free entry into such an industry offered no guarantee of production at the point of maximum "technological" efficiency — quite the contrary, in fact. For since the sales curve of each firm in such an industry is less than perfectly elastic, the tangency of the average-cost and average-revenue curves (which results from complete freedom of entry and exit of factors) must occur at a point where the average-cost curve is sloping downward, i.e., at an output smaller than that indicated by maximum "technological" efficiency. For the most part, this argument was not stated in this precise form; as applied to the transportation field, for example, it appeared in the form of an objection to freedom to set up parallel railway lines on the ground that this would merely result in "underutilization of the facilities" of the companies involved, bringing about either an uneasy compromise at a high rate level or sporadic rate wars possibly culminating in combination and monopoly.

At first, the attainment of optimum conditions in such industries (at least in the railway field) was looked upon almost entirely as a rate problem; attention was focused on the receipt of excess returns, and it was thought that the primary aim of regulation should be to attack this problem directly through the reduction of rates to a point where these returns would be eliminated. (This view is the forerunner and counterpart of a more recent version which completes the picture by insisting that the regulator should remedy lower-than-normal returns in the regulated industry by raising the rate level.)

Now it is clear that, although the adjustment of investment

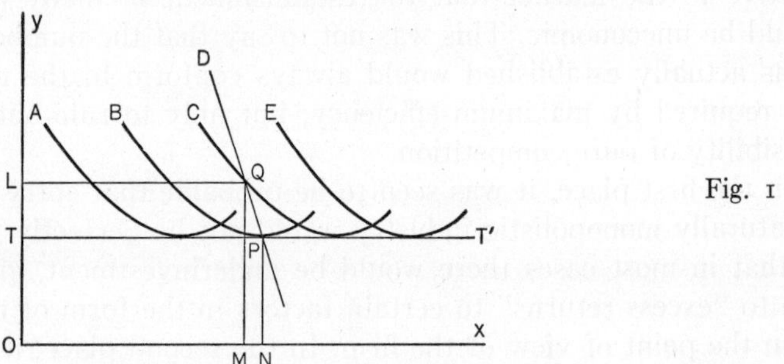

Fig. 1

to the optimum level will also solve the problem of higher-than-normal returns, the reverse is not necessarily true. For example, if in the period prior to regulation the number of firms in the industry has become too large or too small for maximum efficiency, then fixing rates that just cover the cost of production even of the maximum profitable output with this organization of the industry will not produce the desired result. Unit costs and hence rates will of course be higher than if the optimum number of firms were established.

This result is illustrated graphically in Fig. 1, where $x =$ output and $y =$ price or cost. The curves A, B, C, and E represent respectively average costs to the industry (excluding rent) with the number of firms fixed at n, $n + a$, etc. The minimum point of curve A thus lies to the left of that of curve B, and so on. It being assumed for the sake of simplicity that there are no external economies or diseconomies, these minimum points lie at equal vertical distances from the x-axis. If the output of each firm is negligibly small compared to the total output of the industry, the line TT' connecting the minimum points will be the industrial cost curve drawn on the assumption of a variable number of firms; if, however, the output of each firm is not negligibly small compared to industrial output, this industrial cost curve will be scalloped, following the course marked out by the lowest fixed-number-of-firms cost curves for all possible outputs. Line D represents the demand curve for the industry.

Optimum output is equal to $TP;$ actual output, where the number of firms has become too large before the imposition of regulation, and a policy of calling for the maximum output capable of being sold profitably with this number of firms is followed, is equal to LQ. (In this example, it is assumed that the number of firms has been fixed at that for which C is the appropriate cost curve.) The vertical distance LT between P and Q is the difference between actual and optimum unit costs; the horizontal distance MN between P and Q is the difference between actual and optimum output.

This analysis indicates that the task of the regulator in bringing about optimum conditions in "monopolistic" industries goes far beyond the manipulation of the rate level to bring about "normal" returns. To perform his task, the regulator would have to be given powers over the regulated industry that greatly transcend the usual permissive powers delegated to actual administrative agencies in this country. He should be empowered not only to approve or disapprove changes in investment and organization (including the creation and extinction of firms) but to order such changes on his own initiative. Furthermore, the required adjustment of investment and organization might well involve the extinction or drastic curtailment of the operations of existing firms; at any rate, the cost estimates and especially the estimates regarding the demand curve on which the actions of the regulator would depend would necessarily be based on imperfect knowledge, so that final conclusions regarding optimum organization and investment could be arrived at only by experimentation, and the results of such experimentation would require varying periods of time to work themselves out. For these reasons, the regulator could probably not perform his task at all unless the property rights of investors were completely subordinated to the "public interest."

The view expressed above is not representative of the policy recommendations that have been derived from the traditional analysis based on a rigid dichotomy between monopolistic and competitive industries, although in the opinion of the writer it does represent the logical outcome of that analysis. The whole analysis has generally suggested nonintervention in competitive industries (usually defined as those containing many firms), and "regulation" of those industries characterized as monopolistic where competition cannot economically be established. The "regulation" actually recommended has ranged from a simple control of the amount of and relations among rates — which is now generally recognized as inadequate — to extensive control of rates, service, entry, exit, and investment, that of the last three being, however, largely of a permissive or "negative" character.

In the transportation field, the traditional analysis may be used in support of two policy recommendations which are mutually exclusive. On the one hand, it could be said that the "transportation industry" has changed in the last few decades from a monopolistic to a competitive industry with the development of new transport agencies, so that the number of firms in the transportation field that can be supported at an efficient level has become large enough to permit effective competition. Hence, although regulation was obviously necessary in the days when inland transportation was largely carried on by the railroads, a "naturally monopolistic" industry, it is no longer necessary at all. On the other hand, it could be stated that the transportation field is in fact occupied by several industries, of which some are competitive and some naturally monopolistic. Thus, for the latter type of industry — e.g., the railroads and the pipelines — the monopolistic analysis applies, and regulation is necessary; for the former type — e.g., the motor-truck-ing and air-transport industries — the competitive analysis is valid, and nonintervention on the part of government is indicated.

The traditional analysis, it turns out, is quite incapable of affording a principle of choice between these views. The difference between them turns on the different scope of the concept of the "industry" on which they are based, and in this dispute traditional analysis cannot arbitrate. Both of these views, moreover, are based on the use of the rigid and unrealistic categories by which all relations between firms in an "industry" are standardized as either monopolistic or competitive, and relations transcending the bounds of these "industries" are ignored.

The Theory of Monopolistic Competition Within the Framework of the Traditional Industry Concept

The theory of monopolistic competition contributes to the solution of this dilemma by calling in question the applicability to markets in the real world of either of the two rigidly distinct categories employed in traditional analysis, and by supplying the seeds of destruction of the old airtight "industry" by calling attention to competition between imperfect substitutes. Thus, the new theory cleared the ground for a more realistic appraisal of the nature of this market.

Once the existence of competition between imperfect substitutes is accorded theoretical recognition, it becomes immediately clear that the analysis of the markets for air, rail, and other forms of transport, as if these were unrelated and isolated "industries," is highly unrealistic; the most superficial examination of the facts reveals a lively competition between firms included in different "industries" so defined. On the other hand, it is equally clear that this competition, which pervades so much of the transport market, does not conform to the pattern of pure competition, where substitutability between the products of various firms is assumed to be perfect.

Thus far, attention has been given only to the negative contribution of monopolistic-competition theory. We turn now to consider the recommendations that are suggested by the use of the new analysis in lieu of the old programs that it helped to displace.

(1) In the first place, the recognition that the theory of pure competition did not provide a realistic analysis of the transport market destroyed the general and categorical argument for nonintervention which that theory had supplied. Indeed, it was thought by some that the mere assertion that the transport market was characterized by monopolistic competition constituted at least a prima-facie case for some sort of regulation. But obviously it is not the form but the result of pure competition — i.e., optimum investment and the most efficient distribution of output among firms — that is the ultimate desideratum. If monopolistic competition could be shown to be capable of producing these results, the prima-facie case for intervention would disappear.

(2) However, monopolistic-competition theory was interpreted as demonstrating that competition between imperfect substitutes could not produce the optimum results that would arise from pure competition. It was contended that with differentiated competition maximum technological efficiency (in the sense of each firm producing at minimum cost) was actually incompatible with the existence of normal returns on investment; although in certain instances the free working of the market might bring about normal returns, maximum technological efficiency would be excluded by this very condition, because where competition is among imperfect substitutes the sales curve of each individual producer in most cases slopes downward to the right. An argument formally similar has been previously discussed in connection with "monopolistic" industries in the traditional analysis. Here again, optimum investment, interpreted as involving the tangency of the demand and cost curves of each firm, can be attained only when each firm is producing at less than the "technologically" optimum scale. Thus, although investment in the industry might possibly be the same as it would have been under competitive conditions, investment *per firm* would always be smaller, and the number of firms would always be too large for maximum efficiency.

Since this analysis is valid wherever the sales curve of the individual producer is less than perfectly elastic, it applies not only to industries containing a few firms but also to the large group, where each firm controls only a negligible part of the total supply of the product and its price-output decisions therefore have a negligible effect on the fortunes of its competitors. Thus by this analysis doubt was cast for the first time on the ability of free entry and exit to produce optimum results in this type of industry, which would undoubtedly have been forced into the "purely competitive" mold by a traditional analyst.

This analytical result has on occasion been interpreted as meaning that free entry, even with large numbers, would bring about within each firm a departure from optimum scale which would be measured in terms of output by the· horizontal distance between the actual average-cost–average-revenue tangency point and the minimum point on the average-cost curve, and that this discrepancy would be manifested as "underutilization" of fixed factors. In the transportation field, this "underutilization" was thought to be exemplified by rail terminals and roadbeds utilized to a degree falling short of their physical maximum. An uncritical acceptance of this interpretation leads to a recommendation that regulation be centered on restriction of entry in order to avoid "dividing the available business among too many carriers," each of which would be "impecunious" and operating at less than capacity. This interpretation is also stated in the following form: since free entry precludes the development of large-scale economies, limitations must be placed on entry in order to enable existing firms to develop to optimum proportions.[2] Without commenting on the apparent implication in the first of these statements that the volume of business is fixed irrespective of the rate level, let us see whether monopolistic-competition theory in fact justifies such an interpretation.

---

[2] Such a view is strengthened by statements like the following on the part of theorists: "When the market is imperfect individual firms do not grow to their optimum size, so that even if there were no possibilities of specialization between firms, production would still not be carried on in the most efficient way." Joan Robinson, *The Economics of Imperfect Competition* (London: Macmillan, 1938), p. 170.

In the authoritative treatise on monopolistic competition, the *large-group* tangency solution is referred to as a "sort of ideal." [3] The view that will be presented here is the following: that only in markets characterized by nonaggressive price policy are free entry and exit necessarily incompatible with maximum efficiency in production, in the sense that a more satisfactory organization by firms could always be achieved by intervention; that in any case the departure from maximum efficiency is manifested in underutilized physical equipment less than would be indicated in terms of output by the horizontal distance between the actual average-cost–average-revenue tangency point and the minimum point on the long-run average-cost curve); and that a mere restriction of entry or of investment can in no case be relied upon as a means of attaining maximum efficiency.

For the major portion of the following argument, I am indebted to J. M. Cassels, who has dealt definitively with this problem in an article published some years ago. [4]

In the first place, the firm average-cost curve that is relevant for the analysis of the ultimate results of the workings of markets is a long-period cost curve (or "envelope curve"), allowing for the possibility of adjustment of all factors of production, including those generally taken as fixed in the short-run analysis; hence, the fact that equilibrium is reached at a point to the left of the minimum point on this curve does not mean that the horizontal distance between the minimum point and the equilibrium point represents the degree of underutilization of fixed factors — the difference between actual and potential output of such factors. This underutilization will be represented in fact by the horizontal distance between the equilibrium point (which must be on the envelope curve) and the minimum point on the short-run (fixed-scale) average-cost curve that is tangent to the envelope curve at the equilibrium point.

Moreover, to interpret *this* underutilization as a departure

---

[3] E. H. Chamberlin, *The Theory of Monopolistic Competition* (Cambridge: Harvard University Press, 1938), p. 94.

[4] J. M. Cassels, "Excess Capacity and Monopolistic Competition," *Quarterly Journal of Economics*, LI, No. 3 (May 1937), pp. 426–443.

from an economic (as opposed to a technological) optimum scale for the firm would be erroneous. This fact becomes evident when it is considered that only a change in basic consumer tastes, or a forced redistribution of consumer expenditures, could bring about coincidence between the minimum point on the short-run average-cost curve and the equilibrium output indicated by the free maximization of factor returns, i.e., the output indicated by optimum investment.

In other words, the "excess capacity" referred to by Chamberlin in his discussion of "equilibrium with excess capacity"[5] must not be interpreted as an underutilization of fixed factors, since in the long run all factors are variable, nor as a departure from the optimum of the actual proportion between factors used, since the long-run cost curve by definition is based on the optimum combination for each output. It must be interpreted, then, not as an excess of one factor as compared with others but as an excess of all factors in the industry, in the sense that if they were organized into fewer firms, with larger output per firm, they could contribute more to the real national income. Now since any departure from the equilibrium condition described by the large-group tangency solution would involve a decrease in the real national income, no "excess capacity" can exist here, and any intervention in such a group could bring about no better result, from the point of view of economic performance, than that achieved by the free market. Free entry combined with aggressive price policy (the distinguishing characteristic of the large group) brings about not only the optimum adjustment of investment but also maximum efficiency of production in terms of organization into firms, it being always assumed that tastes are given, i.e., are not subject to criticism by the economist.

The same cannot be said, however, of the small group, which is generally characterized by a nonaggressive price policy because of oligopolistic interdependence among the firms. In this case, although free entry would still be expected to bring about tangency between the average-cost and average-revenue curves of each constituent firm, the point of equilibrium would be

[5] Chamberlin, *Monopolistic Competition*, pp. 104–109.

higher on the cost curve than that which would result from free entry with aggressive price policy. In this case, the number of firms would indeed be larger and investment per firm smaller than required by the satisfaction of the preferences of buyers at lowest possible cost. This case, then, is similar to the "monopolistic" case discussed above, and would call for a similar regulatory policy, which would be beset with similar difficulties. Where the achievement of price competition would be feasible, it would still be desirable since it could be expected to bring about the solution described in the large-group case. Such a policy might be indicated especially where the nonaggressiveness of price policy was due not to any "natural largeness" of firms relative to the market but to agreements to live and let live, loose associations, and the like.

It should be pointed out that in neither instance does the existence of "impurity" in competition mean a tendency to overinvestment in the sense that returns to factors in such an industry tend to be less than in other uses. With free entry, it is to be expected that returns to homogeneous factors will be equalized as between this and other fields; with closed entry, the possibility for higher returns is, as usual, present.

If the foregoing analysis is correct, then it is obvious that a restriction of entry is certainly not to be relied upon to achieve optimum results in an industry characterized by monopolistic competition. Such a restriction would indeed be necessary if it could be shown that free entry would always produce overinvestment, but no such thing has been or can be shown. In the "large-group" case, a policy of assuring free entry is obviously called for. In the "small-group" case, much more than a mere restriction of entry will be necessary. A contention that unregulated competition, including free entry, in monopolistically competitive industries may lead to undue poverty on the part of all firms makes an admirable rationalization for recommendations that such measures as restriction of entry and minimum-rate controls be adopted to maintain profits. For example, a belief that this contention is true apparently underlies the following statement:

Suffice to say that circumstances such as a limited number of sellers, differentiated services . . . tend to send prices and costs above the equilibrium point of pure competition. If additional resources and sellers are attracted into the field as a consequence, the available business is divided among greater numbers, with perhaps no appreciable profits for the group as a whole . . . Minimum price or rate control, it may be noted, is likely to foster the same result with respect to increasing the number of sellers in the field; and that is one reason why the prescription of minimum rates requires implementation by control of entrance if the carriers are not to be chronically impecunious and their facilities underutilized.[6]

In the first place, the effect on investment of fixing minimum rates is certainly not determinable without any knowledge of the basis on which such rates will be fixed; here it seems to be assumed that the minimum rates will be fixed so as to attract new investment, or, in other words, so as to permit the earning of more than a normal return on existing investment. In the second place, the practical effect of entry control is similarly not determinable without any knowledge of the principle governing control. If the policy followed is to permit entry of any firm capable of earning a normal return on investment, the effect aimed at would be similar to the equilibrium situation toward which uncontrolled entry would tend; the actual effect would differ from that of uncontrolled entry to the extent that possible miscalculations on the part of the regulatory authority differed in amount or direction from the mistakes that might have been made by the uncontrolled entrants. If the test employed is more stringent, so that fewer firms are permitted to enter than would persist without control, the result will not necessarily be the expansion of the output of existing firms (their sales curves might well be less elastic than if more firms had entered), but will most probably be the earning of supernormal returns by factors within these firms. It is quite certain that with neither type of entry control will the optimum or ideal output per firm necessarily be achieved.

[6] B. N. Behling, "The Nature and Control of the Transport Market," *Transportation and National Policy* (Washington: Government Printing Office, 1942), p. 249.

It may be argued that overinvestment will result from free entry under conditions of monopolistic competition even with large numbers if prices are set with reference to costs rather than with reference to the maximization of profits, the amount of sales being regarded as given. However, even in this case it is not demonstrated that the returns to the factors within the industry will be reduced below a normal level. The "overinvestment" referred to here is of the same type as that resulting from nonaggressive pricing in the small group.

It has also been contended that the existence of impurities in competition, regardless of the type of price policy adopted by individual firms, causes a departure from maximum efficiency in production by giving rise to a divergence between the earnings of any "hired" factor and the value of its marginal physical product, which is defined as the price of the product multiplied by the marginal physical product of the factor. Because of this divergence, it is argued that an entrepreneur drawing factors from uses in which competition is impure will receive earnings in excess of the value of his marginal physical product; hence the adjustment of factor distribution in accordance with the maximization of returns will result in the existence of too many entrepreneurs (i.e., too many firms) in proportion to the amount of "hired" factors in uses where it is possible for the entrepreneur to draw factors from imperfectly competitive industries.[7] Accepting for the sake of argument the implied identification of the firm with the "entrepreneurial factor," let us see whether this contention may be regarded as valid.

An example of this view may be found in an article by Kahn, where the marginal physical product of the entrepreneur is defined as "the physical increment of output which society obtains as a result of the application of an *additional* entrepreneur to a particular type of production, the natural units of

---

[7] In one version of this argument, it is contended that there will always be too many firms in industries that are themselves characterized by imperfect competition. However, this version is based on the assumption that entrepreneurs in such industries draw factors from within the industry (it being supposed that competition is uniformly imperfect throughout the industry) or from other industries that are similarly imperfectly competitive. Hence this version is merely a particular species of the general argument treated in the text.

all other factors employed by industry as a whole remaining the same as before." It is further explained that this product "may be a hotch-potch, consisting of an increment of output in the one particular use and decrements of output in other uses, from which hired factors may be diverted to the new entrepreneur." [8] Thus the value of the marginal physical product of the entrepreneur is in this theory taken to be equal to the value of the total output of his firm minus the value of the product of the hired factors in the uses from which they were drawn. The earnings of the entrepreneur are regarded as equal to the total value of his firm's output minus the amounts paid out to the "hired" factors. If the earnings of the "hired" factors in this firm were precisely equal to the value of their output in the *other* uses, then the earnings of the entrepreneur would be precisely equal to the value of his marginal physical product. The supposed difference between the entrepreneur's earnings and the value of his marginal physical product arises from an alleged difference between the amounts paid out to these factors and the value of their product in these other uses.

It is clear that in order to draw a factor from an alternative use the entrepreneur must pay it an amount at least equal to its earnings in this alternative use, which will, in turn, be equal to its marginal revenue product in this use. If the value of the product of the factor in the alternative use may be taken to be equal to its marginal *revenue* product, then there will be no possibility of the entrepreneur's paying less than the value of its product and hence no difference will arise on this account between the entrepreneur's earnings and the value of his marginal physical product. In the argument under consideration here, however, the value of the product of the factor is taken to be equal not to its marginal revenue product, but to the value of its marginal physical product, defined as the marginal physical product of the factor multiplied by the price of the product. Under this interpretation, the earnings of the hired factors in the firm in question will differ from the value of their output in the uses from which they are drawn to the extent that their

---

[8] R. F. Kahn, "Some Notes on Ideal Output," *Economic Journal*, XLV, No. 177 (March 1935), pp. 22–23.

marginal revenue products differ from the value of their marginal physical products in these uses. This difference will, of course, vary directly with the imperfection of competition in these uses. Thus the decrement of output caused by the diversion of factors to the new entrepreneur will not be fully reflected in his costs — i.e., the payments that he must make to the "hired" factors — and to the extent that this is true the earnings of the entrepreneur will exceed the value of his marginal physical product.

It will be seen that the whole argument rests upon the valuation of the product of the "hired" factors in the uses from which they are drawn as being equal to their marginal physical product multiplied by the price of the product. However, as Chamberlin has demonstrated, this method of valuation is applicable only under conditions of pure competition.[9] But if the entrepreneur draws factors from purely competitive industries, then it is clear, as is explicitly recognized by Kahn, that there can be no difference between the minimum amounts that must be paid out to these factors and the value of their products in these industries.[10] Without the illegitimate application of a pure-competition norm in a context of imperfect competition, the entire argument vanishes.

A similar argument, open to similar objections, has been advanced by J. R. Hicks,[11] who contends that under certain conditions the number of firms in an imperfectly competitive industry will always be excessive so long as price exceeds marginal cost anywhere in the industry. Hicks postulates that the redistribution among other firms of the factors employed by a firm in an imperfectly competitive industry would generate a producers' surplus at the margins of the new uses, a surplus which would have to be offset against any "initial loss" that might be occasioned by the elimination of such a firm from the economy. This "initial loss" would be made up of any loss of consumers' surplus arising from the elimination of the removed

---

[9] Chamberlin, *Monopolistic Competition*, ch. viii, "Monopolistic Competition and the Marginal Productivity Theory of Distribution."

[10] Kahn, "Some Notes on Ideal Output," p. 24.

[11] J. R. Hicks, "The Foundations of Welfare Economics," *Economic Journal*, XLIX, No. 196 (December 1939), pp. 696–712.

firm's product and any loss to factors measured by the excess of their earnings in the firm from which they were removed over those that they would receive in the uses to which they were transferred. The producers' surplus allegedly generated by redistribution of the factors is apparently the same surplus that we have met with above (in Kahn's argument) in the form of excess entrepreneurial earnings in firms drawing factors from imperfectly competitive uses, and will disappear immediately if a correct valuation is applied to the product of the factors.

Hicks's subsequent argument, which is supposed to demonstrate that the number of firms is necessarily excessive in an imperfectly competitive industry under certain conditions, is entirely based on the postulation of the "redistributive" producers' surplus. It is contended that under these conditions it can be shown that the removal of a firm from an imperfectly competitive industry must always result in a net social gain so long as price exceeds marginal cost anywhere in the industry. (Since marginal cost must be equal to marginal revenue, the difference between price and marginal cost will be an index of the difference between factor earnings and the value of their marginal physical products.)

These special conditions appear to be designed to eliminate the other surpluses against which the alleged redistributive producers' surplus must be offset. Producers' surplus within the firm is presumably supposed to be eliminated by free entry (involving the equation of average cost to average revenue); consumers' surplus occasioned by the firm is eliminated by supposing the preference of consumers for the firm's product to be irrational, or the difference between this product and the next best substitute to be slight (apparently so slight as to be negligible), so that no consumer would be really worse off because of the disappearance from the market of the firm's particular product.

(3) Growing out of the destruction by monopolistic-competition theory of the traditional criteria for the judgment of market mechanisms in many fields, including that of transportation, there has arisen a sort of antitheoretical reaction favoring

the "pragmatic" judgment of markets in terms of their "actual results." It is of course true that in one sense such "actual results" have always been recognized as the only valid measure of the performance of markets; for example, the case for non-intervention in purely competitive markets was based on the belief that in such markets uncontrolled economic activities would produce optimum results. The reaction referred to here represents not a reaffirmation of this traditional view, but a partial revolt against it, probably arising in some degree, at least, from the unpalatability of the conclusions related to policy which are supposed to be suggested by the application to real situations of the usual criteria of economic performance. It has already been said that monopolistic-competition theory has been interpreted as a justification for intervention in all markets characterized by competition between imperfect substitutes, both (*a*) because of its demonstration of the very narrow applicability of pure-competition theory, and (*b*) because of its supposed demonstration that imperfect markets necessarily produce results that depart from the optimum. Persons who accept either interpretation, but who are apparently not prepared to recommend the indicated intervention, have resorted to minimizing the importance of the usual criteria of economic performance and casting about for other criteria to replace them, characterizing their new approach as "practical" and "realistic."

In so far as they are really new, and not partial and misleading presentations of the old criteria, these new norms usually are based on the maintenance of "stability" and "order" or "financial soundness," meaning the protection of vested interests from competitive injury. These aims, it is pointed out, are promoted by monopolistic elements in markets that hamper price competition and prevent the establishment of competitive firms. Thus, it is contended, in the determination of policy, these "benefits" must be weighed against the evils arising from monopolistic elements. It is, of course, true that a case can be made for the suspension of competition as a stabilizing factor in an economy threatened by a downward spiral of prices and incomes, and not equipped with more direct and efficient devices of control,[12] or even as an adjunct to these more direct devices. Otherwise, there seems to be little reason for holding the "financial soundness" of existing firms to be a good in itself (except from the point of view of the existing firms, of course).

(4) Because of its emphasis on competition between imperfect substitutes, and the consequent demonstration of the inappropriateness of treating the markets of various agencies of transport as distinct and unrelated entities, monopolistic-competition analysis has been used as a basis for defending the extension of the scope of regulation to include the entire transportation field, rather than limiting regulation to certain portions of it. It is said that the transport market is an "interrelated whole," the implication being that if one sector of the market needs regulating, the whole market should be subjected to regulation.[13]

This view is based in part on a general conception of the transportation field as one "industry" characterized by monopolistic competition, which conception will be discussed more fully below. It is also based on a contention that regulation of one sector or a few sectors of the transport market cannot be effective without regulation of the whole, a contention whose validity depends on the specific content of the regulation referred to. The usual example of a regulatory policy that was ineffective in part, at least, because of failure to regulate competitors is the rate-making rule of the Transportation Act of 1920, involving the provision of a fair return on the fair value of railroad property in this country. It is obvious that certain other types of regulatory policy can be and have been made effective without regulation of competing industries; thus safety requirements and maximum-rate regulation were imposed on interstate railroads before regulation of their competitors. Indeed, it would seem that the only type of policy that does actually require regulation of all significant competitors

---

[12] See K. E. Boulding, "In Defense of Monopoly," *Quarterly Journal of Economics,* LIX, No. 4 (August 1945), pp. 524–42.

[13] See Behling, "The Nature and Control of the Transport Market," especially p. 241.

is one that aims at the protection of the revenues of the regulated firms from inroads by competitors. Even a policy of maintaining a particular rate structure, conceived to be in itself just and desirable, does not *as such* require regulation of competitors; the argument that without such regulation traffic is transferred to competitive agencies would carry no weight in this context if protection of the regulatee's revenues were deemed to be no object.

In summary, it may be said that monopolistic-competition theory has been of inestimable value in casting aside the old categorical type of market analysis as inappropriate in general in the judging of transport markets, and contributing thus to the solution of the dilemma regarding policy created by the traditional theory. It has, however, been misinterpreted so as to produce a new oversimplification of the problems involved in market analysis. On the one hand, it has been interpreted as showing that regulation of most markets is necessary; on the other, it has provoked a reaction in which such aims as "financial stability" are raised to the status of goods in themselves. Related to both of these views is a comparatively new and popular policy recommendation that the transport market be subjected to comprehensive regulation; this recommendation also stems directly from the destruction of the theoretical barriers between transport agencies by the recognition of competition between imperfect substitutes.

Apart from these views, which are largely based on misinterpretations, can any positive conclusions relevant for policy be drawn from monopolistic-competition theory as it has here been presented so far? As has been previously indicated, the analysis of the uncontrolled operation of monopolistic competition in the "large group" shows that the preservation or creation of free entry into such a group would result in the attainment of the best possible economic performance, tastes being regarded as given. Investment as a whole and investment per firm will be at optimum levels; there will be the largest possible output consistent with cost coverage. Here again, as in the case of pure competition, the adjustment of total investment brought about by free entry also suffices to bring each firm to optimum size.[14] When existing firms have reached individual equilibrium, the existence of supernormal profits (denoting underinvestment) also means that output per firm is larger than optimum, i.e., that there are too few firms in the industry.[15] Similarly, subnormal profits with equilibrium of each firm would mean too many firms. Although this result might *conceivably* be attained where the market is only large enough with relation to the firm to support two independently acting firms (provided each of these firms actually did not take into account the probable repercussions on its own business of reactions by the other to changes in its price-output decisions), actually it would be consistent with enlightened self-interest on the part of each firm only when the number of competitors was so large that no appreciable reaction would in fact occur.

Where the latter type of industrial organization is actually feasible, but firms do not act independently, because of agreements or associations, the correct public policy would be to destroy such agreements and prevent them from arising again. Where a nonaggressive price policy is followed because of inertia, ignorance, custom, and the like, it will admittedly be difficult (and perhaps impossible) to overcome; however, an attempt should be made to destroy the root causes. Where such attempts cannot succeed, and also where a nonaggressive price policy arises from a natural largeness of firms with relation to the market, the scope of intervention required to attain optimum economic performance goes far beyond mere price manipulation and permissive entry control. Regulation must aim not at the direct extinction of supernormal profits, but at the adjustment of investment and the improvement of the distribution of output among firms.

[14] The optimum size attained with free entry into the "large group" of monopolistic competitors does not, of course, correspond to the minimum point on the average-cost curve, as does the optimum size attained under conditions of pure competition. It is nevertheless a genuine optimum, since it represents the largest output that would be taken by consumers at a price covering average costs.

[15] Cf. Chamberlin, *Monopolistic Competition*, p. 94: "With fewer establishments, larger scales of production, and lower prices it would always be true that buyers would be willing to pay more than it would cost to give them a greater diversity of product."

In the absence of a more precise definition of the "industry" or "group" than has so far been presented, one might apply the foregoing analysis to all groups of firms producing more or less similar products; this approach might well lead to the treatment of the transportation industry as such a group. From this standpoint, it is perfectly clear that the transportation market is capable of supporting a very large number of firms, each controlling a small portion of the total supply of transportation; it might then be contended that the removal of all obstacles to entry and exit and of all institutions blocking price competition should be undertaken, instead of regulation as now carried on. (It should be emphasized that neither this policy recommendation nor those discussed earlier may be correctly attributed to monopolistic-competition theory *as developed by Chamberlin*. They are, on the contrary, based on analyses that take into account neither an accurate interpretation of the initial presentation of this theory nor its subsequent evolution.) Even at this stage, however, recognition of the diversity of the transport market — divided geographically and otherwise into a multiplicity of sectors — renders this conclusion dubious. The essential problem of the proper unit of market analysis remains unsolved.

The next step indicated is a more thorough investigation of the content of the concept of "industry," and the related ideas of the "market" and the "commodity."

CHAPTER II

CLARIFICATION OF CONCEPTS USED
IN MARKET ANALYSIS

THE BREAKDOWN OF THE TRADITIONAL INDUSTRY CONCEPT

THE INVESTIGATION of the concept of "industry" is one of the major contributions to market analysis made by Triffin in his *Monopolistic Competition and General Equilibrium Theory*.[1] Triffin points out that, once the perfect substitutability between products of constituent firms that is the essential characteristic of the competitive industry is abandoned, the concept of "industry" loses its place as an unambiguous and significant element in value theory. Competitive relations between firms can no longer, by the simple expedient of declaring these firms to belong to the same "industry," be assumed to conform to a simple, standard pattern, and it cannot be postulated that there exist airtight groups of firms all related to each other, none of which have significant competitive relations outside the group.[2]

Since all the policy recommendations discussed so far have been based on the a priori group pattern here rejected, it will be seen that except where such a pattern of competitive relations actually exists — and only factual investigation can show that it does — these recommendations will not be appropriate without revision. This development represents a logical evolution of monopolistic-competition theory, as was recognized by Chamberlin.[3] It will also be seen that the ambiguity attaching to the idea of "industry" also extends to the old concepts of

---

[1] Robert Triffin, *Monopolistic Competition and General Equilibrium Theory* (Cambridge: Harvard University Press, 1940).

[2] *Ibid.*, p. 86.

[3] E. H. Chamberlin, "Monopolistic or Imperfect Competition?" *Quarterly Journal of Economics*, LI, No. 4 (August 1937), pp. 567–568 (or *Monopolistic Competition*, 5th ed., pp. 201–202); cf. also *Monopolistic Competition*, 1st (and later) eds., pp. 102–104.

market, commodity, entry, and investment, all of which were defined with reference to the industrial group. Without perfect substitutability, for example, the "industrial" demand and supply curves, with respect to which optimum investment in the "industry" was defined, cease to have any precise meaning, and the significance of "free entry," which in the "industrial" context could almost always be relied upon to bring about optimum investment, is open to question. Both "optimum investment" and "free entry" must be redefined without reference to the "industry" concept if they are to retain unambiguous general significance.

A Reconsideration of Optimum Investment: Distinction Between Conditional and Unconditional Optima

In order to discover the essential nature of the "optimum" level of investment that is implied by an output corresponding to the intersection of the "industrial" demand and supply curves, it is necessary to inquire further into the exact content of the schedules represented by these curves. It is first of all evident that each of them must be defined on the basis of a homogeneous product. If this condition is met, the "industrial" demand curve may be used equally well in the analysis of all markets for economic goods, whether produced by one firm or by many.[4] The precise nature of the "supply prices" for various amounts of output that are represented by the "industrial" supply curve, however, requires further clarification.

By definition, the industrial supply curve indicates, for each quantity of output, the price that will cause this amount of product to be offered for sale. Given perfect freedom of factors to move out of the industry, it is clear that this price cannot be less than the sum of the transfer prices of the factor units that must be employed to produce the marginal unit of the given

---

[4] The difficulties inherent in the definition of a demand curve for one product that will be applicable over all possible ranges of output, once the assumption of the complete independence of markets for different products has been dropped, arise whether the product in question is produced by one firm or by many. These difficulties are discussed further in Chapter V.

output; for at any lower price, certain factor units would be able to find more remunerative employment elsewhere, and the given amount of output would not be forthcoming. Given perfect freedom of factors to move into the industry, it is also clear that the upper limit of supply price must be the sum of the transfer prices of the factor units necessary to produce an additional unit of output by the formation of an additional firm (i.e., the extensive marginal cost of the amount of output plus one); for at this price (or, strictly, at a price higher than this price) factors outside the industry would enter it and more than the given output would be produced. These upper and lower limits of supply price are perfectly general, given perfect freedom of factor movement. Under conditions of pure competition, however, it may also be said that supply price cannot be greater than the *intensive* marginal cost of another unit of product; since each firm, confronted by a perfectly elastic demand curve, fixes its output at a point where marginal cost (i.e., the transfer prices of the factor units that it must employ to produce an increment of output) is equal to price, a price in excess of this marginal cost would cause it to expand its own output. Thus it may be said quite generally that the *competitive* supply price cannot be greater than the transfer cost of an additional unit of output, whether produced by an expansion of existing firms or by the creation of new firms.

When demand price is equal to supply price, as it obviously must be at equilibrium, the total amount paid out by consumers can be neither less than the sum of the transfer prices of the factor units required to produce the marginal unit of this output multiplied by the amount of product, nor more than the sum of the transfer prices of the factor units required to produce an additional unit of output multiplied by the amount of product plus one. If output is capable of being expanded in very small increments, the difference between the upper and lower limits of equilibrium price will be negligible, and it may be said that the total amount paid out by consumers is to all intents and purposes equal to the transfer cost of the marginal unit of output multiplied by the amount of product.

In what sense does this equilibrium position constitute an optimum? Given the free (i.e., uncontrolled) market determination of returns to factors, the output determined by the intersection of the industrial demand curve and the competitive supply curve is the maximum for which consumers are willing to pay the necessary cost, and the amount paid out by consumers is no more than is necessary to call forth this amount of product. At this output, no factor owner could put his factor to more productive use by transferring either into or out of the industry in question, and no consumer could better his position by taking either more or less of the product of this industry. Thus, given the free-market determination of returns, the equilibrium output is that required for the most productive employment of factors and the maximization of consumer satisfactions.[5]

If, however, the free-market determination of factor returns is not taken as an unalterable datum, the equilibrium position defined by the equality of demand price and supply price does not necessarily constitute an optimum in the sense indicated. This proposition is true because the equality of demand price and supply price does not, except under certain special conditions of factor supply, imply that every factor unit employed in the industry is receiving returns no larger than would be necessary to retain it in this use. In other words, the competitive industrial equilibrium, although incompatible with the receipt by any factor unit of rent from the point of view of the individual firm, is perfectly compatible with the receipt of rents from the point of view of the industry. It is only where the transfer cost of the marginal unit of equilibrium output is no greater than that of any other unit of output that the equilibrium position is incompatible with the existence of rent from the point of view of the industry.

The special conditions under which there will be no rent at equilibrium may be summarized as follows: (*a*) all factors employed in the industry are available in the quantities de-

---

[5] Another line of argument which might be used to defend the view that output under pure competition is always at the optimum level, namely, that argument provided by "welfare" economics, is considered in the Appendix.

manded at an unchanged unit price;[6] (*b*) all factors employed in the industry, although available in the quantities demanded only at a rising unit price, are composed of units that are perfectly substitutable for each other with respect to both the uses from which they are drawn and the industry in question, so that the transfer prices of all units of a given factor are equal; and (*c*) not all factors employed in the industry are available in the quantity demanded at an unchanged unit price, but imperfect substitutes for each factor are available in the quantities demanded at prices sufficiently lower to offset exactly their lower productivity. Unless the supply of factors to the competitive industry satisfies one of these three conditions, the equilibrium output will be an optimum in the sense described above only if the market determination of factor returns is accepted as an unalterable datum.

In other words, the same output could be called forth, at a lesser total expenditure by consumers, through outside intervention designed to hold the returns to each factor down to a level equal to its transfer earnings (or, strictly speaking, to a level only very slightly above its transfer earnings); the price necessary to cover unit cost would then be lower than the competitive equilibrium by the average amount of rent per unit product, and consumers would be willing to pay *this* necessary cost for a larger amount of product; and certain factor units, previously extramarginal to the industry, could improve their productivity by entering it. Such intervention would of course involve much more than the mere fixing by an outside authority of the contractual payments to factors employed in each firm; this type of action in itself would obviously leave the price and output of the product at its former level, and would result only in the transference of rents formerly earned by various

---

[6] In this discussion, all factor units considered as one factor from the point of view of the industry are, by definition, homogeneous from the point of view of this industry. It is believed that the definition of a "factor" as made up of perfectly substitutable units avoids ambiguity in the analysis of factor markets in the same way as the definition of a "product" as made up of perfectly substitutable units clarifies the analysis of commodity markets. The "heterogeneous factor" is here treated as several factors, less than perfectly substitutable for each other. For a discussion of the same problem treated in terms of "factor heterogeneity," see Robinson, *Economics of Imperfect Competition*, ch. viii.

factors to whatever factor happened to be in a position to receive residual returns within each firm. To achieve the desired result it would be necessary to fix prices and to distribute the total proceeds from the sale of the product among the various firms in such a way that each would receive enough, and no more than enough, to cover the transfer earnings (from the point of view of the industry) of the factors included within it. (It should be noted that various levels of earnings might have to be allocated to various units of a factor employed by the same firm, since their transfer earnings from the point of view of the industry might be different.)

It is, then, only with the proviso that the market determination of returns to factors is regarded as an unalterable datum that pure competition with perfect freedom of factor movement inevitably brings about optimum investment within an industry. Without this proviso, it cannot be said that equilibrium investment necessarily corresponds to that required for the most productive employment of factors and the maximization of consumer satisfactions.

The Tangency Condition, Free Entry, and Optimum Investment

Although the achievement of equilibrium investment in a pure-competition industry is, as has been indicated, perfectly compatible with the existence of rents from the point of view of the industry, it is nevertheless always incompatible with the existence of rents from the point of view of the firm; that is to say, there can under no circumstances be at equilibrium any difference between average revenue (price) and average cost to the individual competitive firms. Thus the condition of optimum investment has come to be generally identified with the condition of tangency between the firm's average-cost curve and its demand curve, and the efficacy of "free entry" in bringing about optimum investment is generally equated to its ability to bring about the tangency condition within individual firms. Moreover, it is generally agreed that in order to necessitate the tangency condition at equilibrium, "free entry" must mean ability to produce perfect substitutes for the products of existing firms. (This is the meaning usually assigned to "free entry" in connection with pure-competition industries.) If this analysis is *generally* valid — that is, if optimum investment may *generally* be defined by the tangency condition and if the ability to produce perfect substitutes is necessary to make tangency inevitable — then it is clear that "free entry" under any definition compatible with a situation where competition is among imperfect substitutes cannot be relied upon to bring about optimum investment; for, as Chamberlin has pointed out, the very definition of the type of competitive relations involved in such a situation presupposes inability to produce perfect substitutes.[7] Let us, however, examine more fully the meaning of the tangency condition and its relation to the condition of optimum investment.

Of crucial importance for the precise significance of the tangency condition is the question of what returns to factors are to be included within the cost curve. If there is to be any possibility at all of nontangency, then obviously not all actual earnings of factors can qualify for inclusion by the mere fact of being paid to them. From the point of view of any economic entity, the cost of any factor unit is usually defined as the payment that is necessary to retain it in the employment of that entity. Hence the cost of any factor unit is equal to the price below which that unit would be transferred to another economic entity. The actual content of this concept will of course vary according to the nature of the entity with respect to which the calculation is being made.

If tangency is taken to mean the absence of any returns to any factor unit above the level at which it would be transferred to the production of another commodity, then it is not necessarily achieved at equilibrium even where there is ability to produce perfect substitutes. As has been noted by Triffin, in order to imply tangency in this sense, "free entry" would have to mean not only the ability to produce perfect substitutes, but also the ability to produce these substitutes at the same

[7] Chamberlin, "Monopolistic or Imperfect Competition?" pp. 567–568.

cost as the firms already in the field.[8] (So defined, "free entry" would correspond to the conditions of factor supply that have been noted above as bringing about the absence of rents from the point of view of the industry at equilibrium, plus the condition that no obstacle outside the circumstances of factor supply prevented the production of the same product by additional firms.)

Furthermore, tangency in this sense is not implied by the existence of optimum investment in its usual meaning, i.e., the meaning under which the competitive equilibrium represents the optimum;[9] for an excess of average revenue over the cost of transfer to another use is not, as has been noted, incompatible with this optimum except under certain special conditions of factor supply. Thus transfer price, defined as the price below which any factor unit would be transferred to the production of another commodity, does not *in general* represent the upper limit of factor earnings consistent with the existence of optimum investment *in the usual sense.*

Generally speaking, this upper limit is in fact represented by the cost of replacement of the factor unit in question, that is, the price at which an additional (perfectly substitutable) unit of this factor could be secured by the economic unit in question, or the price at which the given factor unit could be economically replaced by an imperfect substitute (the difference in revenue productivity of the two factor units having been exactly offset by the difference in their prices). Under the conditions of factor supply in which the competitive industrial equilibrium is incompatible with the receipt of rents from the

[8] Thus Triffin prefers to reserve the term "free entry" for a condition in which additional firms are able to produce perfect substitutes at the same cost as existing firms. Ability to produce perfect substitutes he designates "homogeneous entry," and ability to produce imperfect substitutes, "heterogeneous entry." **Triffin,** *Monopolistic Competition and General Equilibrium Theory,* p. 120.

[9] It is, of course, generally recognized that the competitive equilibrium does not represent an optimum if the calculations of individual producers do not adequately reflect the total costs and benefits arising from their activities in the field in question. Thus, the entry of an additional producer into the field might result in industrial economies or diseconomies that would not enter into the calculations of a prospective entrant, and investment in the field might therefore be smaller or larger than would be ideal.

point of view of the industry, and only under these conditions, this upper limit is precisely equal to transfer earnings for any factor unit.

In the usual analysis of pure-competition industrial equilibrium with free entry, the tangency between the average-cost and average-revenue curves of the constituent firms is not intended to imply the absence of returns to any factor unit above the price at which it would be transferred to another industry; the tangency condition represents the absence of rents from the point of view of the firm, but not from that of the industry. The incompatibility of rents from the point of view of the firm with equilibrium investment in the industry results from the fact that each firm is competing for factors with other firms producing exactly the same product. Because this is true, the transfer earnings of any employed factor unit are for each firm determined by the price that would be paid for this unit by other firms within the industry. It follows that these transfer earnings cannot be lower than the price that must be paid to draw the marginal unit of the factor into the industry, or the price (of this factor) at which the least satisfactory substitute actually employed has been attracted to this use. Competition for factors among the individual firms will bring the transfer earnings of each factor unit (from the point of view of the firm) to a level at which its net revenue productivity (i.e., the difference between its transfer earnings and its gross revenue productivity) will be equal to that of the marginal factor unit. Thus there can in any case be no difference between the amounts of rent (from the point of view of the firm) earned by substitutable factor units, and there can be no rent from the point of view of any firm unless the marginal factor unit is itself earning revenues in excess of transfer price, that is, unless investment in the industry is at a lower-than-equilibrium level.

The "monopolistically competitive" firm, however, is by definition not competing for factors with other firms producing the same commodity; in one sense, the firm has here become coextensive with the industry, so that "optimum" investment is as compatible with rents from the point of view of this type of firm as it is with rents from the point of view of the pure-competition industry. Therefore, if the average-cost curve for the "monopolistically competitive" firm is drawn up to include only those payments that are necessary to retain factors within this firm, there is no reason to suppose that there necessarily must be tangency between the average-cost and average-revenue curves when investment is at the "optimum" level. The "optimum" here referred to is, of course, that qualified optimum which corresponds to the general implication of equality between demand price and supply price in the pure-competition industry, that is, that investment at which, *given the free-market determination of returns to factors,* no factor unit could increase its productivity by transferring either into or out of the use in question, and consumers are receiving the maximum output for which they are willing to pay the necessary price, the maximum return to any factor unit being, in general, not transfer cost but replacement cost. Here again, as in the case of the pure-competition industry, this "optimum" implies the nonexistence of rent only under certain special conditions of factor supply.

These supply conditions correspond to those that lead to the no-rent result in the pure-competition industry. If all factors employed by the firm are available in any quantity desired at an unchanged unit price, if imperfect substitutes for all factors are available in any quantity at prices that exactly offset their difference in productivity, or if the transfer price of all substitutable factor units goes up uniformly with the expansion of output, then any departure from tangency would indicate a departure from "optimum" investment in the usual sense. For under any of these conditions of factor supply, an excess of average revenue over average (transfer) cost would indicate that certain factor units not employed by the firm could increase their productivity by entering this use, and that an additional amount of product could be obtained by consumers at the prevailing price, without any outside interference with the free-market determination of factor returns. But under these conditions, it is clear that, in the absence of adventitious obstacles to the interoccupational mobility of factors, the situation described above (i.e., one firm producing the given product at revenues in excess of transfer cost) would not represent a stable equilibrium. There being nothing in the nature of factor supply to hinder the setting up of a new firm producing the same product, and at the same cost, as the existing firm, factors outside this use would hasten to enter it via the establishment of a new firm, until the supply of the product had increased to a point where no further factors could improve their productivity by entering this use — that is, to the point where in every firm average revenue would be equal to average (transfer) cost.

With the postulated conditions of factor supply, the only situation in which the existence of only one firm would represent a *stable* equilibrium would be one in which demand was sufficient to support only one firm at one level of output at a price equal to average (transfer) cost. Here tangency would have been attained; and here, as was the case with regard to the pure-competition industry, the optimum conditional upon the free-market determination of factor returns corresponds to the unconditional optimum. If demand is sufficient to support one firm at a price in excess of average cost, but insufficient to support two firms at a price as high as average cost, there will be no stable equilibrium unless the one firm fixes its price at a figure equal to average cost. Here there would not be *tangency*, but there would be investment equal to both the conditional and the unconditional optimum. This equilibrium would of course occur only if the profit-maximizing activity of the firm, which would ordinarily result in the fixing of price and output at the point indicated by the equality of marginal cost and marginal revenue, were modified by a desire to fend off potential competition.[10]

Under any other conditions of factor supply, the attainment of optimum investment in the usual sense does not imply equality between average (transfer) cost and average revenue. For

[10] This absence of a determinate stable equilibrium under the assumption of ordinary profit-maximizing activity, which arises from the fact that the firm cost curve may be (and, indeed, would ordinarily be expected to be) downward sloping over the first phase of the expansion of output, may occur from 2, 3, . . . , n firms, as well as one; the element of indeterminacy obviously applies to the pure-competition industry as well as to the "monopolistically competitive" firm.

example, if perfect substitutes for the factor units employed by the firm were available only at higher prices than those paid by it (because of imperfect substitutability from the point of view of other uses), there might obviously be a stable equilibrium with one firm producing at a nontangency level. But in this case, the equilibrium situation would correspond to the conditional optimum; there would be no possibility of returns to factors in excess of replacement cost.

Similarly, if imperfect substitutes for the factors employed by the firm are available only at prices that do not offset their lower revenue productivity, the conditional optimum might be reached with one firm at nontangency.

So far, the conditions of factor supply have been considered only as affecting the cost at which a new firm might enter the production of the same commodity as is currently being produced by existing firms. There may frequently arise, however, a situation in which the production of a given commodity requires the employment of a certain unique factor unit — a unit for which, *from the point of view of this use,* there exist no substitutes, perfect or imperfect, at any price. A familiar example of such a situation would be the retailing of commodities at a unique site. (It should be emphasized that, in this analysis, the terms "use" and "commodity" are strictly limited by the requirement of perfect substitutability among the units of product included within them.) In such a situation, there would obviously be no possibility of pure competition among firms engaged in the production of *this* commodity, since in the nature of things there could exist only one firm in this use. Moreover, it is evident that equilibrium might be attained with a difference between average revenue and average (transfer) cost. Nevertheless, it remains true that the equilibrium level of investment here, as well as in the foregoing examples, corresponds to the conditional optimum. For here again there exists no possibility that the unique factor may receive returns above its replacement cost (which is infinite); given the free-market determination of returns to factors, there exists no factor unit that could increase its productivity by entering this use, and consumers are obtaining the maximum output for which they are willing to pay the necessary price.

This conclusion may be demonstrated by the example of the unique retail site. At equilibrium output (demand being assumed to be more than adequate to support this firm at a price equal to transfer cost), a certain rent in excess of transfer cost will accrue to the owner of the site. But unless there is intervention on the part of an outside authority involving the fixing of the return to this factor at a lower level, there will be no possibility of lower prices, of increased employment of other factors, or of larger output at prices that consumers will be willing to pay. Without such intervention, any attempt on the part of the policy determiners within the firm to lower prices and increase output would result in the withdrawal of the site from their employment: it would always be possible for the site owner to establish his own firm and secure the equilibrium rent.

It is, of course, possible to make a distinction between the type of rent accruing to the owner of a unique retail site and that accruing to, say, the owner of a superior manufacturing site used by a firm that produces a commodity perfectly substitutable for that of various other manufacturers, on the ground that the former arises from the inability of other firms to enter the industry, whereas the latter arises only from a cost advantage conferred by the site. This distinction, although genuine and interesting, is of no significance from the point of view of economic performance. Both types of rent indicate a departure from the unconditional optimum, and both are perfectly consistent with the conditional optimum, for investment in the particular use in question.

If, then, the tangency condition is not necessary for optimum investment (in the usual sense) in the "monopolistically competitive" firm, except under certain special conditions of factor supply, can it still be said that the inability to produce perfect substitutes that is implied by the definition of monopolistic competition must preclude the achievement of optimum investment (in the usual sense)? The answer to this question would seem to depend in any particular case on the underlying condition responsible for this inability. It cannot, after all, result from a definition.

If the inability of an additional firm to enter any particular field of production results from the fact that the necessary factors may be obtained only at prices that preclude profitable production in this field — that is, that the necessary factors can be more remuneratively employed elsewhere — then this inability does not prevent the attainment of the conditional optimum. A similar conclusion applies if the inability arises from the absolute uniqueness, from the point of view of the use in question, of any factor unit necessary for entry. If, on the other hand, the inability is the result of some adventitious obstacle to the interoccupational mobility of factors, it may prevent the attainment of the conditional optimum; it may result in an equilibrium situation in which, given the free-market determination of factor returns, certain factor units outside this use could improve their productivity by entering it, certain factor units within this use are receiving returns in excess of the cost of their replacement, and consumers are not able to buy the amount of the product for which they are willing to pay the necessary price. Such adventitious obstacles include any impediments to entry that do not form an inherent part of the economic nature of factor supply, such as a legal restriction on the entry into any particular use of factors owned by foreign nationals.

The absence of any adventitious obstacles, direct or indirect, to the interoccupational mobility of factors is all that is necessary for the achievement of the conditional-optimum investment in any use. It is evident that this general condition must include the absence of obstacles to the formation of a new firm producing any given product, which particular aspect of factor freedom might be designated "free entry" with respect to any use. It is also true, however, that "free entry" in itself is not sufficient for the attainment of even the conditional optimum, for this result may be indirectly impeded by the pursuance of nonaggressive price-output policies on the part of individual firms.

By the adoption of this type of policy, the firm itself may block the attainment of the conditional optimum through making it impossible for certain factor units that could, given the free-market determination for returns, be more productively employed within it than in the production of any other commodity or in the production of the same commodity within an additional firm. This result will occur if the nonaggressiveness represents an actual underestimation of the elasticity of the firm's demand curve; in this event, if the conditions of demand and of factor supply are such that no more than one firm may participate in the production of the commodity in question, the investment in the firm itself will obviously constitute underinvestment in this use in the sense that it will be lower than the conditional optimum. If more than one firm may participate, the adoption of nonaggressive policies will tend to hold prices and costs above the optimum level, the ultimate result being underinvestment in the same sense as in the one-firm case. (It should be noted that in both cases investment is measured by the amount of factors employed valued at their transfer prices rather than at the returns to them in this use. The former valuation is evidently the relevant one in this instance, since it is investment in this sense which is maximized when the optimum level is reached. Whether the total returns to factors in this use would be greater or less than at the optimum level would depend on the elasticity of the demand for the product.)

In summary, it may be said that no possible state of competitive relations among firms — not even pure competition — can in itself be relied upon to result in the attainment of the unconditional optimum for investment in the use in question; on the other hand, it may also be said that the attainment of the conditional optimum — that which is inherently implied by the equality of demand price and supply price in the pure-competition industry — is brought about regardless of the state of competitive relations for the participant firms, provided only that there are no adventitious obstacles to the interoccupational mobility of factors. The latter statement must of course be qualified to take into account the influence of nonaggressive price-output policy on equilibrium investment. Such policies arise from a "nonatomistic" hypothesis of the impact of the individual firm's policies on its rivals and of the impact of their reactions on the fortunes of the firm itself; it is therefore obvious that a competitive situation in which the individual producer is confronted with one or more weighty rivals, of whom he is himself a weighty rival, will be necessary, although perhaps not sufficient, for the existence of such policies.

REDEFINITION OF THEORETICAL CONCEPTS WITHOUT RECOURSE TO THE IDEA OF THE GROUP

It will have been noted that in the discussion of nonaggressive price-output policy, no reference has been made to the distinction between "large groups" and "small groups" that formed the basis for certain policy recommendations discussed in Chapter I. In the latter case, it will be recalled, it was contended that an uncontrolled market would produce an equilibrium condition corresponding to a "sort of ideal"; "free entry" was relied upon to result in the universal tangency condition, and the "largeness" of the "group" to insure optimum size for each firm. In the former case, it was contended that although "free entry" would result in universal tangency, the "smallness" of the "group" would prevent optimum size for each firm at equilibrium investment.

The foregoing discussion has already shown that "free entry" cannot be relied upon to produce a condition of no rent from the point of view of any use, even under pure competition, except under certain special conditions of factor supply. However, it has also been shown that "free entry" can be relied upon to produce the conditional optimum for investment, except where the policies adopted by individual firms correspond to those characteristic of the "small group."

Since, as has been indicated, the theory of monopolistic competition, in eliminating the assumption of perfect substitutability among products of various firms in competition with one another, did away with the unambiguous criterion for the demarcation of the limits of the "group," it is evident that the distinction between "large groups" and "small groups" must be redefined if it is to retain any analytical significance. This distinction may be, and in fact has been, rescued from the wreckage of the monopolistically competitive "industry" by discarding the "numbers" criterion with which it was linked, and by directing attention to its essential significance in terms of the price-output policies of individual firms.

This essential significance may be precisely defined by the use of the Triffinian analytical apparatus. (In providing the tools for the analysis of markets in terms of the competitive relations of individual firms, Triffin has made another major contribution to economic theory.)[11] In Triffin's terminology, the condition of nonaggressiveness may be defined as one in which the hypotheses governing the policy of the firm are such that both the first and the second Triffinian coefficients describing its competitive relations with one or more other firms are regarded as significantly different from zero. That is to say, the firm's policy determiners assume that both the effect on its own revenues of a price change by one or more rivals and the effect on the revenues of these rivals of a price change on its own part will be significantly large in terms of the proportion of total revenues affected. In this terminology, the state of competition among a group of firms whose relations were characterized by this condition, and whose products were imperfectly substitutable, would be designated general circular heteropoly; if the products of these firms were perfect substitutes, the term descriptive of their relations would be general circular homeopoly. The term "circular" is used to identify the condition of oligopolistic interdependence; the absence of such interdependence is identified by the term "atomistic."

The redefinition of market classifications in terms of particular relations between firms, although preserving the distinction between "atomistic" and "circular" policy formerly linked with the concept of group numbers, focuses attention on the *particular* position of each individual maximizing unit, at once illuminating the nature and calling into question the probability of the assumption of uniformity in competitive relations that underlies market analysis in terms of industrial groups. Included in this assumption is the concept that each firm's signifi-

---

[11] Triffin, *Monopolistic Competition and General Equilibrium Theory*, ch. iii.

cant competitive relations are all of one type. Once the particularity of each firm's position is recognized, it becomes evident that many firms are faced with various degrees of competitiveness by different rivals.[12] It is also evident that a firm's competitive position cannot be fully analyzed without reference to its relations with potential as well as with actual competitors, and in this manner the problem of "oligopolistic interdependence as to entry" was brought into the theoretical framework.[13] A firm might conceivably be in a position of "isolated selling" as regards all existing firms, and yet be unable to raise its price above a point just covering minimum unit expenses, because of potential homogeneous competition (under the same cost conditions).

Furthermore, recognition that each firm is subject to diverse competition from producers of various products more or less substitutable for its own brings out the fact that the effect of the creation of a new firm cannot be isolated by the assumption that its impact will be felt only by the members of an a priori group to which the new firm is added. In this sense, the concept of entry itself takes on a different significance in the theory of general competition than in the analysis of pure competition or monopolistic competition in terms of the traditional "industry" concept. In the latter two types of analysis, "entry" means the addition of a maximizing unit to an "industry," the defining characteristic of which is that all the firms within it are producing what may be regarded as the same "commodity," although in monopolistic competition this product is regarded as "differentiated." The third type of theory recognizes the general substitutability among all products, and thus reveals the arbitrary character of the a priori "industrial" grouping with respect to which "entry" was defined.

The concept of "entry" is thus reduced in essence to the addition of a maximizing unit to the economic collectivity. However, the theory does not merely envisage the collectivity as a group of maximizing units all competing to the same degree with each other, which would amount to the substitution of

---

[12] See Chamberlin, *Monopolistic Competition*, pp. 102–104.

[13] Triffin, *Monopolistic Competition and General Equilibrium Theory*, p. 121.

an even more unrealistic standard pattern of competitive relations for the discarded "industrial" pattern. The "localization" of each firm's position in the collectivity is recognized in terms of varying values of the Triffinian coefficients describing its competitive relations with each other firm, actual and potential. Since hardly any conceivable firm's activities can be meaningfully analyzed in isolation, and since at some point on the scale the competitive relations of any firm become of negligible importance, any firm may be said to be a member of a competitive group, composed of itself and those firms with which it has significant relations. But the extent of this group may not be the same for any two firms, and the difference between relations within and without the group is recognized to be one of degree, not of kind.

The acceptance of the individual firm as the basic unit of market analysis makes even more essential the clarification of the precise content of the concept of the firm. As Triffin has pointed out, the definition of the firm as a *maximizing unit* reveals the essential content of the concept, and provides the principle by means of which the "frontier of the firm" may be determined.[14] Thus an organization under unified control that produced two or more commodities for which decisions with respect to price and output were made independently of each other would have to be regarded as two or more firms, whereas an organization nominally composed of several units, but actually governed by the same price-output decisions designed to maximize profit *for the group* would be one firm.

Multidimensional Profit Maximization

Recent theoretical developments have also paved the way for a more comprehensive theoretical treatment of the maximizing activities undertaken by actual enterprises, and thus for a more complete analysis of the organization of production into maximizing units, than was possible within the restrictive assumptions that characterize traditional theory. In this connection, the new tools for the analysis of the firm's competitive position provide media for the theoretical treatment of dimen-

[14] *Ibid.,* p. 94.

sions of the maximizing process that were largely ignored in traditional theory, and that have an important bearing on the actual determination of distribution of output among firms.

Chamberlin's recognition of the availability of "product variation" and the related activity of incurring "selling costs" to the individual firm as avenues of profit maximization has greatly expanded the analysis of the activities of the individual enterprise as compared with the two-dimensional treatment provided by traditional theory. In the latter type of analysis, on account of the rigid immutability of the individual demand curve from the point of view of the maximizer, his task was confined to the determination of output at the point indicated by the intersection (from below) of the marginal-revenue curve by the marginal-production-cost curve and the achievement and maintenance of the lowest possible production costs for any indicated output. (The latter activity tends to be obscured by being taken for granted — the cost curve is drawn on the assumption of lowest possible production costs for each output.)

All the avenues of maximization can be translated into alterations of individual demand or cost curves; however, the use of the Triffinian coefficients provides perhaps a more elegant method of formulation. By the "differentiation" of product or by incurring "selling costs," the maximizer obtains some "shelter from the competitive blast" — that is, he alters the first Triffinian coefficient from an infinite to a finite value, or reduces its value within a finite range. It is clear that this coefficient can be reduced in value in many other ways, including the very expansion of the output of the firm relative to that of its competitors.[15] Means of altering the coefficient include agreements for the division of markets, legal tactics designed to hamper the initiation or expansion of production by competitors, cutthroat competition aimed at driving competitors out of business, and many other types of strategy resulting in the elimination or reduction to insignificance of *independent* price-output decisions of competitors, such as the formation of trade

---

[15] On this point see Theodore Morgan, "A Measure of Monopoly in Selling," *Quarterly Journal of Economics,* LX, No. 3 (May 1946), pp. 461–463.

associations, combinations, or "communities of interest." The determination of the equilibrium size of firm rests to a large extent on the availability and profitability to the firm of the use of these methods of maximization, and it is seen that an analysis of firm equilibrium that does not take them into account is apt to yield unrealistic results when applied to real situations. In general, the more the "strategic" determinants of size of firm become evident, the less weight will be given in analyses of firm equilibrium to considerations of productive efficiency.

Summary and Conclusions

In summary, the preceding discussion has brought out the fact that market analysis and policy determination are arduous and complex tasks which cannot be evaded by the use of generalized prescriptions such as were derived from traditional economic theory.

(1) In the first place, the critical examination of the content of the concepts "industry" and "commodity" has eliminated once for all the possibility of treating the "transportation industry" or any particular agency of transport as a significant unit for analysis. There is no grand formula describing the workings of the "transportation market" from which a national transportation policy can be deduced. On the contrary, it is necessary to investigate particular markets in terms of the conditions confronting particular participant firms.

(2) Even in the examination of these markets, the touch-stone arrived at above — namely, the distinction between the large group, with aggressive price policy, and the small group, with nonaggressive price policy — has been shown to be incapable of providing a simple criterion for policy, even though it can be redefined in terms of particular competitive relations. It has been shown that "free entry" in the sense of the absence of adventitious obstacles to the establishment of a new firm producing the *same commodity* as existing firms (the Triffinian "homogeneous entry") can in no case be relied upon to produce the no-rent condition implied by the unconditional optimum for investment, except under certain special conditions of factor supply. From

this it follows a fortiori that "free entry" in the sense of the absence of adventitious obstacles to the establishment of a new firm producing an *imperfect substitute* for the product of existing firms (the Triffinian "heterogeneous entry," which is the type of entry envisaged in the monopolistic-competition analysis) cannot be relied upon to product this result. There is therefore no airtight case for the limitation of regulatory intervention to the elimination of obstacles to entry and the encouragement of aggressive price policy whenever feasible.

(3) It has become even more evident that the fact that resources engaging in a given activity (such as transportation) are earning no rent cannot be taken to mean that either investment in the field as a whole or investment per firm is at the optimum level, and that no addition or subtraction of investment or of firms competitive with the existing ones would be warranted. Apart from the fact that this condition may have resulted from the combination of oligopolistic pricing and the existence of too many firms, it is clear that the returns earned within existing firms accurately indicate returns available to new firms only where the latter would produce identical products at identical costs. The indication is likely to become progressively inaccurate as substitutability and similarity of cost conditions decrease.[16] Indeed, the very concept of "investment in the field as a whole" loses its precise content where the field itself is heterogeneous and without definite boundaries.

(4) The bringing to light of avenues of profit maximization usually ignored in economic theory has the general effect of calling into question the usual analysis of the distribution of output among firms (and hence equilibrium investment) in uncontrolled markets; the emphasis on "strategic" factors tends to cast additional doubt on the actual weight of considerations of productive efficiency in the determination of the size of real firms. Furthermore, since the "frontier of the firm" is determined by the scope of the maximizing unit rather than by that of the productive or managerial unit, it is seen that considerations pertaining to the determination of the size of the latter have no necessary bearing on the determination of the

[16] Triffin, *Monopolistic Competition and General Equilibrium Theory*, p. 120.

size of the former, except through the fact that the minimum component of a firm would seem to be one producing unit.

(5) As a result of the more precise definition of the firm, the problem of control of entry and exit is seen to be more complex than is usually supposed, and to embrace certain activities usually regarded as internal to the firm as well as some that are generally treated as interfirm relations. It becomes evident that the appearance or disappearance of firms need not take the form of the appearance or disappearance of a certain name from the list of companies engaging in a certain type of business. The conclusion of an agreement among officers of several companies, or the formation of a community of interest by financial groups, may effectively reduce the number of independent maximizers, and the breaking up of such a group may increase it. Similarly, the extension of a company's operations into fields competitively unrelated to its existing activities involves the creation of a new maximizing unit, and its withdrawal from such a field the extinction of one, though the number of corporate entities remains the same.

(6) Finally, the problem of "entry" may no longer be analyzed as merely the addition of a maximizing unit to an "industry," its impact thereby being assumed to be confined to the markets of other firms within this "industrial" group and, within this group, to have a uniform influence on all of the affected markets. In general, the establishment of a new firm will be expected to affect the competitive positions of various existing firms according to the degree of competitiveness between its product and the commodities produced by each of them.

Here it may well be asked what tests of economic performance remain as appropriate for the suggested analysis of particular markets. The former touchstones having been discarded, is there any further definite basis by which to judge markets, or is it necessary to fall back on generalizations about "order" and "change" or to adopt some approximate and imprecise notion of desirable market conditions to substitute for the precise standards formerly supposed to be afforded by pure competition?

The latter course seems to have been adopted by Wilcox in a recent work, where it is maintained that the new market standard should be "effective" competition, and that competition is "effective or workable whenever it operates overtime to afford buyers substantial protection against exploitation at the hands of sellers and to afford sellers similar protection against exploitation by buyers." [17] Although this statement seems to point in the right direction, it has no precise meaning without accompanying definitions of "substantial," "overtime," and especially "exploitation."

Fortunately, it is not necessary to adopt either of these expedients. As has been said, it is not the mere form of pure competition that makes it desirable but its (supposed) implications regarding the allocation of productive resources, and these implications remain as fundamental criteria of economic performance.

These implications are referred to as "supposed" because, as has been demonstrated in the preceding discussion, not even pure competition with "free entry" (i.e., homogeneous entry) can be relied upon to produce the unconditional optimum for investment in the production of any given commodity except under certain by no means universal conditions of factor supply. It has also been shown that the conditional optimum — that is, optimum investment within the framework of the free-market determination of factor returns — is brought about regardless of the competitive relations for the participant firms (with the qualification that these relations may result in the adoption of nonaggressive price-output policies and hence in relatively inefficient organization of production among firms and in underinvestment), provided only that there are no adventitious obstacles to the interoccupational mobility of factors. It remains only to observe that any complex of competitive relations, from isolated selling with respect to every other firm in the economy to homogeneous competition with all significant competitors, for the firms producing any given commodity may be consistent with the achievement of the unconditional optimum level of

[17] Clair Wilcox, *Competition and Monopoly in American Industry,* T.N.E.C. Monograph No. 21, 76th Congress, 3rd Session, p. 9.

investment in the production of this commodity, and it becomes clear that neither the performance of uncontrolled markets nor the correctness of regulatory policies may be judged by the competitive relations present in these markets or resulting from these policies. Accordingly, regulatory policy should not have as one of its ultimate aims the achievement of a certain type of competitive position for the firms regulated.

This last statement is valid so long as the attainment of a static optimum for investment is conceived as the sole aim of regulatory policy, or so long as the power and wisdom of the regulators are regarded as unlimited; once these assumptions are removed, it must be qualified to take into account the stimulus afforded by genuine competition, whether homogeneous or heterogeneous, to the efforts of the firm's policy makers to vary the product and improve production techniques, i.e., to the institution of innovations that are by definition ruled out in static analysis and that the regulators may be legally or otherwise unable to bring about.

Putting aside these considerations for the moment, let us take up in detail the positive guides for public policy that may be derived directly from our analysis of the nature of the conditional and unconditional optima.

In the first place, the obtainment by consumers of the maximum amount of product for which they are willing to pay the necessary cost (i.e., average transfer cost), and the corollary condition that each factor unit be placed in accordance with maximum revenue productivity, must be regarded as the ultimate economic desiderata; hence it is the unconditional rather than the conditional optimum that provides the appropriate standard for the judgment of economic performance of uncontrolled markets and of the economic influence of regulatory policy. It should be noted that this unconditional optimum, defined as it is with reference to a particular product, does not necessarily correspond to the investment that would be arrived at should the production of all commodities be planned to conform to the same essential requirements. In defining the optimum for any particular product, the transfer cost of any factor unit is taken to be the earnings that it would receive in the next best use; thus if rent (from the point of view of this use) is received in this use, or if the earnings of the factor differ from its revenue productivity because of (1) the receipt by it (through its strategic or contractual position) of revenues that should be imputed to another factor unit or (2) monopolistic exploitation by some other factor, its transfer cost from the point of view of the use for which the optimum is defined will differ from that which would obtain if all uses were considered together.

From the economic point of view, the method by which returns to factors are determined is entirely immaterial. Thus no special economic value can be attached to the conditional optimum merely because it represents the outcome of the free-market determination of factor returns. This is not to say, of course, that this method of determination of returns may not often turn out to be the best possible instrument for the allocation of investment among various commodities and the distribution of factors among firms in accordance with the unconditional optimum, but only that its results, like those of a controlled market, must be judged from the economic point of view by reference to the unconditional standard, without weighting the scales for it or against it because of the particular method by which returns are fixed.

It is indeed possible that the free-market determination of factor returns may be regarded as in itself desirable or undesirable by some noneconomic (e.g., political, ethical, or religious) standard of value, and such considerations must of course at some point be taken into account in the making of policy decisions.

Secondly, although the uncontrolled market may, under certain conditions of factor supply, result in the attainment of the unconditional optimum, it will not even under these conditions do so unless there are no artificial obstacles to the interoccupational mobility of factors. Hence it may quite generally be said that, from a purely economic point of view, one of the objectives of public policy should be to remove any such obstacle, whatever its origin. It may be, of course, that certain noneconomic objectives of public policy may be of sufficient importance to overrule this course of action; for example, it might well be thought desirable to place direct obstacles in the way of the expansion of investment in the production of harmful narcotics, or to expand deliberately the quantity of resources devoted to the production of goods or services essential for national defense. Moreover, since the investment of resources in any market cannot be expected to conform to the unconditional optimum unless demand conditions represent rational choice on the part of consumers, a further generally desirable objective for public policy is the promotion of exact consumer knowledge of the nature of the products offered to them — an objective that would involve the elimination of falsification as an avenue of profit maximization by individual enterprises, just as the first objective would involve the elimination of the creation of obstacles to factor mobility as a means of making money. It is, then, clear that some control over the particular means of profit maximization open to firms will in general be necessary. This proposition has, of course, always been accepted as a basis for policy; it has been given its proper place in economic theory by the new multidimensional approach to the theory of the firm.

Thirdly, it is clear that the adoption of nonaggressive policies by individual firms may impede the achievement of the unconditional optimum by resulting in an inefficient distribution of resources among firms. Although there appears to be no direct or infallible method by which these policies may be reversed by public action, it may be said that the existence of trade associations and the like would probably reinforce any tendency to nonaggressiveness that may already be present among the members of any competitive group. There is here perhaps a prima facie case for the elimination of such associations; however, this case must be weighed against the facts that (1) the dissolution of formal associations could not be expected to do away with informal conferences on trade problems; (2) formal or informal conferences are not necessary for the adoption of nonaggressive policies; and (3) some of the activities of such associations may be conducive to the achievement of the optimum.

The desirability of any further intervention by government in any particular market will depend (*a*) upon the degree of departure from the unconditional optimum brought about by the conditions of factor supply or by the policies adopted by individual firms; and (*b*) upon the probable success of government intervention in achieving a closer approximation to the unconditional optimum than would be attained with the free-market determination of factor returns.

In the absence (either initial or as a result of government action) of nonaggressiveness on the part of individual firms, the departure from the unconditional optimum will depend upon the special conditions of factor supply. If these are such that no returns above transfer cost will be earned by any factor unit at equilibrium, there will be no need for further intervention. If, on the other hand, these special conditions are not present, the degree of departure from the unconditional optimum (that is, the amount of underinvestment, the size of the total return to factors above transfer cost, and the amount paid by consumers in excess of the necessary price) will depend upon the actual conditions of factor supply. Such a departure may result from the (technically unstable) equilibrium situation brought about by demand and supply conditions such that a certain number of firms may be supported at a level of returns above transfer cost, but more could not be supported at a level of returns equal to transfer cost, as well as from the other conditions of factor supply, the nature of which has already been indicated.

Given an appreciable departure from the unconditional optimum, the recommended course for public policy will depend upon whether or not it is probable that government intervention will achieve a closer approximation to the unconditional optimum than would be attained with the free-market determination of factor returns. If the achievement of this optimum were a simple task, or if the regulators were all-powerful and perfectly informed, this question of course would not arise at all.

It must be pointed out, however, that even the concrete formulation of the actual level of investment aimed at is an exceedingly complex task, and it might well be expected that even the best regulation humanly possible would in most cases be able to arrive at such a formulation only through trial and error. The difficulties surrounding this task are multiplied, and its eventual accomplishment thus made less probable, when commodities subjected to regulation are in close competition among themselves or with other commodities. The content of the optimum must in any case be subject to alteration as a result of autonomous changes in demand and cost conditions; the task will be more difficult and less likely to be accomplished the more frequent and the more quantitatively important are these autonomous changes. Moreover, by fixing returns to factors at (or a little above) the transfer-cost level, regulation would remove the profit incentive to innovation; the development of new types of product and of new techniques of production would be dependent upon the initiative that might come from outside the regulated firms and the initiative of the regulators. Although it is not inconceivable that these two sources might originate improvements on the same scale as without regulation, it seems probable that the net result would be a slowing down in the rate of "economic progress" in the field.

Taking these considerations into account, it may be said that, other things being equal, the departure from the unconditional optimum needed to justify intervention in firms producing commodities subject to close competition or frequent and large changes in demand and cost conditions would be larger than in firms not so situated. The same proposition might reasonably be applied to fields in which possibilities for innovations are more likely to occur, although it is admittedly very difficult, if not impossible, to distinguish such fields in practice. Among the other things that are supposed equal is the "social importance" of the particular commodity produced by these firms. It might, for example, be thought of little or no importance that investment in the production of champagne was at less than the optimum level. However, this type of consideration cannot be dealt with by use of the tools provided by economic theory.

Finally, it should be noted that the powers that would have to be given to the regulators to accomplish their end would in many cases be much more comprehensive than are ordinarily delegated to regulatory bodies in the United States, and would most probably have to be accompanied by government ownership of the regulated properties to avoid constitutional objections.

PART II
REGULATORY POLICY

CHAPTER III

THE CIVIL AERONAUTICS ACT

The discussion in this study regarding regulatory policy in the field of interstate air transportation will be primarily concerned with the administration of the Civil Aeronautics Act of 1938.[1] As will be seen, the investment in and organization of the air-transport industry in the United States had been affected to a very important extent by the policies of the Federal Government for many years prior to its passage; however, this Act is the first measure applying economic regulation to all interstate commercial air carriers, since previous legislation dealt with mail carriers only. The 1938 Act subjected interstate air carriers to regulation with respect to virtually all phases of their economic activities: the approval of a regulatory agency was required for the initiation or abandonment of service on individual routes; intercompany relations such as mergers, leases, and interlocking directorates had also to be approved; and provisions substantially similar to those already governing rail and motor rates were made applicable to rates charged to the public by the air carriers.

Although, as has been indicated, the Civil Aeronautics Act represented in several respects an innovation in the policy of the Federal Government, it is easy to overestimate the novelty of its provisions and to misconstrue the motives of their framers. A consideration of the major elements of policy contained in the Act should serve to clarify these motives, and hence to provide a valid basis for the interpretation of the Act in the light of Congressional intent, and will also bring out the main features of the nature and development of Federal policy toward air transportation before 1938. The elements to be considered will be: (1) the subsidization policy; (2) the rejection of competi-

---

[1] 52 Stat. 973 (1938).

tive bidding in favor of choice of carrier by a quasi-judicial process; (3) the subjection of air transportation to a regulatory regime similar to that already provided by the Interstate Commerce Act for other types of carrier; and (4) the extension of the certification requirement to cover all interstate air-transport routes, including nonmail as well as mail-carrying services. The last-named provision is, of course, an integral part of the regulatory system dealt with in point (3), as is the method of choice of carrier (point 2); but the particular importance of these aspects of the regulatory system in the air-transportation policy embodied in the Civil Aeronautics Act warrants special treatment of them in this discussion.

The Subsidization Policy

One of the most important features of the Act is its definite setting forth of a rule for the determination of air-mail payments which clearly did not limit them to the cost of carrying the mails, thus marking the first clear-cut Congressional declaration of the policy of subsidization of commercial air-transport companies by means of the mail rate.[2] It has been argued that the Watres Act,[3] passed in 1930, envisaged the subsidization of passenger services through air-mail payments in excess of the cost of carrying the mails,[4] but reference to this Act itself reveals no clear-cut declaration in favor of the subsidization principle. The lack of any such declaration is emphasized by the fact that even representatives of the Post Office Department, which apparently administered the Act with the intention of subsidizing passenger transport, referred to the Depart-

---

[2] Section 406(*b*) of the Act includes a provision requiring that the administrative agency consider in the determination of the mail rate the "need of each such [air-mail] carrier for compensation . . . sufficient . . . together with all other revenue of the air carrier, to enable such air carrier under honest, economical, and efficient management, to maintain and continue the development of air transportation to the extent and of the character and quality required for the commerce of the United States, the Postal Service, and the national defense."

[3] 46 Stat. 259 (1930).

[4] See, for example, P. T. David, *The Economics of Air Mail Transportation* (Washington: The Brookings Institution, 1934), p. 161.

ment's own interpretation of the Act as resting on a "belief" as to Congressional intent rather than on a clear mandate contained in the law.[5]

Nevertheless, the legislative history of the Civil Aeronautics Act does not indicate that either its industrial or its Congressional proponents realized the full significance of the new rule of mail-rate making; furthermore, air-mail payments had most probably actually included an element of subsidy for many years before 1938.

Throughout the discussions immediately preceding the enactment of the law, the question of the mail rate was generally overshadowed by the regulatory aspects of the bills that were the forerunners of the Act; it was the regulatory apparatus, rather than the mail payment, which was emphasized as the salvation of the airlines. The following statement of Colonel Edgar S. Gorrell, President of the Air Transport Association and the most prominent spokesman for the carriers in connection with the proposed legislation, is enlightening. Speaking before a Congressional Committee in the spring of 1938 of the need of the airlines for immediate refinancing, he said:

There are only two ways whereby the necessary capital can be provided to this industry. One is the way toward which the governments of foreign lands increasingly tend — the way of mounting Governmental subsidies, whereby public funds are poured without stint into air transport. The other way is the traditional American way, a way which invites the confidence of the investing public, by providing a basic economic charter that promises the hope of stability and security and orderly and intelligent growth under watchful governmental supervision.

It is the second way, the traditional American way, which H.R. 9738 proposes. It is a way which protects the public through stringent regulation. It is a way which encourages the investor through provision for order and stability. It is a way which challenges management by making it possible to exercise the type of business foresight and planning which has made our country great. It is a way which, I am convinced, will put an end to the unprecedented and wasteful mortal-

____
[5] *Ibid.*

ity that has unfortunately accompanied the growth of the industry heretofore.[6]

In the same Hearings, the following colloquy is recorded:

MR. HOLMES: To what extent, then, under this new Authority or new Federal help is your industry going to recoup some of its losses — by subsidies?
COLONEL GORRELL: No; the principal thing is to reëstablish confidence in the industry, so that we can refinance the companies and get capital to carry out the sound types of business practices that are needed in order to increase the income of the industry.
MR. HOLMES: But you will still expect some subsidy?
COLONEL GORRELL: We expect adequate mail pay, sir . . .[7]

Before 1938, the policy of subsidization had most probably been carried out in the *administration* of legislation dealing with the carriage of the mails by air, even though this legislation itself seems to have envisaged the determination of these payments on a mail-cost basis. Let it be said, however, that the probable inclusion of the subsidy by administrative action was for the most part, at least, accomplished within the letter of the law; consequently the governing legislation must also be held responsible to some extent for the subsidization policy.

For example, it seems to be generally agreed that in the period immediately prior to the passage of the Watres Act in 1930 Congress was opposed to the subsidization principle,[8] but the specific content of this Act was such as to permit the Postmaster General to nullify the intent of Congress. The adoption in the Watres Act of the space-mile basis of compensation for air-mail service, although not in itself indicating any departure from the mail-cost principle (quite the contrary, in fact), enabled the Postmaster General to disregard this principle completely in fixing mail payments, even to the extent of permitting him to award contracts on routes where there was no mail to be

---

[6] *To Create a Civil Aeronautics Authority*, Hearings before the House Committee on Interstate and Foreign Commerce on H.R. 9738, 75th Congress, 3rd Session, 1938, pp. 338–339.

[7] *Ibid.*, p. 301.

[8] On this point, see David, *The Economics of Air Mail Transportation*, p. 94.

carried. This official proceeded to fix these payments in accordance with the need of existing carriers for revenue to make their current operations profitable.[9] In addition, the discretion permitted to the Postmaster General under the Watres Act allowed him to adopt "formulas" for the determination of mail payments which, in so far as they were of any practical effect, were probably in contravention of the mail-cost principle.[10]

A similar situation may have existed in the case of the Air Mail Act of 1934,[11] which superseded the Watres Act. The rule of rate making governing the determination of mail payments in the 1934 Act did not indicate any adoption of the subsidization policy, but in administering this provision the Interstate Commerce Commission explicitly rejected the view that mail payments should be limited to the cost of carrying the mails.

The fact that the statute provided no clear mandate to the Commission to subsidize the mail carriers is well brought out by the statements of Commissioner Joseph B. Eastman before official bodies participating in the formulation of the Civil Aeronautics Act. For example, testifying before the Interdepartmental Committee set up by the President in 1937 to consider proposed aviation legislation, Eastman declared that the question of whether the mail payments should or should not contain a subsidy was for Congress and not for the Commission to decide, and continued:

. . . the only position that the Commission has taken on that [i.e., on subsidization] is that if we are to be given that job we want the rule stated with the utmost clarity so that we will know just what Congress wants us to do . . . To some extent the present rule in the law is subject to that criticism, that is, capable of varying interpretations, as no one knows exactly what is meant by it.[12]

---

[9] *Ibid.*, p. 99: "That the amount of space purchased was not to be determined by the amount needed for mail was clear from the Postmaster General's statement that . . . 'We would try to take sufficient space to keep the carriers from going into bankruptcy until they could get people to fly.'"

[10] For the details of these formulas, see the *Annual Reports* of the Postmaster General for the years 1931 and 1932.

[11] 48 Stat. 933 (1934).

[12] *Hearings* before Interdepartmental Committee To Consider Proposed Aviation Legislation, p. 519 of typed copy.

One of the amendments to this Act that were adopted in 1935[13] serves to strengthen the presumption that Congress had not abandoned the mail-cost principle; this amendment provided that in fixing mail payments the Commission should not take into account carrier losses on nonmail schedules where the gross receipts from their operation did not suffice to cover additional operating expenses chargeable to them.

In administering the Act, however, the Commission explicitly rejected the contention of the Postmaster General that only costs definitely allocable to the mail service should be considered in the determination of mail payments. Although the very doubtful economic validity of the results of the usual methods of cost allocation might well justify the position of the Commission even from the point of view of the mail-cost principle, it is significant that the reason actually given by the Commission for the rejection of the Postmaster General's proposal was that its application might remove the incentive for the development of nonmail services, it being implied that an alternative system of rate fixing (presumably that employed by the Commission itself) was designed to provide an incentive for such development. In fact, the principles which governed air-mail rate making by the Commission appear to have been broadly similar to those later employed by the Civil Aeronautics Board.[14]

In general, it can be said that wherever the mail rates were administratively determined, whether by the Postmaster General or the Commission, the mail-cost principle was most probably not followed in administration. Congress could have avoided this result by a steadfast adherence to the policy of genuine competitive bidding for the award of mail routes, inasmuch as this would have eliminated to a large extent administrative discretion in rate determination. However, it should be emphasized that other than this there is no necessary connection between the award of routes on the basis of competitive

---

[13] 49 Stat. 614 (1935).

[14] See C. E. Puffer, *Air Transportation* (Philadelphia: Blakiston, 1941), pp. 341–342.

bidding and the mail-cost principle. It is clear that competitive bidding could be used to award contracts for the operation of routes certified on the basis of commercial demand, or on any other basis, just as readily as in the award of mail contracts; it is also clear that payments to the carriers could be administratively determined so as to cover only the cost of carrying the mail just as readily as in covering the cost of commercial *and* postal services.

It should be noted that throughout much of the period before the passage of the Civil Aeronautics Act the legislation governing mail payments contained provisions designed to limit such payments on each route to the amount of revenue (or a specified fraction thereof) received by the Government for postal service on that route. When in 1925 the Kelly Act[15] for the first time authorized the letting of air-mail contracts to private operators, payments on each route were limited to 80 percent of Government revenues for services on that route. The 1926 amendment to the Kelly Act,[16] although changing the formulation of the legal maximum from a percentage of receipts to a fixed sum per pound (with mileage differentials), was intended to embody the same principle as the original Act, the formal alteration being adopted for the sake of administrative convenience. The maxima imposed by the Watres Act and the Air Mail Act of 1934 seem to have been less closely related to postal receipts, but the latter measure reaffirmed the intent of Congress to limit payments to the amount of receipts by requiring the Interstate Commerce Commission so to fix airmail rates that after July 1, 1938 the mail payments on any route should not exceed the total of postal revenues expected from the service on that route. These limitations do not in themselves constitute an antisubsidization policy on the part of Congress, since they do not necessarily prohibit payments in excess of the cost of carrying the mails. They are rather to be interpreted as legislative safeguards against the authorization of excessive expenditures by administrative action.

[15] 43 Stat. 805 (1925).
[16] 44 Stat. 692 (1926).

The Rejection of Competitive Bidding

The Civil Aeronautics Act's final rejection of competitive bidding in favor of a quasi-judicial method of choice of carrier did not, as has often been thought, result from any demonstrated shortcomings of the competitive-bidding procedure as such, nor did it represent a complete break with the methods actually employed before 1938.

The so-called "defects of competitive bidding," which indeed played a part in discrediting this procedure itself in the eyes of the public and of Congress, were actually defects belonging to legislatively formulated systems of awarding contracts that retained only the form rather than the substance of genuine competitive bidding. Furthermore, these systems, especially that provided under the Watres Act, apparently had permitted administrative action regarding choice of carrier in which not even the form of competitive bidding was observed.

The Kelly Act, as well as all succeeding relevant legislation until 1938, required that the original award of air-mail contracts be made by competitive bidding. The specific procedure followed at first appears to have been well adapted to the achievement of genuine competitive bidding on the part of the carriers, and thus quite satisfactory from the point of view of securing the most efficient performance of the advertised service; contracts were let for periods of four years, with no provision for extension or renewal without a new submission of bids. In 1928, however, the practical force of competitive bidding in determining the operators of routes was weakened by an amendment to the Kelly Act,[17] providing that the Postmaster General might extend the contracts after two years of satisfactory performance to cover a total length of time of up to ten years (beginning on the date of the original award), and might also renegotiate the mail rate at the time of the extension.[18]

---

[17] 45 Stat. 594 (1928).

[18] The purpose of this provision was to furnish a convenient means for reducing the rates of compensation to the carriers when, as was anticipated, such reductions would become feasible as a result of the increase in the volume of air mail expected to arise from the decrease in the air-mail postage rate authorized in the same amendment.

Although this provision did reduce the influence of the competitive principle by extending the period in which contract holders were protected from competition (only as regards mail carriage, of course), it did not entirely vitiate this principle, because the amendment also required that renegotiated mail rates should not exceed the rate originally bid. Thus it could still be expected that the competing carriers would submit bids based on their actual anticipations of the cost of rendering the service.

By the provisions of the Watres Act, the practical effectiveness of the competitive-bidding system of route awards was all but destroyed, despite the fact that Congress apparently still favored this system and had specifically rejected a proposal by the Postmaster General that it be replaced by a process of administrative negotiation.[19] The Act permitted the Postmaster General, in extending the contracts, to authorize mail rates higher than those originally bid; thus the carriers could look forward to making up later any losses incurred in the first two years of operation under any mail contract, at least to the extent that this could be done by mail rates within the legal maximum. (The maximum extension period remained the same as under the amended Kelly Act, as did the requirement of two years' satisfactory operation before the extension.) This provision of course placed a premium on the ability of any competing firm to weather substantial temporary losses, and gave a decisive advantage to established companies with strong financial backing. The efficacy of the bidding process as a means of insuring the most efficient performance of the subsidized service was evidently destroyed.

Other provisions allowed the Postmaster General to circumvent the bidding process and carry out his own (contrary) policy of awarding contracts to favored established carriers in order to strengthen their financial position. The power granted

[19] David, *The Economics of Air Mail Transportation*, p. 101: "Opposition to the bill centered around the provision permitting award of contracts without competitive bidding. It was referred to in the minority report as follows: 'This provision, making the Postmaster General a law unto himself, eliminates competition, and is nothing more than a subsidy in the interest of the aircraft industry.' "

to the Postmaster General to make extensions and consolidations of routes without resorting to competitive bidding, despite the Comptroller General's rather restrictive interpretation of the meaning of "extension" under the law, was used to by-pass the competitive system in the award of contracts for almost 9000 miles of new route, about 44 percent of the previous mail-route mileage.[20] A special provision allowed the Postmaster General to give preference in the award of contracts for light-traffic routes to companies that had already carried on at least six months' operation of scheduled service over a distance of at least 250 miles. The Postmaster General furthermore used his legal power to specify eligibility requirements for bidders in such a manner as to eliminate all but well-established carriers from bidding on the transcontinental routes, the award of which by the extension method was deemed legally infeasible or at least difficult.[21] In addition to the weakening of the competitive principle permitted or embodied in the law itself, many believe that the Postmaster General insured the ineffectiveness of competition by a direct and illegal encouragement of collusion among the air carriers.[22]

The process by which the mail contracts were originally relet to private carriers after the cancellation of contracts in 1934 evidently was one of genuine competitive bidding; however, the Air Mail Act passed later in that year was fatally defective in this respect. Even more than the Watres Act, the new law in itself vitiated the competitive process: after satisfactory performance of the service contracted for during the original period (the legal *maximum* for this period being at first set at one year, and then, in 1935, at three years), the contracts were automatically to be extended for an indefinite period, the subsequent mail rate and any other additional conditions governing the extended contract to be prescribed by the Interstate Commerce Commission. As was clearly affirmed by one of the 1935 amendments to the Air Mail Act, the Commission was

---

[20] *Investigation of Air Mail and Ocean Mail Contracts,* Hearings before the Special Committee on Investigation of Air Mail and Ocean Mail Contracts, Senate, Sen. Res. 349, and Sen. Res. 143, 1935, pp. 1483–1485.

[21] *Ibid.,* p. 1638.

[22] *Ibid.,* passim, especially p. 1584, and pp. 1674–1675.

empowered to raise the mail payments above the original bid rate as well as to lower them.

In view of this prescribed procedure, other parts of the Act designed to prevent collusion among the carriers and favoritism on the part of the Postmaster General were of no avail in bringing about genuine, effective competitive bidding. These provisions included: (1) a limitation on the total number of routes and also on the number of "primary routes" (important lines enumerated in the Act) which could be held by any one carrier; (2) eligibility requirements effectively excluding from bidding companies whose officers or directors had participated in the so-called "spoils conferences" sponsored by the former Postmaster General; (3) grave penalties for persons attempting to restrain competition in bidding by prospective mail contractors; (4) a requirement that the Postmaster General award contracts to the lowest bidder unless this bidder was thought to be not responsible or properly qualified, in which case the final decision was left to the Comptroller General. There were also other provisions limiting the discretionary power of the Postmaster General, and the sections of the Act regarding business relations among mail carriers were at least in part designed to insure genuine competitive bidding.

It must be admitted that in so far as profitable operation of commercial air transport was dependent on the possession of a mail contract, as it seems to have been on many routes in the period before the 1938 Act, this condition raised difficulties with regard to competitive bidding. For since it is necessary to the success of this process that the contracting authority have evidence that the bidders are qualified to render the desired service and are "responsible," actual eligibility for contract awards is almost inevitably limited to going concerns, and among these, to firms whose previous operations have been at least somewhat similar to those for which the contracts are being let. Thus, in a situation where no commercial air carrier could remain a going concern without a mail contract, the field of competitors might well be effectively limited to companies that had previously operated mail routes.

This consideration, however, did not figure prominently in

the policy discussions leading to the final abandonment of competitive bidding in 1938. One argument used in those discussions was the contention that competitive bidding had produced "disastrous rate wars" and absurdly low bids, and had thus been proved unworkable. It is, of course, true that some of the bids received under the system of awards actually in effect had been indeed absurdly low and bore no conceivable relation to the cost of operating the routes. But this was only to be expected where the original bid rates were almost certain to be replaced by administratively determined payments after a comparatively short period of time.

Secondly, it was contended that competitive bidding placed undue emphasis on low-cost as opposed to high-quality operation.[23] This is a familiar argument against price competition in general; as usual, it is open to the obvious objection that standards of service no less than cost of service are subject to the buyer's choice. If the specifications are adequately defined by the contracting authority, there need be no fear of inferior service.

The Federal Aviation Commission, a body created by the Air Mail Act of 1934 to make recommendations regarding the policy of the United States Government toward aviation, maintained that competitive bidding was unsuitable for the award of air routes because the specifications could not be made satisfactorily complete and flexible, and also because such services should be established on a long-term basis. The Commission stated that no set of specifications could possibly be complete enough to cover all the aspects of the operation of an airline, and that, even if this were not so, the specifications could not be altered rapidly enough to keep the service up with the latest technological changes in such a continuously advancing industry. Thus, the Commission concluded, "We can see no way of introducing an adequately flexible control over a rapidly developing art unless the flexibility be extended to commission power to select operators for new routes and to determine from time to time the conditions under which they must render serv-

---

[23] See, for example, the *Report* of the Federal Aviation Commission, 74th Congress, 1st Session, 1935, p. 55.

ice." [24] Where continuous governmental control of an exhaustive character over all aspects of airline operation is desired, it is indeed improbable that competitive bidding would prove to be a satisfactory instrument of policy. However, it is just as improbable (if not more so) that the usual certification and regulation process would serve; the most suitable method of assuring such detailed and positive control over operations would seem to be government ownership of the airlines.

The Commission's second argument — that airline routes should be established on a "substantially permanent basis" — in so far as it is not merely a bare assertion that replacement of certain firms by others from time to time would have a "disastrous effect on the service," seems to spring from a contention that such replacement would entail excessive waste of resources. It is, at least by strong implication, argued that the fixed investment in an airline, or at any rate in an airline of a desirable type, is so large that a competitive policy, permitting the "air transport map . . . [to] be redrawn every few years," would be intolerable. "An airline," says the Commission, "cannot be casually torn up and transplanted. The fixed investment in land, buildings, and equipment, of major airlines ranges, according to the best information that we can secure, from $200 to $500 per mile of route. While there are lines that have not a penny of such investment, and that depend entirely on rental of existing structures and services, they do not seem to us to offer an ideal example of the type of service that ought to be developed in future." [25]

Although it is of course true of an airline, as well as of almost any business enterprise, that its relocation will probably involve some loss of fixed investment, it is highly doubtful that this loss will be necessarily so great as to make it a preponderant factor in the determination of government policy as to choice of carrier. The mobility of the overwhelming proportion of airline assets indeed appears to be much greater than that of the resources employed in most industries, and this is true of the scheduled trunk-line carriers as well as of the smaller firms.

[24] *Ibid.,* p. 56.
[25] *Ibid.,* pp. 55–56.

Further, the absolute amount per carrier of such immobile investment that is necessary for the efficient performance of scheduled air service is relatively small.

The Commission was undoubtedly right in its belief that the allocation of routes by competitive bidding was incompatible with the guaranteed holding of such routes on a "substantially permanent basis" by particular carriers. It is of the essence of the competitive-bidding process that particular carriers shall be periodically subject to replacement by lower bidders (which are, given proper specifications in the contract, presumed to be more efficient performers of the required service). It was the inherent incompatibility between competitive bidding and the protection of particular carriers from competition by long-term certification that produced manifestly absurd results in the systems of contract awards in force before 1938, and the abandonment of competitive bidding in that year represented a victory for the policy of protecting particular carriers.

THE COMPREHENSIVE REGULATION OF AIR TRANSPORT

The fact that the Civil Aeronautics Act subjected the scheduled interstate air carriers of this country to a regulatory scheme similar to that already provided by the Interstate Commerce Act for other types of carriers, a scheme including provisions outlawing unreasonable or discriminatory rates, might be taken to mean that competition in this industry had been found to be unworkable as a protector of the public from extortion and discrimination, and that Congress had decided to abandon "competition as regulator" in the airline field on the traditional grounds of "natural monopoly." This impression might be strengthened by the consideration of the new provisions as to intercompany relations in the industry; instead of the rigid legislative prohibitions included in the 1934 Act (applying, of course, to mail carriers alone), these relations are subjected to the permissive discretion of a regulatory authority. There is even a provision for the exemption of the carriers from prosecution under the antitrust laws in connection with combinations, pooling agreements, and the like that have received the approval of the authority.

In fact, however, there is little evidence that any of the proponents of the Act, least of all its Congressional advocates, had accepted the "natural monopoly" theory as applicable to air transport, and there is abundant evidence to the contrary.[26] There is similarly no evidence that airline users, or persons speaking in their interest, were calling for rate or service regulation, and it is a fact that the Act's provisions regarding rates and services offered to the public remained for a long time almost inoperative. Although there was indeed some relaxation of the law relating to intercompany relations and of previous limitations on the expansion of particular (mail) carriers, these changes were due, at least in part, to the defective operation of the more rigid provisions; it was thought that the new measure would be more effective than these provisions in preventing the domination of the industry by a few firms.

This point is clearly brought out in the Congressional debate on the Act. The sponsors of the Act were emphatic in their denial of statements to the effect that it was designed to render the policy of the antitrust laws inoperative in the airline field, and explained that the provision for exemption from these laws was included merely in order to permit the administrators to authorize purchase of small moribund airlines by their competitors where the traffic could in any event not support the former.[27] The restrictive proviso limiting the Board's authority in approving consolidations and the like (the first proviso of Section 408(b)) was actually strengthened by amendment on the floor of the Senate.[28]

Protection of small carriers, whose existence was held to be threatened by the existing system of competitive bidding for air-mail routes, was repeatedly mentioned as one of the aims of the Act. For example, Senator McCarran stated: "The whole object, so far as I am concerned, in initiating this legislation has been to establish an independent agency so that airlines such as the Braniff Lines, and other lines of similar character,

---

[26] A qualified adoption of the "natural monopoly" theory as applicable to air transport is indicated in the *Report* of the Federal Aviation Commission. This point is discussed in the last section of this chapter.

[27] 83 Cong. Rec. 6728–6732.

[28] 83 Cong. Rec. 6770.

may have a secure place in the picture for their service." [29] Similarly, Representative Boren declared: "The independent air lines are compelled to fight for route security, and it is a defensive war that compels the interest and respect of the American Government. Some great air lines are grasping for monopolies on all profitable route territories, and their motives are sufficiently sinister to the public interest to demand the Government's attention. Public interest demands that American air transportation, which is the leader of the world, be preserved as an industry instead of being destroyed by accumulative monopolies in its infancy." [30]

Moreover, the 1938 Act itself contains important affirmations of the competitive principle.

As will be brought out in the subsequent discussion of the Act's certification provisions, the proponents of the Act generally accepted (indeed, insisted upon) the fact that the investment necessary to render airline service was comparatively very small.[31] On many routes the market for air-transport services would also be small, so that the necessary minimum investment would be large in relation to the market, the result being that only one or two carriers could be sustained; but even in such a situation the factor of potential competition would be a powerful deterrent to price-output policies designed to secure large excess returns. The high degree of mobility of most airline assets, which was also brought out in the discussions prior to the 1938 Act, would further assure this protection against monopoly power. As further evidence that the proponents of the Act did not believe that air transport *as such* constituted a "natural monopoly," it should be pointed out that, according to

[29] 83 Cong. Rec. 6849.

[30] 83 Cong. Rec. 6406.

[31] See, for example, the testimony of Col. Edgar S. Gorrell before a Congressional committee: "The third distinctive characteristic of air transportation relates to the nature and cost of the capital goods necessary to institute service. This is a feature often overlooked. It is literally possible to institute a common-carrier service by renting a second-hand plane, many of which are available, and calling up an airport to make arrangements for landing and departure. It is not necessary to accumulate the millions requisite to the construction of a vessel or a line of railroad." *Aviation*, Hearings before the Committee on Interstate and Foreign Commerce, House of Representatives, on H.R. 5234 and H.R. 4652, 75th Congress, 1st Session, 1937, pp. 65–66.

one of the Act's leading Congressional advocates, its framers intended specifically to exempt nonscheduled carriers from economic regulation. This exemption was not stated in the law, and the degree of economic regulation to which these carriers have been subjected has been a matter of administrative discretion; but Senator McCarran has asserted that the regulation of nonscheduled carriers under the 1938 Act was never contemplated.

The fact that there was no public demand for the regulation of air-transport rates, together with the virtual inoperativeness for an extended period of the rate provisions of the Act, leads to the conclusion that these provisions were regarded by its sponsors as a distinctly secondary feature, entirely subordinate to the certification provisions which, as will be seen, were of primary importance in the eyes of the principal proponents of the Act. It is not too much to say that these groups accepted the entire regulatory paraphernalia for the sake of the certification provisions, and the provisions governing rates charged to the public were incidentally accepted as a part of the traditional regulatory scheme. It is important to note, however, that some of the administrative agencies of the Government advocated comprehensive regulation of air carriers on the ground that the whole national transport system should be subjected to such regulation. This view was ardently espoused by the Interstate Commerce Commission, e.g. in its *Annual Report* for 1936: "While the present scheduled air transport service began as an exclusive mail service, the transportation of persons and property has grown to such volume and extent in recent years that transportation by air has become an integral part of the transport system of the Nation and should be regulated as such." An expansion of this view is found in a publication of the Federal Coördinator of Transportation:

It has become evident that the entire transportation industry, including the other agencies as well as the railroads, is in need of the guiding hand of Government control if a threatening chaos is to be transformed into order; and this is the conclusion that has been reached quite generally in other countries. The object of such control is not the protection of the railroads only but the proper protection of every form of transportation. They all have their parts to play, for each one of them can do certain things better than any other agency. The problem is to find their appropriate functions, protect them in the performance of such functions, prevent wasteful duplication of service without eliminating such competition as is economically sound, and promote a system of stable rates which will reflect the lowest costs of good service but afford the necessary foundation for credit.[32]

The foregoing statement by the Federal Coördinator makes it clear that the main aim of the comprehensive regulation advocated by the Commission was the protection of carrier revenues, and from this point of view the maximum-rate and antidiscrimination features of the law are of minor importance.

Neither the abandonment of the 1934 limitation on the routes to be held by any particular firm nor the less rigid character of the 1938 provisions concerning intercompany relations can rightly be interpreted as evidence that Congress had adopted the "natural-monopoly" concept. Although the direct limitation on the number of mail routes and of primary routes to be operated by any one carrier was abandoned, the award of routes by the Civil Aeronautics Board, as well as its other regulatory activities, is still subject to the general declaration of policy in Section 2 of the 1938 Act, which requires that the Board shall consider, among other things, "competition to the extent necessary to assure the sound development of an air transportation system properly adapted to the needs of the foreign and domestic commerce of the United States, of the Postal Service, and of national defense," as being "in the public interest, and in accordance with the public convenience and necessity." It is true that this statement appears to leave the degree of competition to be promoted entirely up to the regulatory authority; in another section of the Act, however, the recommended policy is somewhat less ambiguous, namely, that regarding intercompany relations such as mergers.

The Air Mail Act of 1934 flatly prohibited the merger of any air-mail carriers operating on parallel routes, as well as any agreement between such carriers bringing about common control or ownership; forbade the acquisition, possession, or con-

[32] Federal Coördinator of Transportation, *Regulation of Transportation Agencies*, S. Doc. No. 152, 73rd Congress, 2nd Session, 1934, p. 96.

trol of an interest in any air-mail carrier by any other company engaged in the aviation industry (including the manufacturing branch of that industry) or by a holding company; and made ineligible for mail contracts any company with stock in or interlocking relations with a holding company or another aviation company. Although these provisions applied only to mail carriers, and were to some extent designed to prevent collusion in bidding for air-mail contracts, they also indicate that Congress disapproved the suppression of airline competition as such, and wished to check the combination movement that had progressed so rapidly in the years preceding the passage of the Act.[33] This latter interpretation is especially borne out by the first provision mentioned above.

As evidence that the policy of enforcement of competition was found to be unworkable, and hence was later modified by Congress, it is sometimes pointed out that (1) the provision limiting the number of primary routes to be opened by any one carrier was altered to permit United Airlines to retain control of two such routes, and (2) that competition between mail carriers was specifically limited by an amendment adopted in 1935 prohibiting any such carrier from operating nonmail services on routes for which another company had a mail contract, unless such services were found by the Interstate Commerce Commission to be required by the public convenience and necessity. On the first point, it should be noted that the two routes concerned were in no sense competitive, so that there was actually no necessary change in the competitive situation. In addition, there was no protest on the part of the other transcontinental carriers, and no evidence that United was gaining any great strategic advantage by the retention of its West Coast route.

In connection with the second point, however, it must be admitted that the amendment in question seems to represent a genuine legal limitation on competition between mail carriers; nevertheless, there is little doubt that the purpose of this amendment was simply to keep down the cost of the mail service to the Government, a cost which could obviously be mate-

---

[33] See Puffer, *Air Transportation*, p. 521.

rially raised by the competitive reduction of the commercial revenues of mail carriers, whether by the diversion of traffic or by the forced reduction of commercial rates. The exact meaning of the amendment cannot be known without reference to the particular content intended for the phrase "public convenience and necessity"; however, in so far as it was intended to exclude firms that would have been self-supporting, its justifiability on economic grounds, as opposed to grounds of governmental economy, is open to question. It is obviously unjust for the Government to penalize commercial users by holding the rates for any type of commercial service above the cost of providing this service separately on a self-sustaining basis. Such action would in effect result in subsidization of the mail service by the users of the commercial services.

If the amendment was intended to be so administered as to protect a monopolistic nonmail rate structure on the part of mail carriers, for the purpose of minimizing the necessary mail payments, it would be economically unjustifiable. On the other hand, even assuming that the commercial rates charged by each mail carrier were fixed at a level equal to the cost of providing a comparable self-sustaining nonmail service, there would be very few cases in which the exclusion of a self-sustaining service would be justified. For if such a service were self-sustaining without the diversion of traffic from the mail carrier, this would mean that the commercial capacity of the mail carrier had not been adequate to serve the traffic available at cost rates; and if its self-support did involve diversion of traffic, this would lead to the presumption that its service was regarded as superior by some of the former patrons of the mail carrier's commercial service. It is no more justifiable to keep mail payments down by depriving the commercial patrons of a preferred service than to do so by charging them rates higher than the cost of providing a similar service on a self-sustaining basis. Only in those cases where there would be a diversion of traffic ascribable not to consumer preference but to chance distribution of patronage between the two lines, and where the commercial "by-product" capacity of the mail carrier was in fact adequate to accommodate all the traffic available at cost rates, would the Commission be justified in refusing certification to the non-mail carrier.

To put these principles into administrative practice would, of course, be enormously difficult. To forecast accurately the state of consumer preference, to estimate the cost of providing a self-sustaining nonmail service comparable to one supplied jointly with mail service, and to calculate the potential demand for service at a given rate — these are all problems impossible to solve with any great degree of certainty, and the conclusions reached on the basis of the necessary processes of estimation must always be open to challenge on the part of interested parties.

At any rate, neither of the above-mentioned Congressional actions can reasonably be taken to show a fundamental change in the attitude of the legislators toward competition in the air-transport field.

The pertinent sections of the Air Mail Act of 1934 were notoriously unsuccessful in breaking the domination of the air-transportation field by a few great groups and in establishing genuine competition among the carriers.[34] In the absence of any specific provisions for investigation and enforcement, such blanket prohibitions were found to be ineffective. The 1938 requirements for administrative approval of mergers, pooling agreements, interlocking directorates, and the like provided a much more direct method for the control of intercompany relations; they should probably be regarded as a reaffirmation and strengthening of the principles embodied in the 1934 Act rather than as a negation of these principles.

The specific provisions governing these relations are so stated as to confirm this view and to demonstrate further that Congress had not accepted the doctrine of "natural monopoly." The regulatory authority may not, for example, approve a merger, acquisition of control, or similar action if shown to be inconsistent with the public interest, or if a monopoly is thereby created that would restrain competition or jeopardize another

---

[34] See J. H. Hamstra, "Two Decades — Federal Aero-Regulation in Perspective," 12 *Journal of Air Law* (now *Journal of Air Law and Commerce*) 105 (1941).

air carrier. With regard to mergers and the like where the proposed relation is between an air carrier and a carrier other than by air, the legal criterion is still more restrictive: the Board may not approve the transaction "unless it finds that the transaction proposed will promote the public interest by enabling such carrier other than an air carrier to use aircraft to public advantage in its operation and will not restrain competition." It has previously been noted that in the Act's general statement of policy it is declared to be in the public interest to maintain "competition to the extent necessary to assure the sound development of an air transportation system properly adapted to the needs of the foreign and domestic commerce of the United States." Thus the provisions regarding interlocking directorates and pooling agreements are also oriented toward the preservation of competition, since in each case the Board may not authorize them if they are found to be opposed to the public interest.

However, the precise significance attached by Congress to the terms "competition" and "monopoly" is very far from being clear, so that it is impossible to deduce from the Act exactly what type of competitive position for the typical firm Congress was attempting to bring about in the air-transportation field by its passage. Additional light on this question will be afforded by an investigation of the background of and motivation for the general certification requirement for entry into the business of scheduled interstate air carriage.

The Certification Provision

In interpreting the significance of the general certification provision, care must be taken not to overestimate the increase in Government influence over the direction of air-carrier investment represented by this measure; but more important than this, it is necessary to investigate carefully the record concerning the views and motives of the proponents of this provision, in order to avoid misconstruction of their purposes.

In so far as the possibility of profitable operation of commercial air transport had depended before 1938 on the obtainment of a mail contract — and this seems to have been true on many routes — the Federal Government through the Postmaster General had effective control over the development of the air-transport network.[35] Furthermore, as has been pointed out, this control was by no means always used to determine routes solely in accordance with the needs of the mail service. It may also be noted that before 1938 the Postmaster General was supposed to determine on his own initiative the routes on which mail contracts would be let, whereas under the Civil Aeronautics Act the carriers initiate certification proceedings by application to the Board. However, given the new policy with respect to the determination of mail payments, it might be expected that the carriers would apply for all routes that had a reasonable chance of being certified by the Board, so that carrier initiative would be adequate to insure the development of the air-transport network in accordance with the objectives of the Act.[36]

A superficial examination of the Act itself might lead to the belief that the certification requirement was designed solely as a necessary adjunct to the general policy of subsidization. Because the chosen method of subsidization was direct payments to the carriers, and the total amount to be paid out in any given period could not of course be unlimited, the policy would certainly involve an administrative determination of the particular carriers that were to receive these payments at any given time. But neither the general policy of subsidization itself nor the method chosen (i.e., direct payments to carriers) required either the abandonment of competitive bidding as a method of carrier choice or regulatory protection of the revenues of par-

[35] The degree to which a mail contract was necessary for continued profitable operation in the years prior to 1938 is reflected to some extent in the high rate of mortality among nonmail passenger airlines in those years. On this point, see Puffer, *Air Transportation*, p. 53, Table II.

[36] The Board itself, however, has requested that it be given power to determine on its own initiative that routes not in operation are required by the public convenience and necessity, even though no application has been made by any carrier to operate such routes. The Board has declared that this power is essential if it "is to develop air transportation in such a manner as to keep pace with the requirements of national defense and our general national interests," and has pointed out the particular importance of such a power in respect to international air routes. *Annual Report* of the Civil Aeronautics Board, 1942, p. 15.

ticular carriers. Indeed, the correct implementation of a rational policy of subsidization would rule out both.

Competitive bidding, with adequate specifications, would appear to be the best method of assuring maximum efficiency in the performance of the services to be subsidized, where the method of subsidization is such that the number of firms receiving aid at any given time must be limited. There are, of course, methods of subsidization that do not require any form of administrative determination of the firms to be aided. These methods include all those forms of aid the total cost of which does not increase with the number of firms benefited, such as the broadcasting of information on weather conditions, or the financing of research on new types of plane. But direct payments to carriers are obviously not of this type.

Under an effective system of competitive bidding the period for which any particular carrier would have to be relied upon to perform the subsidized service would be relatively short, and competitive inroads on its revenues during this period would presumably be to a large extent foreseen when its bid was made; hence there would appear to be no necessity for the protection of its revenues even in the short run in order to assure performance of the service. To the extent that prospective competition increases the payment necessary to compensate bidders for the subsidized service, it represents a legitimate addition to the cost of this service to the Government. The achievement of governmental economy at the expense of limiting the choice of service available to commercial users cannot in general be defended on economic grounds; it merely shifts the cost of the subsidization program from the Government, which should bear it in full, to the consumers deprived of their preferred service.

The foregoing argument is, of course, based on the idea that the direct payments to carriers are in fact to be the minimum necessary to obtain a quantity and type of air-transport service that have been found to be essential in the public interest — a method of determination that would be a logical corollary to a general policy of air-transport subsidization. In fact, however, the particular policy of subsidization embodied in the

Civil Aeronautics Act was not based on any independent consideration of the amount and type of air-transport investment needed in the interests of national defense or of efficient mail service; similarly, there was no serious consideration by the framers of the Act of the precise meaning of the "extent . . . character and quality" of air transportation "required for the commerce of the United States." Instead, the amount of the total mail payment and its distribution among carriers were apparently determined in the first instance by reference to the financial needs of the then existing mail carriers at their existing levels of operation. Thus there was not (and has not yet been) prescribed any definite standard by which the publicly desirable amount and direction of air-transport subsidy might be determined, except the financial needs of the mail carriers. One obvious consequence of this lack of any independent consideration of the amount and type of air transport required in the public interest is the absence of any specific statutory guide for the Board to apply in determing what *new* routes should be supported. Thus the Board has been compelled to devise its own standard, and the standard which it has devised represents the most logical possible extension of the principle *in effect* adopted by the Congress. This point is further discussed in the following chapter.

Thus the assurance of the financial welfare of a particular group of air carriers, rather than the subsidization of air transport in general, emerges as the major objective of the promotional program. Unlike the general promotional aim, this objective does require the abandonment of competitive bidding; it would be absurd to attempt to choose carriers to be subsidized by this method where the amount of the subsidy is to be whatever turns out to be necessary to make up any deficit incurred by the carrier. Moreover, in the absence of any limiting principle whereby the amount of investment to be supported by the Government could be ascertained independently of the investment decisions of the supported carriers, it was obviously desirable that some control over their expansion be provided through regulatory machinery. However, even this "need-rate" subsidization program does not in fact justify the application to unsubsidized (nonmail) carriers of a certification requirement designed to protect the commercial revenues of the subsidized enterprises. As has been pointed out above, such restrictive regulation merely serves in part to shift the burden of subsidization from the Government, which should bear it in full. Thus even the "need-rate" subsidization program can provide at best only an excuse, rather than a justification, for the imposition of a *general* certification requirement such as was embodied in the Civil Aeronautics Act.

In pointing out that the subsidization program embodied in the Act was oriented toward the promotion of the financial welfare of the mail carriers rather than the achievement of independently defined national aims, the writer certainly does not mean to suggest that the legislative sponsors of the Act were conspiring with the air carriers in a raid on the public treasury, or that they were motivated by any considerations other than the advancement of the public interest. Their statements suggest that they were deeply impressed with the importance of civil air transport from the point of view of the national defense and of commerce, and conceived the Act's promotional and protective program as a means of preserving an air-transportation industry in accordance with national need. The following statements are illustrative of this point:

Senator McCarran: We are not only dealing with a proposed law that will regulate industry . . . but as we promote the industry of aviation and the industry of air transport we also promote the national defense. Every time we encourage an airline to be established over the terrain of this country, just to the extent that airline operates we are building for national defense. Every air-line pilot is today a potential soldier, ready to serve his country when and if the call should come. Every established line in this country from one airport to another constitutes in itself a method of defense, because such air line, surveyed, laid out, and traversed, will be a route known to American soldiery at a time when this country may — God forbid, but may, nevertheless — require every arm to be extended for its defense.[37]

---

[37] 83 Cong. Rec. 6635.

Representative Boren: We need a national aviation program. National defense, American commerce, and the United States Mail Service demands that we have such a program and that we have it now. America leads the world in aviation progress. Our leadership must not be lost by inaction . . . This bill offers the proper program for our present and future national policy.[38]

However, there was (and is) no necessary equivalence between the amount and type of air-transport investment provided by the scheduled carriers and that which an independent consideration of the nation's needs would prove to be required; in the absence of such an independent consideration, the program of Government support was left without adequate orientation. Moreover, the adoption in effect of the "need" of particular carriers as an ultimate promotional standard can be used to provide a superficially respectable argument for a program of restrictive regulation to protect the revenues of subsidized firms. It reflects a confusion between the sustained profitability of particular firms and the soundness of the industry in general which also was of great influence in gaining acceptance for the economic regulatory features of the Act.

Thus, the proponents of the Act appear to have been far more concerned with the potentialities of the certification provision as a means of securing the positions of existing carriers and of preventing the establishment of new services in competition with existing routes than as an instrument of administering the subsidization program. The promotion of investment and of "sound economic conditions" in the air-transport field figures prominently in their arguments as one of the aims to be accomplished by certification, but it is actually the promotion of investment in particular (existing) carriers and the improvement of the financial status of these carriers that is advocated; the certification provision is to further these aims by entrenching the position of the established carriers and suppressing new competition. The confusion of these two distinct concepts is one of the major characteristics of the debate preceding the passage of the Civil Aeronautics Act; another is the practically

[38] 83 Cong. Rec. 6405.

complete absence of any reference to the special position of interstate scheduled air transport as a subsidized (or to-be-subsidized) industry, and of the use of this special position as a basis for advocating the certification policy. These two characteristics appear not only in arguments made by spokesmen for existing air carriers, but also in those advanced by representatives of government agencies and members of Congress.

Among the arguments that were based on an implicit assumption that the profitability of the existing carriers — and hence the restriction of new competition — was essential to the financial well-being of the air-transport industry was the contention that such restriction was necessary to attract capital needed for the expansion of the industry and for technological progress. This point of view was advanced by Colonel Gorrell, who maintained that in the state of "economic anarchy" existing before the Civil Aeronautics Act was passed the only sources of capital accessible to the industry were of an undesirable character and sure to become inadequate to enable the airlines to take advantage of available technological improvements. "The consequences of the existing lack of economic controls over the industry are serious," he stated. "As long as the present state of affairs continues, there will be no adequate new capital available to the industry. Few people realize that the air lines have been built up hitherto almost entirely as a result of capital furnished by a few individual or corporate patrons which have been willing to take long chances." [39] And again: "The industry, as a whole, and particularly the smaller lines, are in critical need of reliable sources of capital among the investing public . . . [The present situation is] intolerable from the public point of view, since it subordinates sound management to the whims of a financial angel and to the exigencies of politics." [40] The only evidence adduced by Colonel Gorrell to substantiate the claim that the industry was in dire need of capital was a statement regarding past losses and anticipated increases in expenses, indicating that more than half of the private capital

[39] E. S. Gorrell, "Rationalization of Air Transport," 9 *Journal of Air Law* (now *Journal of Air Law and Commerce*) 41, 44 (1938).
[40] *Ibid.*, p. 46.

invested in air transport had been lost, and that costs were expected to rise substantially in the following year (1938). The prime importance attached by the industry to the certification requirement in its advocacy of the Civil Aeronautics Act is clearly shown in Colonel Gorrell's statements.[41] A similar view was often expressed by the Congressional proponents of the Act.[42]

With regard to the alleged inadequacy of the supply of capital available to the air-transport industry, it may be said that if the private-capital market was indeed so irrationally frightened by previous losses as to be incapable of financing economically justified technological improvements, a more direct and defensible remedy for this condition would have been the furnishing of credit by the Government through the Reconstruction Finance Corporation or some similar agency. It is also significant that Colonel Gorrell himself laid great emphasis on the threat to the industry of the entry of too many new enterprises, pointing out that the excessive ease of entry arising from the fact that only a small amount of capital is necessary to begin operations "promises haphazard growth" and "threatens unbridled competition."[43] The situation described here would certainly not indicate that the air-transport field as such was not attractive to investors; quite the contrary, in fact. The shortage of capital, if any, apparently was confined to established carriers.

The attraction of capital into the air-transport field has also been mentioned as one of the objectives of the Civil Aeronautics Act by Senator McCarran, who has said that the Act "was nurtured in the spirit of equity and fair play so as to lend encouragement to fearless, venturesome men who might be interested in investing in an industry that was and is as to its vicissitudes

---

[41] *Ibid.*, p. 47.

[42] See, for example, the remarks of Representative Lea, 83 Cong. Rec. 6407.

[43] "A line which has precariously developed traffic between two cities is always faced with the real possibility that another operator may institute service on comparatively brief notice . . . The essential point is that it is possible to start a service on but a minor amount of capital, and this possibility has actually become an actuality from time to time in the past. With the great increase in traffic, the temptation thus to begin new services is becoming stronger." Testimony of Col. Gorrell, *Aviation*, p. 66.

and changes unknown and unmeasured." [44] This statement, in so far as it is based on the excessive riskiness and "unknown" character of the air-transport industry because of its early stage of development, is in apparent contradiction to another argument advanced by Colonel Gorrell in support of governmental protection of the financial status of the carriers: "a measure of stability and the promise of a financially sound future" are said to be demanded by the industry because it has "passed beyond the experimental stage." [45] These two points of view can be reconciled by interpreting Colonel Gorrell's assertion to mean that the existing carriers had become well enough established that their interest in the protection of the *status quo* from new competition was greater than their interest in their own freedom to enter new fields, the threat of new competition being the greater because of the ever-present possibility that a rival might employ hitherto unknown techniques of physical operation or service.

The testimony and views of Colonel Gorrell with respect to the necessity for government action to protect the existing carriers in order to attract capital were cited with approval in the report of a House Committee on the new legislation:

The result of this chaotic situation of the air carriers has been to shake the faith of the investing public in their financial stability and to prevent the flow of funds into the industry. Col. Edgar S. Gorrell . . . testified . . . that $120,000,000 of private capital has been invested in the present air transport system and that 50 per cent of this investment has been lost. He further testified that unless legislation is enacted which would give the carriers reasonable assurance of the permanency of their operation and would protect them from cut-throat competition, a number of the airlines would soon be in serious financial trouble.[46]

In its first Annual Report the regulatory authority created by the Act echoed the view that the "chaotic" pre-1938 situation of

[44] C. S. Rhyne, *The Civil Aeronautics Act Annotated* (Washington: National Law Book Co., 1939); foreword by Sen. Pat McCarran, pp. vi–vii.

[45] Testimony of Gorrell, *Aviation*, p. 66. See also the *Report* of the Federal Aviation Commission, p. 54.

[46] *Civil Aeronautics Bill,* H. Rep. No. 2254, 75th Cong., 3rd Session, 1938, p. 2.

the air-transport industry "was preventing the flow of greatly needed funds into this industry." [47]

The protection of the financial status of existing carriers through restricting new competition was also advocated as necessary for the preservation of desirable labor standards and safety of operation. This argument might be advanced, apart from a contention that uncontrolled competition would result in general impecuniousness on the part of all air carriers, on the ground that labor and safety standards maintained by any particular carrier would be impaired should it find itself in financial straits, regardless of the profitability of air transport as a whole. Nevertheless, the argument was usually so generally stated as to imply that uncontrolled competition would result in a debasement of these standards throughout the industry, thus necessitating as an intermediate step the assertion of general impecuniousness.

With regard to labor standards, Senator McCarran has said that the Civil Aeronautics Act "was fostered so that a brave American youth, giving its best in the way of labor to its country's business in the air, might be encouraged and protected." [48] In a similar vein, the report of a Senate Committee on the pending regulatory bill stated that "aviation in America today, under present laws, is unsatisfactory to investors, labor, and the air carriers themselves." [49] Colonel Gorrell said that the "rationalization" of the industry by *"appropriate governmental controls, coupled with cooperative and farsighted action by the lines"* was *"imperative . . . if the present flight and technical personnel is to remain upon the pay-rolls, [and] if just wages are to be paid."* [50]

With regard to safety standards, the Senate Committee reported that "competition among air carriers is being carried to an extreme, which tends to jeopardize the financial status of the air carriers and to jeopardize and render unsafe a transporta-

---

[47] Civil Aeronautics Authority, *Annual Report,* 1939, p. 1.

[48] Rhyne, *Civil Aeronautics Act,* p. vii.

[49] *Civil Aeronautics Act of 1938,* Sen. Rept. No. 1661, 75th Congress, 3rd Session, 1938, p. 2.

[50] E. S. Gorrell, "Rationalization of Air Transport," p. 45.

tion service appropriate to the needs of commerce." [51] Colonel Gorrell agreed that the impoverishment of the carriers "could lead to competition for traffic of such intensity that the accident ratio might accelerate instead of decline." [52] The threat of excessive competition to safety in operation was also alluded to by Commissioner Eastman.[53]

The labor standards and safety arguments were both presented as pointing out a possible threat rather than an actual condition, and the proper enforcement of legislation dealing directly with each of these problems would have sufficed to avoid any danger along these lines.

As has been noted, the above-mentioned contentions were based on an implicit identification of the profitability of particular carriers with the financial well-being of air transportation as a whole, since it is implied that the consequences to be expected from general industrial unprofitability can be avoided only by measures designed to protect particular carriers. In addition, arguments were advanced that sought to justify this identification in terms of the economic characteristics of air transportation. In general, these arguments stated that without governmental restriction on new competition the uncontrolled operation of the profit motive would result in intolerable economic waste through needless duplication of facilities. It is clear that this statement in itself merely asserts either that there is a permanent tendency toward overinvestment in air transportation, or that in this field the normal competitive process of adjustment of investment to demand involves a waste of economic resources on an intolerable scale. In either of these cases, of course, there would be some reason for the protection of existing carriers from new competition; the preservation of the profitability of these carriers could be regarded as a necessary step in the maintenance of investment in the field at a satisfactory level. However, the reasoning on which these assertions are based remains to be considered.

[51] *Civil Aeronautics Act of 1938*, p. 2.
[52] E. S. Gorrell, "Rationalization of Air Transport," p. 44.
[53] *Aviation*, p. 40.

The frequency with which the economic-waste argument has been employed by the partisans of the Act contrasts strongly with the weakness of the supporting reasoning. In its *Annual Report* for 1939, the regulatory body created by the Act manifested its acceptance of this argument as the primary justification for the certification requirement in the following statement: "For the first time the American air carriers and the public are safeguarded against uneconomic, destructive competition and wasteful duplication of services by the statutory requirement that no person or company may engage in air transportation without first receiving a certificate of public convenience and necessity." [54] Later in the *Report* it is again indicated that without the certification requirement there was a "possibility of needless and economically wasteful duplication of services." [55]

It has already been noted that neither Congress nor any of the nonlegislative proponents of the Act (with the possible exception of the Federal Aviation Commission) had accepted any version of the "natural monopoly" concept as being applicable to air transportation; it is thus not surprising to find that no attempt was made to base the reasoning in support of the economic-waste argument on this concept. Similarly, references to "destructive competition" between air carriers such as that made by the Civil Aeronautics Authority in the above quotation are not based on any idea that the air-transport industry is characterized by lumpiness over large stretches of the cost function which presents a temptation to below-cost rate fixing. In so far as there was any substantial basis in past experience for these references, it was apparently in the bidding for mail routes, where, as we have seen, the absurd lowness of some of the bid rates was a result of inherent defects in the legislation.

The usual basis employed for the economic-waste argument was in fact an analogy with other forms of transportation. For example, the Civil Aeronautics Authority in an early decision made the following statement:

[54] Civil Aeronautics Authority, *Annual Report,* 1939, p. 2.
[55] *Ibid.,* p. 17.

It is . . . apparent that Congress intended the Authority to exercise a firm control over the expansion of air transportation routes in order to prevent the scramble for routes which might occur under a "laissez faire" policy. Congress, in defining the problem, clearly intended to avoid the duplication of transportation facilities and services, the wasteful competitive practices, such as the opening of non-productive routes, and other uneconomic results which characterized the development of other modes of transportation prior to the time of their governmental regulation.[56]

The Federal Aviation Commission also relied in part on the analogy argument to justify the restriction of competition. "To permit an orderly development of air transportation and adequately to safeguard its patrons," the Commission said, ". . . there should be a check on development of any irresponsible, unfair, or excessive competition such as has sometimes hampered the progress of other forms of transport."[57]

And again,

Air transport has grown up to the point where at least one administrative device common in other forms of transportation should be introduced. Following the precedent of the Federal supervision of the railroads and of practically every state in the Union in dealing with passenger transport services on the highways, we are recommending that [certification be required for new services] . . . even though no question of governmental aid be involved.[58]

In the Senate debate on the Civil Aeronautics Act, Senator King drew an analogy between air and railway transportation; in this connection, the Senator stated:

If . . . during the period of railroad building mania a few years ago we had had an instrumentality to determine whether many of the roads were necessary, and that question had been determined adversely, millions and hundreds of millions of dollars of capital which have been wasted would have been saved.[59]

[56] 1 **C.A.A.** 573, *Northwest Airlines Inc. — Certificate of Public Convenience and Necessity* (Duluth–Twin Cities Operation), March 6, 1940, pp. 577–578.

[57] *Report* of the Federal Aviation Commission, p. 54.

[58] *Ibid.*, pp. 54–55.

[59] 83 Cong. Rec. 6852.

Attention was also drawn to the fact that the Federal Government had already applied the certification requirement to interstate motor carriers, an industry that resembles air transportation in the relatively small investment necessary to enter it and the high degree of mobility of the resources invested.[60] This argument has been summarized by Puffer as follows:

The field of common carrier by truck is probably more easily entered than the field of common carrier by airplane. Therefore, if it seems necessary to require certificates for motor carriers, it is only a step to carry the analogy or the precedent to the air carriers.[61]

At this point it should be said that the arguments used in justifying the certification provision in the Motor Carrier Act (1935) were very similar to those cited here in connection with the Civil Aeronautics Act; if these arguments cannot stand on their own merits, then the appeal to precedent also fails.[62]

Closely similar to the argument by analogy with other transportation agencies were those lines of reasoning which favored the certification requirement on the ground that the air-transport industry had become a "public utility," or that air carriers had become "common carriers." For example, the Federal Aviation Commission stated:

Even after air transport shall have attained a purely commercial footing, needing no direct support from the Government, we consider that it will still require control as a public utility, and one which in some cases must take on a monopoly character.[63]

In so far as this contention is intended to be an economic argument, and not a purely legalistic one, it needs to be justified by a more specific consideration of the economic characteristics of the industry. The Commission's reference to "some cases" where the "public utility" known as air transport "must

---

[60] *Aviation*, p. 39.

[61] Puffer, *Air Transportation*, p. 250.

[62] An excellent discussion of these arguments is to be found in J. C. Nelson, "New Concepts in Transportation Regulation," in *Transportation and National Policy* (Washington: Government Printing Office, 1942), pp. 197–237.

[63] *Report* of the Federal Aviation Commission, p. 52.

take on a monopoly character" indicates that this "monopoly character" is not deemed essential to the "public-utility" character of the business; however, the necessity for regulation seems nevertheless to be regarded as somehow related to this "monopoly" characteristic. The Commission presumably had in mind the numerous air routes on which traffic was too light to support more than one carrier at an efficient level of operation. But, as has been suggested, it is of course impossible to define the competitive position of any firm without reference to its *potential* competitors; and in an industry characterized by extreme ease of entry and extreme geographical mobility of resources, potential competition should in most cases provide a strong restraint against the exercise of monopoly power.

A more explicit interpretation of the "public-utility" concept is offered by Puffer. Realizing that the argument advanced for the restriction of competition to avoid financial losses might, in the absence of some unusual characteristics on the part of the air-transport industry, equally well be applied to "the corner drugstore or the neighborhood filling station that may be threatened by disastrous competition," he asserts:

It should be made clear that the chief reason it is more applicable to the air transportation industry is the fact that this industry is a public utility where continuity of service is demanded and irregularities of service are more opposed to the public interest than in the case of other industries consisting of many local small-scale units where one unit more or less makes little difference to the public in general.[64]

It seems to be a perfectly defensible view that regularity of service is more important to the public in transportation industries than in some others; it is also quite conceivable that an uncontrolled market *might* result in undesirable irregularity. However, it is by no means *necessary* that such a condition should occur at all; it even seems improbable that it would occur in a situation of stable or rising national income. At any rate, since publicly undesirable irregularity of service is only

---

[64] Puffer, *Air Transportation,* p. 250.

a possibility, reference must be made to the actual extent and frequency of such irregularity in the air-transport industry, and the resulting inconvenience to the public must be weighed against the probable ill effects of restricting competition. There seems to be little evidence that there was any great degree of irregularity in air-transport service before 1938; at any rate, such irregularity as may have occurred was apparently insufficient to evoke protests on the part of the flying public.

The proponents of the Act attempted to justify governmental protection of the profitability of particular existing carriers by asserting that such protection was necessary for the financial health of air transportation as a whole, or for the achievement of a publicly desirable type of service; in general, their arguments did not draw upon the considerations regarding the state and tendency of the level of national income that played such an important part in gaining support for governmentally promoted restrictions on competition under the N.I.R.A. Since the desired restrictions under the Civil Aeronautics Act were to be of a permanent character, it is entirely understandable that their advocates should not resort to arguments based on temporary cyclical conditions. Furthermore, since these restrictions were to apply to only one field of economic activity, neither the cyclical-aggregative nor the secular-stagnation theories would have been entirely appropriate, unless the proponents of the Act had been ready to extend their recommendations to cover industry in general.

Nevertheless, the hostility to uncontrolled competition that had been built up as a result of depression conditions had its effect in evoking support for the Act, particularly among representatives of interested government agencies. Prominent among these representatives was Commissioner Eastman, whose views on the general undesirability of free competition are found in the following passages from a report issued by him as Federal Coördinator of Transportation:

Any plan of free and unrestrained competition in transportation would be in the teeth of experience. In the case of the railroads it was given a prolonged trial and found wanting many years ago. The results were bad for both the railroads and the country. *The present tendency is to place competition under some measure of restraint in industry generally* [emphasis supplied].[65]

And again:

It is believed that the experience of the past, *not only with the railroads but with all industry* . . . shows which course to take. We relied in the early days of railroading upon free competition as a means of public protection, and the result was bankrupt and unsafe railroads, bad labor conditions, flagrant favoritism in rates with the benefit going to the big shipper and the big community, and an uncertainty and instability which were demoralizing to industry in general . . . Public regulation was imposed quite as much to cure the ills of unrestrained competition as to curb the exactions of monopoly. *Of late the country has begun to discover that competition can also require restraint in industries which were not supposed to be affected, like transportation, with the public interest* [emphasis supplied].[66]

Similarly, there seems to have been no explicit reliance on the popular misinterpretation of monopolistic-competition theory which asserts that competition between imperfect substitutes leads to an oversupply of facilities and "chronic impecuniousness" on the part of the participant firms, although, as has been pointed out in Chapter I, this misinterpretation has been used by students of transport problems to justify comprehensive regulation of the transportation market. On the contrary, the view that free competition would result in waste and duplication was generally based on uncritical analogies and appeals to dubious precedents.

The prevalence of emphasis on the certification requirement as a means of quashing new competition to protect existing carriers is confirmed by the comparative scarcity in the debates of arguments embodying a concept of the requirement as an adjunct of the subsidization policy, and the related idea of

[65] *Regulation of Transportation Agencies,* p. 58.

[66] *Ibid.,* p. 96. These passages also illustrate the point of view which based advocacy of regulation of all forms of transportation, including air transportation, on an analogy between other agencies and the railroads.

keeping down the cost of such subsidization to the Government. There are some incidental references to the necessity of preventing "haphazard growth" of the air-transport network by the process of certification.[67] The Federal Aviation Commission used the governmental-economy argument to give additional support to its general advocacy of the certification requirement and pointed out the specific undesirability of having "inferior" services in competition with more expensive types subsidized by the Government.[68] Finally, it was argued in favor of the requirement that public convenience and necessity be shown for the inauguration of new services that an agency charged with the duty of making such a finding would be better able to withstand political pressure in favor of particular routes than was the Post Office Department, and so would be "in a better position to arrange for an orderly development of the air transportation map." [69] According to David, the Post Office Department was "notoriously open to all the political and commercial winds that blow." "Pressure from the carriers and from politicians was resisted only feebly, if at all, and there was every reason to fear a large and permanent loss on air mail service." He suggested that "resistance would have been easier if it had had some kind of standard by which to judge proposed routes and services." [70] Such considerations as these appear to have been of distinctly subordinate importance as compared with those directly concerned with the protection of existing carriers.

Summary and Conclusions

In the light of the preceding discussion of the significance of the major features of the Civil Aeronautics Act, it is now possible to attempt to determine the precise content of the policy toward the organization of the air-transport industry that the framers of the Act intended to be pursued by the regulatory authority it created. The intended policy toward investment in

---

[67] Testimony of Gorrell, *Aviation*, p. 66.
[68] *Report* of the Federal Aviation Commission, pp. 54 and 61.
[69] Puffer, *Air Transportation*, p. 251.
[70] David, *The Economics of Air Mail Transportation*, p. 155.

the field is indicated by the Act's clear-cut declaration in favor of subsidization — i.e., promotion of investment beyond current demand — by fixing mail payments to each carrier at a level "sufficient . . . together with all other revenue of the air carrier, to enable such air carrier under honest, economical, and efficient management, to maintain and continue the development of air transportation to the extent and of the character and quality required for the commerce of the United States, the Postal Service, and the national defense." [71] As has been stated, the general policy and method of subsidization (i.e., direct payments to carriers) indicated by the Act itself required some form of administrative determination of the carriers to be aided at any given time, but did not necessitate either the regulatory protection of the revenues of particular carriers or the permanent award to any particular carrier of the right to perform any given subsidized service. However, the policy of subsidization in effect adopted by the framers of the Act — i.e., the determination of the amount of the subsidy payment by reference to the need of particular carriers for revenues to enable them to remain solvent — did, of course, involve the abandonment of competitive bidding as a method of carrier choice. It has been pointed out that this policy was in effect embodied in the Act by default of any independent consideration of the needs of the nation for air-transport services and does not in itself justify the regulatory protection of the commercial revenues of the subsidized carriers by a general certification requirement.

Although narrow considerations of governmental economy in connection with this policy can be employed as an argument for such regulatory protection, even this argument did not figure prominently in the Congressional discussions relevant to the economic regulatory features of the Act. In fact, these discussions reflect the same general confusion of the "financial health" of particular carriers and the welfare of air transportation as a whole that accounts for the adoption of the subsidization policy which was embodied in the Act.

The importance ascribed by the proponents of the Act to the

[71] Sec. 406(*b*).

protection of the revenues of particular carriers becomes evident upon examination of the arguments adduced in support of the certification requirement as applied to all new services in interstate scheduled air transport. Great emphasis was placed on the role of this requirement as a means of restricting new competition with existing firms and relatively very little emphasis on the positive role of certification as an adjunct to the subsidization policy. Furthermore, the arguments in favor of restricting new competition do not seem to have been based on any belief (1) that in the absence of control there had been demonstrated a tendency toward permanent overinvestment in the air-transport field, either as a whole or in any relatively homogeneous sector; (2) that the business of air transport was characterized by a very large immobilized investment per firm, making the competitive process of adjustment of investment too costly to be tolerated; or (3) that the cyclical or secular tendency of the national income was such as to make undesirable the instability in the fortunes of particular enterprises which is characteristic of free competition, because of the possible aggregative repercussions of this instability. On the contrary, these arguments were generally based on uncritical analogies and appeals to dubious precedents.

Similarly, it has been seen that the application to air transport of the whole paraphernalia of public-utility regulation did not reflect a view of the industry as a "natural monopoly" (i.e., an industry where the most efficient size of firm is so large relative to the market that actual competition cannot be relied on to protect the public from monopolistic pricing and discrimination, and where also the necessary investment per firm is so large absolutely as to prevent effective protection by potential competition); nor did it result from any public protest regarding the rates or practices of the air carriers. The provisions regarding rates and practices were apparently written into the Act as an incidental part of a general regulatory scheme desired primarily because it included the certification provision.

Moreover, the sections of the Act dealing with intercompany relations cannot be fitted into any pattern of intended "natural monopoly." Although the substitution of administrative discretion for rigid legislative prohibitions and the provision for exemption from the antitrust laws might be thought to reflect such an intention, upon examination it is seen that both the specific norm provided for the judgment of mergers and the like and the general declaration concerning the public interest in the light of which the pertinent sections must be administered indicate that Congress favors the preservation of "competition" in some sense of the term. There is at least as much evidence that the method of administrative discretion was adopted to insure more effective control of these relations as there is to show that it reflected Congressional abandonment of competition in the airline field.

Now if it is true that the framers of the Act regarded the requirement for certification of new services as a means of protecting the revenues of particular carriers from the inroads of competition, and if the same point of view was reflected in the abandonment of competitive bidding as a method of choice of carrier, it may well be asked how such a view can be reconciled with the provisions regarding intercompany relations, and the general declaration of policy in Section 2 of the Act, which apparently favor the maintenance of competition in the air-transport field. For if "competition" is interpreted in any familiar sense of the term, it would seem to be essentially incompatible with the protection of the revenues of particular carriers by administrative action from the effects of the price-output policies followed by firms producing perfect or imperfect substitutes, the inauguration or abandonment of production of such substitutes being included as an extreme aspect of these policies. In this sense, the "protection-of-particular-carriers" view might seem to require a policy on the part of the regulatory body regarding competitive relations which would be directly opposed to that suggested by the competitive norm.

In so far as the "procompetitive" provisions of the Act represent isolated concessions to groups fearful of the results of the certification requirement, or mere bows in the direction of a traditional and popular idol, they need of course have no consistency with the rest of the Act. However, it is possible to interpret these provisions in the light of a concept of "competition" that is not incompatible with the protection of particular carriers, and it seems probable that such an interpretation would give a truer picture of the regulatory policy envisaged by the proponents of the Act, or at any rate by those proponents who represented governmental agencies, than would a view that simply characterized these provisions as minor inconsistencies.

For example, such a concept of "competition" is to be found in the *Report* of the Federal Aviation Commission, especially in the following passage:

We have been fully convinced by all that we have seen and heard that the present high quality of American air transport is due in large part to the *competitive spirit* that has existed throughout its development. There has been *little direct point-to-point competition on identical routes* and what has existed has been comparatively unimportant. *Of much greater benefit has been the availability of two or more alternative routes, served by different companies, between widely separated centers.* The transcontinental run, where at least two and in some cases three companies can be considered as directly competitive for passenger and mail traffic, offers the best example. *Perhaps of even greater importance, however, is the spirit of emulation that exists even between organizations that could not by any conceivable possibility be in direct competition with each other.* If an airline running from coast to coast acquires faster and more comfortable airplanes, it takes but a little time for the patrons of a line running up and down the Mississippi Valley to complain if it fails to make the same advances [emphasis supplied].[72]

This same concept is revealed in a recommendation by the Commission regarding the administration of the certification requirement: although it is suggested that the regulatory body be given the power to decide in each case whether parallel services should be allowed, and that each certificate should be so framed as to "carry no explicit guarantee of exclusiveness of franchise," it is asserted that "a direct duplication of certificates for the same route should normally be avoided."[73]

The "competition" advocated by the Federal Aviation Com-

---

[72] *Report* of the Federal Aviation Commission, p. 6.
[73] *Ibid.*, p. 55.

mission clearly bears only a remote resemblance to any familiar concept of the competitive process. Its desirability and effectiveness appear to be considered as in inverse proportion to the substitutability between the products of the firms involved. In the Triffinian terminology, the most desirable relation is isolated selling; homogeneous competition is regarded as "normally" to be avoided; heterogeneous competition is considered beneficial, but "perhaps" not so much so as isolated selling. Except in so far as public opinion may exert an effect on the revenues of a firm through other means than that of substituting for its product the goods or services produced by a rival, or vice versa (and such an influence conceivably might be exerted through hostile or friendly political action), the profit-maximization motive seems to play a subordinate part in the "competition" most highly regarded by the Commission. There is instead a sort of sportsmanlike emulation in quality of service to the public, which obviously contains but little threat to the profitability of the participant carriers.

Nevertheless, the Federal Aviation Commission seems to consider this type of "competition" as the antithesis of monopoly, which, it says, is exemplified by that type of organization of air transportation adopted by most European countries. On this point, the Commission has this to say:

The common rule in Europe has been the formation of national monopolies to operate all domestic and foreign air transport under close governmental supervision. A similar scheme has at times been suggested for the United States. We have given it careful consideration. We are convinced that the results of anything of the sort would be intolerable, and that the abandonment of competition would endanger an early frittering away of that preëminence in quality of service which American lines now appear to hold.[74]

The Commission's concept of monopoly apparently is of that orthodox but unsatisfactory category which defines the term as the existence of one firm in a vague and highly heterogeneous "field." There is the characteristic disregard of the possibility of

---

[74] *Ibid.*, p. 61.

competition between producers within and without the selected boundaries of the "field" — for example, between the various national companies in the operation of international routes. This concept is indeed a symmetrical antithesis to the Commission's idea of competition, which envisages *many* firms in a vague and heterogeneous field; there is in the competitive concept a similar disregard for the realities of the competitive relations involved.

The Commission's recommendations regarding the regulation of intercompany relations are evidently designed to preserve the approved gentlemanly emulation between carriers. The Commission advises on this point that "there should be a permanent provision for checking air transport financing, with the primary purpose of avoiding any undue concentration of control or merger of interest";[75] and again, "neither the holding company nor any other device should be allowed any use which could by any possibility restrict competition. There should be no merger of aeronautical enterprises in such a way as to make competition unfair."[76]

In a similar vein, the Commission recommends that the strategic position of particular carriers in relation to control of the routing of traffic be closely scrutinized so as to avoid giving one carrier the ability to starve out its rivals, although the quality of the service is to be considered:

The degree in which the ownership, by one of two competitors, of certain cross-lines that feed traffic to both main systems is a menace to fair competition has to be looked into for each case separately. In some instances such a community of ownership seems to us definitely advantageous, and sure to give the area covered by the feeder line a far better service than it could ever get in any other way. In other cases it would be as clearly objectionable, but we can formulate no general rule.[77]

It is interesting to note that the Federal Aviation Commission believed that for the operation of the national air-transport

[75] *Ibid.*, p. 52.
[76] *Ibid.*, p. 69.
[77] *Ibid.*, p. 62.

network *at a given level of technological development* a "national monopoly" would be the type of organization permitting maximum efficiency. The Commission based its case for the maintenance of a number of different carriers in the field on the anticipated beneficial effects of this maintenance on the progress of techniques of operation and service, effects which presumably were deemed important enough to offset the higher cost of operation at any one stage of technological development.[78] From the "static" point of view, then, it would seem that the Commission regarded the national air-transport network as a "natural monopoly," not only in the sense that each sector of the market could be served most efficiently by one firm the relations of which to all other air-transport firms preferably could be characterized as "isolated selling," but in the sense that the whole air-transport network should be subject to unified control.

It seems impossible to determine with any great degree of certainty the precise nature of the competitive relations between air-transport firms that the Congressional sponsors of the Civil Aeronautics Act intended the regulatory body to bring about in its administration of this law. These sponsors placed great emphasis on the prevention of competition tending "to jeopardize the financial status of the air carriers"[79] and on the guarantee to established lines of "reasonable assurance of the permanency of their operation,"[80] from which it can be inferred that the competitive relations that it was desired to establish were not to be such as to endanger these aims. Nevertheless, the evidence is not sufficient to establish the view that the Congressional proponents of the Act agreed with the Federal Aviation Commission in assessing the desirability of competitive relations between air carriers in inverse proportion to the value of the Triffinian coefficients that would represent their significance in terms of the potential effect of the price-output policy of each firm on the revenues of each other firm.

Thus it may well have been that the Congressional sponsors

---

[78] *Ibid.,* pp. 61–62.
[79] *Civil Aeronautics Act of 1938,* p. 2.
[80] *Civil Aeronautics Bill,* p. 2.

of the Act occupied a sort of compromise position, in which approval of a certain degree of protection of the revenues of particular carriers was reconciled with the attachment of a positive value to the availability to the public of genuinely substitutable services supplied by independent firms. Such a compromise position would be exemplified in a policy of certifying the establishment of a new service parallel to an existing one when, but only when, it could be expected that the revenues of the existing firm would not fall below a level sufficient to keep its resources permanently under its control. This policy would assure the profitable maintenance of its previous output by the existing firm, so far as the effects of competitive service were concerned; it would eliminate any possibility of the displacement of an old firm by a newcomer in the market, either by a forced curtailment of the output of the old firm or by its actual bankruptcy. Nevertheless, it would not entirely prohibit new competition — it would not reserve to existing firms the exclusive right to operate any new services potentially competitive with their current operations.

In view of the impossibility of determining from an examination of the provisions of the Civil Aeronautics Act or of the statements of its framers any precise and indisputable pattern designed to govern the regulatory authority in its control of competitive relations between firms in the air-transport field, it is clear that the actual policy that has been followed has depended to a great extent on decisions made by the authority itself in interpreting the Act in the course of its administration. In the following chapters, an attempt will be made to discover the nature of this policy by examining this administrative interpretation of the Act.

CHAPTER IV

ENTRY CONTROL BY THE CIVIL
AERONAUTICS BOARD

THE FOLLOWING TREATMENT of the regulatory policies of the Civil Aeronautics Board will be undertaken in the light of the theoretical analysis of the problem of entry presented in Part I, which offers certain guiding principles that may be briefly recalled at the outset of this discussion.

In the first place, it has been seen that the problem of entry into a branch of economic activity that cannot be regarded as equivalent to the traditional definitely demarcated "industry," within which competitive relations are homogeneous, is not confined to the mere addition or subtraction of companies to or from the list of those engaged in this activity. With regard to air transportation in the United States, for example, the policy of the Civil Aeronautics Board in the control of entry cannot be discovered merely by inquiring whether and under what terms any new companies have been permitted to engage in the "air-transport business" since the passage of the Civil Aeronautics Act. Even if such an inquiry were limited to a somewhat more "homogeneous" field than the air-transport business as a whole — e.g., long-haul scheduled air transportation between major traffic centers — it would still be unsatisfactory in determining entry policy.

Although the decisions of the Board in cases involving the proposed inauguration of services by "newcomers" must certainly be considered in determining the entry policy of the Board, it is clear that the investigation must also include cases involving the inauguration by existing carriers of new services; it would in fact appear that the latter type of case has been vastly more important than that involving "newcomers" in the Board's actual shaping of competitive relations in the air-transport field. Despite its relatively subordinate role, however, the

Board's treatment of "newcomers" appears to be in itself significant in demonstrating the inherent tendency of economic regulation to favor the established company as compared with the "newcomer," a tendency which may have important implications for both the productive organization and the competitive pattern of the regulated group. Because of its particular significance in these respects, the Board's policy toward services proposed by "newcomers" will be treated in a separate section of the present chapter.

In the second place, the theoretical treatment of the problem of entry control has shown that this question is properly to be analyzed as a part of the more general problem of the control of competitive relations of the regulated firms. Although a distinction may be drawn between alteration of the coefficients describing such relations from zero to a finite (or infinite) value and alteration in the value of coefficients that differ from zero at the outset, the practical significance of this distinction is open to question. Indeed, it might well be that a change of the latter type would be of greater import for the competitive position of the carriers involved than one of the former. For example, the initiation of nonstop service as a substitute or supplement for "local" service over a route paralleling that of another carrier between two major traffic centers might involve a relatively large change in the competitiveness of the two services, whereas the initiation of a new "local" service between these centers might involve very little genuine substitutability between the old and the new products. Similarly, a change in the strategic position of one competitor regarding control over the routing of traffic might also be of great importance in altering competitive relations. Thus the inauguration of a new service by a carrier, even though the service itself might be only slightly or not at all competitive with any other, might result in a change in the competitive position of this carrier with respect to routes already operated; in many cases both types of competitive change would be involved. Other types of economic activity which may greatly influence competitive relations between carriers include the formation or alteration of direct-control relations, such as mergers, acquisitions of control, and the like.

Furthermore, it is evident that the Board's policy toward the competitive pattern in air transport cannot be fully determined without reference to its position regarding the degree of "oligopolistic interdependence" between the firms, which is of major importance in influencing the price-output policies that the carriers tend to follow. Although relatively few of the Board's decisions bear on this problem, some light can be thrown on its policy in this respect by a consideration of its treatment of such organizations as the Air Transport Association (U.S.) and the International Air Transport Association, whose activities reinforce the tendency toward nonaggressiveness inherent in the fewness of firms in direct competition with one another that characterizes the air-transport field.

The present chapter will be concerned with the policy of the Board toward competitive relations as revealed in its treatment of the problem of entry. The discussion will be directed toward ascertaining the principles that have governed the Board's decisions on proposed competitive relations among maximizing units not previously so related, or, more precisely, among two or more proposed or among existing and proposed maximizing units.[1] Through the investigation of the basis upon which the Board has approved or disapproved such proposed relations, or by its own action has imposed conditions upon them as a prerequisite to its approval, the major principles which have governed the Board's action and the effect of their application may be determined. Chapter V will deal with a particular aspect of entry regulation, namely, regulation by exemption. The Board's policy as shown in decisions affecting the alteration of existing competitive relations and in those which bear on the problem of oligopolistic interdependence will then be considered.

THE INAUGURATION OF PARALLEL SERVICES

The most common type of case involving competitive relations among air carriers, and probably the most important in terms of the influence of the decisions rendered on the actual

---

[1] Not, of course, *necessarily* between existing and proposed *business enterprises:* this distinction has been dealt with at the beginning of the present chapter.

shaping of these relations, is that concerned with the inauguration of parallel services. This category includes both the initiation of new services competitive with (substitutable for) existing ones and the simultaneous initiation of two or more new services competitive with each other.

Both of these types of case are subdivisions of the general regulatory field of the authorization of new services, which also includes authorization of individual new services not competitive with any existing or proposed air service. In discussing the basic criteria for authorization of new air services in general, the Board has followed an adapted version of the formula developed previously by other regulatory bodies in the administration of similar statutory provisions. In an early decision the Board stated that, in determining whether or not proposed new services are in accordance with the public convenience and necessity, "the primary questions to be considered are, in substance, whether the new service will serve a useful public purpose responsive to a public need; whether this purpose can and will be served adequately by existing routes or carriers; whether it can be served by the applicant without impairing the operations of existing carriers contrary to the public interest; and whether the cost of the proposed service to the government will be outweighed by the benefit which will accrue to the public from a new service." [2] All of these factors are relevant to the Board's policy on the inauguration of competitive services.

Degree of Self-Support. The last-named factor, of course, does not generally enter into the deliberations of the usual regulatory commission, since no subsidy to the proposed operation is usually directly involved. The inclusion of this factor among the "primary questions" to be considered by the Board indicates the principal difference between the criteria applicable to new air-transport routes and those usually employed in determining the "public convenience and necessity" of public-service operations. The major consideration in the usual new-service

---

[2] Eastern Air Lines, Inc., St. Louis–Nashville–Muscle Shoals Operations, 1 C.A.A. 792, 796 (1940). For a similar formula advanced by the Interstate Commerce Commission, see Pan-American Bus Lines Operation, 1 M.C.C. 190, 203 (1936).

case, that is, the estimation of probable revenues and costs with a view to determining whether the proposed operation will be immediately self-supporting, is replaced under the Civil Aeronautics Act by a consideration of the extent to which the new service will be dependent upon Government subsidy. As the Board has said,

It is apparent that one of the ordinary standards of measurement of public convenience and necessity — namely, that there shall be a demand for the proposed service which will remunerate the carrier to an extent sufficient to justify him in maintaining it — does not possess its customary force in new route applications under the Civil Aeronautics Act. Section 406(b) which provides for the fixing of compensation for the carriage of mail at a level which takes into consideration, among other things, the need of the carrier for revenues sufficient to insure the maintenance of the mail service, substantially alters the conventional standard. Under the Act the question of the public convenience and necessity involves a determination of the amount of government expenditures which would be justified by the degree of public interest and value attaching to the particular route, and by the amount of service that such a route might be expected to render.

Although it is, of course, to be anticipated that all parts of the air transport system of the United States will make continuing progress toward independence of Government support, it would not only seem an unsound administration of the Act but also a policy contrary to its intent to require that each addition to the existing system of air routes should be independent of Government assistance through mail payments at the time of its establishment or at any early stage of its operation. Only on a small part of the existing route mileage could such a standard be met, and to establish it for the future would, in effect, freeze the present air transport map, allowing very minor modifications or none at all over a protracted future period.[3]

Thus, in determining whether a proposed operation "will serve a useful public purpose responsive to a public need," the major criterion applied by the Board has been not the immediate self-sufficiency of the service, but whether it can be operated without at the outset imposing upon the Government "an un-

<hr>

[3] Continental Air Lines, Inc., Roswell–Hobbs–Carlsbad Operation, 1 C.A.A. 598, 600–601 (1940).

duly large proportion of the total operating cost," and whether it can be expected ultimately to be independent of Government subsidy.[4] Although the Civil Aeronautics Act did not explicitly require the Board to authorize only those routes which appeared to be capable of progress toward economic self-sufficiency, this policy was adopted early in the administration of the law and has been consistently followed, certain qualified exceptions having been made in the case of experimental services and those required by overriding considerations of national defense or similar aspects of public policy. In considering the authorization of so-called "local" and "feeder" services, the Board has emphasized the experimental nature of these operations, and has not required a showing of probable future self-sufficiency of such character as would be necessary for the certification of the more orthodox "trunk-line" operation between major traffic centers. In justification of this exception to its usual policy, however, the Board has pointed out the desirability, in the interest of developing an air-transport system as required by the Act, of discovering by actual experience to what extent such "local" operations can be expected to be ultimately self-sufficient, and has generally limited the duration of the certificates for such service to periods of three years. For example, in the Board's decision in the Texas Air Service case, it is stated:

The rendering of local air transportation service such as Essair has proposed presents a difficult economic problem to which a great deal of study is being devoted and it is desirable that this study be supplemented by the accumulation of actual experience with new types of operation of particular interest or of potential importance. The service which will be rendered by local carriers concentrating upon the problems of a limited region in which the terrain and climate are generally favorable to such operations, and emphasizing service to intermediate points rather than competition for through traffic, seems to be sufficiently distinctive in character and of sufficient interest in relation to the general planning of future development to justify

---

[4] See, for example, Northwest Airlines, Inc., Duluth–Twin Cities Operation, 1 C.A.A. 573, 579 (1940), and National Airlines, Inc., *et al.*, Daytona Beach–Jacksonville Operation, 1 C.A.A. 612, 616 (1940).

its establishment in the West Texas area on an experimental basis. The results during the designated life of the experiment can determine whether the experimental service should thereafter be converted into a permanent one, and the carrier's ability to make substantial progress toward self-support will be an important factor in determining its future as a certificated operator of services of the type proposed.[5]

And again, in referring to its program of authorizing a number of experimental "feeder" services, the Board has said:

The purpose of the experiment . . . is to determine to what extent feeder air transportation is practicable; to what extent it will be self-supporting; and to what extent it should be continued.[6]

Operations justified primarily on the basis of national defense or similar aspects of public policy have also been limited to temporary periods.[7]

In justification of its adoption of this principle, the Board has in effect argued that it is required by the general declaration of policy set forth in the Act, and particularly that part of the declaration ordering the regulatory agency to "consider . . . as being in the public interest, and in accordance with the public convenience and necessity . . . the regulation of air transportation in such manner as to . . . foster sound economic conditions in such transportation." [8]

Thus, the Authority prefaced its initial endorsement of the principle of ultimate self-sufficiency in a new-route case by the following statement:

The Authority, in determining whether the inauguration of a new service will result in carrying out the objectives of the Act as set forth in the declaration of policy, must consequently consider not only the need of the particular community or section for the proposed

---

[5] Continental Air Lines, Inc., *et al.*, Texas Air Service (Supplemental Opinion) 4 C.A.B. 478, 481 (1943).

[6] Thomas E. Gordon, d.b.a. Orlando Airlines, Transfer of Certificate, 7 C.A.B. 429, 432 (1946).

[7] See, for example, Pan American Airways Co., United States–Africa Service, 3 C.A.B. 47 (1941).

[8] Civil Aeronautics Act, 1938, Section 2.

operation but also the relationship which such service bears to the development of a nationally adequate and economically sound air transportation system from the broad standpoint of the Postal Service, commerce, and the national defense. Furthermore, this determination must be made in the light not only of the cost to the public incident to the inauguration and operation of the service but also of the regulation of the expansion of the industry at a crucial period of its development in a manner which will not only foster sound economic conditions in air transportation at the present time but also in the future. One of the factors directly related to the interests of the public and to the economic welfare of the industry is the relationship between the estimated commercial revenues and operating costs of the proposed service.[9]

In connection with the determination of mail rates, the Board has also held that the promotion of economic self-sufficiency on the part of each carrier is a primary objective and has again appealed to the Act's general declaration with reference to the promotion of "sound economic conditions" in air transport as implying such a policy. In its *First Annual Report*, the Authority declared:

The Authority at the outset of these [mail-rate] proceedings recognized the fact that the fixing of fair and reasonable rates of air-mail compensation under sections 406(a) and (b) of the Act involved the delegation of a broad discretionary power which was to be exercised in the light of certain considerations which Congress had specifically prescribed . . . It was the conclusion of the Authority in the formulation of its rate-making policy that the development and encouragement of air transportation through the air-mail rate which takes into consideration the general factors of the public interest, as set forth in the Act, required that the rate-making provisions of the Act should be administered in such manner as to expedite the attainment for air carriers of an economically sound and stable condition. The belief of the Authority is that as this objective is approached, there will be an accompanying reduction of the dependence of air carriers upon air-mail revenue and a progressive decrease in government aid to the carriers in the form of air-mail compensation.[10]

---

[9] Northwest Airlines, Inc., Duluth–Twin Cities Operation, p. 579.
[10] *First Annual Report* of the Civil Aeronautics Authority, pp. 20–21.

The Board's endorsement of the general policy of promoting carrier self-sufficiency has been reiterated in subsequent *Annual Reports;* for example:

> During the past year, the Board has continued to pursue its policy as stated in previous annual reports of endeavoring to promote the approach of the air carriers to the point at which they will no longer be dependent upon substantial economic aid from the Government, in so far as such policy is consistent with the declared objective of the Act of developing and maintaining an air transportation system adequate to meet the requirements of our national interests.[11]

Certain statements made by the Board in decisions involving new-route applications by reputedly self-sufficient carriers might seem to indicate that its consideration of revenue-cost ratios as relevant to the promotion of "sound economic conditions" in air transport has not been exclusively based on the interpretation of such "sound" conditions to mean economic self-sufficiency on the part of individual carriers. The Board has declared that such ratios are relevant to its deliberations "not only because of the possibility of their effect on mail rates payable to . . . carriers, but also from the standpoint of efficiency and economy as those matters affect the question of an economically sound and efficient air-transport system." [12] At the same time, however, the Board has also indicated that its consideration of revenue-cost ratios, even in cases where all the applicant carriers have attained economic self-sufficiency, is at least in part made necessary by the possibility that operations applied for might cause them to relapse into dependence on Government support.[13]

At any rate, it seems evident that the usual requirement that a new route should show promise of self-support has not been based entirely on considerations of governmental economy, or, more particularly, on the theory that all subsidy payments should as a matter of general policy tend to disappear over a

<hr>

[11] *Annual Report* of the Civil Aeronautics Board, 1941, p. 14.

[12] Eastern Air Lines, Inc., *et al.,* Additional Washington Service, 4 C.A.B. 325, 335 (1943).

[13] *Ibid.,* pp. 334–335.

period of years, since such a showing has apparently been required even where no mail payment was being given to or requested by an applicant for a new route.[14]

In summary, it may be said that the Board, in determining whether a proposed operation "will serve a useful public purpose responsive to a public need," has generally required that the new service show traffic potential in relation to cost of operation such as to impose no undue proportion of the total expenses on the Government at the outset and to justify an expectation of progress toward ultimate self-support; and that the latter requirement has been based primarily on an appeal to the Act's mandate to "foster sound economic conditions" in air transport, which has generally been interpreted as implying economic self-sufficiency on the part of each air-transport company as a whole.

In giving precise content to the idea of a proper degree of Government support, the Board has in fact certificated only such new routes as were anticipated to require a rate of mail payment not out of line with that already prevailing for existing services. Because this existing rate had *in effect* received the approval of Congress, and since no further standard was suggested by it, the Board's standard seems to have been the only one that it could have adopted without taking upon itself the responsibility of developing independent notions of the needs of the national defense, the postal service, and the commerce of the United States. In the foreign field, the existing or "approved" level of mail payment was, of course, much higher than that for domestic operations; also, special considerations of national policy have been of greater importance in connection with foreign operations.

The above reasoning does not apply with equal force to the Board's requirement of a promise of ultimate self-sufficiency. Furthermore, the public statements of the Congressional sponsors of the Act contain no explicit mention of self-sufficiency as a standard for administration of the subsidization policy. Indeed, where the concept of self-sufficiency entered at all into

---

[14] See, for example, New England Case (Supplemental Opinion), 7 C.A.B. 439, 442–443 (1946).

the Congressional debates, it was in an entirely different context: on several occasions, prominent advocates of the Act suggested that the regulatory protection that was to be afforded to existing carriers was justified and necessitated by the fact that the air-transport industry had already arrived at, or was on the eve of, a stage of its development where nonsubsidized operation was economically feasible. However, support for the self-sufficiency aim can be found in the statements of certain nonlegislative governmental spokesmen in the period preceding its enactment, and, more important than this, this particular aspect of the Board's policy can be defended as a not unreasonable corollary of the Congressional mandate to promote "sound economic conditions" in air transport.

Adequacy of Existing Services. The second "primary question" in connection with the new services has been stated by the Board to be "whether this [useful public] purpose [responsive to a public need] can and will be served adequately by existing routes or carriers." In so far as this statement merely implies that services rendered by "existing routes or carriers" should be considered in calculating the traffic potential of proposed new operations, it may be regarded as an amplification of the first "primary question"; from this point of view it involves no necessary presumption in favor of such existing routes or carriers either with regard to their continued performance of the services presently rendered (i.e., retention of all or any specified portion of their existing traffic) or with regard to the initiation of additional service which may be found to be potentially self-supporting (i.e., obtainment of additional traffic found to be available in the market served by them).

As it stands, however, this statement is capable of at least two more restrictive interpretations. In the first place, it may be taken to mean that no new operation should be authorized in any given market unless the services currently rendered by the existing routes or carriers in that market were quantitatively inadequate to serve the traffic available at remunerative rates; only to the extent that such services were inadequate could additional operations be authorized. Under this interpretation, the approval of new competitive services would be contingent upon a showing that additional traffic not served by existing routes or carriers was available in sufficient quantity to support these new services to the required extent. Such an interpretation would imply a presumption in favor of the existing routes and carriers with respect to the retention of all of their existing traffic, in that no new operation would be authorized which would require diversion of traffic from the existing services to attain the necessary degree of self-sufficiency. In the second place, the statement may be taken to mean that no new operation should be authorized in any given market, even though there existed in that market sufficient additional traffic to support it, unless it could be shown that this additional traffic could not be adequately accommodated by the expansion of services by existing routes or carriers. Such an interpretation would imply a broad presumption in favor of the existing routes or carriers with respect to all available traffic in markets served by them.

As to the Board's own interpretation of this principle, it may be said with some assurance that both of the restrictive interpretations outlined above have been definitely rejected. The general principle that the authorization of competitive services does not require a showing of inability or unwillingness of existing carriers (or, more precisely, carriers rendering existing services in the market in question) to render adequate service has been consistently upheld by the Board in many cases involving the inauguration of new operations.[15]

Moreover, the Board has argued that the acceptance of a contrary view would have been in contravention of one of the major policy objectives of the Civil Aeronautics Act. Thus, the Board declared that this Act was designed not only to provide for the protection of the public by economic regulation of air transport, but also "to foster and encourage the maximum development of air transportation." The latter objective, according to the Board, "in some instances . . . calls for something more than mere

[15] See, for example, Northeast Airlines, Inc., *et al.*, Additional Service to Boston, 4 C.A.B. 686 (1944); Colonial Airlines, Inc., *et al.*, Atlantic Seaboard Operation (Supplemental Opinion), 4 C.A.B. 552 (1944); Transcontinental and Western Air, Inc., *et al.*, Additional North-South California Services, 4 C.A.B. 254 (1943), and the Supplemental Opinion in this case, 4 C.A.B. 373 (1943).

attainment of adequate service under protective regulation; it demands improvement and achievement through developmental pioneering." [16] Regulation alone cannot be expected to bring about the "full development and technological improvement of air transportation" envisaged in the Act; "to achieve improvement an incentive is necessary and under the Act that incentive should flow in part from competition between air carriers." [17] In the same sense, the Board has stated:

It is generally recognized that economic regulation alone cannot be relied upon to take the place of the stimulus which competition provides in the advancement of technique and service in air transportation. Competition invites comparison as to equipment, cost, personnel, organization, methods of operation, solicitation of traffic, and the like, all of which tend to insure the development of an air transportation system as contemplated by the Act. That the domestic air transportation system of this country has reached its present position of preeminence is in large part due to the competitive spirit which has existed throughout its development. The continued maintenance of that position as well as the further development of the industry demands the encouragement of free initiative and enterprise subject only to the condition that the competitive services shall not be wasteful.

The Act has clothed the Board with full power and machinery by which it may require the performance of safe and adequate service. However, a service which is just adequate, as that term is used in the statute, will not provide the public with the full advantages which should be expected from the most modern form of transportation nor will it encourage the development contemplated by the Congress. The improvements which flow from a competitive service cannot be obtained by administrative fiat. There is no regulation conceivable which could assure courtesy by a carrier's employees, for example, and it would be extremely difficult to attempt to dictate many other matters affecting the quality of the service rendered. A sound competitive system should encourage and give added impetus to the development of each competing air carrier's enterprise to a much greater extent than would a monopolistic system.[18]

[16] Transcontinental and Western Air, Inc., *et al.*, Additional North-South California Services (Supplemental Opinion), 4 C.A.B. 373, 375 (1943).

[17] *Ibid.*

[18] Colonial Airlines, Inc., *et al.*, Atlantic Seaboard Operation (Supplemental Opinion), p. 555 (1944).

If the authorization of competitive services were required to be justified by "the inability or unwillingness of an existing carrier to render adequate service," the Board argued, "no competition would ever be authorized for there is no limit to the extent to which an existing carrier could expand to meet increased demand;" and thus the achievement of maximum development would be thwarted. As conclusive evidence that Congress did not intend that regulation should entirely supplant competition in the air-transport field, the Board noted that the Act "expressly directed the Board to consider 'competition to the extent necessary to assure the sound development of an air transportation system' as being in the public interest." [19]

Although the above argument would seem to apply primarily to the broader type of presumption in favor of existing routes or carriers, the Board has applied the same general principle in cases where adequate service by the carrier already in the field clearly required no expansion of the service that it was currently rendering. That is, competitive operations have been authorized even where existing services were not found to be quantitatively inadequate to accommodate all the available traffic.[20] In such cases, the authorization of the new services would seem necessarily to involve some diversion of traffic from existing operations. Instances in which the Board has approved competitive services despite an anticipated diversion of traffic explicitly recognized by it will be discussed at a later stage.

In addition to holding that the initiation of new competitive operations does not have to be based on a showing of present or prospective inadequacy of service by carriers already in the field, the Board has also explicitly endorsed the corollary principle that the ability or willingness of existing carriers to render sufficient service does not in itself preclude inauguration of competitive services.[21] Perhaps the most notable instance of the application of the latter principle is in the American Export

[19] Transcontinental and Western Air, Inc., *et al.*, Additional North-South California Services (Supplemental Opinion), pp. 374–375 (1943).

[20] See, for example, Northeast Airlines, Inc., *et al.*, Additional Service to Boston, p. 689.

[21] See, for example, Hawaiian Air Lines, Ltd., *et al.*, Hawaiian Case, 7 C.A.B. 83, 103 (1946).

case, where Pan American, at that time the only existing trans-
atlantic United States-flag carrier, contested the authorization
of a competitive service partly on the ground that precedents
developed under other regulatory statutes similar to the Civil
Aeronautics Act precluded such authorization when it, the existing carrier, was prepared to supply whatever additional service should be found to be required.[22]

In support of this view, Pan American cited certain decisions
of the Interstate Commerce Commission in interpretation of the
Motor Carrier Act,[23] which, it contended, is similar in intent to
the Civil Aeronautics Act, particularly in that it embodies, in
Section 202(a), a statement of purpose including the development and preservation of "a highway transportation system
properly adapted to the needs of the commerce of the United
States and of the national defense."[24] In justifying its certification of a new competitive service on the transatlantic route, the
Board relied primarily on the declaration of policy in Section 2
of the Civil Aeronautics Act, advancing an argument similar to
that used in the North-South California case, discussed above.[25]
The Board also agreed with the contention advanced by American Export that Section 2, and especially that paragraph relating to "competition to the extent necessary to assure the sound
development of an air transportation system properly adapted
to the needs of . . . commerce . . . of the Postal Service, and
of the national defense," served to differentiate the Civil Aeronautics Act from the Motor Carrier Act and similar regulatory
statutes.[26]

Nevertheless, the Board did not concede that precedents developed under other regulatory statutes, even if they could be
assumed to be controlling, would require the denial of certification to American Export; on the contrary, it asserted its
belief that authorization of this service "is entirely consistent

[22] American Export Airlines, Inc., Trans-Atlantic Service, 2 C.A.B. 16, 30
(1940).

[23] 49 Stat. 543 (1935).

[24] Pan American cited the Commission's opinion in Clark Common Carrier
Application, 1 M.C.C. 445, 448 (1937).

[25] American Export Airlines, Inc., Trans-Atlantic Service, p. 32.

[26] *Ibid.,* p. 30.

with general principles of public utility regulation," since the transatlantic air-transport market could not be regarded as "served . . . to the point of saturation." [27] The Board pointed to a decision of the Interstate Commerce Commission embodying a doctrine similar to its own view, namely, that because regulation could not entirely substitute for competition in the promotion of good service, the authorization of operations competitive with existing ones might be required by the public interest even though the existing service might be adequate, provided that available traffic was sufficient to support such competitive operations.[28] An additional qualification was made by the Commission: that no "worthy competitor" already exist in the field; but this qualification has neither been explicitly endorsed nor adopted in practice by the Civil Aeronautics Board, although the lack of existing competitive service has been cited apparently as a subsidiary consideration strengthening the case for the authorization of parallel services.[29]

Nor did the Board accept the contention of American Export that the "competitive" paragraph of Section 2 of the Act makes the establishment of competition mandatory in air transportation, or, a fortiori, in any particular air-transport market.[30] In accordance with this view, the Board has repeatedly held that the Act leaves considerable discretion to the Board in determining to what extent in any particular case competition is necessary to the achievement of the statutory objectives, especially in refutation of claims by applicants for parallel routes that the Board is required by the statute to authorize such services where traffic is sufficient to support them. For example, the Board reiterated this point in the Atlantic Seaboard case, where two applicants for operations paralleling an existing service contended that "the philosophy underlying the Act requires the Board to authorize competition where there is sufficient traffic to profitably support another operation and where such

[27] *Ibid.,* p. 34.
[28] *Ibid.,* p. 34–35.
[29] Colonial Airlines, Inc., *et al.,* Atlantic Seaboard Operation (Supplemental Opinion), p. 554.
[30] American Export Airlines, Inc., Trans-Atlantic Service, p. 31.

competition will not be destructive." [31] In this case, as well as in the American Export case, the Board followed up its statement of the "nonmandatory" doctrine by a reference to the principle first set forth in the United–Western Air Express Acquisition case, namely, that the true statutory policy with respect to competition requires the Board "to safeguard an industry of vital importance to the commercial and defense interests of the Nation against the evils of unrestrained competition on the one hand, and the consequences of monopolistic control on the other." [32]

The general significance of this principle as developed by the Board will be brought out at a later stage in the discussion. In this particular context, the precise content of the principle is not developed in detail; at this point, it can only be said that the evidence at hand indicates that the Board does *not* regard the institution of competitive services in every market as necessary to safeguard the industry against the "consequences of monopolistic control," and, in addition, that the mere availability of sufficient traffic to support a parallel service is *not* deemed by the Board to be a sufficient safeguard against the "evils of unrestrained competition." These two propositions seem to be implied by the Board's use of the principle in question in an argument designed to refute contentions such as were advanced by applicants in the Atlantic Seaboard case.

Nevertheless, while maintaining that the Act itself does not make competition mandatory in any particular air-transport market or provide any definite formula for the determination of whether parallel services should be authorized in any individual case, the Board has held that the general policy embodied in the Act, interpreted in the light of the circumstances surrounding its enactment, leads to the conclusion that, "since competition in itself provides an incentive to improved service and technological development," the Board should recognize "a strong, although not conclusive, presumption in favor of

---

[31] Colonial Airlines, Inc., *et al.,* Atlantic Seaboard Operation (Supplemental Opinion), p. 554.

[32] United Air Lines Transport Corporation, Acquisition of Western Air Express Corporation, 1 C.A.A. 739, 749–750 (1940).

competition on any route which offered sufficient traffic to support competing services without unreasonable increase of total operating cost." [33] In support of this view, the Board has relied on the argument discussed above in connection with the criterion of "adequacy of existing service" in parallel-service cases, namely, that the encouragement of the maximum development of air transportation, which is one of the major objectives of the Act, requires that competition supplement regulation in the achievement of this aim. This objective, together with the declaration of policy in Section 2 of the Act, is taken to imply "the desirability of competition in the air transportation industry when such competition will be neither destructive nor uneconomical" and, furthermore, to mean that "the Board is directed to implement such competition as will fulfill the purposes of the Act." [34]

Although the Board had frequently in previous cases elaborated on the benefits to be derived from competitive services, and insisted upon the view that regulation alone could not provide a satisfactory incentive to progress in air transport, the first explicit formulation of the "presumption" doctrine cited above was in the supplemental opinion on the North-South California case. By this opinion, a new operation directly duplicating an existing service was authorized, despite no showing of inadequacy on the part of the latter, where the creation of competition was virtually the only positive justification advanced for the authorization.

It will have been noted that the actual significance of the presumption doctrine as stated by the Board is far from clear.

In the first place, the presumption itself is characterized as "strong . . . but not conclusive," which would seem to indicate that even though on a particular route traffic was sufficient to support a proposed parallel service at a cost not unreasonably higher than that of the existing service, and despite the fact that "competition in itself provides an incentive to improved service and technological development," the authoriza-

---

[33] Transcontinental and Western Air, Inc., *et al.*, Additional North-South California Services (Supplemental Opinion), p. 375.

[34] *Ibid.*

tion of this proposed service would not necessarily be justified. In explanation of this point, the Board has said:

> The reason that such presumption is not conclusive is because the Board considers all the circumstances surrounding each case . . . The over-all public interest is the principle by which we measure each decision. The public interest can only be determined after the Board has considered all of the factors and circumstances surrounding the case, and in such consideration the Board does not give weight to any empty phrase, but rather to such factors as volume of potential traffic, total operating costs, benefits to the public in the form of improved service, financial condition of the carriers, and many other factors which contribute to the constant improvement of air transportation.[35]

It is difficult to see how either of the first two enumerated considerations, i.e., volume of potential traffic and total operating costs, could afford a basis for the doctrine of the inconclusiveness of the presumption, since both of these factors are explicitly treated in the statement of that doctrine; similarly, at least one aspect of the "improved-service" factor (the incentive provided by competition as such) has already been specifically related to the problem of parallel services. Thus it would appear that the "circumstances surrounding each case" that do in fact render the presumption inconclusive would have to be sought primarily in connection with the "financial condition of the carriers" and with such "other factors" as may be found to "contribute to the constant improvement of air transportation."

Both the ambiguity of the "inconclusive presumption" doctrine as outlined in the Boston Service case and the implications of a clear-cut presumption in favor of parallel operations on any route offering "sufficient traffic to support competing services without unreasonable increase of total operating cost," have been strongly criticized by two members of the Board in a separate concurring opinion.[36] It is there urged that the policy objectives embodied in the Civil Aeronautics Act, particularly that part of Section 2 dealing with "competition to the extent

[35] Northeast Airlines, Inc., *et al.*, Additional Service to Boston, p. 691.
[36] *Ibid.*, pp. 700–703.

necessary . . . ," offer no basis for a prima facie case in favor of parallel services on every route where such services could be supported.

It is not argued that Congress intended that regulation should supplant competition in the air-transport field, but rather that the competition favored by Congress was not necessarily that between genuinely substitutable services. As evidence that Congress did in fact have in mind at the time of the passage of the Act "indirect" rather than "direct" competition among air carriers, the two Board members cite the *Report* of the Federal Aviation Commission, which was available to Congress at that time, where the benefits of emulation between nonparallel services are given major emphasis. In opposition to the presumption doctrine, the two members proposed that the establishment of parallel services be authorized only when "affirmative evidence of record" shows that there is a public need for such action; when securing the "benefits of competition" on any route is positively demonstrated to be dependent upon the establishment of parallel services, then and only then should they be authorized. Here a sharp distinction is made between the Board's reasoning in the North-South California Supplemental Opinion and that in the American Export Case. In the latter, it is argued, the Board in fact based its decision on an affirmative showing that certain specific "benefits of competition" could be attained only by the certification of an additional carrier for transatlantic operation. Among these benefits were opportunities for comparisons between costs, operating methods, equipment, and the like not present where no other carrier was engaged in comparable service; the contribution to the national defense represented by the research and development activities of an additional carrier; the stimulation of manufacture of more and better equipment for overocean flying; the training of additional personnel in transoceanic aviation techniques; and the protection of the public from high rates and inadequate service in foreign operations, over which the Board's economic regulatory powers are much more restricted than with regard to interstate and overseas air transport.[37] In the absence of

[37] American Export Airlines, Inc., Trans-Atlantic Service, pp. 32–33.

such a specific showing, the minority opinion holds, it cannot be said that such general benefits of competition as the stimulus to improved service and technological advance so often extolled by the Board are dependent upon the existence of actually substitutable services.

The similarity between this argument and that advanced by the Federal Aviation Commission is evident. Furthermore, it is clear that despite the fact that the language used in majority opinions dealing with the general benefits of competition has on occasion been very similar to that used by the Commission,[38] the prevailing view of the Board, as exemplified in the North-South California Supplemental Opinion, differs significantly from that of the Commission; the Board's appeal to the general benefits to be derived from "competition" in support of a presumption (however ambiguous) in favor of parallel services indicates that it regards these benefits as contingent upon genuine substitutability between the rival services.

The Board's rejection of the view that existing routes or carriers are entitled to any additional traffic available at profitable rates in the markets that they serve, so that no competitive operations should be authorized unless the existing ones are shown to be unable or unwilling adequately to carry such traffic, is in itself sufficient to demonstrate that the Board has not regarded a condition of universal isolated selling as the optimum competitive pattern in the air-transport field.

In the second place, even the "inconclusive presumption" in favor of parallel services is held to exist only on routes offering "sufficient traffic to support competing services without unreasonable increase of total operating cost"; and competition in the air-transport industry is in general held to be desirable only "when such competition will be neither destructive nor uneconomical." It is obvious that the precise significance of these statements cannot be ascertained without defining what is meant by an "unreasonable" increase in cost, and what characteristic or result of competition is required to make it "destructive" or "uneconomical." Unfortunately, these concepts

---

[38] See, for example, Colonial Airlines, Inc., *et al.*, Atlantic Seaboard Operations (Supplemental Opinion), p. 555.

have not so far been explicitly defined by the Board in any opinion, so that their meaning must be sought by reference to instances of their application. Nevertheless, the Board has evidently declared itself to be prepared to approve competitive services where *some* increase in operating cost will be involved as compared with a one-carrier operation; which is to say not only that the determination of the competitive pattern is not based *solely* on considerations of maximum efficiency (as of a given stage of "technique"), but that such considerations are not necessarily of overriding importance even in cases where they point clearly to a particular decision.

This conclusion is supported by a consideration of the American Export case, where the Board ruled that additional service found to be required by the public convenience and necessity should be rendered by a second carrier (American Export), even though the cost of the operation involved was apparently expected to be very much larger than would have been the case had the additional service been rendered by the carrier already in the field (Pan American).[39] The Board justified its action in this case primarily on the basis of the benefits to be derived from competition in the transatlantic service. Other instances may be cited where similar considerations have been used to justify the certification of parallel services despite their apparent higher cost, although in general the evidence as to comparative cost is not so conclusive as in the American Export case.[40]

Cost Considerations. It is very difficult to determine the degree to which cost considerations have actually been subordinated to the competitive principle in cases involving the certification of parallel services, since in such cases the Board typically does not cite evidence showing the expected cost of accommodating probable additional traffic by the expansion of

---

[39] American Export Airlines, Inc., Trans-Atlantic Service, pp. 35–37.

[40] See, for example, the North-South California case, where the institution of competitive service by Western apparently involved at least some capital costs that would not have been incurred had additional local traffic been routed via the existing carrier. Transcontinental and Western Air, Inc., *et al.*, Additional North-South California Services, p. 263, and the Supplemental Opinion in this case.

existing services, such specific cost evidence as is cited generally being limited to estimates of additional costs on the part of the carrier applying for the new parallel operation.[41] Furthermore, such evidence as is cited is usually made up of estimates developed by the carriers concerned, and it is often far from clear to what extent the Board regards these estimates as accurate. It is also important to note that any precise calculations of additional cost in relation to either expansion of existing services or inauguration of new ones must be based on definite quantitative estimates of traffic potential, and such estimates are seldom if ever made by the Board itself in its stated opinions.

A notable series of cases in which the carrier (Pan American) already serving the markets concerned has presented evidence designed to show that the continuation of a one-carrier service would be less costly than the certification of additional carriers to accommodate traffic expansion is that dealing with United States-flag foreign air services.[42] In these cases, however, the Board has indicated that it does not regard this evidence as conclusive,[43] and has furthermore argued that the chief economic advantages claimed for the one-carrier service can probably be more properly expected from service by more than one carrier.[44] It is thus not possible to determine in these cases to what extent, if any, the expected benefits of competition have been allowed to overrule cost advantages regarded by the Board as genuine.

Moreover, the general significance of these foreign-route cases may be somewhat limited by the fact that the "benefits

---

[41] See, for example, Continental Air Lines, Inc., *et al.*, Denver–Kansas City Service, 4 C.A.B. 1 (1942); and Transcontinental and Western Air, Inc., *et al.*, Additional North-South California Services, and the Supplemental Opinion in this case.

See also Colonial Air Lines, Inc., *et al.*, Atlantic Seaboard Operations (Supplemental Opinion), where no evidence as to cost of operation by either the new or the old carrier was cited in the decision regarding additional service from Florida to New York and Philadelphia.

[42] See, for example, Northeast Airlines, Inc., *et al.*, North Atlantic Route Case, 6 C.A.B. 319, 324 (1945).

[43] *Ibid.*, pp. 324–325.

[44] *Ibid.*, p. 325.

of competition" involved here are not entirely comparable to those which would be relevant in the ordinary domestic case. It has already been pointed out that the original decision in favor of parallel transatlantic services was based at least in part on special considerations related to the national defense and on the fact that the Board's regulatory powers over foreign operations are relatively limited. Similar special considerations have played a part in subsequent foreign-route cases. In the North Atlantic Route case, in particular, the Board stated its belief that a finding in favor of one-carrier service on this route would be tantamount to restricting all United States-flag international air service to operation by one company, and based its decision at least in part on the objectionable political consequences of such a restriction.[45] However, neither this consideration nor the lack of any comparable transoceanic service which figured in the Board's American Export opinion have been relevant in later foreign-route cases dealing with other geographic areas, where similar economic arguments have been advanced by Pan American, although the limited nature of the Board's regulatory powers over international operations would, of course, be pertinent to these cases.

Some additional light on the meaning of "unreasonable" cost increases in relation to parallel services can be obtained from decisions in which applications for such services were denied primarily because of cost considerations. In several cases the Board explicitly indicated that the cost of institution of parallel operations by a new carrier was so large in comparison with the cost of expansion by the existing carrier "as to outweigh any benefit which might accrue by the inauguration of a competitive service"; one of these cases was that involving additional service from the United States to Cuba and Central America, where this service was awarded by the Board to Pan American rather than American Export, a prospective newcomer in this market.[46]

As usual, it is impossible precisely to estimate the Board's

---

[45] Northeast Airlines, Inc., *et al.,* North Atlantic Route Case, pp. 324–326.

[46] Pan American Airways, Inc., *et al.,* Service from New Orleans to Cuba and Central America, 4 C.A.B. 161, 177 (1943).

idea of the cost difference involved. Some idea of the order of magnitude of this difference can be obtained from forecasts considered in connection with probably necessary mail compensation on the new route. On the basis of its own cost and revenue estimates, Pan American calculated that annual income from the proposed and finally certified operation between New Orleans and Guatemala City would exceed annual expenses by about $130,000; however, this figure was arrived at by excluding depreciation charges on equipment, the inclusion of which would have produced an annual *deficit* of $40,000. The data cited by the Board are not adequate to show comparable figures for American Export; it is noted that a total annual deficit of about $830,000 was estimated by the carrier, but this figure included operations not finally found by the Board to be required by the public convenience and necessity. Statistics prepared by Pan American, as corrected by the inclusion of depreciation charges, indicated that for operations more closely comparable to those included in the American Export calculation Pan American would incur an annual deficit of only $190,-000. Moreover, in addition to the fact that the traffic and hence the revenue estimates of the two carriers were not precisely comparable, the comparison is further obscured by the fact that the Board indicated that both cost and revenue forecasts were open to question because of "changes in conditions since the estimates were prepared," including considerable increases in current and anticipated volume of traffic.[47]

In its conclusion on the selection of a carrier, the Board singled out the fact that the capital costs that would have to be incurred by American Export would be much higher than those of Pan American; here again, however, the actual figures cited ($177,000 for Pan American; more than $1,200,000 for American Export) were estimates made by the carriers, apparently not on a strictly comparable basis. Even were the evidence as to the exact cost difference more clear, the general applicability of any conclusions drawn from it on the significance of "unreasonable" cost increase in connection with parallel services would be open to question, since the Board indicated that,

<hr>

[47] *Ibid.*, pp. 171–172.

because of the difference in the type of service that could be offered by American Export and Pan American, the former could not be expected to offer really effective competition to the latter.[48]

A second case in which the institution of a competitive service was denied approval because of cost considerations is that involving the application of Canadian Colonial Airways, Ltd., to operate on the Montreal–New York route; this case, which, as usual, does not contain evidence sufficient to show the Board's estimate of the relative cost of operation by one carrier as opposed to two, is chiefly interesting because the addition to the number of firms in the market in question would have been brought about by the splitting up of one firm composed of two affiliated companies.[49] Certain savings that would be expected from the one-carrier operation were enumerated; these were administrative expenses connected with supervision and bookkeeping. It was also indicated that greater economy in the utilization of equipment might be expected from the one-carrier operation; this consideration was apparently held to be of particular importance because of the relatively short route mileage between the terminal points, a factor tending in itself to limit the opportunity for efficient use of equipment.[50]

Utilization of equipment as well as savings in administrative overhead were also relied on in the Board's decision in favor of single-carrier service in the Puerto Rican case,[51] which is of particular interest in that it involved the "exit" of an existing firm rather than the denial of entry to a new one.

Although none of these decisions affords a basis for determination of the precise relative weight accorded to considerations of cost and to the competitive principle in decisions on parallel operations, certain important conclusions can be drawn from them regarding the Board's general policy on such services. In the first place, the fact that the Board has certified

<hr>

[48] *Ibid.*, pp. 175–176.

[49] Canadian Colonial Airways, Ltd., Permit to foreign air carrier, 3 C.A.B. 50 (1941).

[50] *Ibid.*, p. 63.

[51] Caribbean-Atlantic Airlines, Inc., Puerto Rican Operations, 3 C.A.B. 717, 725 (1942).

parallel services where the cost of a one-carrier operation was clearly regarded as much lower strengthens and extends the conclusion already pointed out with respect to the Board's attitude toward the broad type of presumption in favor of existing carriers: not only does the Board consider such carriers to have no prior claim to additional traffic available in their markets which they can and will serve adequately; they have no such claim even when they can serve this traffic at lower cost than could a new carrier.

Furthermore, it is possible to eliminate at least one explanation that might be offered for the Board's differentiation between the cases in which cost considerations were allowed to outweigh the benefits of competition and those in which the opposite result was arrived at. Since the Central American, Puerto Rican, and Montreal–New York cases all involved a decision in favor of service by a single carrier, it cannot be said that the distinction has been based on a prejudice against having a particular market occupied by only one firm. Another possible interpretation is that the Board has attached overriding weight to cost considerations where additional cost to the Government in the form of mail payments was expected to be involved, and to competitive benefits where considerations of governmental economy either were irrelevant or tended to favor the parallel service; this interpretation could be supported in particular by reference to the Atlantic Seaboard and North-South California cases, and to the three cases cited in which certification was denied on the basis of cost. However, it would then have to be argued that the American Export decision, which approved a competitive service where a very large additional cost to the Government was involved, was extraordinary, and hence of no general significance, on account of special considerations such as those related to the national defense, the limitations on the Board's regulatory powers over foreign operations, and the unique "yardstick" value of the competitive service.

The three cases cited in which parallel service was denied on the basis of cost are also important because, even though the Board's opinion as to the precise cost difference at stake cannot be determined, the decisions seem to have been based on genuine comparisons between the probable efficiency of a one-carrier operation and service by two carriers; in these cases, the Board appears to have decided against the institution of competitive services on the basis of a calculation, however imprecise, of the most efficient distribution of a given volume of traffic between firms.

At this point, it will be well to summarize what has so far been discovered regarding the criteria used by the Board in passing on the authorization of new competitive services. In the first place, the Board requires that such services, in common with all new operations, shall not impose an undue proportion of the total cost on the Government at the outset, and shall show promise of ultimate economic self-sufficiency. It has been suggested that the latter requirement has been based primarily not on mere considerations of governmental economy, but on a concept of "sound economic conditions" in air transportation, which means essentially the achievement of profitable operation by each carrier subject to the jurisdiction of the Board.

Secondly, although the Board has recognized the adequacy of existing services as a relevant consideration in connection with new competitive operations, it has consistently held that carriers rendering existing services in any market possess no prior right either to operate any additional services that may be found to be required in that market, or to retain all of the traffic that they are currently serving. Thus, the authorization of a new parallel service is not contingent upon a showing that existing routes or carriers are unable or unwilling to render adequate service, whether or not an expanded service is found necessary to accommodate traffic in their markets. The Board has adopted this view on the ground that a contrary opinion would preclude the achievement of the maximum development of air transportation by ruling out the authorization of new competition (i.e., the availability of new genuinely substitutable services provided by different firms), such competition being regarded as necessary to provide a stimulus to progress in techniques of service and operation.

In the third place, the Board has held that the Act does not make the authorization of competition mandatory in any particular transport market where there is adequate traffic to support it, but leaves considerable discretion to the Board in this connection, subject to the broad requirement that it safeguard the air-transport industry "against the evils of unrestrained competition on the one hand, and the consequences of monopolistic control on the other." In exercising this discretion, however, the Board has declared that the achievement of one of the Act's major objectives, namely, maximum development of air transport, requires that it recognize a "strong, although not conclusive, presumption in favor of competition on any route which offered sufficient traffic to support competing services without unreasonable increase of total operating cost." The Board's own statements leave the exact status of this presumption far from clear; however, it is suggested that the "inconclusiveness" of the presumption arises from the necessity of considering the effect of new competitive services on the financial condition of the carriers concerned. Furthermore, competition is apparently not to be authorized where it will be "destructive" or "uneconomical," or where the market does not afford "sufficient traffic to support competing services without unreasonable increase of total operating cost."

The exact nature of the factors that render the presumption in favor of competition inoperative in any given instance must be sought in an investigation of particular cases in which the Board has dealt with proposed new competitive services. The cases so far considered indicate (1) that new competitive services have been authorized on occasion despite some anticipated excess in total operating cost as compared with an operation of the same services by the existing carriers, although it is not possible to determine the exact cost difference estimated by the Board; (2) that in a few cases the higher cost of a two-carrier service has been the ruling consideration in the denial of authorization to the competitive service (here again, it is impossible to discover the precise cost differences anticipated); (3) that the distinction between these two types of case cannot be explained in terms of a prejudice on the part of the Board against having any market occupied by only one firm; (4) that it can be argued, although not conclusively, that the actually operative distinguishing principle has been the question of comparative cost to the Government, that is, that cost considerations have generally been given superior weight where the excess cost of competitive services would have involved an additional burden to the Government in the form of mail pay, and competitive considerations in the opposite case. It has also been suggested that the three cases in which a proposed competitive service was denied because of cost considerations are significant in that the Board's decisions appear to have been based on calculation, however imprecise, of the most efficient distribution of a given volume of traffic among firms.

In the majority of parallel-service cases, however, there is no such simple relation between the Board's decisions and considerations of relative efficiency. The denial of authorization to proposed services competitive with existing ones has typically been based either (1) on a contention that the available traffic is inadequate to support such services, or (2) on an argument that their authorization would occasion undue diversion of traffic from existing operations. It is evident that neither of these criteria is inherently incompatible with the distribution of traffic in accordance with maximum efficiency; however, it is also evident that neither of them as it stands necessarily requires such distribution.

In fact, the precise meaning of "inadequate" traffic or "undue" diversion in this context cannot be determined without reference to an independently arrived at concept of the optimum distribution of traffic among competitive firms. For it is clear that demand in any market is in most instances adequate to support service by two or more firms at *some* levels of output, and, therefore, that a contention that traffic in any market is "inadequate" to support more than one service must be interpreted to mean that the distribution of traffic involved in supporting two or more services differs from some predetermined optimum. Similarly, an argument that the authorization of additional services would result in an "undue" diversion of traffic from existing services implies some standard from which the resulting traffic distribution would differ.

It is in the opinions involving the extent of permissible diversion that the Board's conception of the optimum distribution of traffic among competitive firms is most definitely indicated. Moreover, it is these cases that are most important in affording a precise idea of the nature of the factors that usually render the presumption in favor of competition inapplicable in particular cases (and, in this connection, in indicating what is meant by "uneconomical" or "destructive" competition and the "evils of unrestrained competition"), and in revealing the significance in administration of the third "primary question" relevant to the public convenience and necessity of a proposed new service, namely, "whether it [i.e., the useful public purpose responsive to a public need] can be served by the applicant without impairing the operations of existing carriers contrary to the public interest."

Adequacy of Available Traffic. Before the Board's specific treatment of the "diversion" issue is dealt with, however, there will be discussed in some detail one notable case in which the certification of a proposed competitive service was denied primarily on grounds of inadequate traffic. This decision, which is particularly interesting in that the argument of the applicant carrier was based in part on a study of the variation of airline operating costs in connection with schedule frequencies, will serve to illustrate the typical difficulties involved in determining the precise standards of traffic distribution relied upon by the Board in connection with the adequate-traffic criterion, as well as the seeming divergence of such standards as appear to have been used from considerations of relative efficiency.

In this case,[52] Northwest Airlines sought authorization to extend its West Coast–Chicago route to New York City, service between the latter two points already being provided by three companies: T.W.A., American, and United. The Board's refusal to approve the proposed Chicago–New York extension

[52] Northwest Airlines, Inc., *et al.,* Additional Service to Canada, 2 C.A.B. 627 (1941).

was based primarily on an argument that traffic potential in this market did not justify service by an additional carrier, in view of the fact that the load factors prevailing on flights by the existing operators showed that they not only could "take care of the existing traffic with a surplus of space still available," but could also be expected to absorb any foreseeable increase in traffic.[53]

If the Board's refusal were based on a contention that any increase in traffic at all could be accommodated by the expansion of service by existing carriers, it would be in apparent contradiction to the usual position taken with respect to the willingness and ability of existing carriers to render additional service found to be required in the markets they serve. A similar apparent contradiction is to be found in another section of the same case, where a proposed competitive service (in this instance, parallel to a route then served by only *one* carrier) was denied authorization not only because of the relatively low load factor on existing schedules, which was taken to indicate that the present service was not inadequate and that there was no need for service by two carriers, but because there was no showing in the record "that the present operator . . . [was] incapable of accommodating the natural growth of air traffic which can be foreseen at this time." [54] "Under these conditions," the Board continued, "the contention that there should be competing, duplicating services between two points merely to prevent one Government regulated carrier from dominating that field is unimpressive." [55]

However, a more consistent interpretation of the Board's opinion, and one that seems on the whole to be more appropriate, would take into consideration the fact that in connection with neither of the above-mentioned routes was the possibility of a traffic expansion that *would* warrant the inauguration of additional competitive service completely ruled out; in both instances, the denial of authorization was justified by reference to the *then foreseeable* development of traffic potential. The

[53] *Ibid.*, p. 639.
[54] *Ibid.*, pp. 651–652.
[55] *Ibid.*, p. 652.

"claim" of the existing carriers to additional traffic available in the markets that they served was not, then, regarded as including any increase in such traffic, however large, but was evidently more restricted. The Board's use of evidence as to low load factors on existing schedules to demonstrate lack of justification for competitive service might be taken to indicate that the existing carriers were believed to be entitled only to such traffic as could be conveniently accommodated *on the then scheduled flights*. Such a view on the part of the Board might, moreover, be at least partially justified on the basis of cost considerations. But this interpretation of the Board's opinion would not be consistent with its reference to the fact that "the existing airlines may be expected to inaugurate such flights [as might be warranted by increases in demand] when the income from the traffic at least equals the out-of-pocket expense of these flights." [56]

Comparative Cost to the Government. Some additional light on the Board's opinion on this point may be obtained from a consideration of its treatment of the question of comparative cost. The case presented by Northwest included an argument designed to justify certification of its proposed service on the basis of the behavior of operating costs of airline firms with varying daily frequencies of schedule. A witness for this carrier contended that unit operating costs do not decrease after a daily frequency of five to seven flights has been reached, so that there is in reality no cost advantage to be obtained by adding schedules to those of existing carriers to accommodate additional traffic after such carriers have reached the designated frequency of service.[57] With regard to the New York–Chicago route, the record showed that the three carriers in the market were then offering a combined total of thirty-four daily flights eastbound and thirty-two westbound.[58]

It is to be noted that the Board did not base its denial of certification on any direct criticism of the validity or applicability of the results of the cost-behavior study. Instead, it

[56] *Ibid.*, p. 639.
[57] *Ibid.*
[58] *Ibid.*, p. 636.

pointed out that in order to institute the service Northwest would have to incur large capital costs, and that a very large mail payment would be necessary to support the new service, whereas the expansion of existing carriers could be expected to involve no additional cost to the Government.[59] The last-named contention was advanced on the ground that these carriers could be expected to inaugurate new schedules only when the additional cost involved would be covered by the additional revenues to be obtained from such schedules, and not on any explicit argument that the three carriers in the field were inherently more efficient than the applicant company. Since the expansion so envisaged must, for the sake of the argument, be regarded as adequate, i.e., including all service actually "warranted" by traffic increases, this argument as it stands would have to be based on a view that only such schedules as are immediately self-supporting are so "warranted," a position that would be contrary to the Board's general policy on the inauguration of new operations. It is obvious that if this position is adopted no new competitive service involving a subsidy of any size whatever could be certified, irrespective of the relative cost of the expansion of existing operations. Indeed, the Board's treatment of this problem seems to be an entirely unsatisfactory substitute for a bona fide calculation of the estimated cost involved in expanding the existing services to the extent deemed to be required by the expected traffic potential; only from this calculation could results have been derived that would be useful in making a genuine comparison with the cost of operation by the applicant carrier.

A similar criticism is applicable to the treatment of the cost issue in connection with the New York–Buffalo route in the same proceeding. With regard to this route, the Board merely indicated that a substantial increase in the necessary subsidy payment to the applicant carrier would result from authorization of the proposed service.[60]

This treatment of the cost issue — i.e., the calculation of the additional cost involved in the inauguration of a new competi-

---

[59] *Ibid.*, p. 641.
[60] *Ibid.*, p. 651–652.

tive operation by estimating the subsidy that would have to be paid to the applicant carrier to support it — is far more typical than that exemplified in the cases discussed above where major emphasis was placed on considerations of operating costs. It will have been noted that in this instance, as well as with regard to the proposed Chicago–New York extension, the Board's discussion of the issue centered on cost to the Government rather than on a direct comparison of operating costs with and without the addition of the proposed new service. Under certain conditions, the use of comparative cost to the Government as a measure of relative efficiency of operation would unquestionably be appropriate.

However, to use the estimated subsidy to the applicant carrier as a measure of the cost difference involved, as was done in connection with the New York–Buffalo route, is open to serious objection, since this procedure must evidently be based on an assumption that the necessary subsidy payment to the carrier or carriers rendering existing services will be as large with the certification of the new competitive service as it would be should the new operation not be authorized; this would seem to imply that the carriers already in the field are expected to continue to provide service at substantially the same level. In regard to the Chicago–New York extension, the Board's treatment of cost to the Government is likewise open to objection, since the comparison of governmental cost with and without the new service was not based on an assumed uniform level of total output.

The relation between anticipated cost to the Government and the general question of optimum investment in a subsidized industry, as well as the nature of the special conditions under which a criterion of comparative governmental cost may be expected to yield valid results, will be brought out in the discussion following the next section.

Diversion of Traffic from Existing Services. We turn now to a specific consideration of the Civil Aeronautics Board's treatment of the question of diversion of traffic from existing services by proposed new competitive operations.

In the first place, the Board has consistently held that the mere fact that a new service will divert "substantial" traffic from existing carriers does not in itself constitute sufficient reason for denying it authorization, and has in many instances approved new operations despite an anticipated diversion of traffic, although the diversion itself seems to have been regarded as undesirable from the point of view of the public interest.[61] From this it follows that the Board does not hold that existing carriers or services are entitled to protection from competitive inroads on their markets to the extent necessary to maintain the existing level of traffic; it can also be said that the Board does not regard the reduction of the traffic available to existing services as itself necessarily constituting an impairment of these operations contrary to the public interest.

In discussing the general status of prospective traffic diversion as an element in the determination of the public convenience and necessity of new services, the Board has typically taken the position that the effect of these services on existing carriers is pertinent because the reduction of revenues of the carriers might impair their "economic stability" and hence affect adversely the "soundness" of the national air-transport system, and also might necessitate the payment of a higher mail rate by the Government to support their operations.[62] In accordance with this view, the extent of the prospective diversion is usually considered with reference to its effect on the total commercial revenues of the carriers rendering existing services. Cases may be cited in which the very low proportions of system revenues (of carriers rendering existing services) that were expected to be diverted by proposed operations have been regarded as evidence sufficient to show that diversion would not be large enough to justify denial of authorization to the new services.[63]

However, it cannot be said that the Board's policy is one of mere restriction of diversion to a fixed percentage of system revenues. The principle governing the Board's decisions is not

[61] See, for example, the Board's statement in National Airlines, Inc., *et al.*, Daytona Beach–Jacksonville Operation, 1 C.A.A. 612, 617–618 (1940).

[62] See, for example, American Airlines, Inc., *et al.*, Additional East-West California and Arizona Services, 4 C.A.B. 297, 305 (1943).

[63] *Ibid.*, p. 312, for example.

that any carrier is entitled to protection of its revenues from competition up to a certain arbitrary proportion of these revenues, but that it has a right to such protection to the extent necessary to permit it to continue to conduct an "economical and efficient operation in the area served by it." [64]

In other words, the Board's policy seems to be to refuse authorization to new services if they affect the revenues of carriers already in the field to such an extent that they would be unable profitably to continue their existing operations at the subsidy rate previously received. In this context, the continuance of "existing operations" appears to include the profitable maintenance of some service not only on all the routes currently being operated, but also at substantially the existing capacity for carriage.[65] This interpretation is supported by the emphasis frequently given to the "economic stability" or "financial stability" of the carriers as such in connection with the problem of diversion; for if, as seems to be implied by this emphasis, the extent of permissible diversion is limited to that which would not reduce the over-all profitability of an existing enterprise to a level below a "normal" rate of return, then it appears to be desired that the level of investment maintained in this enterprise shall be the same after as before the initiation of the competitive service.[66]

An interesting example of the Board's usual practice of evaluating diversion by reference to its effect on the total operations and profitability of carriers rendering existing services, rather than on the basis of the proportion of total revenues affected, is found in Alaska Air Lines, Inc., et al., Service to Anchorage, Alaska.[67] In this case, a proposed service by Pan American Air-

---

[64] National Airlines, Inc., *et al.*, Daytona Beach–Jacksonville Operation, p. 617.

[65] In support of the view that the maintenance of service on all existing routes is envisaged, see in particular the Daytona Beach–Jacksonville case, pp. 624–25; and Service in the Rocky Mountain States Area, 6 C.A.B. 695, 740 (1946).

[66] See, for example, the statement in Additional East-West California and Arizona Services cited in note 62; and also, Service in the Rocky Mountain States Area, p. 740; and Northwest Airlines, Inc., *et al.*, Chicago-Milwaukee-New York Service, 6 C.A.B. 217, 223 (1944).

[67] 3 C.A.B. 522 (1942).

ways between Fairbanks and Anchorage was denied approval because of the extent of the anticipated diversion of traffic from Star Air Lines, Inc. (a local Alaskan carrier), even though only a small proportion of the latter's total business would have been affected. Through the purchase of Lavery Airways, another local carrier already operating between Fairbanks and Anchorage, Pan American proposed to extend its Seattle-Juneau-Fairbanks operation to Anchorage, thereby providing a "more luxurious service" than was then available between the last two points, and at a reduced rate to through passengers. In view of the superiority of the proposed service, the Board pointed out that Star's traffic "between these points would be practically lost if it were forced to compete with Pan American for this business," and that the line would be "placed in a position where it . . . [could not] render effective competition for traffic between Anchorage and Fairbanks." The denial was justified primarily on the ground that local carriers such as Star should be protected from outside competition on the relatively lucrative routes between major towns in Alaska, in order to assure their continued ability to provide other services "highly essential to the economic life of the Territory," at least until the Board was able to ascertain whether the latter type of service could be independently self-supporting.[68]

The same principle has apparently governed the Board's restrictions on new services specified in the certificates authorizing them. These restrictions have included requirements (1) that the carrier not participate in local traffic between points served by it on a through route, (2) that the carrier's service between certain points on its route be limited to flights originating or terminating at certain other points, (3) that all or a specified number of points on the carrier's route be served on every flight, and (4) in the case of the Alaskan carriers, that charter and special services, and services authorized under an "irregular" route certificate that are directly competitive with

---

[68] *Ibid.*, pp. 527–528. The same line of reasoning is apparent in the Board's treatment of proposed through carrier service to Greeley and Laramie in *Service in the Rocky Mountain States Area*, p. 740.

regular scheduled operations, be "casual, occasional and infrequent," the former also being limited to flights to or from a point that the carrier is specifically authorized to serve.[69]

Although the explicit justification for such restrictions has on occasion been made in terms of the "adequacy" of existing services,[70] and more frequently by a general statement that the traffic available was not sufficient to justify such additional service as would have been possible in the absence of the restriction,[71] there seems to be no real evidence of a departure from the principle outlined above in connection with the certification of competitive services. The aim and effect of these restrictions are primarily to limit the amount of diversion from and hence protect the revenues of carriers rendering existing services; in no case is there any indication that the Board has adopted a criterion of "undue diversion" which is inconsistent with that described above, and in some cases it is quite clear that this same criterion has been used.[72] The effect of this principle on the functioning of the regulated markets, as well as its relation to the minimization of cost to the Government, will be dealt with in the following section.

Optimum Investment and Number of Firms in a Subsidized Market

As has already been said, the usual major criterion of public convenience and necessity, namely, immediate economic self-sufficiency, has been replaced in the airline field by a consideration of the degree to which the proposed service can be expected to be supported by commercial revenues, it being postulated that any service that can be maintained at a rate of subsidy not notably larger than those already authorized is required by the

---

[69] An "irregular route" certificate designates a certain area within which the carrier is authorized to serve all points. All carriers may engage in charter and other special services to points throughout the Territory. Ackerman Air Service, *et al.*, Alaska Air Transportation Investigation, 3 C.A.B. 804, 820–821 (1942).

[70] See, for example, Continental Air Lines, Inc., *et al.*, Additional Air Service in Texas, 4 C.A.B. 215, 234 (1943).

[71] See, for example, Colonial Airlines, Inc., *et al.*, Washington-Ottawa-Montreal Service, 6 C.A.B. 481, 502 (1945); Transcontinental and Western Air, Inc., *et al.*, Additional North-South California Services, 4 C.A.B. 373, 377 (1943).

[72] See, for example, American Airlines, Inc., *et al.*, Additional East-West California and Arizona Services, pp. 307–308, 313.

public convenience and necessity. In the determination of the level of output in any particular market, application of this principle would mean that in each case optimum output would be the maximum that could be supported with a Government subsidy to cover no more than the approved proportion of the total operating cost.

This principle may be applied to the problem of the service of one homogeneous market by various numbers of firms as well as to the distribution of output among various markets. With reference to a demand curve showing the market for homogeneous air transport on a given route, various supply curves may be drawn, each showing the unit cost of providing various amounts of such transport with a given number of firms, optimum distribution of output among these firms being assumed at every point on each curve. Optimum output will then be shown by the point at which maximum service can be provided at whatever cost-revenue ratio has been settled upon as being not unduly burdensome to the Government; the particular supply curve upon which the relevant unit-cost point is found will indicate the optimum number of firms. *For any given output,* the optimum number of firms will be that for which the unit cost of operation is lowest; *if the cost to the Government per unit of service is computed as the vertical distance between the commercial demand curve and the various cost curves drawn up as indicated above,* then the optimum number of firms for any given output will be that for which the (total or unit) cost to the Government is least.[73]

From this analysis, certain conclusions as to the conditions under which the use of relative cost to the Government as an inverse measure of the economic desirability of service by various numbers of firms is valid may readily be derived. In the first place, it is evident that such a procedure is appropriate only with a given level of output, and cannot be relied upon in judging the relative desirability of, say, service by two carriers as opposed to one where the actual choice to be made involves

---

[73] Throughout this discussion, possible real losses arising from the immobility of certain resources among various firms are disregarded. No modification in the principles underlying the argument would be necessary in order to take such losses into account; moreover, it seems highly probable that they are of very slight importance in the air-transport business.

different levels of output. To make this choice on the basis of minimum cost to the Government, either total or per unit of service, would be inconsistent with the promotional investment policy embodied in the Civil Aeronautics Act.

This point is illustrated graphically in Fig. 2, where $x =$ output and $y =$ price or cost. Line D represents commercial demand (average commercial revenue). Line D_1 represents total demand (average commercial revenue plus per-unit subsidy). Curves C_1, C_2 and C_3 represent average transfer cost with one, two, and three firms, respectively.

For the sake of simplicity, this diagram is drawn on the assumption of a fixed per-unit subsidy rate, the vertical distance between D and D_1 being the same for any output. If a fixed

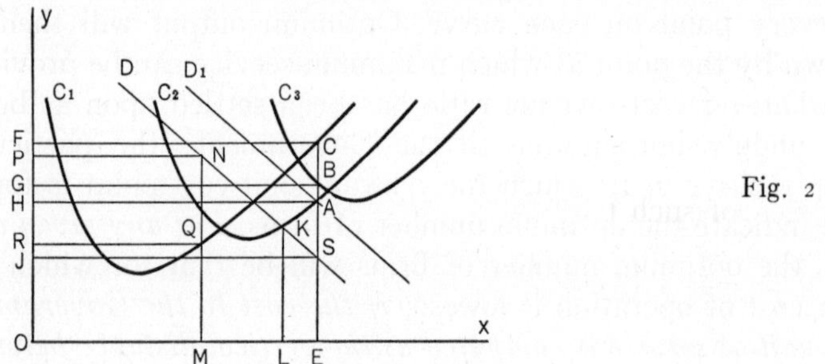

Fig. 2

proportion of total (or average) revenue were contributed by the government, the vertical distance between the two curves would diminish steadily with the expansion of output.

At the optimum output OE, average total revenue is AE, average commercial revenue SE, and subsidy per unit of output AS. The total subsidy payment is $ASJH$. The optimum number of firms is two. For this output, if the cost to the Government per unit of output is computed as the vertical distance between the commercial demand curve and the various cost curves, two firms will be the number for which both per-unit and total subsidy is smallest. With one firm, the per-unit subsidy for this output would be CS, and the total cost to the government $CSJF$; with three firms, the per-unit subsidy for this output would be BS, and the total cost to the government $BSJG$.

If the primary criterion for output determination were the minimization of cost to the government, either per-unit or total, then it is obvious that output OE would not be chosen. At output OL, for example (which would be the optimum output if there were no subsidy), it would be possible to eliminate subsidy payments altogether; but it is equally obvious that the choice of such an output would not be in accordance with the Government's promotional policy. Similarly, if a choice were being made between, say, output OM with one firm and output OE with two, the minimum-subsidy criterion, either per-unit or total, would obviously favor the former alternative. At output OM, the Government's liability would be zero, as compared with $ASJH$ at output OE.

In the second place, the obligation of the Government to each firm must be actually limited to and measured by the difference between the firm's total cost of operation and total revenues *at the level of output indicated for it by the optimum distribution of production among the carriers*. Just as a valid conclusion as to the relative desirability of supplying a particular quantity of a good by one, two, or more firms on the basis of minimum production cost must be based on a completely flexible distribution of this output among the firms, which is to say a distribution unlimited by any "presumption" (not based on cost considerations) regarding the "right" of any particular firm to supply any absolute amount or predetermined proportion of the total quantity or to receive any absolute amount or predetermined proportion of the revenue obtained from its sale, so a calculation of the optimum number of firms on the basis of minimum cost to the Government must, if it is to offer a genuine guide to maximum efficiency, involve no obligation on the Government's part to support the output or revenues of any particular carrier at a predetermined level.

For example, suppose that service on a particular air route is being rendered by one carrier at the rate of seven round-trip flights per day, this service having been found to be the optimum on the basis of a certain plane-mile rate of subsidy determined to be "not unduly burdensome," demand having been so estimated that, although seat-mile cost for one carrier would have been minimum at a daily frequency of five round trips, this service would have had more than the required degree of economic self-sufficiency, whereas any operation by more than one carrier would have involved either less than the required degree of economic self-sufficiency (a higher rate of subsidy than the approved level) or the provision of fewer than seven round-trip flights per day (less service supplied at higher commercial rates).

Now suppose demand to increase to such an extent that ten daily round-trip flights could be supported at the approved subsidy rate provided that unit costs of operation were at the minimum — a condition that would obtain if the service were rendered by two carriers each operating at maximum efficiency — but that only eight such flights could be supported if they were all operated by the existing carrier, because of the higher unit costs of such an operation. It is clear that on the basis of promotional policy and maximum efficiency the correct course of action would be to authorize the provision of five schedules by an additional carrier and, by the limitation of subsidy payments to the existing carrier, bring about the necessary curtailment of its services.

It will be seen that the decision whether or not to authorize service by a second carrier, if presented in a form involving different levels of output, could not be correctly made by reference to the criterion of minimum governmental cost. If, for example, the choice were presented between a seven-flight service by one carrier and a ten-flight service by two, the minimum-subsidy principle (interpreted either as minimum total or minimum per-unit service) would probably point to approval of the former (since the increased demand would make possible higher commercial rates for the seven-flight service); if the choice were between an eight-flight service by one carrier and a ten-flight service by two, a criterion of minimum *total* subsidy would result in approval of the former, and a criterion of minimum *per-unit* subsidy would offer no basis for choice.

This example is illustrated in Fig. 3, where x = output in terms of flights per day and y = price or cost. Line D_1 represents initial commercial demand (average commercial revenue prior to change in demand). Line D_1' represents initial total demand (average commercial revenue prior to change in demand plus per-unit subsidy). Line D_2 represents new commercial demand. Line D_2' represents new total demand. Curves C_1 and C_2 represent average transfer cost with one and two firms, respectively. This diagram is drawn on the assumption of a fixed per-unit subsidy.

The initial equilibrium output is OG, with one firm operating at seven flights per day. With commercial demand as indicated by D_1, any service by two firms would require more than the approved rate of subsidy, since C_2 lies above D_1' throughout.

With commercial demand as indicated by D_2, the new optimum would be at output OJ, with two firms each operating at

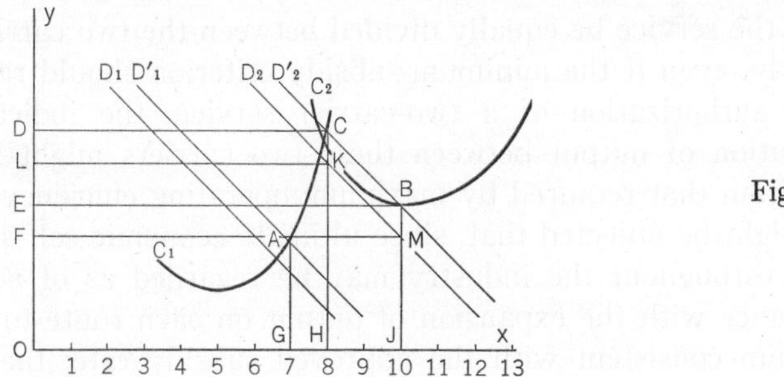

Fig. 3

five flights per day. As between output OJ with two firms and output OG with one, the minimum-subsidy criterion would obviously indicate the latter, since no subsidy at all would now be required to support this service. As between output OJ with two firms and output OH with one, the minimum-total-subsidy criterion would indicate the latter, since $CKLD$ (the total subsidy at output OH with one firm) is smaller than $BMFE$ (the total subsidy at output OJ with two firms). The minimum-per-unit-subsidy criterion would offer no basis for choice between output OH with one firm and output OJ with two firms, since BM (the per-unit subsidy at output OJ with two firms) is equal to CK (the per-unit subsidy at output OH with one firm).

Secondly, it is evident that the minimum-subsidy principle

may be expected to produce results identical with those dictated by maximum efficiency with reference to the optimum number of firms to operate the ten-flight service only if the ultimate obligation of the Government to the existing carrier could be measured by the deficit incurred in the operation of a five-flight service. If the Government were committed to provide a certain level of revenue to the existing carrier higher than it would receive from the five-flight service, as would be the case, for example, if the Government were obliged to make up any deficit incurred in, or to provide a "fair return" on the *entire* investment required for, the operation of the carrier's existing seven-flight service, it might well be that the total subsidy payments involved in authorizing the existing carrier to operate even a ten-flight service might be less than would be required should the service be equally divided between the two carriers. Similarly, even if the minimum-subsidy criterion should result in the authorization of a two-carrier service, the indicated distribution of output between these two carriers might well differ from that required by maximum operating efficiency.

It might be objected that, since ultimate economic self-sufficiency throughout the industry may be regarded as of equal importance with the expansion of output on each route to the maximum consistent with the approved subsidy rate, the increase in demand that has been assumed need not be taken to imply that more services should be authorized but might better be utilized to provide larger commercial revenues per unit for existing operations, with an accompanying reduction in the necessary rate of subsidy. It is certainly true that the above argument should take into account both of the coördinate aims of governmental policy. However, no fundamental modification of the principles developed above is needed to satisfy this requirement. Thus, it could not be said that the introduction of the aim of gradual extinction of the subsidy serves to make the minimum-subsidy criterion of overriding importance in the determination of optimum output, but only that a suitable compromise should be struck between the policy of encouraging "overinvestment" in air transport and the gradual adjustment of this investment to a level justified by the commercial demand. Such a compromise could be effected by a progressive dimunition of the approved rate of subsidy used in the calculation of optimum output.

Moreover, the introduction of the extinction aim does not in itself require any modification of the conclusion arrived at regarding the validity of the minimum-subsidy criterion in the determination of the number of firms that should participate in the production of any given amount of service. Despite the fact that if this aim were attained every carrier existing at that time would be earning a "fair return" on the entire investment actually required for the performance of its services, this condition does not imply that any particular carrier would be entitled to profitable operation at any predetermined level of output, or that any adjustment in the output of the carrier in the attainment of this condition must be upward rather than downward.

Similar conclusions may be drawn with respect to the Board's typical line of decision involving the certification of new firms only where diversion from existing services is not sufficient to reduce the revenues of the carriers furnishing them below a fair return at the existing level of investment. This principle, be it noted, is not the same as that necessarily involved in the use of minimum cost to the Government, calculated on the basis of an obligation to support all existing operations, as a criterion for decision on the addition of new firms, since additional "need" on the part of the old firm might in some instances be more than offset by operating economies resulting from the certification of a new firm. The strict limitation on diversion imposes a condition on the distribution of output among firms that is similar in direction but more restrictive in effect than the calculation of governmental cost on the basis of a fixed commitment to the existing firm.

Although the above discussion has dealt with the determination of output and numbers of firms in a single homogeneous market, the principles developed may also be applied to situations involving nonhomogeneous competitive services. In such cases, possible combinations of cost, revenue, and number of firms cannot be organized two-dimensionally by a single demand schedule and various supply schedules as described above, since there is no homogeneous product with reference to which the curves may be drawn. The "determination of output as a whole" in such a market ceases to have any precise meaning; instead, the combination of various outputs that will most nearly conform to the optimum must be determined.

It is therefore evident that this optimum can no longer be defined *for the market as a whole* as the maximum "output" that can be supported at the approved subsidy rate; this definition could apply only in the case of a (homogeneous) service considered in isolation. Furthermore, although the problem under consideration here may be regarded as a special case of the more general problem of the distribution of output among various internally homogeneous markets, it is impossible to determine optimum output for each of the competitively related services in isolation, since the demand for each service is in part dependent upon the supply and the price of each other service. Thus the distribution of output among such related markets must be determined on the basis of a simultaneous consideration of all possible combinations of output of the various services; for each combination, unit revenues and unit costs under various assumptions as to the number of firms in operation will be determinate for each service. The assumptions underlying the various cost estimates should of course include the possibility that more than one type of service could be rendered by the same firm.

In the selection of the optimum combination of outputs from among all the possibilities, it is evident that the principles developed above with regard to cost to the Government are also applicable: (1) the optimum combination of outputs cannot be defined as that which would occasion the least cost, either per unit or total, to the Government; (2) for any given output combination, the minimum-subsidy criterion will give satisfactory results only if the Government's obligation to each carrier (and, of course, to each homogeneous service as a whole) is measured by the difference between its actual cost of operation at the output indicated by the optimum distribution and the commercial revenues received at this output level. Similarly, the choice of output combination and number of firms on the basis of a fixed limitation of diversion will not conform to the optimum result.

A determinate solution regarding the optimum output combination cannot be arrived at by the application of the requirement that in *each* of the component markets output be at the maximum consistent with the approved subsidy rate; if the maximization of output in each market is considered as an absolute end in itself, the solutions arrived at with respect to the various markets separately considered will be inconsistent with each other. This is true because of the substitutability that exists among the related services — the fact that the demand for each service is in part determined by the price and output of the others. If, for example, the problem is approached with the sole aim of providing the maximum output of service A that can be supported at the approved subsidy rate, it may well be that the accomplishment of this aim would require that none of service B be available at any price; and conversely, the same aim applied to service B considered separately might lead to elimination of service A, or at least to an output of A smaller than that indicated by the maximization of A as an end in itself.

Thus it is clear that in determining whether or not to authorize a new service heterogeneously competitive with an existing one, it cannot be assumed that the amount demanded of the existing service at the existing price either will be or should be maintained at its previous level after the new service has become available. A determinate demand curve for the service B may be drawn up on the basis of the availability of the existing output of service A at the existing price, and used to estimate the maximum output of B that can be supported at a price equal to unit cost plus subsidy; nevertheless, the availability of this amount of B will inevitably react on the demand for A, so that both the amount demanded at the existing price and the output that would fulfill the optimum requirement for the individual market will be different from their previous levels. (It has been assumed that the price and output of *A* have been determined in the first place with reference to a demand curve drawn up on the assumption that no *B* is being produced.)

The maintenance of the demand for service *A* could be assured by determining the price and output of *B* with respect to a demand curve drawn on the assumption that no "diversion" of traffic from *A* should be permitted; such a demand curve would take into account only the part of *B*'s potential market made up of buyers for whom *A* did not constitute an acceptable substitute at each relevant price ratio. For each price for *B*, the amount demanded would be set at the amount that would be taken by buyers for whom *A* did not constitute an acceptable substitute under the condition that it (*A*) was offered at the given existing price. However, it is clear that the output of *B* so determined would not be a defensible "optimum," since it would involve an arbitrary restriction (1) on the freedom of consumers to choose between the alternative services, through the limitation of the available amount of *B* to the quantity required to accommodate only part of its potential market, and (2) on the freedom of factor owners to direct their resources into the most profitable employments, through the arbitrary limitation of investment to the quantity that could earn returns equal to the average transfer cost of the indicated output within an artificially restricted market for the factors.

Such a procedure, although it would produce results nominally consistent with the achievement of optimum investment within the framework of a general subsidization policy, would in fact interfere with this result. The mere requirement that in each of the competitive markets the returns to factors be equal to average transfer cost does not in itself provide a satisfactory criterion for the optimum output combination; for if the price and output of service *B* are determined with reference to a demand curve drawn up under an artificially restrictive condition, e.g., that there be no "diversion" from *A* or that it be limited to a predetermined portion of the traffic or revenues of *A*, then there will be no "excess return" to factors employed in the production of *B* even though "excess demand" exists at the price-output level determined by this method.

In addition, it will be recalled that the supply schedules used in the determination of optimum output in each market have been drawn on the assumption that the distribution of output among firms is the most efficient possible. This assumption involves the condition that the expansion of production in any given firm is not restricted by the adoption of an oligopolistic or "nonaggressive" price-output policy on the part of the individual maximizing unit. In the absence of this condition, it would be possible to adjust output in any market to the point at which returns to factors were just equal to average transfer cost, and still not attain optimum investment, since the allocation of consumer expenditures as well as of productive factors to the oligopolistic firm would be limited to a lower level than would be possible on the basis of an "aggressive" price-output policy. Additions to investment that could most efficiently be made by the expansion of such a firm would be either precluded entirely or forced into a less efficient channel, namely, the addition of another firm. In the latter case, the number of firms would be larger than that required by the economic optimum.

An analogy may be drawn between this situation and that described above where the operative demand curve for any product is subjected to an artificial restriction; in this case, the operative *firm* demand curve is similarly restricted. Only if both types of artificial restriction are absent can the optimum condition be adequately defined as the level or combination of output at which the return to the factors is just equal to average transfer cost.

In practice, the application of this criterion to the authorization of competitive services is admittedly difficult, since the ordinary uncertainties involved in the *ex ante* estimation of demand are multiplied by the complications introduced by the interdependence of the markets for these services. As has been indicated, the demand for service *B* cannot be estimated without assuming the availability of a definite amount of service *A* at a given price; yet unless the assumption as to *A* has been fortuitously based on an assumed demand for *A* consistent with the price and output of *B* determined by reference to the demand curve based on the availability of this quantity of *A* at this price, the appearance of the indicated amount of B on the market will in turn alter (1) the demand for A and (2) the amount of A that can be supported at the approved subsidy rate — and hence (3) the demand for B. With perfect knowledge on the part of the regulatory authority, it would of course be possible to consider in turn all possible price-output decisions as to A — price in each case being fixed at unit cost minus subsidy; to determine for each of these possibilities the demand for B and, with reference to this demand, the price and output of B consistent with the requirement that the marginal factors earn no more than their transfer costs; and to determine on the basis of this price-output decision as to B the optimum output and price of A; when this final decision as to A coincided with the initial assumption, then the optimum output combination would have been discovered.

It is obvious, however, that there is no practicable means whereby the necessary demand schedules based on the various assumptions as to the output of competitive goods can be accurately determined. Furthermore, these estimates, as well as the cost schedules, which are also basic to the analysis, must be subject to constant revision; it is especially true in the air-transport field that both demand and cost conditions may be expected to change in significant degree over relatively short periods of time.

These difficulties, formidable enough in themselves, would arise even though the regulatory authority possessed full power to determine the direction and volume of the flow of investment in the regulated field. The limitations on the power of actual regulatory agencies constitute additional practical obstacles which will be more fully discussed at a later stage. However, it may here be noted that the Civil Aeronautics Board's powers in connection with the initiation of services over new routes or by new firms are only permissive; that is, the Board can in no case order the performance of any such new service, but can only approve or disapprove proposals made by the carriers. Moreover, once a carrier is authorized to operate over a particular route, it has a very considerable degree of freedom in determining what amount of service shall be supplied. Although the

Board's power to fix mail rates gives it some control over the services offered by "non-self-sufficient" carriers, and although the Postmaster General is empowered to order the establishment of additional flight schedules where these are required for the transportation of air mail, the determination of schedules and of the type and size of equipment used is largely in the hands of the carriers.[74]

Nevertheless, the general approach to the problem indicated by this discussion — that is, the consideration and comparison of all possible output combinations on the basis of their relative contribution to the most efficient utilization of productive resources and the maximization of satisfactions received by consumers per dollar spent — would seem to be an acceptable pattern for the guidance of any regulatory authority in its decisions on competitive nonhomogeneous services, and a model by which the actual performance of such an authority may fairly be judged.

It might be objected that the subsidization policy itself involves a deliberate departure from the distribution of output that would be required for the realization of the unconditional optimum, since in a subsidized field production is carried to a point beyond that at which price would be equal to average transfer cost, so that both consumer expenditures and productive factors are directed into such a field in larger amounts than would be indicated by the unconditional optimum in a free market. This is certainly true; nevertheless, it may still be said that optimum distribution of output from the point of view of the carrying out of the intended policy is indicated by the realization of the unconditional optimum within the conditions determined by the approved rate of subsidy. For the fulfillment of this condition means that investment in each of the component markets of the subsidized field is at the maximum consistent with the approved subsidy rate *and with the preservation of freedom of choice on the part of consumers and factor owners.*

[74] Section 401(*f*) of the Civil Aeronautics Act provides that "No term, condition, or limitation of a certificate shall restrict the right of an air carrier to add to or change schedules, equipment, accommodations, and facilities for performing the authorized transportation and service as the development of the business and the demands of the public shall require."

Under these conditions, neither consumers nor producers as such are called upon to bear the cost of the departure from the free-market optimum that results from the carrying out of public policy; this cost is borne in full by the Government.

The definition of the optimum that has been used in connection with the isolated homogeneous market (i.e., maximum output consistent with the approved subsidy rate) is itself a particular version of the more general criterion, a version that could be used in that context because of certain simplifying assumptions. These assumptions served to provide a unique demand curve which could be regarded as stable irrespective of variations in output and number of firms in the particular market for which the optimum was calculated. The assumption of homogeneity of product sufficed to rule out any variation in the demand in connection with the distribution of output among various numbers of firms; that is, it was assumed that no inherent preference existed on the part of consumers for a service rendered by x firms over one rendered by $x + y$ firms, or for a service rendered by firm A over one rendered by firm B. A second assumption served to eliminate any variations in the demand curve as a result of changes in the output of this particular service through repercussions induced by the effect of such changes on the demands for related products; it was assumed that the product in question was sufficiently "isolated" from substitutes to make it feasible to ignore such repercussions.

Under these assumptions, the condition that output in this particular market be at the maximum consistent with the approved subsidy rate provides a unique solution which also implies the realization of the unconditional optimum within the conditions determined by the policy of subsidization. For at this output, defined with reference to stable demand and supply curves, consumers are provided with the maximum of this service for which they are willing to pay the necessary price (which price is equal to average transfer cost minus the approved rate of subsidy), and investment in the field is carried to the point where no more factor units could earn as much here as they would in the next best alternative use.

In the discussion of markets for heterogeneously competitive air-transport services, it was recognized that no such unique and stable demand curve was available either for the services considered as a group or for any of them separately. However, the analysis was still limited to the demand and supply schedules of the particular services for which output was to be determined. This limitation can be justified only by an assumption that these services as a group can be meaningfully analyzed in isolation — that is, that the recognition of the interdependence among them is sufficient to take care of all the significant competitive relations of each of the services concerned. In fact, any or all of these services might be in close competition with other types of transport agency, so that changes in their output would induce repercussions in their markets from outside the group, which would significantly alter the relevant demand schedules and hence the indicated optimum outputs. A completely valid determination of these optima would have to be based on simultaneous consideration of all possible combinations of output in all the markets that are significantly related — not only those of the air-transport services directly concerned, but also those of the competitive surface-transport operations.

Finally, it should be noted that the validity of any result based on a consideration of various demand and cost schedules, as well as that of any conclusion based on a single pair of curves, must of course depend on the extent to which these schedules could be taken to indicate respectively "rational" preferences and actual transfer costs. The degree of "rationality" of the preferences reflected in the demand schedules determines the extent to which the amounts that would be spent by consumers for various quantities of the service in question are based on genuine valuations of this particular service in terms of other available channels of expenditure. There seems to be no reason to suppose that in general "irrationality" of consumer preference would cause the result to differ to any great extent from the actual optimum in the case of air-transport services. With regard to the cost schedules, the ever-present possibility of imperfections in the factor market justifies greater doubt as to the validity of decisions made on the basis of those schedules taken at their face value. In most cases it will be impossible for a regulatory authority of the usual type by its own action alone to correct the departure from the optimum occasioned by discrepancies between factor prices and transfer costs, since it does not have full power to deal with their root causes.

Summary and Conclusions

The major principles developed by the Board in its interpretation of public convenience and necessity in connection with the authorization of competitive services may now be brought together with a view to determining the conception of optimum competitive relations that they embody. As has been noted, the Board's position with regard to the "adequacy" or "inadequacy" of existing services or carriers, as well as its doctrine of "presumption" in favor of parallel services by different carriers, clearly demonstrates that it does not regard universal isolated selling as the optimum competitive pattern in the air-transport industry, and that it attaches a positive value to the availability of genuinely substitutable services to the public. The Board's refusal to recognize any right on the part of a carrier already in the field to any additional traffic therein which it is capable of serving has not, however, been based on any explicit contention that recognition of such a right might interfere with the attainment of the most efficient possible service from the point of view of given techniques of service and operation; nor has the Board required that the authorization of competitive service by new firms be contingent upon a showing that prospective costs of operation will be lower than if the proposed service were performed by carriers already in the field. On the contrary, the Board has justified its stand primarily because of various benefits which it expects will be obtained from the availability of substitutable services through their alleged stimulus to progress in the techniques of operation and service, these benefits being deemed significant enough to offset a not "unreasonable" increase in the total cost of service. Since it is almost always impossible to determine the probable level of the Board's estimate of operating costs with and without the authorization of the competitive service, there is little evidence to show exactly what increase in cost would be just "unreasonable" enough to preclude the authorization.

This lack of information on anticipated comparative costs also precludes any quantitative evaluation of the departure of the decisions reached by the Board from those which would have resulted from the application of a strict minimum-cost criterion in the choice of the number of firms that should participate in the production of any given homogeneous output; together with the similar lack of data on estimated demands, it precludes an evaluation of the Board's decisions on the amounts supplied and numbers of firms participating in the production of nonhomogeneous competitive services in terms of the "economic optimum." Nevertheless, the mere fact that such estimates are nowhere to be found in the Board's reports serves to indicate the divergence of the line of reasoning followed from that which would have been required to arrive at the "economic optimum." Except in a few isolated cases, what is actually considered by the Board appears to be the additional cost involved in the operation of the parallel service on the assumption that carriers already in the field continue to provide service at substantially the same capacity, and more especially the additional cost to the Government under this assumption.

It is in its treatment of the specific question of diversion of traffic from existing firms that the Board's conception of the optimum distribution of output among competitive services is most clearly revealed, since the point directly at issue is the permissible impact of new services on the output of the carriers already in the field. On this point, the Board has consistently refused to hold that these carriers are entitled to absolute protection from competitive inroads, i.e., to the maintenance of their traffic and revenues at the existing level. Nevertheless, it has apparently based its decisions on the view that competitive inroads should be limited to an extent consistent with the profitable maintenance of operations by existing carriers at substantially the existing level of investment, without the necessity of additional support in the form of Government subsidization.[75] The effect of this principle is similar to, but not identical with, that of the use of additional cost to the Government as a criterion by which to judge the proposed inauguration of parallel services, the additional cost being calculated on the basis of a commitment to support existing services so that a fair rate of return continues to be earned by them. Even with such a commitment, it might in some instances be less costly to the Government to certificate a new firm for the provision of additional services if an additional mail payment required by the existing firm were more than offset by operating economies brought about by the certification of the new carrier. The limit on diversion imposed in the Board's general line of decision implies a more rigid inflexibility of the distribution of output among firms than is involved in the governmental-cost criterion as defined above, and a consequent wider departure from optimum investment and number of firms in the subsidized market.

It should be noted that this concept, although sufficient in any given instance to provide a principle by which the proposed competitive relations (i.e., the proposed value of the first Triffinian coefficient) may be judged, does not prescribe any particular value of the coefficient as an a priori generally applicable optimum.[76]

Because the concept embodies a predilection in favor of the availability of genuinely substitutable services provided by different firms, or, in other words, a value of the first Triffinian coefficient that differs significantly from zero, it might be thought that the value of this coefficient in itself is relied upon as at least a partial guide to the Board's action. However, it

[75] It is in this sense that the Board's broad statement as to the statutory policy with regard to competition in air transport must be interpreted; that is, the Board apparently regards the above course of action as equivalent to safeguarding the air-transport industry "against the evils of unrestrained competition on the one hand, and the consequences of monopolistic control on the other."

[76] The concept is sufficient to provide such a principle, since its application will determine which relations between the outputs (and prices) of the competitive services will be approved. Given the "demand" characteristics of these services, these price-output relations fix the value of the first Triffinian coefficient.

would appear that this predilection is not of coördinate importance with the general principle that competition should be limited to the degree that is consistent with the maintenance of the
operations of carriers rendering existing services at substantially the same level. This is true because in practice the predilection is never allowed to overrule the general principle, but
is applied only within the limits set by it. Instead of qualifying
the accepted principle of competitive limitation, then, the predilection serves only to rule out any other more restrictive
principle that might conflict with it (such as the limitation of
competitive services to the traffic that could not be accommodated by the expansion of existing operations).

The accepted principle itself does not involve any generally
applicable optimum value for the first Triffinian coefficient,
because it is based on a consideration of a total rather than a
marginal effect; it has reference to an absolute rather than a
proportional change in revenues; and it is concerned with the
total revenues of the participant carriers rather than with the
revenues received from the competitive services alone.

In this *general* characteristic (i.e., in not prescribing any
particular value of the first Triffinian coefficient as a generally
applicable optimum), the general principle employed by the
Board is similar to that implied by the definition of the "economic optimum" which has been suggested earlier in the discussion. For it is clear that the distribution of output among
various markets and firms in accordance with the unconditional
optimum may result in various degrees of competitiveness
among the firms in question.

It is important to distinguish the concept accepted by the
Board from another that would be quite different in its practical implications, namely, that genuinely substitutable services
should be available in all markets to the extent that this is consistent with the over-all profitability of operations (in a subsidized industry, within the framework of the approved rate of
subsidy) by all carriers in the field at the level of investment
indicated by the distribution of output in accordance with the
economic optimum. Whereas the latter concept is based on a
completely flexible distribution of output among firms and mar-

kets, the former is at any given time rigidly conditioned by the distribution that has developed as a result of past circumstances.

It would seem that any apparent predilection of the Board in favor of "indirectly" as opposed to "directly" parallel new services could be adequately explained in terms of the above ideal. Although certain statements of the Board, especially in the early years of its existence, might be interpreted as indicating such a predilection,[77] the Board has refused to approve a contention that direct duplication is generally inconsistent with the Act itself or with "the pattern for air transportation . . . laid down by the Board," [78] and in at least one case where an indirect parallel service has been authorized in preference to a direct parallel, it is quite evident that this was done in accordance with the optimum concept developed above.[79] Similarly, in determining the route patterns for various foreign areas, the Board has been guided by considerations of anticipated degree of self-sufficiency rather than by any autonomous presumption in favor of indirect parallels.[80]

The major principle governing the Board's regulation of competitive relations between firms in the air-transport industry would appear to arise directly from its interpretation of its duty under the Act — to promote sound economic conditions in the industry — to mean the promotion of the financial welfare of existing air-transport companies. It has been seen that the adjustment of the distribution of output to the economic optimum might well require a large curtailment of output of a carrier already in the field, with an accompanying reduction in justifiable investment which would involve a decrease in the return on the existing investment. It is equally evident that this adjust-

[77] See, for example, Mid-Continent Airlines, Inc., *et al.*, Twin Cities–Des Moines–Kansas City–St. Louis Operation, 2 C.A.B. 63, 93 (1940), and Pennsylvania-Central Airlines Corporation, Pittsburgh-Youngstown-Erie-Buffalo Operations, 1 C.A.A. 811, 815 (1940).

[78] Transcontinental and Western Air, Inc., *et al.*, Additional North-South Services, p. 264.

[79] Eastern Air Lines, Inc., *et al.*, Great Lakes to Florida Service, 6 C.A.B. 429, 444–449 (1945).

[80] See, for example, Northeast Airlines, Inc., *et al.*, North Atlantic Route Case, p. 337.

ment might in some cases require the retirement of an existing carrier from a particular field: for example, where a new applicant could render the same service more efficiently, or where the existing number of firms in the field was too large for maximum efficiency, or where the provision of a new service heterogeneously competitive with the existing one would reduce the demand for the latter to a point where no amount of it could be supported at the approved subsidy rate. If the abandoned field made up the whole or perhaps a large part of the business of the company operating the existing service, this curtailment of its operations might mean its total extinction. The Board's conception of its statutory duty would seem to rule out not only those adjustments which would eliminate an existing carrier from the air-transport business or from any particular market, but all those which would require an increase in the mail payment required to support such a company at its existing level of investment.

As has been illustrated, there is no incompatibility between a general policy of subsidization — even when carried out by means of direct payments to particular firms — and an administration of economic controls so as to attain the best possible economic performance at any given level of support; and this is true even though a progressive decrease in the general level of support is regarded as one of the major aims of the program.

Under the particular subsidization policy embodied in the Civil Aeronautics Act, however, no standard was provided for the determination of direct payments to mail carriers apart from the financial needs of the benefited firms. Thus, although the Board has never recognized any binding legal obligation to provide a fair return on the entire investment of any firm,[81] and has insisted that the Act gives it broad discretion with respect to

---

[81] The Board has held that any mail rate which covers the cost of carrying the mails, including a reasonable return *on the investment allocable to the mail service,* would fulfill its obligation to any carrier under the Fifth Amendment. See, for example, Pan American Airways Company (of Delaware), Mail Rates, 1 C.A.A. 220, 252 (1939). Furthermore, it has maintained that the provisions of the Civil Aeronautics Act governing mail-rate determination do not require that such rates shall be fixed so as to include a return on the total investment of the carrier concerned (*ibid.*).

the payments made to any "non-self-sufficient" carrier,[82] mail rates have actually been fixed so as to avoid bankruptcy on the part of any mail carrier. Under this policy, the actual obligation of the Government may be in fact measured by the amount required to keep the carriers going at substantially their existing level of operations. As has been shown, the cost calculations made in some instances by the Board have employed this measure of governmental cost in connection with existing firms, and thus have not led to economic decisions that make for the best possible economic performance at any given level of support. It has also been noted that the more typical procedure followed by the Board in deciding new-route cases does not involve a mere comparison of costs to the Government, but is rather based on a decision as to the effect of the new-route authorization on the revenues of competitive carriers. Thus the minimum-cost criterion might favor the authorization of a new service even though the Government's liability to the prior occupant of the field, measured by the amount needed to keep it out of bankruptcy, should thereby be increased; the major principle espoused by the Board would not permit such an authorization. The effect of this doctrine is evidently to impede the achievement of optimum results to an even greater degree than the above measurement of governmental costs, since it imposes an even greater inflexibility on the distribution of output among firms.

The question then arises whether the particular subsidization policy embodied in the Act required that the Board follow the economic policy described above. In so far as this policy merely reflects the calculation of governmental costs on the basis of "need-rate" liability to existing firms, the answer is, of course, yes. Thus the "need-rate" subsidy program would have represented an obstacle to the achievement of the best economic results at the approved rate of subsidy even if the Board had authorized new competition whenever required to bring about maximum output at an average subsidy equal to the accepted

---

[82] See, for example, Pan American-Grace Airways, Inc., Mail Rates, 3 C.A.B. 550, 568–569 (1942); American Airlines, Inc., Mail Rate Proceeding, 3 C.A.B. 323, 334 (1942).

rate. But the more typical ruling principle of absolute protection of the solvency of the existing firm at the existing mail rate does not necessarily follow from the "need-rate" program, but rather from the Board's construction of the promotional policy of the Act as involving a continuous progress toward self-sufficiency on the part of each mail carrier. As has been noted, this construction is not required by the subsidization program itself, and does not follow from the subsidy standard *in effect* adopted by Congress in the same sense as does the Board's use of the going mail rate as a measure of the maximum estimated payment to be authorized for new routes. It is rather based on a not unreasonable interpretation of the Act's mandate that "sound economic conditions" be promoted in air transport as demanding the progressive achievement and maintenance of profitable operations on the part of each carrier subject to the Act. Thus it is this latter principle, rather than the Act's "need-rate" subsidization policy itself, that has formed the broad basis of the regulation of competition under the Act. To permit new competition that would put an end to the commercial profitability of any carrier at the existing mail rate would be obviously contrary to this principle. It is of course true that, given the "need-rate" subsidization program, the protective policy of the Board *with respect to mail carriers* might be explained in terms of a long-run program of *eliminating the Government's liability to these carriers,* on grounds of governmental economy. However, the view that governmental economy is not the *ultimate* explanatory principle behind the Board's regulatory policy is supported by the following considerations: (1) this policy may be fully explained, as it is in fact usually explained by the Board itself, by the Board's interpretation of the "sound-economic-conditions" mandate,without any intermediate appeal to the consideration of governmental economy in any sense; and (2) considerations of governmental economy would not in any way explain the application of protective regulation to nonsubsidized carriers.

Hence, the Board's action placing a floor under air-cargo rates may be cited to show that its general policy of protection of carrier revenues is based ultimately not on the "need-rate" subsidy program, but on its obligation to maintain "sound economic conditions" in air transport. This action was taken as a result of protests by the noncertificated (non-mail-carrying) cargo carriers against rates instituted by certificated (mail-carrying) carriers; the protection of the former from possible bankruptcy was cited by the Board as an important reason for its action.[83] Thus it may be predicted with some confidence that the same broad regulatory criteria would continue to be employed by the Board if and when all carriers subject to its jurisdiction attain unquestionable commercial self-sufficiency, and even though the "need-rate" subsidization program should be stricken from the Act.

That the Board's policy of limiting new competition in air transport with reference to its effect on the profitability of carriers rendering existing services has arisen primarily from a conception of a special obligation to promote the financial welfare of air-transport companies, rather than from a general theory of the nature of "workable" or desirable competition, is demonstrated by the usual treatment accorded to competitive surface-transportation facilities in new route cases. As a rule, the Board has considered such facilities only in connection with calculating the traffic potential of proposed air services; surface traffic is considered as one index of the "community of interest" between localities, and the speed and frequency of existing surface facilities are compared with those of the proposed air operation to discover whether the advantages of the latter are sufficient to justify an expectation that it could compete successfully with the former. The anticipated diversion of traffic from surface carriers is very seldom considered from the point of view of its effect on the profitability of these companies, and has never occasioned the denial of authorization of any new air service.[84]

The policy outlined above has been followed with a remarkable degree of consistency throughout the period of regulation by the Board. There is, however, some evidence that in the very

[83] Air Freight Rate Investigation, Orders Serial No. E–1415, April 21, 1948, p. 5.

[84] See Northeast Airlines, Inc., Consolidation of Routes Nos. 27, 65 and 70, 6 C.A.B. 541, 545–546 (1945), and Northeast Airlines, Inc., *et al.*, North Atlantic Route Case, p. 341.

recent past consistency has been sacrificed to a notable extent to the pressures of the moment. For example, in the Additional Service to Puerto Rico Case,[85] a new competitive service was authorized without the usual careful consideration of the diversion issue; in the Southern Service to the West Case,[86] on the other hand, it appears that possibilities for a new competitive service were given inadequate consideration.

Of greater potential importance than these apparent aberrations, however, is a possible new approach to the question of competitive service that is indicated by way of dictum in the latter decision. After pointing out that the absence of competition on any route does not mean that it is necessarily "isolated against the competitive incentive and its benefits," the Board said:

Undoubtedly, where it appears on the record of a particular case that an air carrier is failing to attain the high standards of public service contemplated by the Civil Aeronautics Act and where only provision for an economic competitive service would contribute effectively to the assurance of such standards, a case is made for competition. . . .[87]

And again:

It behooves us, in considering the structure of a sound airline industry, to remember that a relatively good earning position at a given time may suggest the need for giving serious consideration to the possibilities of reducing transportation rates and fares rather than the need for expanding competitive services . . . Our aim and that of the carriers must always be to provide the public with the benefits of safe and modern air transportation at the lowest rates and fares that can be economically provided. The most effective means of achieving this objective is the development of an air route pattern which will enable the individual carriers to enjoy the highest load factors. The creation of uneconomic, duplicating services will not encourage the development of such load factors.[88]

[85] Orders Serial No. E–5075, January 23, 1951.
[86] Orders Serial No. E–5090, January 30, 1951.
[87] *Ibid.*, p. 23.
[88] *Ibid.*, p. 24.

If these dicta mean that henceforth new competition will be authorized only where it can be shown to result in specific service improvements not obtainable by any other means, and that excess returns on any route will be eliminated by rate reductions, a radical change in policy has obviously taken place. That such a change has in fact occurred, at least for a temporary period, is indicated by the following statement by Board Chairman Delos W. Rentzel to a Senate Committee in March, 1951:

The basic objective of the Board, in addition to reaching a current level in its workload, is to achieve a stabilization of the air transportation system through the finalization of mail rates and lowering of subsidy requirements through mergers, elimination of uneconomic services and refusal, in general, until such time as the system is stabilized, to award additional routes except where the existing services cannot meet the public need. This does not mean that the Board is committed to any system of monopoly. It does mean that the Board does not believe that any substantial additional competitive routes are required during this period of mobilization.[89]

The economic effect of such a new policy would differ greatly from that of the old. This point is further discussed in Chapter VII.

TREATMENT OF "NEWCOMERS"

There will now be considered an aspect of the "entry" problem which is perhaps of greater significance in showing the general implications of economic regulation for the competitive process than in throwing light on the Board's conception of optimum competitive relations, namely, the treatment of "newcomers" to the air-transport field. Since its inception, the Board has authorized no "long-haul" or "trunk-line" scheduled domestic passenger service by any new air-transport company (i.e., any company that did not originally qualify for certification under the grandfather clause), though certificates have

---

[89] Statement of Delos W. Rentzel, Chairman, Civil Aeronautics Board, Before the Interstate and Foreign Commerce Committee of the United States Senate, March 15, 1951, p. 5 of mimeographed copy.

been granted to new domestic carriers for the operation of feeder passenger services and for exclusive freight carriage.

In view of the comparatively small degree of substitutability between conventional air services and those of the feeder and all-freight variety, these facts might be interpreted as an additional manifestation of the protective orientation of the Board's general policy on competitive relations, and it seems very probable that this orientation has played some part in weighting the evidence in particular cases against the authorization of services by "newcomers." Such an interpretation might be strengthened by reference to the Atlantic Seaboard Case, in which a proposed unsubsidized operation by a "newcomer," involving the institution of a low-rate cargo service independent of the Railway Express Agency, was denied certification primarily on the ground that it would divert substantial traffic from and interfere with the financial strengthening of an existing carrier.[90] In support of the interpretation, one might also cite a statement made by the Board early in 1941 which might seem to indicate that the Board recognized a general presumption against the certification of operations by "newcomers":

In reaching this conclusion [that is, the choice of an established carrier rather than a "newcomer" for the operation of a particular route] we recognize the fact that the considerations which lead us to this determination would be equally applicable in any case in which an existing air carrier is competing with a company without operating experience for a new route or service. The number of air carriers now operating appears sufficient to insure against monopoly in respect to the average new route case, and we believe that the present domestic air-transportation system can by proper supervision be integrated and expanded in a manner that will in general afford the competition necessary for the development of that system in the manner contemplated by the Act. In the absence of particular circumstances presenting an affirmative reason for a new carrier there appears to be no inherent desirability of increasing the present number of carriers merely for the purpose of numerically enlarging the industry. In the instant case there is no indication that the operation of this route by

---

[90] Colonial Airlines, Inc., *et al.*, Atlantic Seaboard Operation, pp. 559–60.

Pennsylvania-Central constitutes a monopolistic condition contrary to the public interest, nor is there any evidence of record as to any unusual factors which make it appear desirable to add a new operator to those presently authorized to engage in air transportation.[91]

However, it is important to note that the Board in this particular case, as in almost all others in which it has dealt with the relative merits of authorizing service by a "newcomer" as compared with an established company, based its decision in favor of the latter on specific and positive advantages other than the protection of existing carriers to be derived from the choice of this carrier — in this case, the availability of convenient one-carrier service to points not on the particular route being awarded, and probable lower operating cost.[92] The superior ability of existing carriers to render through service was also apparently the main reason for the rejection of a "newcomer" in the Great Lakes to Florida case,[93] as well as being a major consideration in this connection in the Latin-American case and in Trans-Southern Airlines, Inc., *et al.*, Amarillo–Oklahoma City Operation.[94] In the last case, economies to be obtained from the integration of the new route into existing operations were also important in the rejection of Trans-Southern in favor of Braniff.

It is clear that both of these factors, i.e., the ability to provide maximum through service and to integrate the new route into existing operations, wherever they are at all relevant, must always favor existing companies as compared with "newcomers." An additional factor that has operated to the advantage of existing carriers, of particular importance in connection with foreign routes, is the fact that these carriers are in a position to demonstrate their capacity to operate successfully by reference to a past record; furthermore, the mere fact that these

[91] Delta Air Corporation, *et al.*, Additional Service to Atlanta and Birmingham, 2 C.A.B. 447, 480 (1941).

[92] *Ibid.*, p. 479.

[93] Eastern Air Lines, Inc., *et al.*, Great Lakes to Florida Service, p. 439.

[94] Additional Service to Latin America, 6 C.A.B. 857 (1946); Trans-Southern Airlines, Inc., *et al.*, Amarillo–Oklahoma City Operation, 2 C.A.B. 250, 271–72 (1940).

companies have had experience in the business counts as evidence of their probable ability to conduct new services efficiently and to develop a maximum of traffic on new routes.[95]

The "newcomer," on the other hand, must present detailed evidence as to plans for financing, organization, and operation, which must meet with the Board's approval before it is found to be "fit, willing and able." [96]

Thus, although it cannot positively be said that the Board has deliberately excluded new companies from the long-haul scheduled air-transport field as a matter of general policy, for the sake of protecting existing carriers or for any other reason, it would appear that the regulatory process by its very nature tends to make it extremely difficult for "newcomers" to compete successfully with existing companies for the right to conduct operations similar to services that are already being performed by the latter. The main reason for this seems to be that the regulatory body in determining what carrier to certify inevitably gives greater weight to such advantages of cost and service as can be clearly foreseen in advance of actual operation than to those which can only be proved by future experience; in connection with operations similar to those already being conducted by existing carriers, such advantages are usually almost wholly on the side of these companies.

Other considerations that have influenced the Board's decisions on choice of carrier are the opportunity to achieve economies through spread of overhead cost,[97] the diversion of a minimum amount of traffic from other existing services,[98] and the strengthening of a financially weak carrier.[99] The last two factors are of course not obviously related to superiority of

[95] See, for example, Northeast Airlines, Inc., *et al.*, North Atlantic Route Case, pp. 339, 341, 342, 326–327.

[96] See, for example, Delta Air Corporation, *et al.*, Additional Service to Atlanta and Birmingham, p. 488 and American Overseas Airlines, Inc., *et al.*, South Atlantic Routes, 7 C.A.B. 285, 306 (1946).

[97] See, for example, Continental Air Lines, Inc., *et al.*, Mandatory Route, 1 C.A.A. 88, 102 (1939).

[98] See, for example, Transcontinental and Western Air, Inc., *et al.*, Reading Operation, 2 C.A.B. 667, 673 (1941).

[99] See, for example, Colonial Airlines, Inc., *et al.*, Atlantic Seaboard Operation, pp. 559–60.

service or cost advantages; nevertheless, they represent typical elements considered by the Board that should tend to favor existing companies. The economical distribution of overhead might not generally be expected always to be a factor on the side of the existing carrier, since it might be anticipated that at some stage in the expansion of such a company there would be reached a point beyond which unit costs would rise. However, the Board's consideration of relative efficiency as among carriers is on a qualitative rather than a precise quantitative basis, and it has taken no cognizance of any possibility that general administrative expenses and the like per unit of service rendered may increase with the growth of operations by any one company. It may therefore be expected that "spread of overhead" as considered by the Board will generally weigh in favor of the existing carrier.[100]

With respect to types of operation that are not comparable to those already conducted by existing carriers, these companies do not enjoy a similar advantage. For example, in the provision of local and feeder services, the superior experience of the existing long-haul intercity carriers in the conventional type of air operation does not carry the same weight in connection with their probable ability successfully to conduct the newer kind of service.[101] Nor are possibilities for achieving economies through utilization of existing facilities and equipment of the same importance with regard to these services. Moreover, the factor of probable ability to develop traffic, which in the conventional type of case also favored the existing long-haul carriers, is here a major consideration on the side of the new company, since, as the Board has repeatedly recognized, it is clearly to be expected that a carrier whose major interest lies in the development of local traffic will exert the maximum effort along this line.[102]

Whether or not the Board's policy on the admission of "new-

---

[100] On the Board's position with respect to the behavior of cost with expansion of operations, see Continental Air Lines, Inc., *et al.,* Denver–Kansas City Service, 4 C.A.B. 1, 18 (1942).

[101] See, for example, Service in the Rocky Mountain States Area, p. 736.

[102] See, for example, Service in the Rocky Mountain States Area, pp. 736–737 and The Florida Case, 6 C.A.B. 765, 786 (1946).

comers" to the air-transport field can be interpreted as demonstrating further the policy of protection of existing carriers that was found to be a ruling consideration in its treatment of new competitive services, the fact that the standards used in the regulatory determination of the choice of a carrier for a proposed route tend to favor existing companies is probably in itself of some consequence for the determination of output distribution and competitive relations among firms in the regulated field. In the first place, the attainment of the theoretical optimum of output distribution would seem to be hindered by the inevitably greater weight given to cost and service considerations that can be clearly demonstrated in advance; in so far as this emphasis obscures the real nature of the possible cost and product combinations that are available in any given case, the decision of the Board will tend to diverge from the economic optimum. In the second place, the tendency to favor existing companies might reasonably be expected to strengthen any existing inclination toward "nonaggressive" price-output policies in the regulated field, in that such companies might well be more likely than "newcomers" to respect any tacit or institutionalized "live-and-let-live" arrangements that might have developed among competitive carriers. In this connection, the recent history of the "air-coach" experiment, which is discussed in the following chapter, is particularly illuminating.

CHAPTER V

GENERAL EXEMPTIONS UNDER THE CIVIL AERONAUTICS ACT

The Civil Aeronautics Board has granted general exemptions from certain of the economic regulatory provisions of Title IV of the Civil Aeronautics Act to four types of air carrier: (1) irregular air carriers, (2) certain air-cargo carriers, (3) air-freight forwarders, and (4) Alaskan air carriers. Three of these are dealt with in this chapter. Because of the special economic and administrative conditions that have governed the Board's policy with respect to Alaskan air carriage, this policy is a separate story and will not be treated here. The term "general exemption" designates those exemptions which apply or have applied to classes of air carriers rather than to individual carriers or operations. Although the latter type will not be exhaustively considered, some of these exemptions will be discussed in connection with the main problem at hand. The first three sections of this study present accounts of the history and purposes of the several exemptions. The last section contains an evaluation of the policy embodied in these exemptions in terms of the Board's statutory duty.

In considering the history and purposes of the three exemptions, it is important to bear in mind that the major regulatory provision to which they apply is the certification requirement.

Irregular Air Carriers

The Board's first general exemption regulation, which became effective shortly after the adoption of the Act, applied to all air carriers engaged solely in "nonscheduled" operations. This regulation contained the following definition of the type of operation in which the exempted carriers might engage:

Within the meaning of this regulation any operation shall be deemed to be non-scheduled if the air carrier does not hold out to the public by advertisement or otherwise that it will operate one or more airplanes between any designated points regularly or with a reasonable degree of regularity upon which airplane or airplanes it will accept for transportation, for compensation or hire, such members of the public as may apply therefor or such express or other property as the public may offer.[1]

The exemption granted by this regulation extended to all provisions of Title IV of the Act with the exception of Section 401 (*l*) (Compliance with Labor Legislation) and the reporting requirements of Section 407. In connection with the latter section, the regulation provided that specific reporting requirements should apply to the exempted carriers only if expressly made applicable to them. In fact, these carriers were not required to report any information to the Board until May 1946.

The description of exempted operations in the original regulation contains two key concepts which are not precisely defined: (1) the concept of "holding out" to the public, in connection with which the regulation does not specify whether such "holding out" must be by express communication with the public (as would be the case if the time pattern of services were described in an advertisement or published schedule) or could be accomplished merely by the actual operation of the services; and (2) the concept of "regularity" or "reasonable regularity," which in all subsequent versions of the regulation continued to be the designated boundary of the exemption. The first of these concepts was definitely clarified by the Board in May 1946; at this time also the Board made explicit the general criterion which it intended to be employed in determining the "regularity" of operations. As will be seen, the very nature of this general criterion was such as to make its application subject to legitimate differences of opinion in particular instances, and

---

[1] Section 292.1 of C.A.B. Economic Regulations, as amended December 7, 1938 (at that time designated Regulation 400–1). The Economic Regulations were recorded effective July 1, 1949. By this recodification, Section 292.1 became Part 291, Section 292.5 became Part 295, and Section 292.6 became Part 296. All references herein apply to the system of enumeration in effect before the recodification.

consequently to require a case-by-case process of clarification in order to give the "regularity" concept a precise and generally valid legal definition.

In its *First Annual Report,* the Board (then Authority) indicated that the original exemption order was a temporary measure intended to be effective "pending completion of studies with respect to this type of [i.e., nonscheduled] operation."[2] In an article published early in 1946, the then General Counsel of the Board asserted that the regulation was adopted "probably more as a means of postponing a problem which could not be handled due to the press of other activities required by the Act than as a reasoned economic policy."[3] Shortly after this, the Board referred to the "limited economic significance" of nonscheduled air transportation at the time the regulation was put into effect, and to the fact that most of the operators "were engaged in air transportation to only a limited degree, chiefly as a byproduct of other air services"; "under the circumstances," the Board explained, "it was incumbent upon the Board to devote all of its energies to the orderly development of the certificated air network within the United States and abroad."[4]

Whether administrative expedient or deliberate policy resulting from an appraisal of the "economic significance" of the affected operations, the original regulation continued in effect for more than seven years;[5] no systematic reëxamination of the regulation was undertaken until mid-1944; and the amended version adopted in May 1946 as an immediate result of this investigation made no substantial change in the regulation. Ac-

[2] *First Annual Report* of the Civil Aeronautics Authority, 1939, p. 26.

[3] G. C. Neal, "The Status of Non-Scheduled Operations under the Civil Aeronautics Act of 1938," reprinted by permission from *Law and Contemporary Problems* (published by the Duke University School of Law, Durham, North Carolina; copyright 1946 by Duke University) XI, No. 3 (Winter-Spring 1946), pp. 508–523; p. 514.

[4] Investigation of Nonscheduled Air Services, 6 C.A.B. 1049, 1051 (1946).

[5] The only change in the scope of the regulation during this period occurred in 1941, when the Board promulgated a special exemption regulation with respect to Alaskan air carriers and rendered the nonscheduled exemption inapplicable to these carriers and to operations within Alaska. Alaska Air Transportation Investigation, 2 C.A.B. 785 (1941).

cording to the Board, it was the anticipation that noncertificated air services would expand greatly in the postwar period which caused it, in July of 1944, to undertake reconsideration of its policy toward these operations.[6] In general, the investigation then instituted was to determine what type of economic regulatory policy toward "nonscheduled" air transportation was desirable; in particular, it was to discover what, if any, changes in the exemption order were necessary to clarify its meaning or to carry out the economic policy found to be desirable.

The data obtained in this investigation pertained for the most part to the "fixed-base" operators, i.e., persons engaged in nontransport phases of aviation who perform transportation services to or from their principal places of business as an incidental activity. The examiners found "no indication that such [transportation] services did not constitute an attractive and valuable service to the public that had occasion to utilize them."[7] Although not even the representatives of the certificated carriers contended that these operators presented any immediate competitive threat to the scheduled airlines, the examiners believed that the transport services of the "fixed-base" operators would probably expand in the future. Hence, they reasoned, the definition of exempted operations should be so written as to "minimize the possibility of competition with existing air services and . . . permit the free and unhampered growth of the transportation activities of the fixed-base operator."[8]

Thus the regulation proposed by the examiners was designed (1) to limit the exemption to typical "fixed-base" operations (trips other than to or from the principal place of business of any exempted carrier were to be made only on a "casual, occasional, or infrequent basis"); and (2) to protect certificated services by a requirement that no exempted carrier make trips "between points between which reasonably direct service is available" on certificated airlines except on a "casual, occa-

---

[6] Investigation of Nonscheduled Air Services, p. 1051.

[7] Investigation of Nonscheduled Air Services, Docket No. 1501, Report of the Examiners, August 22, 1945, p. 21.

[8] *Ibid.*, p. 22.

sional, or infrequent basis." The latter type of operation (i.e., trips competitive with "reasonably direct" certificated services) was further to be subject to a definite quantitative limitation of ten trips in any calendar month.[9]

The "nonscheduled" or "irregular" concept was, then, to be replaced by a "fixed-base" concept fortified by a direct restriction of activities competitive with the certificated carriers. The examiners found that the abandonment of the former concept was necessary to permit maximum development of "fixed-base" transportation, and was therefore desirable in view of the fact that protection of certificated airlines could be accomplished without restricting the frequency or time pattern of the typical noncompetitive services of the "fixed-base" operators.[10]

The examiners conceived the problem of recasting the exemption as one of adapting it more closely to the type of operation which the Board had had in mind when it adopted the original order, and which had in practice enjoyed the exemption privilege since that time. Accordingly, the scope of the economic regulation to which the exempted carriers were to be subject under the examiners' proposal was very limited: these carriers were to be exempted from all of Title IV with the exception of Sections 401 (*l*) (Compliance with Labor Legislation) and 412. The latter Section, which makes certain types of contracts and agreements subject to Board disapproval, was to be made applicable in order to prevent evasion of the operational limitations provided in the regulation by the pooling of frequencies by two or more "fixed-base" operators between the same two points.[11] To obtain information regarding these operators, each was to be required to file with the Board a statement containing such data as its name, address, principal place of business, and the type of air-carrier services to be offered, and also to file any periodic reports of operations that the Board should prescribe.

The Board, on the other hand, apparently saw the major problem as one of adapting the regulation to the relatively large-scale noncertificated air-transport enterprises which had

---

[9] *Ibid.,* Appendix III, p. 2.
[10] *Ibid.,* pp. 24–25.
[11] *Ibid.,* p. 24.

sprung up in the immediate postwar period and were conducting full-time transport services on an essentially different basis
from the incidental activities of the "fixed-base" operators.
This development had indeed for the most part occurred after
hearings had been held by the examiners, and thus, as has been
noted, figured hardly at all in the record developed by them.
Thus the Board rejected the examiners' proposed new definition of exempted operations, and reaffirmed the distinction
between "scheduled" and "nonscheduled" air carriers as "a
fundamental one," serving "as a basis of distinction between
two different types of service having different regulatory problems." [12] The Board also proposed at this time a much more
comprehensive regime of economic regulation adapted to the
large-scale services of the new operators: although the amended
version of the regulation adopted concurrently with the issuance of the opinion on the investigation provided for very limited economic controls, a draft proposal released at the same
time envisaged the subjection of nonscheduled carriers using
large aircraft to virtually all provisions of Title IV except the
certification requirement and some other sections and parts of
sections which obviously would not apply to them. The adopted
new version, Amendment No. 2 of Section 292.1 of the Economic Regulations, effective June 15, 1946, exempted all the
affected carriers from all of Title IV except Section 401 (l)
(Compliance with Labor Legislation), 407(a) (reporting requirements under this section were limited as before to those
expressly stated to be applicable to the exempted carriers),
and 411 (Methods of Competition). The draft proposal, proposed Amendment No. 3 of Section 292.1, circulated May 17,
1946, divided the nonscheduled carriers into two classes, according to the gross weight of all aircraft or of any individual
aircraft utilized in air transportation. Exemptions for carriers
falling within the smaller classification were to be the same as
those provided by Amendment No. 2. The larger class, however, was to be exempt only from Section 401 (Certificate of
Public Convenience and Necessity) except (l) (Compliance
with Labor Legislation), certain provisions of Section 404(a)

---

[12] Investigation of Nonscheduled Air Services, p. 1054.

(Carrier's Duty to Provide Service, Rates and Divisions); Section 405 (Transportation of Mail); Section 406 (Rates for Transportation of Mail); and Sections 408, 409, and the filing requirements of 412 with respect to mergers, interlocking relations, agreements and the like between nonscheduled air carriers.

Both this proposal and Amendment No. 2 contained definitions of exempted operations substantially similar to that in the original regulation. The only changes contained in the Amendment were (1) the substitution of the words "expressly or by a course of conduct" for the original "by advertisement or otherwise" — a revision that did away with one of the essential ambiguities of the original regulation; and (2) the addition of a paragraph expressly excluding indirect air carriers from the exemption — a revision that was also for purposes of clarification rather than alteration of intended meaning.

This definition was in substance incorporated in the proposed Amendment No. 3, with (1) an additional proviso (not finally adopted) setting forth a presumption against allegedly "nonscheduled" operations consisting of more than ten round trips per month in two consecutive months between the same two points, and (2) a definition of the term "point" designed to prevent evasion by slight variation in locations of take-offs and landings. In addition, the geographical scope of the exempted operations was to be restricted to trips within the United States and between the United States on the one hand and Alaska, Canada, or Mexico on the other.

In rejecting the examiners' proposal that a special restriction be placed on operations directly competitive with services of the certificated carriers, the Board by no means repudiated the general idea that these carriers should be protected from noncertificated competition. With respect to the examiners' proposal, the Board pointed out that "the pattern of local service" by certificated operators was then in process of determination in the so-called area cases; and that until these new local routes had been established and tested, "it would not be appropriate to permit the inauguration and operation of services without express authorization simply for the reason that no service is now available." [13]

The Board believed that a properly defined *general* restriction (that is, one not limited to particular routes already served by certificated carriers) by means of a definition of the type of operation to be offered by the noncertificated carriers would provide a legal framework within which they would develop operations serving essentially different markets from those of the certificated lines, and would therefore bring about the desired insulation of the revenues of the certificated carriers. This belief was clearly shown in the findings that accompanied the promulgation of the finally adopted third version of the Regulation, where the Board stated:

In addition to the public demand and need for air transportation services furnished by the certificated air carriers on regularly scheduled operations, there is public demand and need at the present time for air services on an irregular basis both to certificated and noncertificated points. Such irregular services vary greatly with respect to type of service, and fill a need which, because of fluctuations in the demand and the impossibility of determining where and when the demand will arise, by its very nature cannot be fulfilled economically by carriers operating on regular schedules and routes . . . Because of the fact that irregular services meet a different need and must be infrequent and irregular, such services, if properly regulated under provisions of the Act other than those relating to certificates of public convenience and necessity, will not under present conditions have adverse competitive effect upon the services performed by the certificated air carriers.[14]

It was here furthermore found that these services should be authorized by exemption rather than certification, because the latter procedure would either (*a*) "impose no substantial limitations upon operations" or (*b*) "substantially reduce the flexibility and usefulness of such carriers." In addition, the Board asserted, "Certification, in the case of many small scale operations, would be uneconomical and would tend to prevent or

[13] *Ibid.,* p. 1057.
[14] Regulations Serial No. 388, May 5, 1947, paragraph 2.

retard the development of new types of services designed to meet special conditions." The intent of the Board to authorize only services essentially noncompetitive with certificated airlines has subsequently been expressly reaffirmed, although the extremely limited character of the markets for the "tramp" type of operation envisaged in the regulation has been increasingly recognized.[15]

Accordingly, the Board undertook to provide such a general definition in its opinion on the investigation.

Here the Board made it quite clear that no "published timetable" or even "preconceived plan" for a "regular" operation was necessary to make a given service fall outside the exemption. "It is," said the Board, "the thread or semblance of consistency which identifies an operation as one conducted with a reasonable degree of regularity." Thus, "the test involves in large part the state of mind of both passenger and operator;" both actual operations and the program directly communicated to the public or planned in advance by the operator are relevant in determining whether or not a reasonably regular service is held out.

The Board stated its general position in the following passage:

The irregularity contemplated for exemption is that which neither directly nor indirectly leads the public to believe that between given points a reasonably certain number of flights per day or per week, or flights at approximately certain times or on certain days, may be anticipated with a reasonable degree of assurance. The irregularity exempted can be reflected only be rare and infrequent flights if between the same two points, and must be of such rarity and infrequency as would preclude any implication of a uniform pattern or normal consistency of operation.[16]

The Board recognized that the boundary between operations permitted and not permitted under the exemption was not sufficiently precise to make its application unquestionable in all

---

[15] On this point, see Orders Serial No. E–2085, October 13, 1948, pp. 6–7 and the *Annual Report* of the Civil Aeronautics Board, 1948, p. 5.

[16] Investigation of Nonscheduled Air Services, p. 1055.

instances, but indicated that its general pronouncements in the opinion, together with current and subsequent decisions in particular cases, would serve to define more clearly the scope of permissible operations.[17]

In summary, then, the Board's intent was to authorize, by the exemption, services essentially noncompetitive with those of the certificated airlines; the "irregular" flights of the exempted companies were expected to carry traffic not available to the services of the scheduled airlines; and it was further expected that the inherent indefiniteness of the regulation itself would not prevent the carrying out of the Board's intent. While recognizing that the regulation would give rise to "borderline" cases requiring specific regulatory action, the Board believed that this problem could be dealt with on a case-by-case basis in such a way that the purpose of the regulation would be effectively implemented. At the same time that the opinion was issued, the Board handed down decisions in two cases in which particular noncertificated carriers were found to be operating outside the scope of the exemption.[18]

In November 1946, the Board circulated to the public a revised form of the proposed new regulation.[19] A major innovation in this version was the introduction of two new proposed classes of exempted carriers: noncertificated air-cargo carriers and noncertificated indirect air-cargo carriers. This development will be dealt with in the two succeeding sections of this chapter. A second major innovation was the proposed requirement that all the exempted carriers obtain, as a condition to enjoying the exemption privilege, "Letters of Temporary Authority" from the Board, a device which would assure the receipt of certain information regarding the exempted carriers and aid in the enforcement of the content and intent of the regulation.

With regard to the irregular carriers, the term "nonscheduled" was dropped entirely from the proposed regulation, pre-

---

[17] *Ibid.*

[18] Page Airways, Inc., Investigation, 6 C.A.B. 1061 (1946) and Trans-Marine Airlines, Inc., Investigation of Activities, 6 C.A.B. 1071 (1946).

[19] Economic Regulations Draft Release No. 14, November 22, 1946.

sumably to avoid misunderstanding as to the legal status of published schedules in connection with these carriers (the proposed designation was "Non-Certificated Irregular Air Carriers"), but the type of operation to be exempted as "irregular" was to be essentially the same as before. The proviso, included in the May draft proposal, creating a presumption against more than ten trips per month between the same two points in two consecutive months was omitted: many protests had been directed against this provision, and some public misunderstanding was evident with regard to it.[20] The definition of a "point" was broadened to include the area within a 25-mile (as compared with the May draft's 15-mile) radius of a landing place, for more effective prevention of evasion. The proposed geographical scope was changed (as compared with the May proposal) to exclude all foreign and to include all overseas air transportation; that is, exempted irregular carriers were to be allowed to engage in interstate and overseas transportation without geographical restriction (except, of course, with regard to operations within Alaska) but not in any foreign air transportation. Like the May proposal, the November draft provided for extensive economic regulation of irregular carriers utilizing large aircraft, the scope of regulation provided for each of the two classes of irregular carrier being substantially the same as that in the earlier proposed version, with the one major exception that the larger class was to be totally exempt from Section 404(a). In addition, this class of carrier would have been required to file with the Board (under Section 412) contracts and agreements for pooling or apportioning earnings, losses, traffic service, or equipment.

In the oral argument on the proposed regulation, considerable attention was devoted to the question of noncertificated operations in foreign air transportation. Although most of the discussion was directed specifically to the Board's proposal that the new class of noncertificated air-cargo carriers be permitted to engage in such transportation, statements made by Board members in this connection suggest the possible rationale of the

[20] See, for example, *Aviation News*, July 1, 1946, p. 27, and September 23, 1946, p. 28.

proposed geographical limitation on the irregular carriers, and throw some light on why this limitation was, in the adopted version of the regulation, made applicable only to transportation of persons. The major concern of the Board was apparently to avoid diversion of traffic which might otherwise be available to the scheduled carriers on recently certificated international routes.[21] It was noted, however, that the certificated routes had been laid out with primary if not sole reference to potential traffic in passengers and mail rather than property,[22] and suggested that the Board should not interfere in the development of new air-cargo routes in international trade.[23] There was also some feeling that the cargo-only exemption would be easier to "police" than the distinction between regular and irregular in the foreign field.[24] It may be conjectured that the original plan to permit the exclusive cargo carriers to engage in foreign operations was conceived as a method of permitting the experimental development of the new field of foreign cargo operations while definitely excluding new competition from the major market (passengers) of the certificated airlines; and that the ultimate decision to permit foreign property transportation by the irregular carriers only was made in the belief that the above objectives could be better accomplished by this means, perhaps in part because the flexible operations of the irregulars would be better adapted to the desired experimentation.

At any rate, the third adopted version of the regulation, effective June 10, 1947, permitted the irregular carriers to engage in the foreign air transportation of property only; the regula-

---

[21] In promulgating the adopted version of the regulation, the Board found that the exemption with respect to foreign air transportation of persons by irregular carriers was no longer justified "in view of the recent substantial extension of our international air transportation system, as well as the recent award of foreign air carrier permits, and in view of the smaller traffic potential which the Board finds to exist in the field of international air transportation as compared with interstate and overseas air transportation." Regulations Serial No. 388, paragraph 5. The same finding was made in connection with the ultimate decision to exclude the noncertificated cargo carriers from foreign air transportation. Regulations Serial No. 389, May 5, 1947, paragraph 5.

[22] Remarks of Board Chairman James M. Landis, Oral Argument on Proposed Revision of Section 292.1, Docket No. 2742, p. 92 (January 6–7, 1947).

[23] Remarks of Chairman Landis, *Ibid.,* pp. 93–96.

[24] Remarks of Board Member Josh Lee, *Ibid.,* p. 245.

tion was subsequently amended (effective July 15, 1948) to permit irregular carriers utilizing small aircraft to carry persons in foreign air transportation.[25] Because of the nature of their aircraft, these carriers were believed to present no significant competitive threat to the certificated airlines.[26] Moreover, under individual exemption orders, several large irregular carriers have been permitted to conduct specified flights in foreign air transportation of persons, these flights having involved virtually no diversion from the certificated carriers, at least in the opinion of the Board.

In addition to this change in scope as compared with the November proposal, the new regulation (1) specifically excluded from the exemption carriers exempted by any other section of the Economic Regulations (as well as those operating pursuant to special exemptions as provided in the November draft). The effect of this change was to prevent any carrier's operating simultaneously as an irregular air carrier and as a noncertificated cargo carrier. It also (2) made the irregularity restriction expressly applicable to operations "within a designated point," and (3) added the following elaboration of the "irregular" concept:

No air carrier shall be deemed to be an Irregular Air Carrier unless the air transportation services offered and performed by it are of such infrequency as to preclude an implication of a uniform pattern or normal consistency of operation between, or within, such designated points.

Thus the regulation now contained in explicit form the general concept or irregularity formulated by the Board in its opinion in the *Investigation of Nonscheduled Air Services*. The basic definition of the type of operation contemplated by the exemption was the same as before. The defining paragraph in its entirety reads as follows:

There is hereby established a classification of non-certificated air carriers to be designated as "Irregular Air Carriers." An Irregular Air

---

[25] Regulations Serial No. ER–128, June 9, 1948.
[26] *Annual Report* of the Civil Aeronautics Board, 1948, pp. 20–21.

Carrier shall be defined to mean any air carrier (1) which does not hold a certificate of public convenience and necessity under Section 401 of the Civil Aeronautics Act of 1938, as amended, (2) which directly engages in interstate or overseas transportation of persons and property or foreign air transportation of property only, and (3) which does not hold out to the public, expressly or by a course of conduct, that it operates one or more aircraft between designated points, or within a designated point, regularly or with a reasonable degree of regularity upon which aircraft it accepts for transportation, for compensation or hire, such members of the public as apply therefor or such property as the public offers. No air carrier shall be deemed to be an Irregular Air Carrier unless the air transportation services offered and performed by it are of such infrequency as to preclude implication of a uniform pattern or normal consistency of operation between, or within, such designated points. Within the meaning of this definition a "point" shall mean any airport or place where aircraft may be landed or taken-off, including the area within a 25-mile radius of such airport or place.

In this connection, however, the Board indicated that there were "probably" certain other kinds of service "which appear to lend themselves to non-certificated air carrier operations" but which might tend to be performed more regularly than would be permissible under the regulation, e.g. "so-called 'air tours' or 'all-expense tours,' conducted, for example, each week-end to some resort region," and suggested that persons desiring to conduct such services might apply for certificates or for individual exemptions.[27] The operation envisaged here was a combination of transportation and other services of a type essentially different from the services performed by the certificated carriers.

Like the proposed drafts, the adopted version provided for more extensive economic regulation of irregular air carriers utilizing large aircraft. Under the regulation, the "larger" class includes any irregular air carrier which utilizes "in its air transportation services any single aircraft unit having an allowable gross take-off weight in excess of 10,000 pounds, or three or more aircraft units (not including any aircraft unit having an

[27] Explanatory Statement, Regulations Serial No. 388.

allowable gross take-off weight of less than 6,000 pounds) having an aggregate allowable gross take-off weight in excess of 25,000 pounds." (The allowable gross take-off weight of a DC-3-type plane is in general between 25,000 and 27,000 pounds.) For these carriers, the applicable sections of Title IV were substantially the same as under the May 1946 proposal; however, the duties of these carriers under Section 404(*a*) were in the adopted version limited to the provision of safe service, equipment, and facilities in connection with air transportation. The only major extension of regulation (as compared with the May proposal) with regard to the smaller carriers was the bringing into effect of Section 404(*a*) with respect to them to the same extent as for the larger carriers. The exempted carriers were required to obtain letters of registration, which were to be subject to immediate suspension when the Board found such action to be in the public interest.

Aside from the amendment, previously noted, which authorized irregular carriers using small aircraft to engage in foreign air transportation of persons, no significant change was made in the general irregular exemption from May 1947 until August 1948. Under this regulation, more than 2000 small irregular carriers and more than 140 large irregular air carriers were issued letters of registration by the Board.[28] The former class was predominantly composed of "fixed-base" operators who engaged only to a limited extent in transport operations and presented no problem in connection with unduly "regular" services. Companies in the latter class, however, were in many cases engaged in relatively large-scale air-transport operations with "transport-type" aircraft, the majority of these services being concentrated on heavily traveled air routes already served by certificated carriers. Although in the domestic field these operations were in the aggregate very small in volume as compared with those of the certificated airlines, they came to be of substantial relative importance both in international and overseas transportation and on those domestic and overseas routes on

[28] Letter from Board Chairman Joseph J. O'Connell, Jr., to Senator Edwin C. Johnson, Chairman of the Senate Committee on Interstate and Foreign Commerce, March 24, 1949, pp. 6–7 of mimeographed copy.

which they were concentrated (see Tables 1 and 2). The passenger operations of these carriers, although utilizing aircraft of types also used in the regular services of the certificated carriers, were in general equipped to carry a greater number of

TABLE 1
SUMMARY COMPARISON OF LARGE IRREGULAR AIR CARRIERS[1]
WITH CERTIFICATED CARRIERS
Third Quarter — 1948

	Domestic Operations		International and Overseas Operations	
	Certificated Trunk Lines	Large Irregulars	Certificated Carriers	Large Irregulars
Percentage Distribution of:				
Aircraft Operated	90.7[2]	9.3	87.0[2]	13.0
Revenue Miles Flown	96.6	3.4	88.3	11.7
Revenue Passenger Miles	97.5	2.5	89.2	10.8
Cargo Ton-Miles	93.5[3]	6.5	60.4[3]	39.6
Total Revenues	97.8	2.2	92.0	8.0
Net Worth	99.3	0.7	95.5	4.5
Average Length of Flight (miles)	197	766[4]	712	1,958[5]
Average Passenger Journey (miles)	459	1,382	1,410	2,526
Revenue Passenger Miles per Employee (000)	30	59	23	45

Source: Letter from Board Chairman Joseph J. O'Connell, Jr. to Senator Edwin C. Johnson. Chairman of the Senate Committee on Interstate and Foreign Commerce, March 24, 1949, Table I,

[1] Includes only 59 carriers for which information was obtained by the Board. These carriers are estimated to have performed about 85 percent of the transportation services of the large irregular air carriers.

[2] Includes 270 aircraft used both in domestic and in international and overseas operations. The distribution of the total fleets of all certificated and irregular carriers, eliminating this duplication of 270 aircraft, is: certificated carriers, 86.8 percent; large irregulars, 13.2 percent.

[3] Express and freight.

[4] Includes Viking, Standard, and Airline Transport carriers only.

[5] Includes Trans-Ocean, Seaboard & Western, and Trans-Caribbean only.

passengers per plane than the scheduled airlines; elaborate services to passengers with respect to reservations, meals, and the like were omitted; and the rates charged were substantially lower than for certificated air service between the same points.[29]

[29] See, for example, letter from Chairman O'Connell, p. 12: "The 'air coach' carriers have been charging $99 for transcontinental coach service, as contrasted with a fare of $157.85 charged by the certificated carriers."

In many cases, these operations were of a degree of regularity which the Board believed to be far in excess of that contemplated by the Regulation. According to Chairman O'Connell, a probable maximum of thirty large irregular air carriers had been conducting such operations as of March 1949.[30] By this time, a total of 111 large irregular air carriers were still authorized to operate under the exemption, the letters of thirty-three having been suspended, some on account of cessation of operations.[31] Despite the vigorous efforts of the Board to cope

TABLE 2

SCALE OF OPERATIONS OF IRREGULAR AIR CARRIERS ON IMPORTANT ROUTES

| | | *Number of equivalent monthly DC-3 flights*[1] | | |
| | | | *By Irregular Air Carriers* | |
Route	*Month (1948)*	*By Certificated Air Carriers*	*Number of Flights*	*Percent of Certificated Carriers*
New York–California	Sept.	1,530	153	10.0
New York–Miami	March	839	49	5.9
New York–San Juan	March	310	19	6.1
Miami–San Juan	March	248	44	17.7
Seattle–Alaska	July	372	90	24.2

Source: Letter from Board Chairman Joseph J. O'Connell, Jr. to Senator Edwin C. Johnson, Chairman of the Senate Committee on Interstate and Foreign Commerce, March 24, 1949, Appendix A.

[1] Each DC-4, DC-6, Constellation, and C-46 flight is here counted as the equivalent of two DC-3 flights. Flights are counted in one direction only, from city first listed. The month selected represents, for each route or area, the period of peak or near-peak traffic. Data for irregular air carriers are furnished by Operations Division; data for certificated carriers are taken from official carrier schedules.

with this problem through ordinary and extraordinary enforcement procedures, these attempts proved ineffective to stop the growth of the operations concerned because of the long periods of time required to bring these proceedings to a close under the requirements of due process, and the limited personnel available for enforcement activities.[32] In August 1948, the Board (1) closed the field of irregular operations under the general

[30] *Ibid.*, p. 7.

[31] *Ibid.*

[32] *Ibid.*, pp. 8–9.

exemption to new entrants proposing to utilize large aircraft,[33] and (2) instituted a comprehensive investigation of the "activities and practices" of large irregular carriers that were believed to be in violation of the Act and requirements thereunder, in order to obtain information on which to base recommendations for proceedings by the Department of Justice.[34]

By December of that year, the Board was apparently ready to admit defeat in its attempts to keep the large irregular carriers within bounds under the general exemption. At this time, a draft regulation was circulated which contemplated the termination of the general exemption with respect to these carriers.[35] This proposal was carried into effect by a revision of the regulation adopted in April and effective May 20, 1949,[36] almost exactly three years after the Board's first decision to allow these carriers to operate under a general exemption and two years after the regulatory framework within which they were to develop had been provided in its completed form.

The Board made it plain that individual exemptions would subsequently be issued to carriers conducting operations of the type intended to be authorized by the general exemption,[37] it also permitted authorized large irregular carriers which should apply for such individual exemptions by a certain date to continue to operate pending disposition of these applications (or until their letters had been revoked or canceled, whichever was sooner). Nevertheless, this new regulation was rightly regarded as a "death sentence" by many of the affected carriers. It meant the end of the indefinite legal boundary which had enabled them to believe in, or at least to rationalize, the legality of their operations and provided for relatively prompt specific official judgment with respect to each carrier's particular

[33] An amendment to the regulation adopted at this time provided that "The Board will not issue a Letter of Registration to any large Irregular Carrier except in response to applications therefor which are received for filing by the Secretary of the Board, on or before 11:00 A.M. (Eastern Daylight Time) August 6, 1948." Regulations Serial No. ER–130, adopted August 6, 1948, effective August 6, 1948.

[34] Orders Serial No. E–1864, August 11, 1948.

[35] Economic Regulations Draft Release No. 33, December 10, 1948.

[36] Economic Regulations Serial No. ER–142, April 13, 1949.

[37] Letter from Chairman O'Connell, p. 11.

services. In addition, in the findings accompanying the regulation the Board stated that it would take into consideration, in the disposition of applications for individual exemptions, "the extent to which the applicant had engaged in regular operations and had otherwise failed to comply with the requirements of the Act and the Board's regulations." [38] Under the new revision, ninety-six large irregular carriers applied for individual exemptions.

The other changes effected by the new regulation were by comparison of minor importance. With respect to small irregular carriers a general exemption was provided with exactly the same stated scope as to type of operation as before. However, both groups (i.e., the small irregular carriers and the large irregular carriers which continued to operate under the general exemption pending disposition of their individual exemption requests[39]), were subjected to greater economic regulation. Thus, the partial exemption from Sections 408, 409(a), and 412 (mergers, etc., interlocking relations, and contracts and agreements) which had been enjoyed by the large irregular carriers was terminated, as was their exemption from the duty under Section 404(a) to establish, observe, and enforce just and reasonable individual rates, fares, charges, classifications, rules, regulations, and practices. This action was taken "in view of the scope of operations being conducted by the Large Irregular Carriers, the extent of violations, and the necessity of protecting the public interest and providing for uniform application of the Act to carriers conducting similar or comparable operations." [40]

Under the new regulation, the exemptions enjoyed by the large irregular carriers are limited to sections 401(a) (the certification requirement), 405 (e) (Mail Schedules) and certain parts of 404(a). Small irregular carriers are exempted

---

[38] Economic Regulations Serial No. ER–142, p. 6.

[39] Before June 20, 1949, the regulation was applicable to large irregular carriers which held letters of registration as such issued to them pursuant to application therefor filed with the Board before August 6, 1948, and not revoked or canceled as of May 20, 1949. From this date, it applied to the above carriers only if they had filed individual exemption applications.

[40] Regulations Serial No. ER–142, p. 6.

from Sections 401(*a*), 403 (filing and observance of tariffs), 404(*a*) (except for the safety requirement), 404(*b*) (discrimination), 405(*e*), 407(*b*) (disclosure of stock ownership), 408, 409(*a*), and 412.

The removal of the large irregular carriers' partial exemption from Section 412 gave the Board a direct veto power over agreements among such carriers by means of which the irregular operations of several companies could be coördinated to provide a regular service. Because Section 412 was still to be inapplicable to small irregular carriers, participation by these carriers in this type of agreement or arrangement was directly prohibited by the Regulation itself. Other provisions with respect to these carriers were included with the intent of preventing the continuation of operations found illegal by means of a mere change in business identity, and to insure the prompt filing of reports required by the Board. For both classes of carrier, changes were made designed to prevent letters of registration from remaining outstanding for significant periods of time after the carriers to which they had been issued had ceased to operate.

At the time the regulation was issued, a proposal for further amendment to prevent evasion by means of the use by several large irregular carriers of a common ticket agency, and other related devices, was circulated to the public.[41] Provisions designed to deal with this problem had been included in the draft circulated in December 1948, but were omitted from the adopted version. Late in 1949, an amendment with this objective was finally adopted by the Board.[42]

The failure of the general exemption to accomplish the expected result as to large irregular carriers — i.e., the large-scale performance under it of operations of a type not intended to be permitted — was attributed by the Board to the facts that large aircraft could be used profitably in truly irregular operations only to a limited extent, and that users of such aircraft necessarily had large overhead and were subject to other cost condi-

---

[41] Economic Regulations Draft Release No. 38, April 13, 1949.
[42] Regulations Serial No. ER–164, Adopted November 4, 1949, effective December 10, 1949.

tions which gave rise to an all but irresistible temptation to engage in unduly regular operations.[43] For this reason, the Board concluded that no user of large aircraft should be permitted to operate unless the temptation to overstep legal bounds was at a minimum, owing to the existence of demonstrated "need" for *irregular* air service, and unless the particular legal bounds applicable to such carrier were defined "with more particularity than is possible under a blanket exemption authority such as §292.1." [44] Under an individual exemption order the Board could accomplish the desired "particularity" of definition: in any such order, the Board stated, it would "expect to insert appropriate conditions relating to the term of the exemption, the nature of the services to be rendered, the areas within which such services may be furnished, and other appropriate conditions intended to confine the carrier to the rendition of an irregular service." [45]

The Board's policy governing the issuance of individual exemptions was further clarified in an opinion made public in May 1950, at which time two applications for such exemptions were approved and eleven others denied.[46] It was stated in this opinion that no carrier which had in the past conducted "route" operations (defined as "a pattern of operations which shows a concentration of relatively frequent and regular flights between a limited number of pairs of points" [47] would be granted an individual exemption, on the ground that such carriers "are not to be entrusted with authority which might permit them, in the absence of unremitting and intensive enforcement effort, to continue in the same pattern." [48] At the same time, it was made clear that individual exemptions would be granted to those carriers which had been furnishing "truly irregular services," consisting "to a large extent . . . of such operations as

---

[43] Regulations Serial No. ER–142, pp. 2–5.

[44] *Ibid.*, p. 5.

[45] *Ibid.*, p. 6.

[46] Orders Serial Nos. E–4240, E–4241, E–4242, E–4243, E–4244, E–4245, E–4246, E–4247, E–4248, E–4249, E–4250, E–4251, and E–4252, May 25, 1950.

[47] *Ibid.*, p. 12.

[48] *Ibid.*, p. 20.

charter flights for athletic teams, business men's organizations, and similar groups; flights involving unusual and generally non-repetitive movement of property," which services "fill, in some respects, the interstices of the certificated route system" and whose "continuance . . . will have no adverse effect upon the certificated carriers." [49] To insure further that the operations of the exemptees would continue to be of the type contemplated, it was announced that each individual exemption would contain a specific prohibition against the operation of more than eight flights in the same direction between any pair of points in a period of four successive calendar weeks, and also against the operation of more than three flights in the same direction in such period between certain specified pairs of points (including most of the high-density routes on which the large irregular carriers had concentrated their services). Moreover, it was indicated that additional restrictions on flight patterns would be incorporated in individual exemptions;[50] that each exempted carrier would be specifically prohibited from entering into any agreement with respect to the conduct of air transportation which would exceed the authority of the individual carrier if conducted by it alone; and that each exemption would be granted for a maximum period of two years. Other requirements applicable to individual exemptees — including economic regulation under the Act and geographical restriction on their operations — are substantially similar to those applicable under the general exemption regulation.

Early in 1951, the Board circulated a proposed regulation

---

[49] *Ibid.*

[50] The two exemptions granted at the time of the Opinion (Orders Serial Nos. E–4246 and E–4247) contained additional prohibitions against: (*a*) "Operation of flights between any two points in the same direction on the same day of two or more successive calendar weeks"; (*b*) "Operation of a total of three or more flights between any two points in the same direction during any period of two successive calendar weeks unless such period is followed by a break of at least one calendar week during which no flights are operated between such points"; (*c*) "Operations so arranged as to result in the observance of breaks required by [(*b*)] . . . at regularly recurring intervals"; and (*d*) "Operations so arranged as to result in any uniform pattern or normal consistency of operations between any two points."

that would temporarily exempt small irregular carriers in the continental United States from virtually all economic regulation, for the purpose of permitting these carriers to operate "air-taxi" services from uncertificated to certificated points without restriction as to regularity.[51] Shortly thereafter, the general exemption applicable to large irregular carriers whose applications for individual exemptions had not yet been processed was amended to include specific flight-pattern prohibitions of the same nature as those applied to individual exemptees.[52] As of July 1951, the effective date of this amendment had been indefinitely postponed by injunction. At the time of the adoption of this amendment, the Board issued a policy statement reiterating the necessity for an *individual* exemption procedure to prevent the large irregulars from engaging in route-type services. However, it was also announced that the large irregulars would be temporarily authorized to conduct certain operations for the Department of Defense without restriction as to regularity or as to the foreign air carriage of persons, primarily because of the extraordinarily high temporary demand for such service.[53]

The very limited character of the effective demand for "tramp" passenger operations by large aircraft seems amply demonstrated by experience. Only a small percentage of the large irregular carriers have obtained individual exemptions, and the operations of at least some of these conform closely to the "fixed-base" pattern. Moreover, as the Board pointed out, representatives of large irregular carriers have themselves admitted — indeed, insisted upon — the general necessity for frequent service over an established route to permit adequate utilization of such aircraft. (These representatives took this position in support of the contention that, since the general exemption regulation contemplated noncertificated operations of some sort by operators of large aircraft, it could not have been the purpose of the Board so to limit the regularity of

---

[51] Economic Regulations Draft Release No. 47, February 14, 1951.

[52] Regulations Serial Number ER–159, adopted March 2, 1951, originally to be effective April 6, 1951.

[53] Civil Aeronautics Board, Statement of Policy, *The Role of the Large Irregular Carrier*, March 2, 1951.

their services that no such operations would be economically feasible.)

The existence of such economic pressures does not, however, afford an adequate explanation for the existence and persistence of noncertificated "regular" services which the Board did not intend to authorize, or absolve the Board from final responsibility for them. In the first place, if there had been no general exemption order covering air transportation under the jurisdiction of the Board in the postwar period, then it cannot be supposed that any significant number of new enterprises would have chosen to face certain prosecution and conviction by engaging in such transportation without certificates. In the second place, if the general exemption had been so drawn up as to leave from the outset no reasonable doubt as to the exact quantitative boundary of the exempted type of operation, it is similarly unlikely that many persons would have deliberately engaged in clearly illegal activities. In either case, the enforcement problem facing the Board would have been of manageable proportions. It is true that some of the offenders had begun operations before the issuance of the opinion in the *Investigation of Nonscheduled Air Services,* and had thus invested substantial sums in large aircraft before the broad definition there outlined and the two specific opinions issued concurrently therewith had become available; but it is also true that even these initial investments were made under the exemption regulation promulgated by the Board in 1938, that essentially the same general exemption was continued by the Board in the second and third versions of the regulation in 1946 and 1947, and that neither the opinion in the *Investigation* nor any subsequent decisions of the Board served as adequate substitutes for a specific quantitative formula embodied in the regulation itself.

As has been noted, the Board did not include in the regulation a precise, quantitative definition of the type of operation contemplated for exemption, but chose to rely on the case-by-case method of developing its content. Given a sufficient number and variety of cases, this method could indeed have served to provide a definition of such precision and unchallengeable legal status as to prevent the existence of any significant number of noncertified services in excess of the prescribed scope. The definition provided by the Board in the *Investigation* opinion *can* be precisely elaborated in a manner reasonably consistent with the general principle there set forth. This principle is that operations shall not be such as to give the public the impression of consistent, normal availability of flights, without special advance arrangement, between any two points. The impression of normal availability of flights without special arrangement can be conveyed in two ways: (1) by the operation of a uniform time pattern of service (e.g., a flight every Sunday), or (2) by frequency of service, in either case continued for a sufficient period of time to enable the public to gain the impression that the availability is normal, i.e., can be expected to persist. In providing a precise interpretation of this standard, it is therefore necessary to answer the following questions: (1) what is a uniform pattern? (2) what number of flights per given unit of time constitutes frequency? (3) how long a time break in the service is necessary to establish discontinuity? (4) how long must a continuous service persist in order to convey the impression of "normality"?

It is clear that all these questions could be supplied with definite answers by the administrative body, and various decisions handed down by the Board have in fact served to make more precise the intended boundary of the exemption.

In the first such case, for example, the Board found the following air-carrier activity to be outside the scope of the exemption: operation of thirty southbound and twenty-nine northbound flights between the same two points in a period of approximately four months, for at least half that time under a demonstratedly preconceived plan to operate two round trips weekly on the same days of the week, which plan was effectively communicated to the public (by means other than printed advertising) so that arrangements could be made "sometimes weeks in advance" for space on definitely dated flights, and carried out at least fairly well in practice. It was also shown that the service "offered many of the features of a certificated and regularly scheduled operation," such as free food aloft, hotel-airport transportation, etc., and that "all efforts [were] directed toward making the service the equal of, or at least comparable to, standard operations of certificated air carriers." [54]

In the second such case, the following air-carrier activity was found to be outside the scope of the exemption: operation of a daily round-trip flight between the same two points Mondays through Thursdays, with two round trips on Fridays, under a preconceived plan carried out with the exception of "cancellations caused by safety and weather conditions, and . . . one proposed trip which was canceled in order to carry a group of service men to New York" (the plan, it was testified, was to operate the flights subject to the availability of passengers as well as weather conditions), which plan was effectively communicated to the public over the telephone after an advertisement had invited inquiries, for a period of about six weeks. In addition to the planned operations, an afternoon round trip on Sunday was provided. The carrier's representatives were instructed to give, and for the most part did give, only "approximate" times of arrival and departure in response to inquiries by the public; but evidence showed that there was a definite uniform schedule of such times which was made available to individual members of the public. [55]

Other proceedings, instituted in the fall of 1946, involving noncertificated air carriers believed to be operating outside the scope of the exemption terminated in the issuance of consent orders or cease-and-desist orders directing these carriers not to engage in "operation of a single flight per week on the same day of each week between the same two points, or . . . recurrence of operations of two round trip flights, or flights varying from two to three or more such flights, between any same two points each week in succeeding weeks, without there intervening other weeks or approximately similar periods at irregular but frequent intervals during which no such flights are operated so as thereby to result in appreciable definite breaks in service: it being intended by this subparagraph to require irregularity in service between any such points but not to preclude the opera-

---

[54] Page Airways, Inc., Investigation, 6 C.A.B. 1061 (1946).

[55] Trans-Marine Airlines, Inc., Investigation of Activities, 6 C.A.B. 1071 (1946).

tion of more than one or two such flights in any given week, nor to prescribe any specific maximum limitation upon the number of flights which may be performed in any one week, if infrequency and irregularity of service is otherwise achieved through variations in numbers of flights and intervals between flights and through frequent and extended definite breaks in service." [56] (This passage was quoted in full by the Board in the explanatory statement accompanying the third version of the regulation issued May 5, 1947; the Board also noted here that similar provisions had been included in cease-and-desist orders entered as to Willis Air Service, Inc., and Trans-Luxury Airlines, Inc.)[57]

Although these last pronouncements constitute fairly clear evidence as to the intent of the Board with respect to the type of operation covered by the exemption, they are still subject to challenge in the courts as being unreasonable and arbitrary interpretations of the language contained in the regulation; for them to attain the same status as a definition included in the regulation itself, this contention with respect to them would have to be rejected by the courts not merely in connection with the individual carriers to which the orders were directed, but in connection with the exempted carriers in general.

The necessarily limited legal significance of an administrative decision in any particular case, and the fact that a long period of time is typically required to bring any such case to final judicial decision, made the case-by-case method ineffective to provide promptly the type of unassailable legal definition that would have been necessary to prevent violation.

For it is also clear that the answers to the above questions are by no means self-evident, that they depend to a considerable extent on estimates of mental processes of the traveling public, and that in the absence of a specific formula incorporated in the regulation its proper interpretation was subject to legitimate differences of opinion. Thus a carrier could argue, or plan to argue, in court that the regulation itself did not make known

[56] Matter of the Non-certificated Operations of Trans-Caribbean Air Cargo Lines, Inc., Docket No. 2593.
[57] Dockets Nos. 2639 and 2589.

exactly what was prohibited, and that the specific interpretations advanced by the Board were unreasonable and arbitrary. In addition, the indefiniteness of the standard in the regulation lent considerable weight to the contention that no duly registered large irregular carrier could violate Section 401(*a*), since this contention was based on an interpretation of the regulation which would have placed on the Board primary responsibility for determining the proper scope of operations in any particular case.

Presumably with the intention of meeting the argument that the purpose of the regulation had not been made sufficiently clear, the Board in December 1948 issued an interpretation of the Regulation containing ten hypothetical examples of operational patterns, eight of which were stated to be outside and two within the scope of the exemption.[58]

Here the following operations between any two points were stated to be outside the scope of the exemption: (1) operation of one flight in one direction on five consecutive Sundays in one calendar month (it was further stated that "if over a period of weeks an occasional Sunday flight is omitted, or is operated on some other day of the week, such minor variations in the general pattern . . . would not cause the service to become an irregular service"); (2) operation of one flight in one direction on every Tuesday and Friday of a calendar month (a similar statement as to minor variations was made in this connection); (3) operation of one flight in one direction on each of seven days in a calendar month, flight days being separated by three, four, or five-day intervals; (4) operation of one flight in one direction on two days of each of eight weeks in a period of approximately nine weeks' duration; (5) operation of one flight in one direction on each of twenty-two days in a period of sixty-one days, the flights being so distributed that the longest intervals without flights are two eight-day periods; (6) operation of one flight in one direction on each of fourteen days in a period of sixty-two days, the weekly frequency never exceeding two, and the two longest intervals without service being

---

[58] Interpretation No. 1 to 292.1, Regulations Serial No. ER–136, December 10, 1948.

of ten and eight days' duration, but six flights occurring on Tuesdays and six on Fridays; (7) operation of one flight in one direction every other day for a period of sixty-two days (there occurring, however, three seven-day periods in which no flights were operated). The above examples all refer to operations by one irregular air carrier. The eighth example of service outside the scope of the exemption was an operation by four large irregular carriers who agreed "to utilize the services of a single ticket agency . . . with respect to service between points *A* and *B*, and to furnish to the agent the dates upon which each will operate between *A* and *B*." In this instance, if the combined flights of the four carriers between *A* and *B* are of a pattern similar to any of the above one-carrier examples, "the combination of flights constitute regular air transportation and each such carrier is deemed to be conducting regular operations between *A* and *B*." The following operations were stated to be within the scope of the exemption: (1) operation of one flight in one direction in each of five succeeding weeks, on different days of the week, with breaks of at least a week between all but two of the flights; (2) operation of fourteen one-way flights in a sixty-one day period exhibiting the following time sequence: (i) eight days without service, (ii) one flight on each of two succeeding days, (iii) seventeen days without service, (iv) one flight, (v) six days without service, (vi) eight flights in a four-day period (at least one flight on each day), (vii) twenty days without service, (viii) three flights in a two-day period, (ix) one day without service.

By the time this interpretation was issued, however, the Board was ready to escape from its self-imposed difficulties by abandoning the general exemption altogether for users of large aircraft.

The decision to terminate the general exemption seems to be the best possible solution of the broad problem confronting the Board, not only because it provided an expeditious method of dealing with existing operations outside the intended scope of the exemption, but also because it is not at all certain that any generally applicable definition of this scope (however precise) based solely on frequency or time pattern of service would constitute a *completely* effective means of preventing all operations significantly competitive with those of the certificated carriers. There is no doubt that the Board intended the regulation to cover a class of operations which would meet needs not served by the scheduled airlines. However, since any regulatory definition of the type under consideration here would not limit exempted operations to routes not served by these airlines, and since the demands met by the continuous services of these airlines are at least in part made up of an aggregate of sporadic and discontinuous individual demands, there is no assurance that such a definition would in fact accomplish the desired end.

Here an analogy may be drawn with the regulatory distinction between common and contract carriage: although a precise distinction *can* be made on the basis of the type of operation conducted, it remains true that the limited services of the contract carrier, however precisely defined in terms of the number of persons served, conditions under which service is made available, and the like, are still essentially in competition with the common carrier serving the same route, in that they meet limited sectors of the general demand available to the latter. Specific regulatory control, by means of legislation providing for individual permits and minimum-rate regulation, over contract carriers has therefore been found necessary to accomplish protection of common-carrier revenues in surface transportation, and in air transportation such specific control is apparently being achieved by administrative interpretation of the law.

For these reasons, the abandonment of the general exemption with respect to large irregular operators appears to be a necessary and proper step toward the carrying out of the Board's intended policy. There remains, of course, the question whether the exempted transport services of the small irregular carriers may cause diversion from short-haul certificated services such as those of the feeder lines; however, since the aircraft used by the small irregulars are not of a type preferred by the traveling public, this effect may be of little quantitative significance.

Noncertificated Cargo Carriers

As early as March 1945, when hearings were held by the examiners in the *Investigation of Nonscheduled Air Services,* the suggestion was made that special regulatory treatment be given to "carriers intending to engage solely in the transportation of cargo, as distinguished from express." Specifically, it was recommended (1) that these prospective carriers be given "as much latitude as possible with respect to the inauguration of such services and revisions of the service after inauguration" and (2) that a special exemption order be adopted which would permit regular common-carrier service by cargo carriers. In rejecting these suggestions, the examiners noted that the studies of potential traffic and costs that were submitted in evidence did not by any means prove that the proposed operations would be profitable.[59] They found that the proposal for special treatment of the cargo carriers was beyond the scope of the proceeding, and that the data presented were insufficient as a basis for recommendations.[60]

In its opinion in this Investigation, the Board at least tentatively rejected the special-exemption proposal. Although all-cargo operations had by this time begun to operate on a significant scale (as the Board noted),[61] it believed that these services, which would necessarily parallel the routes of certificated airlines (in all cases authorized to carry property), should be subject to the certification requirement. At the time of this opinion, the Board had already instituted the Air Freight Case proceeding in which applications for cargo routes throughout the continental United States were being considered.[62] Accordingly, neither the revised exemption regulation nor the proposed draft issued concurrently with the opinion in the Investigation provided for a special exemption for cargo lines. These were to be subject to the same irregularity requirement as the noncertificated passenger carriers, despite the fact that the Board

[59] Investigation of Nonscheduled Air Services, Report of the Examiners, pp. 19–20.

[60] *Ibid.,* p. 25.

[61] Investigation of Nonscheduled Air Services, p. 1053.

[62] *Ibid.,* p. 1056.

foresaw that this restriction would "preclude the operation of a cargo service between major cities with sufficient regularity to attract shippers."[63]

By November 1946, the Board had reconsidered its position: the new draft regulation released at this time contained a proposal for a special exemption permitting cargo carriers to operate regular common-carrier services pending disposition of their applications for certificates.[64] Although exempt from the certification requirement, the cargo carriers were to be subject to the remainder of Title IV of the Act with the exception of Sections 404(a) (Carrier's Duty to Provide Service, Rates, and Divisions), 405 (Transportation of Mail), 406 (Rates for Transportation of Mail), and such accounting and reporting requirements under Sections 407(a) and (d) as were not expressly made applicable to them. As in the case of the irregular carriers, letters of temporary authority were to be required as a condition to the exercise of the exemption privilege, and special provision was made to prevent the public's being misled as to the nature of the service.

As written at this time, the exemption was without limitation as to routes, and, with respect to interstate and overseas transportation (1) would have been extended to all noncertificated cargo carriers which should have filed with the Board an application (or applications) for a certificate authorizing such transportation within thirty days after the effective date of the regulation and (2) would have continued for any such carrier until sixty days after final disposition of its application (or applications). With respect to foreign air transportation, the exemption (1) would have been extended to all noncertified cargo carriers which should have filed with the Board *at any time* an application for a certificate authorizing such transportation and (2) would have continued for any such carrier until sixty days after final disposition of any one application, or part thereof, for a certificate authorizing foreign air transportation (other proposed foreign routes for which application by the same carrier was pending at the time of the hearing on the one

[63] *Ibid.*
[64] Economic Regulations Draft Release No. 14.

disposed of could at that time also be disposed of as the Board saw fit). The exemption, however, was not to be available to any noncertificated cargo carrier which had at a previous time been exempted under the regulation and had had its exemption wholly terminated.

This proposal, "coming while the Board [was] bearing down on nonscheduled passenger and passenger-cargo operators, apparently took the entire industry by surprise." [65] Orders were issued by the Board in October and November of 1946 directing twelve noncertificated carriers other than exclusive cargo carriers to show cause why they should not be ordered to cease and desist from engaging in scheduled air transportation (one of these orders involved an intrastate carrier allegedly engaging in interstate commerce).[66] Enforcement action was not undertaken against the cargo carriers before the issuance of the regulation allowing them to engage in regular common-carrier service. This may or may not have been because the Board thought that they were performing only contract services (outside the scope of Title IV). It has been asserted, however, that "to at least a considerable degree such operations were in fact common carriage, and subject to regulation as such";[67] and it may be noted that even special "charter" flights of large irregular carriers in foreign air transportation have been held by the Board to be common rather than contract carriage.

The Board's change of heart coincided with the collapse of the hopeful postwar boom in new air-cargo operations. It was evident that most if not all of the new carriers were facing grave financial difficulties. Indications were that few would be left in the field by the time the Board reached a decision in the Air Freight Case, hearings on which were only beginning when the new proposal was made. At this time, these carriers had under the law to confine themselves to contract carriage or to irregular services; this was believed to be a serious obstacle

<hr>

[65] *Aviation News,* December 2, 1946, p. 7.

[66] *Annual Report* of the Civil Aeronautics Board, 1947, p. 27.

[67] Air Freight Case, Boston–New York–Atlanta–New Orleans Case, Tentative Opinion, April 25, 1949, Dissent of Board Member Harold A. Jones, Orders Serial No. E–2759, p. 18.

to profitable operations. The Board has said that the primary purpose of the special exemption was simply to enable the cargo carriers to remain in business until their applications for certificates could be passed on, although certain statements made by it might be taken to indicate that at least one objective of the exemption was to provide for regular common-carrier operations on an experimental basis in order to determine the economic feasibility of such all-cargo services.[68]

Thus in promulgating the final version of the exemption regulation (Section 292.5 of the Economic Regulations), the Board found that the inability of the cargo carriers to develop sufficient traffic and obtain return loads while engaging only in contract carriage had resulted in a situation in which

many of such carriers . . . may be required, for financial reasons, to terminate operations if they are required to continue to operate only upon an irregular or non-common carrier basis . . . The probability of dissipation of the operating staff and experience of such carriers, interruption of operations, loss of revenues and probable loss of part of their capital funds during the aforesaid interim period [i.e., the period in which the certificate applications were pending] constitute unusual circumstances affecting the operations of such carriers and would impose an undue burden on such carriers.[69]

The Board has also specifically rejected the contention that Section 292.5 was intended to or did in fact afford an opportunity for the cargo carriers to demonstrate adequately the full economic potentialities of their operations. In this connection, the Board pointed out that because of the temporary character of their authority under Section 292.5 the applicants had reasonably adopted "an interim policy of conservation of capital, which necessarily meant an absence of appreciable effort to develop additional traffic" and shippers had been loath to make any "considerable change in . . . customary business methods or facilities" to utilize the services of these carriers.[70]

In accordance with the limited objective of the new regulation, the version finally adopted by the Board restricted the

[68] See, for example, Regulations Serial Number 389, May 5, 1947, paragraph 3.

[69] *Ibid.*, paragraphs 2–3.

[70] Air Freight Case, Tentative Opinion, p. 9.

availability of the exemption to those noncertificated carriers of property only which on May 5, 1947 had applications for certificates on file with the Board, and who on that date were actively engaged in the carriage of air cargo. Operations under the exemption were further restricted for any carrier to transportation between its "established points," defined to include "any point to or from which such carrier has transported property by air, for compensation or hire, on other than merely a casual, occasional or infrequent basis, at any time during the twelve-month period ending May 5, 1947 . . . [and which] is a point, or is located in a region, proposed to be served" in the carrier's application pending on May 5, 1947. Provision, however, was made for additional exempted service (subject to Board approval) to points which were located in "the area immediately adjacent to any established point." Exemption with respect to any carrier was to terminate completely sixty days after final disposition of any one of its certificate applications or part thereof, unless otherwise extended by order of the Board. The exemption thus became a genuine grandfather type without the opportunities for expanded operations available in the November proposal.

The proposed exemption with respect to regular foreign transportation of cargo by applicants for certificates was completely omitted from the final form of Section 292.5. The Board gave as its reason for this omission "the recent substantial extension of our international air transportation system . . . the recent award of foreign air carrier permits, and . . . the smaller traffic potential which the Board finds to exist presently in the field of international air transportation as compared with interstate or overseas air transportation." [71] This aspect of the regulation has already been discussed in connection with the irregular carriers.

The exempted carriers were made subject to almost all of the provisions of Title IV except the certification requirement; as compared with the November draft, the only significant change in this connection was the subjection of these carriers to those parts of Section 404(a) which make it the duty of an

[71] Regulations Serial No. 389, paragraph 5.

air carrier "to establish, observe and enforce just and reasonable individual and joint rates, fares, and charges, and just, reasonable and equitable divisions thereof, and just and reasonable classifications, rules, regulations, and practices relating to air transportation" and "to provide safe service, equipment and facilities in connection with air transportation." Like the irregular carriers, the cargo companies were required to obtain letters of registration.

The Board's broadening of the exemption to permit regular common-carrier operations by the cargo carriers to enable them to stay in business pending the disposition of their applications for certificates is in sharp contrast to the course followed with respect to the large noncertificated carriers of passengers. As has been noted, when it became evident that many of these companies could not operate profitably within the intended limits of Section 292.1, the Board's response was to terminate the general exemption and provide for individual judgment to make sure that nobody would remain in business who would be tempted to operate regularly. Several of these carriers had at this time already applied for certificates of public convenience and necessity.

The basis for this different treatment of the two types of carrier is suggested in the Board's findings accompanying the promulgation of the cargo exemption regulation. Here the Board stated that, unlike the transportation of passengers and express, which had for a long time been performed by the certificated airlines, "the carriage of property in aircraft specially adapted or used solely for that purpose, and by companies devoting all or a major portion of their efforts to the solicitation and carriage of property constitutes a new and developing business." [72]

The certificate applications of nine cargo lines that were authorized to operate under Section 292.5 were dealt with by the Board in its tentative and final opinions in the Air Freight Case, which were issued on April 25, 1949, and July 29, 1949, respectively. Five of these carriers did not participate in the proceedings from the spring of 1948, when the examiners' re-

[72] *Ibid.*, paragraph 1.

port was issued recommending denial of their applications, until the issuance of the tentative opinion in April 1949. Three of the remaining four were granted temporary five-year certificates, in all cases for routes paralleling those of certificated carriers. A fourth certificate was issued to Airnews, Inc., for the operation of a combination truck-plane service entirely within the State of Texas. The certification of Airnews, Inc., involved issues essentially different from those related to the other three carriers, which had been operating under the exemption. However, it should be noted that the Board found that "the proposed service of Airnews will result in little if any diversion from the existing carriers." [73]

In justification of this action, the Board leaned heavily on the fact that during the period when the noncertificated cargo carriers were operating under Section 292.5 the freight traffic of the certificated airlines as well as that of the applicant cargo lines had expanded. (The relatively static volume of freight carried by the noncertificated carriers was taken by the Board as a demonstration that these companies had directed their efforts to "holding their own in the air freight market pending a decision in this case." [74]) Thus, said the Board, the noncertificated carriers had "in the past developed their traffic from the traffic potential; they did not divert it from the certificated carriers"; both types of carrier had "drawn their traffic from the common reservoir of the air freight potential." [75] This fact, plus the "likelihood" that the air-freight market would continue to grow, in the Board's opinion served to "negative any contention of diversion in the ordinary sense of the term." [76] The "ordinary sense" was apparently "diversion of *past* or *present* business" as opposed to the obtainment of additional traffic which might otherwise be acquired by the certificated carriers.[77]

This view was reinforced by the considerations that (1) "only a few of the presently certificated air carriers have even

---

[73] Air Freight Case, Boston–New York–Atlanta–New Orleans Case, Opinion, July 29, 1949 (Orders Serial No. E–3085), p. 58.

[74] Air Freight Case, Tentative Opinion, p. 9.

[75] *Ibid.*, p. 22.

[76] *Ibid.*

[77] *Ibid.*, p. 25.

yet paid any substantial attention to freight carriage in all-cargo equipment," and (2) "that a portion of the air freight market [i.e., traffic not between major centers which would not warrant all-cargo plane service but could profitably be served on combination flights] will remain reserved at least for the present, for development by the existing certificated carriers."[78]

Having disposed of the diversion issue in the usual sense, the Board proceeded to deal by implication with the position that the entire air-cargo market, including traffic yet to be developed, should be reserved for the certificated airlines in order to enable them to improve their financial situation. This view was rejected on three grounds: (1) that reservation of the air-freight market was not necessary to enable the certificated carriers to operate at a profit; (2) that at any rate it would not be desirable as a matter of public policy to enable these carriers to make up losses on their passenger business with profits on freight; and (3) that the development of air freight as a mere "supplement" to passenger traffic would also be undesirable.[79]

In his dissenting opinion, Board Member Jones argued strongly in favor of the rejected view;[80] but the majority's approach (whatever one may think of the factual support adduced for the decision) is in this respect far more consistent with the Board's usual treatment of the diversion issue.

As for the measurement of diversion, the majority's treatment was, as Mr. Jones pointed out, unprecedented.[81] There was no attempt to determine on a route or carrier basis the effect of the proposed services on existing operations. However, to reconcile the majority's argument with the usual method of dealing with this problem, it is only necessary to assume that the Board believed that not only in general, but on the particular routes certificated, the expansion of air-freight traffic would be such that no diversion of past or present business would result.

[78] *Ibid.*
[79] *Ibid.*, pp. 25–26.
[80] *Ibid.*, Dissent of Board Member Jones, p. 39.
[81] *Ibid.*, Dissent of Board Member Jones, pp. 37–38.

Since a large part of the traffic that had been carried by the applicant cargo carriers was in fact on these routes, such a belief would be a not unreasonable extension of the Board's position with regard to freight traffic in general.

The Board in effect admitted that the available evidence on past and estimated future demands for and costs of air-freight transportation did not give conclusive support to its position as to the probable over-all future growth of the business (a position essential to its conclusion regarding "diversion in the ordinary sense of the term"). As against this inconclusiveness, it pointed to the wide latitude on occasion allowed to administrative agencies by the courts in matters of evidence and proof, and, more emphatically, to the "promotional" orientation of the Civil Aeronautics Act. Under the Act, broad considerations related to the development of the air-transportation industry were properly to be taken into account in determining "public convenience and necessity"; and this approach "must necessarily be predicated upon future estimates as well as present facts for it is keyed to future goals and an effort to envisage the shape of things to come." [82]

The particular broad considerations which the Board found relevant were as follows: (1) the possibility that the cargo carriers, unsupported by passenger and mail revenues, would be impelled to develop new markets, techniques, and equipment which would expand the air-freight business to the benefit of the certificated carriers and of air transportation as a whole; (2) the fact that the exclusive cargo carriers would "provide a valuable yardstick for measuring the alertness and efficiency of other carriers of cargo"; (3) the fact that the exclusive cargo carriers would also "provide a valuable yardstick of costs," since the freight costs incurred by the certificated lines were difficult to ascertain because of allocation problems, and the Board, faced with the problem of deciding whether the mail carriers were achieving maximum economy and efficiency, could not do so without the standards that would be provided by an unsubsidized operation; and (4) the likelihood that the exclusive cargo carriers would afford "a continuing spur of

[82] *Ibid.*, pp. 26–28.

competition to presently certificated carriers." Considerations of national defense were not accorded primary emphasis in this decision; however, it was found that the certification of the freight carriers was "consistent with and in furtherance of the interests of the national defense" in that it would "bring about a more rapid development of the air freight market and lead to a commercial demand for air freight transportation greater than if the air freight field were left exclusively to the certificated carriers." [83] No promotion of the interests of the postal service was expected.

The Board did not authorize any of the carriers to carry mail, and regarded the absence of mail payment as an essential part of the case for certification. At the hearings, a representative of the Post Office Department declared that it was neutral with respect to the issue of certification, but that it found the services of the existing certificated airlines superior as regards mail carriage to those proposed by the cargo lines. It was also indicated that the Post Office was interested in seeing the certificated airlines attain economic self-sufficiency so that mail payments might be reduced.[84]

Temporary certification was regarded as desirable because of the still experimental state of air-cargo operations: the award of certificates was regarded primarily as an experiment that would "supply evidence to chart the more distant course." A five-year period was deemed necessary in order to "give the new carriers a fair chance to develop . . . traffic." Temporary certification was preferred to continuation of the exemption in that the former would put the applicants on a "comparable basis" with the certificated airlines and make possible the establishment of "stable relationships" with financial institutions and shippers.[85]

The tentative opinion was finally reaffirmed, after further oral argument, on July 29, 1949. The only substantial change in the final as compared with the tentative decision was the inclusion of a provision prohibiting the certificated cargo carriers

---

[83] *Ibid.*, pp. 29–31.
[84] *Ibid.*, pp. 32–35.
[85] Air Freight Case, Tentative Opinion, pp. 35–36.

from carrying air express shipped by the Railway Express Agency.[86] The purpose of this action was to remove any possibility of diversion of air-express traffic from the existing certificated carriers; in this connection, the Board asserted that "the potential traffic available [to air-express service] is not such under present circumstances as to warrant further competition and the additional service which would be provided the public would not be substantial."[87]

Air-Freight Forwarders

In the immediate postwar period, which saw the initiation of operations on a large scale by noncertificated direct air carriers of passengers and cargo, there also were inaugurated a substantial number of enterprises that acted as intermediaries between shippers of air cargo and direct air carriers. Although some of these companies shipped freight via the certificated as well as the noncertificated airlines, the latter benefited much more extensively from their services,[88] and favored regulatory authorization of common-carrier operations by them. The certificated carriers have consistently opposed any extension of the operating authority of the intermediary enterprises, as well as any broadening of the air-transportation activities of the Railway Express Agency, in part on the ground that services proposed to be performed by these companies could better be furnished by the certificated airlines themselves with the assistance of their joint subsidiary, Air Cargo, Inc.[89] The services performed by the new enterprises varied in scope;[90] however, they would have been in violation of the Act had they not con-

---

[86] Air Freight Case, Opinion, pp. 78–79.

[87] *Ibid.*, p. 26.

[88] Air Freight Forwarder Case, Docket No. 681 *et al.*, Report of the Examiner, April 21, 1948, pp. 37–38.

[89] This subsidiary, which was set up in 1941 primarily as a research organization, and was inactive during the war, in 1947 was authorized to undertake certain operating activities including participation in ground handling of air cargo. The Board found that its actual and proposed operations "are so limited that it will not operate as an indirect air carrier and consequently will not take over the functions of REA in the air transportation of property nor will it operate as an air freight forwarder." Air Freight Forwarder Case, September 8, 1948, pp. 22–23 (Orders Serial No. E–1968).

[90] *Ibid.*, p. 37.

fined their activities to contract operations or to acting as agents for carriers or shippers.

Under the Act, indirect as well as direct (common) carriers are subject to Title IV, including the certification requirement (as well as to other parts of the Act), and the Board early decided that this definition covered such air-cargo operations as those of the Railway Express Agency[91] and of ordinary freight forwarders.[92] The Act also contains specific authorization for the relief of such indirect carriers from the Act's provisions "to the extent and for such periods as may be in the public interest."[93] This provision has been interpreted by the Board as reflecting a recognition that some parts of the Act which apply to "air carriers" are "obviously inapplicable" to indirect air carriers (as, for example, those requirements specifically designed to regulate the actual operation of aircraft.)[94] Although the Board has never certificated any indirect air carrier, and has referred to the certification requirement as being especially adaptable to direct air carriers,[95] it has not taken the position that this requirement is "obviously inapplicable" to indirect carriers, but has rather based its exemptions in this regard largely on special circumstances existing at the time such exemptions were granted.

Therefore, in order that they might legally engage in indirect common carriage by air, many of these postwar enterprises, as well as some established surface forwarders and subsidiaries of such forwarders and of surface carriers, applied to the Board either for exemption from Section 401(*a*) or for certificates. Seventy-eight such applications were considered in the Air Freight Forwarder proceeding. In order to obtain full information on these services and on questions relevant to the proper regulatory policy to be followed with respect to them,

[91] Railway Express Agency, Inc. — Certificate of Public Convenience and Necessity, 2 C.A.B. 531 (1941).

[92] Universal Air Freight Corporation — Investigation of Forwarding Activities, 3 C.A.B. 698 (1942).

[93] Section 1(2).

[94] Railway Express Agency, Inc. — Certificate of Public Convenience and Necessity, p. 537.

[95] Air Freight Forwarder Case, p. 34.

the Board instituted a comprehensive investigation and consolidated the applications into this proceeding. Also included in the proceeding were the application of the Railway Express Agency for broader and more permanent authorization than it held under its exemption order. The opinion in this case was issued in September 1948.

Meanwhile, the suggestion had been made that the intermediary enterprises be permitted to operate as common carriers under a temporary general exemption order, pending the outcome of the freight-forwarder proceeding. Accordingly, the Board included in the draft version of Section 292.1 circulated to the public in November 1946 a proposal which would have permitted such carriers so to operate until sixty days after the Board should have made final disposition of this proceeding.[96] These carriers would have been exempted only from Sections 401, 405 (Transportation of Mail), 406 (Rates for Transportation of Mail), and the accounting and reporting requirements of Sections 407(a) and (d) except where expressly made applicable to them. They would, like the other classes of carrier dealt with in the draft, have had to obtain letters of temporary authority in order to exercise the exemption privilege, and to display a summary statement of their operating authority in their advertising and in offices where they transacted business with the public. The regulations adopted in May 1947 did not, however, include any exemption for indirect air carriers.

In October of that year, the Board released a new draft regulation which again would have permitted temporary exemption pending the outcome of the freight forwarder proceeding.[97] Under this proposal, the exempted carriers were not to be permitted to use for air transportation the facilities of non-common carriers, or (with the exception of Alaskan Air Carriers and irregular air carriers utilizing small aircraft) the services of any other carriers at rates not included in tariffs filed with the Board. They were to be subject to all provisions of Title IV of the Act which were applicable to them, with the exception of Sections 401 (except (l)) and 408; as will be seen, the latter

---

[96] Economic Regulations Draft Release No. 14.

[97] Economic Regulations Draft Release No. 22, October 15, 1947.

provision presented difficult problems in connection with these companies. Letters of registration were to be required as a condition to enjoyment of the exemption privilege, but there was no provision with respect to display of a statement of operating authority. Although temporary, this proposed exemption, like the previous proposal, was to be of an unlimited open-end variety: that is, unlike the direct air-cargo-carrier exemption, it was not limited to a particular group of carriers which had applied for certificates, but was to be open to all enterprises desiring to engage in indirect air transportation. There was also no limitation on routes or on broad geographical location of the service. This plan was presented in the form of a proposed new section (292.6) of the Economic Regulations.

On April 2, 1948, the Board issued an order[98] denying certain petitions for temporary exemption of indirect air carriers and finding that such action would not be in the public interest. The Board here found that the issues presented by the temporary-exemption proposal were "basic" and were "also presented by the applications in the Freight Forwarder Case"; that "hearings covering a period of several months and resulting in thousands of pages of testimony and exhibits" had been held in that proceeding; that "in reaching a decision on such issues and establishing a policy with respect to indirect air carrier operations, the Board should have the benefit of the proceedings in the Freight Forwarder Case, and interested parties should be granted an opportunity to present their views on such issues on the basis of the record in the Freight Forwarder Case, if such procedure can be followed without causing undue delay"; that this proceeding could "if accorded expedited treatment . . . be disposed of without undue delay"; and that the Board had "determined to expedite proceedings in the Freight Forwarder Case to the greatest extent possible, consistent with fair procedure."

In his dissenting opinion, Board Member Josh Lee characterized the majority's failure to adopt the proposed regulation as "not consistent with the public interest" [99] largely because the

---

[98] Orders Serial No. E–1343.
[99] Dissent of Board Member Lee, p. 1.

experience that could have been accumulated under it would constitute a "practical — and probably the only available — method for testing the merit of the indirect carriers' claims for authorization." [100] He noted that the "basic factual material needed for a decision on the indirect air carrier question is not available" and that the record in the freight-forwarder proceeding "on many of the all-important points . . . supplies only the conclusions of witnesses, pro and con, based on questionable assumptions and analogies." He further pointed out the probability that the ultimate decision in the freight-forwarder proceeding would in fact be to grant an exemption under which the forwarders might operate for an experimental period, and concluded that "if this be true, the decision of the majority here can have only one result — to delay the proper and orderly development of air cargo and air freight." [101] In view of the actual outcome of the proceeding, the above criticism seems in large part justified.

Shortly after the issuance of this order, the examiner in the *Air Freight Forwarder Case* submitted a report proposing (1) that air-freight forwarders be allowed to engage in common carriage under a general exemption of indefinite duration, (2) that the Board recommend to Congress the passage of an amendment to the Act providing for the regulation of entry into the air-freight forwarding business on the basis of permits similar to those provided for surface forwarders under Part IV of the Interstate Commerce Act; (3) that "further recommendations for additional legislation be withheld until the expiration of a reasonable period of experimentation under the proposed legislation"; (4) that the current Railway Express Agency exemption be continued but expanded to allow it to enter into contracts with noncertificated cargo carriers; and (5) that the Railway Express Agency and the direct carriers undertake to renegotiate their contracts "so as to provide for the payment by Railway Express Agency, Inc. to the air carriers a fixed amount per ton-mile of air express carried and so as to permit Railway Express Agency, Inc. to fix and determine the rates for air ex-

[100] *Ibid.*, p. 7.
[101] *Ibid.*, p. 6.

press which will be stated in the tariffs of Railway Express Agency." [102] This last recommendation was designed to prevent the continuance of a situation in which the Railway Express Agency and the carriers could each blame the other for high express rates and alleged failure to develop maximum traffic under the air-express system, and to give the Agency a relatively free hand to develop the express service that the carriers proposed ultimately to abandon. (Under the existing contracts, the rates in the Railway Express Agency's tariff were set by a Traffic Committee representing the underlying carriers, and receipts from air express were divided between the Agency and the carriers on a fixed percentage basis after the deduction of "out-of-pocket" expenses of the Agency.)

The examiner took the view that there was in general no need to impose the certification requirement on companies desiring to enter the air-freight-forwarder field. Despite the fact that indirect air carriers had been held to be subject to regulation under the Civil Aeronautics Act, it appeared to the examiner that this Act had been "specifically drawn with the purpose in mind of regulating the direct carriers," and that "there are no regulatory provisions specifically relating to air freight forwarders." [103] Thus the Board was confronted not only with the problem of deciding whether an essentially new type of service, on which only "limited empirical data" could in the nature of things be available, should be allowed to be rendered, but also with the problem of drawing up *de novo* a plan for the regulation of these services, if permitted, without any specific guidance in the Act itself.[104] As to the first issue — whether or not a public need existed for the proposed air-freight-forwarder operations — the examiner found that the very existence of the applicants, plus the testimony of businessmen and of the non-certificated cargo carriers who desired to utilize these services, established that such a need did exist.[105] As to the second, in the asserted absence of any guidance in the Civil Aeronautics Act itself, the examiner drew an analogy with the policy established

[102] Air Freight Forwarder Case, Report of the Examiner, pp. 85–86.
[103] *Ibid.*, p. 80.
[104] *Ibid.*, p. 51.
[105] *Ibid.*, pp. 53–55.

by Congress with respect to surface-freight forwarders, and recommended a plan of regulation substantially identical with that provided in Part IV of the Interstate Commerce Act, pending specific action by Congress with respect to air-freight forwarders.

Under this plan, persons desiring to enter the air-freight-forwarder field would not be required to prove public convenience and necessity; in this connection, the examiner declared that "as in the case of surface freight forwarders, it appears that there should be no limitations upon the amount of competition among air freight forwarders." [106] However, since Part IV of the Interstate Commerce Act provides for specific authorization of particular surface-forwarder services without such proof, on a showing that the applicant is "ready, able, and willing" to provide them, and since the Civil Aeronautics Act contains no provision for this type of authorization, the examiner proposed that the Board recommend that such provision be made by Congress.

The specific provisions of Title IV from which the forwarders were to be exempted were the same as under the October proposal, except that they were to be made subject to Section 408; in addition, specific exemption was to be made from Title VI of the Act (Safety Regulation). As compared with the October proposal, the major innovations in the examiner's suggested regulation were (1) the inclusion of a new and more specific definition of the type of carrier to be exempted;[107] (2) a re-

---

[106] *Ibid.,* p. 82.

[107] Whereas the October proposal had applied to "Noncertified Indirect Cargo Carriers" defined to include "any noncertificated air carrier which indirectly engages in interstate, overseas or foreign air transportation of property only," the examiner's regulation applied to "air freight forwarders" defined to mean "any person who holds himself out to the general public to transport or provide transportation of property only by air for compensation, in interstate, overseas, or foreign commerce, and who, in the ordinary and usual course of his undertaking, (A) assembles and consolidates or provides for assembling and consolidating of such property, and performs or provides for the performance of break-bulk and distributing operations with respect to such consolidated shipments, and (B) assumes responsibility for the transportation of such property from point of receipt to point of destination, and (C) utilizes, for the whole or any part of the transportation of such shipments, the services of a direct air carrier subject to the Civil Aeronautics Act."

quirement that a minimum amount of insurance be maintained to protect the public; (3) a requirement that transportation bills from direct air carriers be paid within a reasonable period after the services are rendered; and (4) a requirement that no operations be conducted until after a valid tariff should have been posted and filed. As in the October proposal, the exempted carriers were to be prohibited from using contract services. The insurance and bill-paying requirements were included to allay fears that a great many freight forwarders would become hard up or fail, with a resulting large loss to the public and the direct air carriers.[108]

The immediate effect of the Board's decision in the Air Freight Forwarder Case, made in September 1948, was substantially the same as that which would have resulted from adoption of the examiner's recommendations. The Railway Express Agency's exemption order was continued in effect, and the company was directed to negotiate new contracts with the carriers accomplishing the same revisions as those proposed by the examiner. The Board, however, did not authorize the Agency to deal with the noncertificated cargo carriers; moreover, in the final opinion in the Air Freight Case, as has been noted, it was decided not to permit the cargo carriers who were certificated to carry express traffic shipped by the Agency. Final action on the Agency's requests to handle air freight and to operate as an air-freight forwarder was deferred.

With respect to the other applicants in the proceeding, the Board adopted a general open-end exemption order [109] very similar to that proposed by the examiner. This order applied only to domestic operations. A substantially similar order was later adopted with respect to overseas and foreign operations.[110]

The major respects in which the Board's action differed from the examiner's proposal reflect (1) the essentially different rationale accepted by the Board regarding economic regulatory

[108] See, for example, the dissent of Board Member Jones in the Air Freight Forwarder Case, who here also indicated his belief that this problem would not be effectively dealt with by the requirements in the regulation.

[109] Regulations Serial No. ER–131, September 8, 1948 (effective October 15, 1948).

[110] Regulations Serial No. ER–155, September 8, 1949 (effective April 24, 1950).

policy toward the air-freight forwarders; (2) the greater weight attached by the Board to possible adverse effects of relations of freight forwarders with surface carriers and other types of enterprise; and (3) greater attention to problems of administration and enforcement.

(1) The Board did not adopt the examiner's position that the regulation of air-freight forwarders presented a problem essentially outside the scope of the Civil Aeronautics Act which should be dealt with on the precedent of Congress' treatment of surface-freight forwarders. Thus, no proposal was made that Congress be asked to amend the law to provide for affirmative authorization of air-freight-forwarder operations on the basis of fitness (or readiness), willingness, and ability. While the examiner envisaged the exemption regulation and the proposed Congressional action as a means of establishing a definitive new regulatory scheme, the Board looked upon the exemption order as a temporary measure under which "essential experience can be developed upon which a permanent policy may be soundly determined." [111] The exemption was therefore limited to a maximum period of five years. Again, in deciding the specific question of the appropriateness of certification as a means of authorization for the forwarders, the Board did not refer to Part IV of the Interstate Commerce Act or draw any general conclusion as to the inherent desirability of limiting competition in the air-freight-forwarder field; on the contrary, its decision was placed squarely within the framework of the Civil Aeronautics Act itself, and the decision to provide for exemption rather than certification was based on particular circumstances existing at the time of the decision.[112] Continued operation of the applicant companies on an agency basis was rejected as inconsistent with maximum competitive incentive and with maximum benefits to shippers.[113] Because of the small investment required to enter the air-freight-forwarder field, it was thought that a type of authorization more permanent than the exemption order was

[111] Air Freight Forwarder Case, p. 52.
[112] *Ibid.*, pp. 53–54.
[113] *Ibid.*, pp. 50–51.

not necessary to assure the validity of the experiment.[114] This point serves to distinguish the forwarder decision from that in the Air Freight Case, where a five-year *certification* was deemed essential to allow the new carriers fully to develop their services.

(2) Unlike the examiner's proposed regulation, the version adopted by the Board made the issuance of a letter of registration to any forwarder conditional upon a finding that "the conduct of air freight forwarder operations by the applicant will not be inconsistent with the public interest." The reason for this condition is indicated by the following statement in the Board's opinion:

> Under this reservation we will carefully examine all applications to insure that Letters of Registration are not issued to applicants whose operations, because of the applicants' affiliations with persons engaged in other modes of transportation or other phases of aviation, might be inimical to the development of a sound air transportation system.[115]

The detailed requirements in the regulation pertaining to information to be furnished by applicants also reflect the Board's concern with such affiliations.

Whereas the examiner's report had contained relatively little discussion of this problem and a conclusion was drawn by him that "there appears to be no justification at this time for making any distinction between forwarders because of surface carrier affiliations," [116] the Board's opinion dealt at length with the complex issues presented by the affiliations of certain applicants with surface-freight forwarders, persons engaged in other phases of aviation, and direct surface carriers. The Board found that the second proviso of Section 408(*b*) and the policy suggested therein are inapplicable to cases where the air carrier to be controlled is indirect rather than direct. The only applicants refused authorization because of their connections were two railroad-controlled companies who were expected, if authorized,

[114] *Ibid.*, p. 52.
[115] *Ibid.*, p. 57.
[116] Air Freight Forwarder Case, Report of the Examiner, pp. 84–85.

to possess substantial competitive advantages as compared with other air forwarders and to be subject to a potential conflict of interest between rail and air transportation activities.[117] In addition, two companies engaged in other phases of aeronautics involving a potential conflict of interest were required to show discontinuance of such activities as a condition to authorization to operate as freight forwarders.[118]

(3) Section 292.6 as finally adopted makes letters of registration subject to suspension after not less than ten days notice, "but without hearing or further proceedings, for failure to comply with the provisions of the Act or with any order, rule, or regulation issued thereunder, or with any term, condition, or limitation of any authority issued thereunder." In addition, issuance or retention of such a letter is conditional upon a showing to the satisfaction of the Board that "the public interest and the carrier's intention and ability to conform to the provisions of the Act and requirements thereunder will not be adversely affected" by any current or proposed (specified) relation with a person connected (in specified manner) with any exempted carrier subject to suspension action at the time of such connection.[119]

Section 292.6 also makes provision for revocation without prejudice of a letter tendered for cancelation by a forwarder who concurrently files a written notice of discontinuance of common-carrier activities, and of the letter of any forwarder who for two successive periods fails to file the periodic reports required by the Economic Regulations.[120]

With respect to the demonstrated public need for the service of the air-freight forwarders, the Board appears to have been somewhat more skeptical than was the examiner. Despite the fact that the opinion included a rather lengthy discussion of the public service which could be rendered by the forwarders, the Board found that evidence presented by the parties "did not

[117] Air Freight Forwarder Case, pp. 72–76.

[118] *Ibid.*, pp. 66–67.

[119] A similar provision was made with respect to small irregular air carriers in the version of Section 292.1 which became effective on May 20, 1949 (Regulations Serial No. ER–142).

[120] Similar provisions were included in the latest version of Section 292.1.

reveal that searching analysis which the importance of the present issue demanded," and that "no empirical basis exists for a determination of the important issues involved." Nevertheless, it was concluded that "the public interest in and need for the services of air freight forwarders has been sufficiently established to justify the authorization of freight forwarder operations for a limited period during which essential experience can be developed upon which a permanent policy may be soundly determined." [121] The lack of affirmative evidence in this regard was strongly emphasized in the dissenting opinion of Board Member Jones, who found that the evidence was entirely inadequate to justify the Board's authorization. That some of the applicants, at least, may have been overoptimistic with respect to demand is indicated by the fact that, although more than fifty companies were specifically authorized to operate at the time the opinion was issued, only ten air-freight forwarders were reported in operation under the exemption early in May 1949.[122] On January 2, 1951 there were 29 air-freight forwarders participating in domestic air transportation under the exemption.

If the applicants' case that a public need existed for their services fell somewhat short of being conclusive, the arguments presented by the certificated carriers as to the undesirable consequences of freight-forwarder authorization were even less persuasive. The examiner rightly characterized these arguments as "an accumulation of apprehensions," and noted that "There has been little or no experience of freight forwarder operations in air transportation and hence no factual material to support these apprehensions." [123]

In addition to the damage which would allegedly result from the nonpayment of transportation charges by the forwarders, a matter specifically dealt with in the regulation, the Board considered several other types of injury to the fortunes of the certificated airlines which, it was contended, would result from the authorization of freight-forwarder operations, including:

---

[121] Air Freight Forwarder Case, pp. 51–52.
[122] *Aviation Week*, May 23, 1949, p. 42.
[123] Air Freight Forwarder Case, Report of the Examiner, pp. 45–46.

(1) direct diversion of air freight by the forwarders from the underlying carriers; (2) loss of revenue through transport-rate reductions to forwarders unjustified by cost; (3) accentuation of the directional unbalance of traffic, concentration of traffic at certain times of day, and underutilization of cargo space on combination flights; and (4) diversion of traffic from one air carrier to another or from air to surface carriers. Although the Board did not in all cases deny that some loss might result from these factors, none of them was found to have been shown to be of significant consequence for the finances of the direct air carriers, and in fact there seems to be no reason to suppose that any or all of them would result in appreciable losses.

With respect to point (1), it is evident that, since none of the forwarders would engage in direct air carriage, any competitive loss which might be incurred by these direct carriers would result from (*a*) loss of profit (or increase of loss) on ground handling operations or (*b*) loss of additional net revenue (or increase of net loss) as compared with that which would have been obtained (or incurred) if the traffic consolidated by the freight forwarders had moved at rates in effect for small shipments. The first of these possible types of loss did not merit or obtain explicit treatment in the Board's opinion. As for the second, it obviously would not occur if the volume spreads in tariffs represented genuine cost differences.

This brings us to point (2), which was expressly found to be not valid, because of the facts that transportation rates would be set by the direct air carriers themselves and that the Board would be in a position to prevent the forwarders' exercising their superior bargaining power to obtain preferential rates.[124]

Directional unbalance of traffic was found to be "due primarily to the economics of production and distribution"; thus it would be "illogical to conclude that either REA or the freight forwarders are or would be responsible for this unbalance."[125] While some accentuation of congestion at the end of the day was

[124] Air Freight Forwarder Case, p. 43.
[125] *Ibid.*, p. 45.

anticipated as a result of the forwarders' operations, it was noted that the general expansion of air freight also resulting from them would produce some nondeferrable traffic which would relieve this situation. It was also pointed out that the availability of air parcel post would alleviate the problem of unutilized space on combination flights.[126]

Apart from special concessions which might be obtained by the forwarders by diverting traffic from one air carrier to another (a point already discussed above), this type of diversion, the Board found, would "take nothing from the industry as a whole and its possibility will be a compelling incentive for each carrier to render service fully adequate to the needs of the shipping public." [127]

It was conceded that "the effect of air freight forwarder operations on the problem of diversion of cargo from air to surface transportation cannot now be determined." [128] However, it was pointed out that delays in ground handling "impose a handicap upon the air-cargo transportation business" and that "the experience of the freight forwarders in this phase of transportation should result in improved air cargo service," [129] although the extent of the improvement could not be known in advance of actual operation.[130] Moreover, the Board expressly found that participation by surface-freight forwarders in air-forwarding activities (as distinguished from participation by direct surface carriers in direct air transportation) would prob-ably not result in substantial diversion of traffic from air to surface carriers.[131]

In addition to their claims of direct injury to themselves, the certificated carriers contended that the forwarders would worsen air-cargo service, make it more expensive, and perform no operation that could not be done better by the carriers themselves with the aid of Air Cargo, Inc. In view of the fact

[126] *Ibid.*, pp. 46–47.
[127] *Ibid.*, p. 47.
[128] *Ibid.*
[129] *Ibid.*, p. 48.
[130] *Ibid.*, p. 50.
[131] *Ibid.*, pp. 59–60.

that the authorization of forwarders involved no restriction whatever on shipper choice or on the activities of the direct air carriers, those contentions do not seem cogent.

CONCLUSIONS

Each of the three general exemptions discussed above was intended to serve a different specific purpose. The irregular-carrier exemption provided in Section 292.1 was designed to permit the performance of direct air transportation of persons and property complementary to that performed by the certificated carriers, this transportation including (*a*) incidental transport services furnished by "fixed-base" operators and (*b*) a "tramp" type of operation to meet discontinuous and sporadic demands not adapted to the kind of service rendered by the scheduled carriers. The cargo-carrier exemption provided in Section 292.5 was designed to enable certain all-freight airlines to remain in business, over specified routes, pending the disposition of their applications for certificates of public convenience and necessity. The freight-forwarder exemption provided in Section 292.6 was designed to make possible development of indirect air carriage with maximum flexibility on an experimental basis, the experience under the exemption being expected to provide data on which a permanent regulatory policy might be based.

The major effect of all of the general exemptions was, however, the same, namely, the creation of an area of air-carrier operation to enter which it was not necessary to prove that the proposed services were required by the "public convenience and necessity" — although in the case of the freight carriers the area was limited, with respect to each entrant, to specified routes and could be entered only by specified carriers. Exemption provisions with respect to other sections of Title IV have been of relatively minor significance, and the special requirements with respect to exempted carriers incorporated in the regulations have been largely for the purpose of obtaining information and for facilitating enforcement.

From the point of view of the Board's duty under the Act, its general exemption policy has been criticized both as too liberal and as too restrictive. Thus, it has been suggested that the cargo-carrier and freight-forwarder exemptions represented unwarranted abdications of the Board's statutory power; and, on the other hand, that the irregular-carrier exemption as interpreted by the Board has been so restrictive as to preclude operations the performance of which is required by the broad policy objectives of the Act. Moreover, it has been suggested that the Board has been inconsistent in according different treatment to the cargo carriers as compared with other noncertificated direct air carriers.

In fact, however, the exemption policy of the Board appears with one major exception to have been both internally consistent and in accordance with its statutory duty and its general past policy in administering the Act. This exception, which was the granting of a too broad and indefinite general exemption for "irregular" air carriage, itself represented no intentional departure from established policy, but rather a mistaken anticipation as to the effect of the action taken. Furthermore, this error has been at least in large part corrected by the termination of the general exemption for large irregular carriers effective May 20, 1949.

In determining the Board's statutory duty with respect to its exemption power, it must first of all be noted that the provisions of the Act which authorize such exemptions, and the legislative history which bears directly on these provisions, do not afford an adequate point of departure.[132] The decision whether to grant any exemption is by these provisions merely made conditional upon a finding as to the public interest; and

[132] Section 416(*b*) provides that the Board may exempt air carriers or classes of air carriers from all or part of Title IV of the Act (with certain specified exceptions) or requirements thereunder if it finds that enforcement of these provisions "is or would be an undue burden on such air carrier or class of air carriers by reason of the limited extent of, or unusual circumstances affecting the operations of such air carrier or class of air carriers and is not in the public interest." The exceptions have to do with the labor provisions contained in Subsection 401(*l*). Section 416(*b*) provides no authority for exemption from requirements with respect to maximum flying hours for pilots or copilots, and exemption from certain other labor provisions are subject to very restrictive limitations. Section 1(2) authorizes relief from any part of the Act (not only Title IV) for indirect air carriers "to the extent and for such periods as may be in the public interest."

there is in them no clue to the meaning to be attached to this phrase. It is of course true that Section 416(*b*) also requires a finding that enforcement is or would be an "undue burden" upon exempted carriers "by reason of the limited extent of, or unusual circumstances affecting," their operations. However, the absence of "undue burden" has never been cited by the Board as a reason for not granting an exemption where enforcement was deemed to be not in the public interest; on a great many occasions the required finding as to "undue burden" seems to have been purely formal;[133] and at any rate, since *some* "burden" must necessarily be involved in conformity to any provision of the Act, and *any* "burden" resulting from enforcement not in the public interest would appear to be "undue," the public interest remains the ruling consideration regardless of the legal necessity for a finding of "undue burden." The circumstances rendering enforcement not in the public interest would of course in themselves constitute "unusual circumstances affecting the operations" of the exempted carrier or carriers.

The legislative sponsors of Section 416(*b*) apparently envisaged the provision of aid to small air carriers where some hardship would result from enforcement of the Act. It might therefore be argued that the Board should have confined its exemption activities under Section 416(*b*) to the carrying out of this limited purpose; however, the Board has not in general interpreted the Act as involving such a limitation and it would seem unreasonable on this account to accuse it of thwarting the purposes of Congress if its exemption policy has been in accordance with the broad intent of the Act. Similarly, although Section 1(2) was primarily intended to provide for the relief of indirect air carriers from provisions "obviously inapplicable" to them, this direct intent has not prevented the Board from exempting these carriers under Section 1(2) from provisions not "obviously inapplicable," nor does it appear that this fact in itself would warrant a charge of contravention of legislative purposes.

Therefore, since the language of the exemption sections

[133] Examples are Orders Serial No. E–2012 and E–2013, September 24, 1948.

leaves very broad discretion to the Board in the administration of these provisions, the only definitive guide being the "public interest," and since the direct anticipations of the framers of the Act provide an unduly narrow standard by which to evaluate the performance of the Board, it is necessary to consider the broad intent of the Act in order to determine whether or not the Board has carried out its statutory duty. More particularly, in judging the Board's general exemptions from the certification requirement — which requirement was the major feature of the economic regulatory program incorporated in the Act — it is necessary to consider the purpose that this requirement was intended to serve.

As has been shown in Chapter III, the legislative history and the provisions of Title IV show that its primary purpose was the promotion of the financial welfare of the mail carriers. In this context, the certification requirement is essentially a device to enable the Board to protect the revenues of such existing services from proposed new competitive operations. However, as has been noted, the Board has recognized no obligation in the administration of this provision to reserve potential as distinguished from present business for carriers already in any particular field; indeed, its general policy has been to permit new competition except where the anticipated diversion of revenues from existing operations was great enough to endanger the profitability of the carrier rendering the existing service.

To perform its intended function, therefore, the certification requirement must be applicable to all new services that may result in appreciable diversion of existing revenues from the certificated carriers. The converse of this proposition establishes the Board's statutory duty with respect to the exemption power: no new services that may result in appreciable diversion of the existing revenues of certificated carriers should be exempted from the certification requirement. Apart from this, the Board appears to be free to exercise its own discretion. Since the certification requirement as interpreted by the Board is not designed to reserve future additional business for existing services, it is not necessary that this requirement be extended to proposed air-carrier operations designed to meet demands that might be in the future but are not at the time of decision met by carriers rendering existing services. In other words, the diversion that must be subject to measurement in a certification proceeding is diversion of past or present rather than future potential traffic.

Judged by this standard, the *intended* policy of the Board with respect to general exemptions is completely justified: the temporary exemption accorded to the freight carriers was to permit noncertificated entry into a market not yet served on any appreciable scale by the certificated carriers; the freight-forwarder exemption was to permit noncertificated entry on an experimental basis into a field with regard to which, at the very least, there was no adequately supported expectation that any diversion of revenues from certificated carriers would be involved; and the irregular-carrier exemption was to permit non-certificated entry into a type of air-transport operation that by its very nature would be noncompetitive with scheduled-air-carrier operations. The Board's treatment of the foreign air-transportation field might be thought to constitute an exception to the rule: the cargo operations of the exempted freight carriers and the passenger services of the irregular carriers were not, under the general exemption order, permitted to extend into the foreign market, and the argument adduced by the Board in support of this limitation seems to favor reservation of future markets for certificated carriers, at least under certain circumstances. However, by the later amendment of Section 292.1 to permit foreign air transportation of persons by small irregular carriers, and by the individual exemptions granted to large irregular carriers, the foreign field has actually been opened on a noncertificated basis to operations not involving appreciable diversion from certificated carriers.

The definitions of exempted operations set forth in the cargo-carrier and freight-forwarder regulations were effectively adapted to carrying out the purposes of the Board. The same cannot be said for the definition contained in the irregular-carrier regulation. As has been noted, the precise meaning of this definition was subject to legitimate differences of opinion, and the case-by-case method chosen by the Board to clarify it was ineffective in providing promptly a definition of such precision and unchallengeable legal status as to prevent violation of the intent of the regulation or to reduce the enforcement problem to manageable proportions. In addition, it is doubtful whether any general definition, however precise, based solely on frequency or time pattern of service would effectively limit *all* exempted operations to those not significantly competitive with certificated services.

In view of the foregoing considerations, the Board cannot justly be accused of discriminatory treatment of the noncertificated passenger carriers as compared with the exclusive cargo carriers in connection with its *general* exemption policy, despite the apparent contrast between the Board's response to situations in which the two types of carrier could not operate profitably under existing regulations pending disposition of their applications for certificates. It seems evident that no general exemption could have been devised which would have permitted the large irregular carriers to operate profitably and which, at the same time, would have defined their operations in such a way as to exclude all possibility of appreciable diversion from certificated services.

Similarly, the granting of individual temporary exemptions to the particular large irregular carriers that had applied for certificates would have gone beyond the precedent established by the freight-carrier exemption: since the operations of these carriers were such as necessarily to involve the possibility of appreciable diversion, authorization by exemption rather than certification would have been contrary to the intent of the Act. Thus, in rejecting the request of one large irregular carrier (Air America, Inc.) for such a temporary exemption, the Board expressly rejected the analogy drawn by the applicant with the freight-carrier exemption. Here the Board found that

the exemptions granted in the past by the Board and cited by Air America as being comparable to the exemption sought herein, differ from the exemption sought herein in numerous respects to which the Board accords substantial weight, particularly in their lesser threat of substantial diversion from existing facilities, and that no air coach exemption comparable to that sought therein has been granted by the Board.[134]

The appropriateness of the certification rather than the exemption procedure has been generally insisted upon by the Board in denying applications of coach carriers for individual temporary exemptions, and in this connection the Board has emphasized the "diversionary aspects" of the proposed services. In the Air America case, the applicant contended that such an exemption would provide experience on which a permanent decision with respect to its authorization could be based. The Board found that

the furnishing of data for a certification proceeding cannot generally be accepted as ground for summary grant of an exemption as distinguished from the grant of a temporary certificate, which certificate under the requirements of the Act is granted only upon a full hearing properly determining and weighing all other factors involved, including possible diversionary aspects.[135]

In a similar proceeding, the Board stated:

The importance and controversial nature of the issues involved, the scope of the operations proposed and their possible significant effect upon existing services, and the paucity of established facts at the present time lead unquestionably to the conclusion that enforcement of the Act is in the public interest.[136]

It has been suggested that such individual exemptions be granted subject to specified limits on the quantity of service to be rendered by the exempted carrier. However, the formulation of limits that would have made appreciable diversion from certificated services impossible would have involved a detailed measurement of prospective diversion such as is ordinarily and properly undertaken in a certification proceeding.

It is true that such a detailed measurement of diversion has

---

[134] Orders Serial No. E–2824, May 16, 1949, p. 2.
[135] *Ibid.*, p. 3.
[136] Orders Serial No. E–2543, March 7, 1949, p. 3.

not been found necessary in connection with those few large irregular carriers that are presently operating under individual temporary exemptions. But the "diversionary aspects" of the operations of these carriers are not comparable to those involved in the operations of the air-coach carriers that had applied for certification on heavily traveled routes.

The above reasoning does not, of course, exclude the possibility that the irregular coach carriers, or some of them, might be allowed to operate profitably under permanent or temporary certificates. In July 1951, there was still pending before the Board a proceeding in which applications by large irregular carriers for certification of transcontinental air-coach services were being considered.[137] All of the broad considerations adduced by the Board in support of its temporary certification of the freight carriers would obviously apply to the noncertificated low-rate passenger carriers. Indeed, it can be argued that the Board's need for unsubsidized "yardstick" operations is more urgent with respect to passenger than to freight carriage, and that the broadening of the passenger market promises more for the quantitative development of air transportation in the foreseeable future than does any probable degree of expansion in air-freight traffic. The effectiveness of low-rate, coach-type operation in providing additional passenger business on a profitable basis, at least on certain routes, appears to be demonstrated by recent ventures in this field by some of the certificated carriers.[138] These ventures, which were undertaken after noncertificated carriers had been for some time engaged in this type of operation, were regarded with caution by the Board, whose own prescription for increasing the profitability of certificated air-passenger services was apparently in the main along such lines as raising commercial rates and limiting competition by regulation or agreement.[139]

One large irregular carrier has in fact been granted a tem-

---

[137] Docket No. 3397 *et al.*

[138] See, for example, statements released by Northwest Airlines and quoted in part in *Aviation Week,* July 4, 1949, p. 54.

[139] Views of Board Chairman O'Connell which are relevant here may be found in his article "Legal Problems in Revising the Air Route Pattern," 15 *Journal of Air Law and Commerce* 397 (1948).

porary (five-year) certificate to engage in nonmail transportation on two routes wholly within the Territory of Hawaii.[140] In this case, the treatment of the diversion issue was similar to that in the Air Freight Case: it was noted (1) that during the period when the applicant carrier had been operating under the exemption the traffic of its certificated competitor had increased despite this competition and (2) that estimates of potential future traffic indicated that the traffic of the certificated carrier would continue at a high level even though the applicant were certificated.

This case is especially significant in two respects. In the first place, the disposition of the diversion issue in such a way as to permit the certification of the irregular carrier was largely made possible by the fact that it had already been operating at a frequency comparable to the services proposed in its certificate application. In the second place, this type of actual operation could only have been performed, and was in fact performed, in violation of the intended scope of the exemption provided in Section 292.1. The applicant carrier had been found by a District Court to be in violation of Section 401 of the Act because of the regularity of its services.[141]

These two points appear to apply generally to irregular carriers seeking certificates: any evidence that would justify the Board in certificating their services would have to come from prior operations comparable to those applied for, and any such operations would necessarily be in violation of the Board's intention with respect to 292.1. In addition to the fact that only by such operation could the necessary evidence as to diversion be supplied with airtight factual support (as in the Hawaiian case), in most cases the irregular carriers would be competing against existing certificated airlines for the right to operate the proposed services. In these instances, the choice of a "newcomer" to render air-coach services, even if they were found

---

[140] Intraterritorial Service in Hawaii, Orders Serial No. E–2496, November 29, 1948.

[141] Hawaiian Airlines, Ltd. v. Trans-Pacific Airlines, Ltd., 73 F. Supp. 68 (1947).

to be required by the "public convenience and necessity," would hardly occur unless the "newcomer" could point to a record of competent operation of services comparable to those applied for.

It seems safe to say that such carriers as the transcontinental irregulars could not have gained initial entry into the markets they served by obtaining certificates. Even apart from the substantial expense involved in carrying on legal activities necessary in a certification proceeding, which typically takes many months to be brought to decision, the apparently inevitable fate of air-coach proposals not backed by experience of actual operations is indicated by the Board's decision with respect to Atlantic Airlines, Inc., where a well-planned and well-financed venture was refused authorization on the grounds that the "risk" of diversion from certificated carriers would be too great and that the applicant's claim of ability to operate at relatively low cost had not been demonstrated.[142]

It may be concluded that if any of these carriers obtain certificates it will be as a result of having operated services that were outside the intended scope of Section 292.1, and therefore ultimately as a result of the Board's mistaken anticipation as to the practical effect of this regulation. For, as has been noted, it is all but certain that these services would not have been undertaken in any great number, and that any violations would have been so few as to have been expeditiously dealt with, if the regulation had been so written as definitely to outlaw them.

It is, of course, not at all certain that any of these carriers will obtain certificates. It appears that at least some of them will be unable to do so as a direct result of the very operations that were necessary to prove their case. Although, as has been noted, one irregular carrier that had operated beyond the intended scope of 292.1 did receive a certificate, the Board's opinion in this same proceeding made it plain that in most cases such operation will be an insuperable barrier to ultimate cer-

---

[142] Middle Atlantic Area Case, Orders Serial No. E–1211, February 19, 1948, pp. 89–90.

tification, regardless of any "worthy objective" that might have motivated the offending carrier.[143] In this case, the Board pointed out, extraordinary circumstances had prompted its action. Having concluded that "an additional carrier of persons and property, between the Hawaiian Islands is required by the public interest," the Board had to certificate the irregular applicant or forego this additional service, since there were no other applicants to render it. The Board concluded that the public need for this additional service was "sufficient to outweigh the disadvantage under which the only available applicant approaches us." [144] It is also significant that the existing certificated airline was the only carrier authorized to render scheduled air service in the Territory, and held a virtual monopoly of all interisland passenger travel; this circumstance was emphasized by the Board in its opinion, where it was also noted that the dependence of the Territory on the facilities of Hawaiian was "fraught with grave significance in the event of any catastrophe, the destruction of facilities from fire, strikes, war emergencies, or other disastrous events producing the disruption of air service." [145]

The already dim prospects for the further certification of large irregulars to engage in passenger transport were rendered dimmer by the Board's decision in the Additional Service to Puerto Rico Case.[146] Here, despite an admittedly conclusive showing that the primary need in this market was for additional passenger service of the low-cost type which had been provided by the irregular carriers, and despite the offers of such carriers to provide this service without participation in "first-class" carriage and without mail pay, the applications of the irregulars were denied. To meet the demonstrated need, Eastern Air Lines was granted a five-year certificate without restriction as to class of service to carry persons, property, and mail. In the Board's Opinion, this action is explained as follows:

[143] Intraterritorial Service in Hawaii, p. 10.
[144] *Ibid.,* p. 11.
[145] *Ibid.,* pp. 4–6.
[146] Orders Serial No. E–5075, January 23, 1951.

While other applicants in the case . . . propose services which will be directed to this . . . need [for low-cost transportation] only, the Board agrees with the Examiner that the carrier selected should be able to provide vigorous competition with Pan American [the carrier already certificated in this market] under an authorization commensurate in latitude with that held by Pan American.[147]

Under this reasoning, it will apparently be impossible for irregular applicants to secure certification as specialized coach operators in markets already occupied by carriers with orthodox certificates. The certification in this proceeding of a noncertificated cargo carrier for the transportation of property only does not, of course, mitigate the effect of the decision on the prospects of irregular applicants for passenger-service certificates.

In conclusion, then, the Board's one (unintended) departure from a proper and consistent general exemption policy in terms of its statutory duty has made possible the operation for a substantial period of time of low-rate air-passenger services not supported by mail payments. It has also in all probability been directly responsible for the operation of low-rate services by certificated airlines, since these services were undertaken only after independent experimentation had been made by the noncertificated carriers. It has enabled a "newcomer" to enter the field of regular air-passenger transportation in Hawaii. It may possibly have provided a foothold by means of which new companies may gain legitimate entry into the trunk-line air-passenger business in the United States or between this country and its outlying territories. At any rate, it is highly unlikely that any of these results would have materialized had the Board been wholly successful in carrying out the regulatory policy embodied in the Act. The absence of such independent experimentation in markets from which substantial revenues are derived by existing certificated air carriers and the virtual impossibility of entry by new enterprises into such markets are direct corollaries of the major purpose of Title IV of the Act.

[147] *Ibid.*, p. 4.

CHAPTER VI

CONTROL OF THE ALTERATION OF EXISTING COMPETITIVE RELATIONS

THE PROBLEM of the alteration of existing competitive relations among air carriers has been dealt with by the Board in connection with three types of decision, namely, those involving (1) the alteration of the physical characteristics of the service rendered by a carrier in competition with other air operations; (2) the choice of a carrier to operate new services in so far as this affects the relative competitive strength of the carriers; and (3) direct intercompany dealings such as mergers and agreements. Although competitive relations might also, of course, conceivably be altered by the formation of interlocking relations such as are subject to the Board's approval under Section 409(*a*) of the Act, the fact is that the Board has so construed this section as to preclude such alteration. In general, significant competition between the companies between which interlocking relations are passed on is regarded as a source of possible conflict of interests affecting the individual whose affiliations are involved, and such conflict is in itself deemed to affect adversely the public interest.

The direct control of relations between rates charged by competitive carriers, which has been one important channel through which regulatory agencies have influenced competitive relations among surface transportation facilities, has not yet figured to any important extent in the regulatory determination of the competitive pattern in air transport. Beginning in the latter part of 1948, the Board has devoted increasing attention to air passenger rates, partly as a result of the postwar financial reverses of the certificated carriers and partly as a result of the new low-rate services initiated by noncertificated carriers. Particular attention has been given to promotional rate devices such as family fares, and the like. Although in one case[1] the adverse effect of the proposed fares on carriers competitive with the chief proponent of the rates in question appears to have played some part in influencing the Board's decision that these rates would be unlawful, in general the ruling consideration both with respect to the limits placed on the applicability of reduced fares and with respect to fares actually found unlawful has so far been the anticipated effect on the profits of the proponent carriers themselves.[2] The Board's intervention in air-carrier freight-rate competition is discussed below.

Alteration of Physical Characteristics of Service

With regard to the first of these types of decision, the general policy followed by the Board appears to be precisely similar to that involved in the "entry" decisions discussed in the preceding chapter. The relevant guiding principles are well brought out in the United-Western Interchange of Equipment Case, where an improvement in through service between Los Angeles and points east of Salt Lake City was proposed to be effected through the interchange of sleeper planes at the latter point.[3] The Board maintained that a showing of inadequacy of service on the part of the carriers already rendering through transcontinental service to Los Angeles was not necessary to justify the approval of the proposed interchange,[4] and that the mere fact that a substantial amount of traffic would be diverted from one of these carriers was not "in itself sufficient to render the improvement inconsistent with, or adverse to, the public interest."[5] The Board stated that to prevent service improvements "solely as a protection to a particular air carrier" would be contrary to the policy of the Civil Aeronautics Act, in that it would retard rather than assure "the development of an ade-

[1] The Hawaiian Common Fares Case, Orders Serial No. E–3625, November 29, 1949.

[2] See, for example, Northern Consolidated Airlines' Passenger Excursion Fares, Orders Serial No. E–3958, March 3, 1950, and The Summer Excursion Fares Case, Orders Serial No. E–4037, April 3, 1950.

[3] United Air Lines Transport Corp. and Western Air Express Corp. — Interchange of Equipment, 1 C.A.A. 723 (1940).

[4] *Ibid.*, p. 731.

[5] *Ibid.*, pp. 730–731.

quate air transportation system in this country," and pointed out that the Act expressly directed the encouragement of co-ordination of air transportation.[6] The approval of the interchange agreement was based in part on a finding that it had not been established that a competitive carrier's "continued existence as a transcontinental operator" would be endangered, or that "unsound economic conditions in air transportation" would result;[7] thus the protection of the competitive carrier was not entirely rejected as a consideration relevant to the authorization of the improvement, but only such protection as did not appear necessary to its continued existence at substantially the same level of operations.

A similar principle is exemplified in another case where improved service was proposed to be effected between Memphis, Birmingham, and Atlanta through the removal of a restriction contained in the certificate originally authorizing operation by Eastern Air Lines, Inc., between Atlanta and Birmingham.[8] Despite the fact that some diversion of traffic from existing services was anticipated, the restriction was modified in such a way as to permit improved service between the three cities, the modification being justified on the ground that it would not jeopardize the operations of other carriers.[9]

An important group of cases involving the alteration of the physical characteristics of competitive services is that concerned with the proposed institution of nonstop operations between points previously served only on flights via one or more intermediate points. Under the Economic Regulations (Section 238.3) prescribed by the Board, a carrier is automati-

---

[6] *Ibid.*, p. 731.

[7] *Ibid.*

[8] Braniff Airways, Inc., *et al.*, Memphis–Oklahoma City–El Paso Service, 6 C.A.B. 169 (1944).

[9] *Ibid.*, p. 178. With respect to Delta Air Corporation, for the protection of whose revenues the restriction had been originally inserted, it was pointed out that the proportion of total passenger revenues affected would be now much less than at the time when the restriction was imposed, owing to the fact that in the interim new route awards had increased this carrier's total route mileage by about 70 percent (*ibid.*, p. 177). The relatively small proportion of the total traffic which would be subject to diversion was also referred to in the case of National Airlines, as indicating that the modification of the restriction would not "seriously affect" this carrier (*ibid.*, p. 178).

cally permitted to conduct nonstop operations between any two points on a route that it is authorized to serve twenty days after filing due notice with the Board, unless the Board notifies it within this period that "a direct straightline course between the points between which such service is to be operated appears to involve a substantial departure from the shortest course between such points as determined by the route described in the certificate," in which event the service cannot be inaugurated "unless and until the Board finds, upon application of the holder and after notice and public hearing, that the public interest would not be adversely affected by such service on account of such substantial departure."

As the Board itself has asserted, this regulation was designed to prevent the uncontrolled initiation of "new and unexpected competitive service which might cause substantial diversion from a large carrier or threaten the very existence of a small carrier" and in connection with which the "harm caused by diversion might be so great as to be contrary to the public interest." [10] Thus, automatic approval was provided for nonstop service not involving a substantial departure from the shortest course between the points concerned on the route described in the certificate because it was thought that under those circumstances "no new or unexpected competitive situations of substance would or could arise"; [11] and the requirement of a showing that a nonstop service that did involve such a substantial departure would not adversely affect the public interest may be interpreted as a safeguard against undue diversion of traffic from carriers rendering competitive services.

In the nonstop cases, the measure of undue diversion appears to be the same as that applied in other decisions involving service improvements and also in those concerned with entry. For example, in the Detroit–St. Louis Nonstop Case, the Board approved the proposed through service on the ground that there was no showing in the record that "the extent of the traffic diversion which might result would be so great as seriously to

---

[10] Transcontinental and Western Air, Inc., Detroit–St. Louis Nonstop Service, 6 C.A.B. 471, 476 (1945).
[11] *Ibid.*

jeopardize the ability of American to render its service to the public." [12]

Choice of Carrier

The choice of a carrier for the operation of a new route involves the alteration of existing competitive relations in that the award of the route may (1) give the chosen carrier an advantage with respect to control over the routing of long-haul traffic originating at or destined to points on the new route, (2) improve its over-all financial position, or (3) by the mere fact of expansion of its operations add to its prestige with the traveling public, thus tending to increase consumer preference for all its services as compared with those of competing airlines.

As to the impact on competitive companies of granting new routes involving control of additional long-haul traffic, it may again be said that the effect of such action on the over-all profitability of the competitive carriers at their existing level of operation is a determining factor in the eyes of the Board. For example, the inclusion of Tulsa and Oklahoma City on the transcontinental route of American Airlines rather than that of Transcontinental and Western Air was in part justified on the ground that "the competitive disadvantage which will result to TWA from the addition of Tulsa and Oklahoma City to American's transcontinental route is not of such magnitude as to affect seriously its financial position or to impair its ability to render service to the public." [13]

A more important aspect of the Board's consideration of the effect of carrier choice in existing competitive relations, however, is not primarily concerned with the extent of traffic diver-

---

[12] *Ibid.,* p. 479.

[13] Braniff Airways, Inc., *et al.,* Memphis–Oklahoma City–El Paso Service, p. 173. TWA had contended "that denial of its application would constitute a serious threat to its transcontinental service and further weaken its competitive position among the three transcontinental carriers;" it had argued that it was "the smallest of the transcontinental carriers, and that through its inability to control traffic originations it is unable to obtain its share of through traffic." The Board indicated that recent additions of new points to the TWA system should be taken into consideration in evaluating the effect on its competitive position involved in the authorization of American to serve Tulsa and Oklahoma City.

sion from the carrier or carriers not chosen to operate the new service, but rather with the positive effect of the award on the over-all competitive strength of the chosen carrier itself, through improvement of its strategic traffic position or its general financial status. This factor has been important in connection with the award of routes to small and weak (i.e., relatively unprofitable) carriers in preference to larger and more profitable companies.

To justify such an award in the Denver–Kansas City case, where considerations of minimum operating cost and maximum through service would have indicated the choice of a larger carrier, the Board has appealed to the provisions of the Civil Aeronautics Act directing it to consider "the development of sound economic conditions in the industry, and the preservation of 'competition to the extent necessary to assure the sound development of an air transportation system properly adapted to the needs of the commerce of the United States.' " [14] To rely solely on cost and service as criteria in the choice of carrier, the Board asserted, would result in awarding all new routes to the larger companies, thus "throttling forever the growth of the smaller carriers." It interpreted the above-cited provisions of the Act as designed expressly to prevent such a result.[15] Although certain other factors were referred to as favoring the choice of the smaller carrier (Continental) in this particular case, the ruling consideration was the fact that this award would "strengthen that carrier by providing it with an additional traffic center of importance" and would "aid it in attaining self-sufficiency," the latter effect resulting in part from enabling it "to spread its overhead costs over an additional number of miles and passenger revenues." [16]

---

[14] Continental Air Lines, Inc., *et al.*, Denver–Kansas City Service, 4 C.A.B. 1, 18 (1942).

[15] *Ibid.*

[16] *Ibid.* The other factors referred to were (1) the reduction of diversion of traffic from other carriers to a minimum (the new route being principally competitive with another route already operated by Continental), (2) service advantages to be derived from the operation of the new route "without the need of giving primary consideration to transcontinental requirements," and (3) the related consideration that maximum development of local traffic could be expected by the local carrier, especially "in view of the fact that the Denver--

The Board has often held that considerations of cost and service are not to be regarded as "controlling" factors in the choice of carrier, and this position seems generally to be based on the same reasoning as that found in the Denver–Kansas City case discussed above, namely, that sole reliance on these factors would interfere with the development of sound economic conditions in air transport and the maintenance of competition as required by the Act.[17]

Moreover, other particular cases in which the principle of "sound economic conditions" has been relied on as a criterion of choice among carriers embody an interpretation of this principle which is precisely similar to that found in the Denver–Kansas City case, namely, that it requires the strengthening of small and weak carriers by expanding their operations and improving their strategic position with regard to the control of traffic. For example, in the Atlantic Seaboard case, the Board pointed out that the selection of National Airlines to operate an additional service between New York and Florida "would not only strengthen a small carrier but would also provide it with access to important traffic producing centers of the North and thus enable it to carry its own through traffic from the Florida area and to share in the through traffic from the northern area," and that this result would be "in accord with the specific statutory duty imposed upon the Board to regard, as in accordance with the public convenience and necessity, the encouragement and development of a sound air transportation system."[18]

In several such cases, the fact that the authorization of another carrier would have resulted in undue diversion of traffic from the one ultimately chosen was also an important con-

---

Kansas City route will represent its best route from the standpoint of traffic carried" (p. 19).

[17] See, for example, Additional Service to Latin America, 6 C.A.B. 857, 900 (1946).

[18] Colonial Airlines, Inc., *et al.*, Atlantic Seaboard Operation, 4 C.A.B. 552, 560 (1944). See also Mid-Continent Airlines, Inc., *et al.*, Kansas City–Tulsa–New Orleans Service, 6 C.A.B. 253 (1945); Colonial Airlines, Inc., *et al.*, Washington-Ottawa-Montreal Service, 6 C.A.B. 481 (1945); Western Air Lines, Inc., *et al.*, Denver–Los Angeles Service, 6 C.A.B. 199 (1944).

sideration; in this connection, it has been held that such diversion itself would be contrary to the development of sound economic conditions in air transport and the maintenance of competition as required by the statute.[19] In so far as the Board's choice of the smaller carrier in these cases was based on the desirability of protecting this carrier in the performance of its existing services, it will be seen that the principle involved is the same as that which has been found to be controlling in the "entry" cases. However, it seems clear that this principle does not provide a sufficient interpretation for the Board's decisions in these cases; there is also involved the desirability of positively promoting the financial welfare of the smaller carriers, i.e., increasing rather than merely maintaining their over-all profitability. Again, it may be said that the Board's policy does not seem to be based on its conception of its legal obligation to the carriers in connection with the subsidization policy, but rather on its broader responsibility to promote "sound economic conditions" in the industry, interpreted as implying a steady progress toward and maintenance of economic self-sufficiency on the part of each individual carrier without any substantial intermediate curtailment of any of its existing operations.

As to the significance of this policy for the determination of competitive relations among air carriers, it is evident that the relative competitive strength of the smaller or weaker carriers is thereby made greater than it would be if considerations of efficiency were allowed to be controlling. Through the competitive advantages received as a result of the control over the routing of additional traffic and the "advertising value" of the new routes in increasing the prestige of the carrier in the minds of consumers, the distribution of output among the firms in any given market tends to be altered in favor of the smaller carriers, and this fact in itself further enhances their competitive position.

An additional factor which has tended to strengthen the position of the smaller carriers is the Board's recognition of "pri-

---

[19] On this point, see Western Air Lines, Inc., *et al.*, Denver–Los Angeles Service, pp. 210–211.

mary loyalty" as a pertinent consideration in regard to choice of carrier.[20] This factor has played some part in the authorization of "regional" rather than longer-haul (i.e., international or transcontinental) companies to operate new routes designed primarily to accommodate "local" traffic (i.e., traffic originating and terminating on the new route itself),[21] and has been of greater importance in connection with the selection of "local" carriers (carriers specializing in short-haul operations serving relatively small population centers) to operate "feeder" routes.[22] However, since it seems reasonable to suppose that operation of such routes by carriers primarily interested in their development would at least to some extent result in the provision of better service than otherwise, it cannot be said that the "primary loyalty" principle in itself has necessarily altered the distribution of traffic among carriers from that which would have been dictated by considerations of maximum efficiency.

The relative competitive strength of the smaller carriers is presumably also enhanced in so far as the award of new routes to large and comparatively powerful companies is denied because of their superior competitive strength. Although the precise nature of the principle involved is not entirely clear, this factor seems to have been important in the denial of an application made by American Airlines, the largest United States domestic air carrier, which would have enabled it to operate

[20] In its general treatment of factors considered in choice of carrier in Additional Service to Latin America, p. 900, the Board discussed this point as follows: "It must appear that the applicant will have every possible incentive to develop to the maximum the potential market for air transportation. It is always pertinent to inquire where lies the primary loyalty of the enterprise and to determine whether there is any conflict between that primary loyalty and the full development of the air transportation market. The importance of air transportation to the American public . . . makes it impossible to overemphasize the importance of this factor in selecting the particular enterprise to be entrusted with the task of developing a new air transportation service."

[21] See, for example, Continental Air Lines, Inc., *et al.*, Denver–Kansas City Service, p. 19; Braniff Airways, Inc., *et al.*, Memphis–Oklahoma City–El Paso Service, pp. 180–181; Hawaiian Airlines, Ltd., *et al.*, Hawaiian Case, 7 C.A.B. 83, 104 (1946); New England Case, 7 C.A.B. 27, 35 (1946).

[22] See, for example, The Florida Case, 6 C.A.B. 765, 786 (1946); Service in the Rocky Mountain States Area, 6 C.A.B. 695, 736–737 (1946); New England Case, pp. 39–40.

single-carrier services between Miami and Detroit, Chicago, and New York.[23] In the Hawaiian Case, although it is very doubtful whether air service by a steamship company would have been authorized in any event, the Board based its denial of Matson's application at least in part on the "undesirable competitive advantage" that this company would have had as compared with the existing air carrier, Pan American.

The Board's statement in this connection is particularly interesting in its indication that a desirable degree of competition must stop short of the displacement of existing carriers:

While competition is to be authorized when required by the public interest, it must be sound competition which will not cause a deterioration in service to the public or impede the development of an adequate system of air transportation. Nor should competition merely result in the substitution of another air carrier by a process of traffic starvation. Because of its dominant position Matson will continue to carry substantially all the steamship traffic in the postwar period. This, together with authorization to engage in air transportation, would give it an undesirable competitive advantage over Pan American. Matson's domination of surface freight transportation between the Mainland and Hawaii would permit it to exercise a persuasive influence over its freight consignors and consignees with respect to air passengers traveling for or on their behalf. The same is true with respect to air cargo. The record shows that Matson has invested several million dollars in Hawaii in hotel facilities and recreational accommodations designed to stimulate vacation traffic; and that it annually spends thousands of dollars with travel agencies and tourist bureaus in advertising Hawaii as a world resort. By reason of its ownership of the two outstanding and most famous resort hotels . . . of the islands, Matson would be in a position to and would naturally favor its own passengers in reservations and service at these hotels. These bargaining influences and advantages which Matson would have over Pan American would not inure to any other applicant in the proceeding.[24]

With respect to the award of the Anchorage-Juneau route in the Pacific Case, the superior competitive strength of the

[23] Eastern Air Lines, Inc., *et al.*, Great Lakes to Florida Service, 6 C.A.B. 429, 438 (1945).

[24] Hawaiian Airlines, Ltd., *et al.*, Hawaiian Case, p. 108.

applicant seems clearly to have been the decisive factor in its rejection in favor of a smaller carrier, despite the evident advantages of the additional through service that could have been provided by the rejected company. Here, as in the Hawaiian Case, the measures by which the competitive strength of the applicant was found to be excessive were the extent and importance of the anticipated traffic diversion from existing carriers that would have resulted from its authorization.[25]

Although in this case, as well as in the Great Lakes to Florida decision, the size of the rejected company as compared with others in the same broad area (Alaska or the United States) was mentioned as if relevant to the issue of carrier choice, the evidence seems insufficient to show that the Board in any of these cases was motivated by any desire to equalize the size of air-transport companies in any area as an end in itself, or by any principle other than that of protecting the financial welfare of the carriers already in the field.[26] Indeed, the Board has explicitly rejected the equalization of the size or competitive strength of the carriers subject to its jurisdiction as a policy objective. This was done in response to a contention by an applicant carrier that it should be awarded a particular new route, which would have given it "access to more of the larger air traffic markets of the country," in order to equalize its competitive position as compared with larger carriers paralleling some of the most important routes on its existing system.[27] Again, the same position was taken by the Board in minimizing the importance of evidence (submitted by an applicant carrier in support of its bid to operate a new route) designed to demonstrate the relative weakness of the applicant with regard to control of traffic, as shown by the smaller amount of traffic originating at points on its routes, the smaller number of cities served, and the larger percentage of its routes paralleled by comparable carriers.[28]

[25] Northwest Airlines, Inc., *et al.,* Pacific Case, 7 C.A.B. 209, 235–236 (1946).
[26] *Ibid.,* pp. 234–235.
[27] Northwest Airlines, Inc., *et al.,* Chicago–Milwaukee–New York Service, 6 C.A.B. 217, 224 (1944).
[28] *Ibid.,* pp. 237–238.

Mergers and Acquisitions of Control

Such direct intercompany transactions as mergers and acquisitions of control affect existing competitive relations in several ways. First, if the carriers concerned have been competitive with each other, such a transaction will eliminate this competition, that is, will involve the "exit" of one firm from each of the markets in which the two companies were competing. Second, if the transaction gives the acquiring carrier direct access to points originating traffic that ultimately travels over its existing routes, or enables it to give through one-carrier service to traffic destined for points on the routes of the acquired carrier, the competitive position of the acquiring company on its existing routes is thereby strengthened. Third, the competitive relations between the firms in the markets formerly served by the acquired carrier will be affected in so far as the larger carrier substituted for the acquired company possesses a greater degree of strategic traffic control, is capable of more efficient service, or possesses greater prestige in the minds of the consuming public. Fourth, the mere enlargement of the operations of the acquiring carrier may enhance its competitive position in some or all of the markets that it serves by improving its general finances, increasing consumer preference for its services, or both.[29]

It will be observed that the "substitution" of the larger carrier mentioned above could equally well be treated as a case of "entry" of a new carrier into the field, inasmuch as the identity of the firm concerned has changed. This point serves to bring out the relative unimportance of the distinction between the entry problem and the problem of the alteration of existing competitive relations, since the analysis of the transaction from the point of view of its effect on the competitive pattern will in no way be affected by its classification as "entry" or non-"entry."

---

[29] The distinction between the "acquired" and the "acquiring" carrier is, of course, of no theoretical importance; it has been used for the sake of convenience in exposition and to give some degree of concreteness to the discussion.

The first type of competitive effect enumerated above has been considered by the Board primarily in connection with testing the consistency of proposed transactions with the first proviso contained in Section 408(*b*) of the Civil Aeronautics Act, in which the Board is prohibited from approving "any consolidation, merger, purchase, lease, operating contract, or acquisition of control which would result in creating a monopoly or monopolies and thereby restrain competition or jeopardize another air carrier not a party to the consolidation, merger, purchase, lease, operating contract, or acquisition of control." Subject to this requirement, the Board is directed to approve such transactions as it shall not find inconsistent with the public interest, "upon such terms and conditions as it shall find to be just and reasonable and with such modifications as it may prescribe."

With regard to transactions involving the acquisition of an air carrier by a surface carrier, there is an additional requirement that the Board find that they "will promote the public interest by enabling such carrier other than an air carrier to use aircraft to public advantage in its operation and will not restrain competition." As originally interpreted by the Board, this latter requirement would have applied only to the acquisition by a surface carrier of an air carrier already operating as such; under this interpretation, the proviso would presumably have been aimed at the prevention of the elimination of existing competition between air and surface carriers.[30] However, this interpretation was subsequently reversed by the United States Circuit Court of Appeals for the Second Circuit.[31] In this decision, the Court appeared to hold that the intent of Congress was to prevent the entrance of surface carriers into the air-transport business through subsidiary enterprises (except in the restricted sphere indicated by the proviso) regardless of whether these enterprises had or had not previously engaged in air transportation. As the Board pointed out, under this con-

---

[30] American Export Airlines, Inc., Trans-Atlantic Service, 2 C.A.B. 16, 46–47 (1940).

[31] Pan American Airways Company *v.* C.A.B. and American Export Airlines, Inc., 121 F. (2d) 810 (C.C.A. 2nd, 1941).

struction of the statute there is no valid basis for distinguishing the inauguration of air-transport operation by a surface carrier through a subsidiary from the inauguration of such operation directly by the surface carrier itself, so far as the general intent of Congress is concerned, although the proviso would, of course, be directed primarily at the former type of transaction.[32] Under this interpretation, the proviso would be aimed not only at preventing the elimination of existing competition between air and surface carriers, but also at excluding surface carriers in general from participating in air-transport operations, except in a restricted sphere, regardless of the effect of this participation on the competitive position of the surface carrier with respect to air carriers. Accepting the position thus dictated by the Circuit Court of Appeals, the Board until recently held that the restrictive proviso was a legal condition governing proceedings under Section 401 as well as under Section 408. Although failure to conform to the proviso was never invoked as a reason for the denial of a certificate to a surface carrier for a proposed air service, all such applications were in fact denied. In March 1947 the Board reversed its former position and declared that the proviso was not a legal condition governing proceedings under Section 401.[33] Nevertheless, it was indicated that the policy embodied in Section 408 was still to be "considered as one of the standards which guides the Board in determining whether the public convenience and necessity requires the issuance of a certificate to a surface-carrier applicant."[34] Thus the Board even now holds that it "has the power and the duty in a proceeding under Section 401 to limit the entry of a surface carrier into air transportation to operations which would enable such surface carrier to use aircraft to public advantage in its surface transport operation unless the record of the case were to reveal that the public interest required service by a surface carrier regardless of the circumstance that it was a surface carrier."[35] Under a similar interpretation of

[32] American Export Lines, Control of American Export Airlines, 3 C.A.B. 619, 624–625 (1942).

[33] American President Lines, *et al.*, Petition, 7 C.A.B. 799 (1947).

[34] *Ibid.*, p. 802.

[35] *Ibid.*, p. 804.

similar provisions of the Motor Carrier Act, the Interstate Commerce Commission has limited its certification of property motor-carrier operations by rail carriers almost entirely to services auxiliary or supplemental to rail service.[36]

The absence of the first type of competitive effect has in some instances been cited by the Board in support of a finding that a proposed transaction is not in contravention of the first proviso. For example, in the Western-Inland acquisition case, the Board stated:

There is no evidence in the record which would lead to the conclusion that the acquisition of Inland by Western would result in the creation of a monopoly and thereby restrain competition or jeopardize another carrier not a party to the acquisition. Inland and Western do not now compete with each other and are scarcely complementary except for their junction at Great Falls. They serve different areas so that the general public will not be subjected to less air service than at the present nor subjected to monopoly through the elimination of competitive services.[37]

However, the mere fact that a transaction *will* result in the elimination of competition between the participant carriers is insufficient to render it inconsistent with the proviso. There have been many cases in which the Board has approved transactions that have involved the exit of one firm from one or more markets; statements made in connection with these cases would seem to indicate that the elimination of competition between the participant carriers could not be in violation of the proviso where genuinely substitutable services in the affected markets would continue to be provided by nonparticipant carriers, or where the market concerned did not appear capable of supporting parallel services. Thus, in the Marine Airways–Alaska Air Transport case, the Board adjudged a proposed con-

---

[36] *Annual Report* of the Interstate Commerce Commission, 1946, p. 44.

[37] Western Air Lines, Inc., Acquisition of Inland Air Lines, Inc., 4 C.A.B. 654, 663 (1944). Similar statements may be found in American Airlines, Inc., Control of American Export Airlines, Inc., 6 C.A.B. 371, 379 (1945) and United Air Lines, Operation of Catalina Air Transport, 6 C.A.B. 1041, 1046 (1946). In the latter case, it was pointed out that "Catalina was not a competitor for traffic with any other air carrier."

solidation to be consistent with the proviso despite its elimination of certain parallel services on the ground that because "other air carriers [had] . . . been operating, and [would] . . . continue to operate" throughout the region served by the consolidating carriers, "the company resulting from the proposed merger . . . will not be able to control air transport generally in that region." In the same case, the Board justified the elimination of competing service on a route where no other carrier was expected to conduct parallel operations by pointing out that in this market the traffic had not been and apparently would not be in the future sufficient to support parallel services.[38]

The former position with regard to the exit of a competing firm is exemplified in the Wien-Ferguson, Wien-Mirow, and TWA-Marquette acquisition cases.[39] In the first of these cases, the Board pointed out that all the points which had been served by both of the participant carriers were also served by other companies, which would continue to offer competitive service.[40] In the second, a transaction that was expected to eliminate a substantial amount of competitive service and to make the consolidated carrier the largest in the immediate (Seward Peninsula) area was nevertheless approved because the "substantial volume of business" handled by other lines in this area was taken to show that the consolidated operator would "continue to receive real competition" there; hence it was held that "the proposed acquisition would not result in giving Wien Alaska Airlines the degree of control of air transportation or some phase thereof within a particular section of the country, necessary to constitute a monopoly therein." [41] Again, in finding the acquisition of Marquette Airlines by TWA not inconsistent with the proviso, the Board relied on a showing that the

[38] Marine Airways, Alaska Transport, Inc., Consolidation, 3 C.A.B. 315, 319 (1942).

[39] Acquisition of Ferguson Airways, Inc., by Wien Alaska Airlines, Inc., 7 C.A.B. 769 (1947); Wien Alaska Airlines, Inc., Sigurd Wien, and Mirow Air Service, Acquisition of Mirow Air Service, 3 C.A.B. 207 (1941); Acquisition of Marquette by TWA, 2 C.A.B. 1 (1940).

[40] Acquisition of Ferguson Airways, Inc., by Wien Alaska Airlines, Inc., pp. 773–774.

[41] Wien Alaska Airlines, Inc., Acquisition of Mirow Air Service, p. 213.

acquiring carrier would "have competition from at least one of its two transcontinental competitors at every point on the [Marquette] route," and that where it would be the only carrier providing service between two specified points on this route, Marquette was then rendering a single-carrier service. In view of this showing, the Board found that the transaction would not give TWA "the degree of control of air transportation or some phase thereof within a particular section of the country, necessary to constitute a monopoly therein." [42]

These decisions, involving as they do the approval by the Board of the exit of carriers from certain markets where genuine competition would continue to be provided by companies not participating in the transaction at issue, or where traffic was deemed inadequate to provide the desired degree of economic self-sufficiency for more than one carrier, may be interpreted as embodying an exit policy on the part of the Board similar to but not entirely symmetrical with its entry policy. There is implied the same attribution of positive value to the availability of genuinely substitutable services in all markets where this is consistent with the maintenance of profitable operations by carriers serving such markets. However, since the Board has approved the elimination of some competitive services that had been profitably carried on, the exit policy exemplified in these opinions would not be entirely symmetrical with the entry policy outlined in the preceding chapter. It is interesting to note that in view of these precedents the action finally taken in the much-discussed North Atlantic route transfer case[43] probably does not represent a reversal in policy, despite the fact that the original decision of the Board, adopted by a vote of three to two, was overruled by the President. The maintenance of two-carrier United States-flag service in the

---

[42] Acquisition of Marquette by TWA, p. 9. Here a table is presented showing that all the cities on the Marquette route would continue to be served by either American or United (in addition to TWA) should the proposed acquisition be approved. It is also shown that with the single exception of Dayton, which before the merger was served by both TWA and Marquette, the acquisition would not result in a reduction of the total number of carriers serving any city, but merely in the substitution of TWA for Marquette.

[43] Orders Serial No. E–4410, July 10, 1950.

principal markets affected by the acquisition by Pan American of the assets of American Overseas was assured by the accompanying authorizations for new service that were specified by the President in his letter to the Board directing approval of the acquisition.[44]

It will have been noted that in considering the consistency of any transaction with the first proviso in Section 408(*b*) the Board has been concerned primarily with the "degree of control of air transportation or some phase thereof" in a particular area that would be enjoyed by the consolidated carrier, and, in particular, in ascertaining whether the degree of control so attained would be so great as to constitute a monopoly. The "degree-of-control" doctrine of monopoly was first developed by the Board in the United-Western interchange case, in refutation of a contention by an intervening carrier that a proposed interchange agreement would "give United a virtual monopoly of all west coast business." [45] In this case, the Board declared that a proper interpretation of the proviso (i.e., an interpretation that would be internally consistent and give meaning to every word contained in the statutory text) requires that the term "monopoly" in this context be defined as a "particular degree of control of air transportation, or any phase thereof, in any territory or section of the country." [46] The question of precisely what "degree of control" would constitute a monopoly did not here arise; since the proposed interchange agreement was found to involve *no* additional control over air transport by a particular carrier, it was held that no monopoly would be created, and therefore the proviso was declared to be "without effect." [47] The other decisions discussed above seem to imply that that "degree of control" which would eliminate all genuinely substitutable air-transport service would constitute a monopoly; however, since there has been no instance in which a proposed transaction has been disapproved on account of prospective violation of the proviso, it is impossible to discover

----

[44] *Ibid.*, pp. 6–7.

[45] United Airlines Transport Corporation and Western Air Express Corporation, Interchange of Equipment, 1 C.A.A. 723, 728 (1940).

[46] *Ibid.*, pp. 733–734.

[47] *Ibid.*, p. 737.

just what degree of substitutability between the remaining services must obtain in order that the elimination of a firm from the market shall not create a monopoly.

Denials of authorization for transactions under Section 408 have always been based on findings of general inconsistency with the public interest. In these cases, the elimination of competition between the participant carriers has usually been of relatively minor importance. However, in the United-Western acquisition case considerable attention was devoted to this point; here the elimination of the acquired carrier as an independent operator was mentioned as one of the two general considerations leading the Board to conclude that the proposed acquisition was not consistent with the public interest.[48]

The Board indicated that the elimination of the acquired carrier as an independent operator would be contrary to the public interest in two apparently distinct, though related, respects: (1) the maximum development of local north-south service in the western region would be prevented, in that the carrier to be acquired could be expected, "especially under competitive stimulus," to promote this service more actively than would the transcontinental company that proposed to acquire it;[49] and (2) the elimination of this carrier would be "undesirable at this stage in the development of a properly balanced system of air transportation."[50]

Although the major relevance of the "balanced-system" concept in this case appears to be in connection with the relative competitive position of the transcontinental carriers (this aspect of the case will be discussed below), it seems also to be directly pertinent to the question of the prospective elimination of competition between the participant carriers. That is, the proposed acquisition was regarded as prejudicial to the development of a "balanced system" in the local (north-south) western markets in which the two participant carriers were the only competitors, as well as with regard to the east-west serv-

---

[48] United Airlines Transport Corporation, Acquisition of Western Air Express Corporation, 1 C.A.A. 739, 750 (1940).

[49] *Ibid.*, p. 747.

[50] *Ibid.*

ices. The prospective elimination of competition between the participant carriers was apparently in itself in part responsible for the Board's disapproval; the "balanced-system" concept seems to involve the maintenance of some competition (i.e., the provision of genuinely substitutable services by different firms) in all markets where these have proved in the past to be capable of the required degree of self-support, and would imply an exit policy similar to that apparently embodied in the cases previously discussed in connection with the proviso.

There is some indication that the elimination of competition between United and Western, as well as the elimination of the local carrier as such, was regarded as undesirable because of its direct effect on the maximum development of air transport in the local market, since the Board did refer, if only incidentally, to the "competitive stimulus" arising from the two-carrier service as a factor in promoting the maximum development of the local service. Thus, it is suggested that the Board's disapproval of the elimination of competition between participant carriers when this would involve suppressing completely the availability of genuinely substitutable air-transport operation in a market capable of supporting such services was based in part of the desirability of maintaining such services because of the stimulus afforded to competitive effort. Such a position would clearly be similar to that adopted by the Board in connection with new-route authorizations.

It may here be noted that in so far as the preservation of genuinely substitutable services is considered as desirable in itself, there is a possible conflict between the criteria used by the Board in passing on acquisitions, etc., and those indicated by maximum efficiency. However, in this particular case, the Board explicitly declared that "the evidence fails to convince us that United could be expected to furnish a more effective or economical local service than that now provided by Western," [51] and the other service and cost advantages claimed for the acquisition as such were held to be of small quantitative significance.[52]

[51] *Ibid.*
[52] *Ibid.*, p. 744.

Of particular importance in the United-Western acquisition case was the effect of the proposed transaction on the competitive relations between the transcontinental carriers through the improvement of the acquiring company's strategic traffic position with respect to transcontinental and other east-west traffic in the western region. As the Board noted, the acquisition of Western would have given United "direct access to the entire Pacific coast area for the origination of transcontinental traffic"; United would have had "direct transcontinental routes to all four major West coast metropolitan areas, whereas no other air carrier has direct entry to more than two of such areas. This advantage," the Board continued, "is particularly significant in view of the fact that United operates the only north and south route on the Pacific coast." [53]

In addition to extending United's already superior contact with traffic centers on the Pacific coast, the Board noted, the acquisition would have extended "United's control over western traffic, and its advantage with respect thereto, eastward to the Rocky Mountains," thus effecting an "increase in the size and control of United in this large area" which "would adversely affect the existing competitive opportunities for western business and would greatly increase United's advantage with respect to such business." In support of this view, the Board pointed out: (1) that the route mileage of United in the area west of the Rockies, which already amounted to 3,068, would be increased by the addition of the Western system to 4,147, as compared with a total of 2,775 operated by American, Northwest, and TWA; (2) that the combined population of cities in this area served by United, which was already much larger than that served by American, Northwest, or TWA, would become almost as large as the combined total served by all three of these lines; (3) that the addition of Western's to United's traffic in the Los Angeles region would result in the latter company's carrying 72 percent of the total passenger traffic originating in or destined for this region, and 50 percent of the air mail; and (4) that United would as a result of the acquisition

[53] *Ibid.,* p. 745.

become the only carrier serving San Diego and Salt Lake City.[54]

This increase in the relative degree of control over traffic in the western region possessed by one carrier, the Board found, would be contrary to the public interest as defined in the Act because it would "seriously endanger the development of a properly balanced air-transportation system in this region." A "reasonably balanced system of air transportation in every section of the country" was held to be required by the Act, in that such a system alone would, at least "at the present state of the industry's development," best serve to maintain the "state of *competition* among air carriers *to the extent required by the sound development of the industry*," and thus "safeguard an industry of vital importance to the commercial and defense interests of the Nation against the evils of unrestrained competition on the one hand, and the consequences of monopolistic control on the other." In further explanation of its position, the Board declared that "size alone cannot be said to be the determining factor in judging a carrier's conformity to such a balanced system"; on the contrary, it is the relative degree of control over traffic in any region that is the pertinent consideration.[55]

What the "determining factor" with regard to "conformity to such a balanced system" actually is, however, is not entirely clear. It could of course be argued that the concept of the "balanced system" involves essentially the limitation of the proportion of traffic served by any one carrier in any given "region" (defined in some more or less arbitrary manner) to a predetermined percentage of the total. But in view of the fact that the Board has based the case for the balanced system on its value in the maintenance of competition, and has generally adopted the idea that competition means the availability of genuinely substitutable services, this interpretation would seem to be of questionable validity. Furthermore, it will be recalled that the Board specifically related its discussion of

[54] *Ibid.*, p. 746.
[55] *Ibid.*, pp. 749–50.

the actual increase in traffic control to be obtained by United to the adverse effect that this increase would have had on the "existing competitive opportunities for western business" and to the enhancement "of United's advantage with respect to such business."[56] Thus it would appear that the degree of control of traffic which is deemed consistent with the "balanced system" is to be judged not by reference to some predetermined percentage of the total traffic in a geographical area, but in the light of its effect on the competitive relations between carriers offering genuinely substitutable services in the markets affected by the transaction that is being passed on.

There are three other notable decisions in which the competitive position to be attained by the acquiring carrier played an important part, and which throw additional light on the real implications of the "balanced-system" concept. In the first of these decisions, involving the acquisition of a small Alaskan carrier by the largest air-transport company in that Territory (in point of route mileage and total revenues), the Board refused to approve the transaction on the ground that it "would further increase that carrier's [i.e., the acquiring carrier's] overwhelming competitive advantage in the territory to such an extent as to make the acquisition inconsistent with the public interest by precluding the development of a proper competitive balance."[57] As in the United-Western acquisition case, the Board pointed out that the acquiring carrier (in this case, Alaska Airlines) was already operating on routes the total mileage of which was much larger than that operated by any other carrier in the territory served by it, and indicated that this superiority in route mileage had given it an "overwhelming competitive position" in this territory.[58] The Board brought out the importance of the competitive relations between Alaska Airlines and each of its two nearest competitors by noting the

<hr>

[56] *Ibid.*, p. 746.

[57] Acquisition of Cordova Air Service, Inc., by Alaska Airlines, Inc., 4 C.A.B. 708, 712 (1944).

[58] The total regular route miles which Alaska Airlines was authorized to serve, including those added to its system by the acquisition of three relatively small carriers, amounted to 6,140, as compared with 2,535 for "its largest competitor in point of mileage," and 1,315 for the next largest. *Ibid.*, pp. 711–712.

large extent to which it paralleled their routes.[59] Furthermore, it was pointed out that Alaska Airlines was authorized to provide irregular-route service to all of Interior Alaska except the region served by Cordova Air Service, the carrier that it proposed to acquire in the instant proceeding.

In finding the proposed acquisition inconsistent with the public interest because of its prejudicial effect on "the development of a proper competitive balance," the Board indicated that the competitive advantage which would have accrued to Alaska Airlines was such that it would "stifle . . . [the] growth" of "strong local systems dedicated to service in the territory." [60] Here it was not the strategic control over the routing of traffic which would have been gained by the acquiring carrier that was expected to bring about the anticipated increase in its competitive advantage, since the traffic in the region served by the carrier to be acquired was of a predominantly local character.[61] This decision affords no indication of the precise nature of the factor that was expected to bring about this result; it can only be conjectured that the relevant consideration was the further enhancement of the prestige of the larger carrier through the enlargement of the territory served by it. However, the decision does provide a clue to the criterion adopted by the Board in judging whether or not the competitive relations resulting from an acquisition are in accordance with the development of a "proper competitive balance"; if the advantage obtained by the acquiring carrier is such as to stifle the growth of its competitors, then these relations are inconsistent with this development.

In the American–Mid-Continent acquisition case,[62] the anticipated competitive position of the acquiring company relative to carriers rendering services competitive with those of the company to be acquired was at issue in determining whether or not the transaction was consistent with the public interest, as well as the increased advantage to be obtained by the acquir-

---

[59] *Ibid.,* p. 712.

[60] *Ibid.*

[61] *Ibid.*

[62] American Airlines, Inc., Acquisition of Control of Mid-Continent Airlines, Inc., 7 C.A.B. 365 (1946).

ing carrier in its existing markets. The transaction was disapproved in part because of the effect that the substitution of American for Mid-Continent would have had on the relative competitive position of carriers competitive with the latter, and in part because of the effect of the extension of American's system on its competitive position in markets already served by it.

Both the superior prestige in the minds of the consuming public enjoyed by American and its stronger position with respect to control over the routing of traffic were recognized by the Board as factors affecting the relevant competitive relations. In connection with the former factor, the Board pointed out that American was already the largest domestic carrier in terms of route mileage, population served, revenue plane-miles flown, revenue passenger-miles flown, total operating revenues, and net operating income; that it considerably surpassed any other domestic air-transport company in these respects; and that the acquisition of Mid-Continent would result in a further substantial enlargement of American's system.[63] Because of the "mere volume and geographical scope of its operations," the Board declared, American inevitably possessed a superior competitive position in the markets that it served through the effect of this consideration on the preferences of consumers in general.[64]

The geographical scope of American's system was also mentioned as relevant to the strategic traffic position of that carrier, and it was pointed out that this control over routing could be expected to be of substantial importance with regard to the relative competitive position of the particular carriers in the markets served by Mid-Continent, as well as those competitive with American (e.g., for traffic between points on the Mid-Continent system and Southern California).[65]

In view of these factors, the Board found that the acquisition of Mid-Continent "must reasonably be expected to produce

[63] *Ibid.*, pp. 377–378.
[64] *Ibid.*, p. 378.
[65] *Ibid.*, pp. 378–379.

so great a diversion of traffic from other air carriers as would be inconsistent with sound economic conditions in air transportation and would impair the competition we deem requisite to assure the development and maintenance of an adequate air transportation system." [66] The criterion by which the competitive relations to be created by the acquisition were found to be inconsistent with the public interest is here clearly shown to be the extent of diversion of traffic from nonparticipant carriers. The Board did not explicitly discuss the extent of the diversion that was anticipated with respect to any of these carriers; although several carriers intervened in the proceeding and presented evidence that the acquisition would subject them to "severe economic disadvantage," the Board, while recognizing the "core of truth" in the contentions of these carriers, did not base its finding on an acceptance of the exact validity of these contentions.[67] Thus it is not possible on the basis of this decision alone to discover what degree of diversion was here found to be "inconsistent with sound economic conditions" and with the maintenance of the desired amount of competition among air carriers. If, however, the doctrine on this point that has been adopted by the Board in the entry cases and in other cases involving the alteration of existing competitive relations can be assumed to apply in this context, as seems warranted by the Board's reference to "sound economic conditions" in the industry, then it would appear that the traffic diversion was expected to be such as to endanger the profitable maintenance of the operations of at least some of the nonparticipant carriers at substantially their existing level. This interpretation is corroborated by the following statement:

Our analysis above demonstrates that this acquisition might seriously threaten the economic foundation of other air carriers and, in that event, would pose the immediate possibility of greater demands on the public treasury in their behalf.[68]

[66] *Ibid.*, p. 379.
[67] *Ibid.*, p. 378.
[68] *Ibid.*, pp. 383–384.

The Board's discussion of the strategic control over the routing of traffic to be attained as a result of the acquisition raises an interesting question with respect to the distribution of traffic that should be regarded as in accordance with the public convenience and necessity, and suggests an additional criterion of this distribution apart from that provided by the effect on the economic welfare of the competitive carriers. It is suggested that access to points of origination or destination of traffic may allow a carrier to direct this traffic over routes that are not the most desirable from the point of view of the public benefit, in that they are longer than other routes provided by connecting service by two or more carriers, and that the routing so effected would be a result of "artificial factors of competitive advantage rather than the establishment of any truly integrated transportation facilities." However, it is evident that if the same connecting services and joint rates were in fact maintained as had been available before the acquisition (and the Board possesses power to insure their maintenance), and if the rates for the one-carrier service adequately reflected its relative cost (again, the powers of the Board are adequate to assure this), any diversion from the connecting services could not be ascribed to "artificial factors," but should be attributed to a rational preference on the part of consumers for a one-carrier service.

At any rate, it is quite evident that the Board's decision provides no evidence that it interprets the Act as requiring either the limitation of the traffic served by any one carrier to a predetermined percentage of the national or regional total, or the achievement of equality in size or competitive strength among the air carriers under its jurisdiction.[69]

The question of the competitive position to be attained by the acquiring carrier is relevant to yet another argument used by the Board in disapproving the acquisition of Mid-Continent by American. It was argued that future alteration of the route pattern in accordance with the public convenience and necessity would be prejudiced if American were allowed to acquire control of Mid-Continent, in that future extensions of the Mid-Continent route pattern otherwise required by the public con-

[69] *Ibid.*, pp. 379–380.

venience and necessity might be found to be undesirable because of the "cumulative competitive effect of such accretions to the combined system." In particular, it was suggested that such extensions might be found necessary to promote the independent profitability of the Mid-Continent system, an objective that would be impeded by the necessity of considering the enhanced competitive effect on other carriers of the extensions if they were to be operated by American.[70] Here again, the language used by the Board indicates that the criterion by which the "cumulative competitive effect" of the new routes might be found to be excessive is its impact on the long-run "economic stability" of other carriers.

There were certain other adverse factors considered by the Board in disapproving the American–Mid-Continent acquisition, namely, the probable discouragement of the development of connecting services maintained by Mid-Continent with carriers other than American, and the lack of "integration" between the operations of the two participant carriers (i.e., the relatively minor volume of traffic that would receive improved service as a result of the acquisition). With regard to the latter factor, it should be noted that lack of "integration" in itself has been found by the Board not to constitute sufficient grounds for disapproval of a proposed acquisition.[71]

An additional decision in which the Board's disapproval of a proposed acquisition was based primarily on the anticipated excessive competitive strength of the acquiring carrier (in this case, only in the market formerly served by the acquired company) has already been discussed in connection with entry policy.[72] As has been pointed out, the resulting diversion from a local carrier competitive with the company to be acquired was expected to be so great as to endanger the maintenance by this local carrier of service on the route in question and on other less lucrative routes currently served by it.

The major features of the Board's treatment of the alteration

---

[70] *Ibid.*, p. 381.

[71] Western Air Lines, Inc., Acquisition of Inland Air Lines, Inc., 4 C.A.B. 654 (1944).

[72] Alaska Air Lines, Inc., *et al.*, Service to Anchorage, Alaska, 3 C.A.B. 522 (1942).

of existing competitive relations through mergers and acquisitions may now be summarized. In the first place, the elimination of competition between the carriers participant in such transactions has been recognized as a relevant consideration both in determining whether proposed transactions are consistent with the public interest in general and in testing their admissibility under the first proviso contained in Section 408(*b*) of the Civil Aeronautics Act.

In the latter connection, the absence of elimination of competition between participant carriers has been cited as evidence that no violation of the proviso would be involved in the approval of a proposed transaction; however, the mere fact that elimination of competition would result from a transaction is insufficient to render it contrary either to the public interest in general or to the proviso. In cases where transactions have been approved despite their elimination of competition between the participant carriers, the Board has indicated that these proposals were acceptable either because the affected markets were incapable of supporting parallel services, or because other (nonparticipant) companies would continue to provide genuinely substitutable services in the affected markets. Moreover, the disapproval of one important proposed acquisition seems to have been based in part on the anticipated elimination of competition between the participant carriers; in this instance, the result would have been the suppression of all competition on several relatively important routes, on which parallel services had previously been rendered by two relatively profitable carriers.

These decisions appear to embody an exit policy on the part of the Board similar in some respects to its entry policy. There is implied the same attribution of positive value to the availability of genuinely substitutable services in all markets where this is consistent with the maintenance of profitable operations by carriers serving such markets. However, since the Board has approved the elimination of some competitive services that had been profitably carried on, the exit policy embodied in these decisions is not entirely symmetical with the entry policy outlined in the preceding chapter.

In the second place, in considering the effect of proposed transactions on the over-all competitive position of the consolidated carrier, the Board has not based its judgments on any arbitrary standard of maintaining certain size relations among the carriers under its jurisdiction, or limiting to a predetermined percentage the proportion of national or regional traffic controlled by any one carrier. Where relative size and degree of traffic control have been taken into account by the Board, these factors have been considered for the sake of and in connection with their implications for actual particular competitive relations among carriers. These factors have been found relevant to such relations in that the increase in size and the enhancement of the strategic traffic position of the acquiring carrier by means of a proposed transaction will strengthen its competitive position in the markets that it already serves, and the substitution of the acquiring for the acquired carrier will affect competitive relations in the markets served by the latter to the degree that the size and strategic advantage of the acquiring company (as enhanced by the acquisition) are superior to those of the acquired carrier.

In passing on alterations of competitive relations brought about by these means, the Board has found such alterations inconsistent with the public interest if they will stifle the growth of nonparticipant carriers or divert such a quantity of traffic from these carriers as would be "inconsistent with sound economic conditions in air transportation," "seriously threaten the economic foundation of other air carriers," or endanger the profitable continuance of existing operations of other carriers. In view of the Board's usual interpretation of "sound economic conditions in air transportation" as meaning the over-all profitability of the operations of the individual carriers, the three formulae used in judging the permissible extent of diversion may be taken to be identical. Moreover, it is evident that the criterion used here is the same as that which has been found to govern the Board's policy in the entry cases and in those involving the alteration of the physical characteristics of competitive services.

Agreements

Another category of intercarrier transactions which may profoundly affect existing or potential competitive relations among the participant firms as well as influence their competitive position with respect to nonparticipant carriers is agreements limiting certain specific maximizing activities of the companies concerned. Proposed agreements of this type that have been passed on by the Board have included restrictions on (1) the routes or general type of traffic to be served by competitive operations, (2) the volume of output of competitive services, (3) rates charged by the participant carriers, and (4) such other channels of competitive effort as advertising and other selling activities.

Agreements limiting the routes or general type of traffic served by competitive carriers have been uniformly disapproved by the Board as inconsistent with the public interest as outlined in Section 2 of the Civil Aeronautics Act, and in particular in paragraph (d) of that section. Thus, a proposed agreement between Pan American, Matson Navigation Company, and Inter-Island Steam Navigation Company, Ltd., which would have resulted in the exclusion of the latter two companies from independent operation between the West Coast of the United States and Hawaii, and would have specifically committed Pan American not to operate more flights between these points than between Hawaii and points beyond, was rejected by the Board as being "likely to tend to impede the development of competition to the extent required by the present and future needs of the nation" and thus thwarting the purposes of the Civil Aeronautics Act.[73] The Board's condemnation of this

[73] Pan American Airways, Inc., *et al.*, Pan American–Matson–Inter-Island Contract, 3 C.A.B. 540, 546–547 (1942). Other considerations which also supported the Board's finding that the agreement was not consistent with the public interest were: (1) the stifling effect on new competition in the West Coast–Hawaii market of the overwhelming strategic competitive position to be enjoyed by the proposed local carrier to be jointly controlled by the three companies participant in the contract (*ibid.*, p. 546); (2) the possibility of difficulties in administration arising "where the interests of air and steamship transportation come into conflict," because of the equal distribution of control between Pan American and the two steamship companies (*ibid.*, p. 548); and (3) the

agreement was generalized to include all transactions "whereby a carrier operating in a particular territory obtains from a prospective competitor an undertaking, express or implied, not to attempt competitive operations."

This line of reasoning was also apparently relied on by the Board in rejecting part of a proposed agreement between American Airlines and American Export Lines under which the latter company would have been bound not to engage in air transportation except to the extent permitted through its minority interest in American Export Airlines, and the former not to engage in international air transport (except on the North American continent) except through American Export Airlines, which it was to control.[74] Similarly, the Board refused to approve an arrangement between Pan American and American Export Airlines allocating the transatlantic, European, Middle Eastern, and North African air-transport markets between the two carriers on an exclusive territorial basis.[75]

The last agreement provided that American Export should not operate in or to Great Britain, Ireland, Bermuda, Holland, Denmark and Iceland, Norway, Sweden, Finland, Estonia, Latvia, Lithuania, Czechoslovakia (as of September 22, 1938) and Hungary; and that Pan American should not operate in or to Italy, Yugoslavia, Romania, Albania, Bulgaria, Greece, Turkey, Western Asia to the Persian Gulf, the Mediterranean Islands, and North Africa. Secondly, it was to be agreed that Pan American should confine any service to the U.S.S.R. to a route or routes through Poland or a country north of Poland, and that operations to the U.S.S.R. carried on by American Export should be through a country south of Poland. Thirdly,

---

danger to the maximum development of air transport inherent in a part of the agreement which awarded exclusive general traffic agencies for Pan American's services to Matson and Inter-Island in territories served by them, and thus made Pan American "entirely dependent upon [the steamship companies] . . . for the solicitation of passenger and express business over its trans-Pacific route" (*ibid.*).

[74] American Airlines, Inc., Control of American Export Airlines, Inc., 6 C.A.B. 371, 379–380 (1945).

[75] Pan American Airways Company (Delaware), American Export Airlines, Inc., *et al.*, Agreement, Orders Serial No. 31, April 7, 1939.

it was stipulated that each party should attempt to negotiate for commercial landing and flying rights in France and Germany on the basis of an equal division of the total schedule frequencies between the two companies; if, however, either party were unwilling or unable within a reasonable time to provide service to France or Germany for which authorization had been secured, such authorization would revert to the other carrier and the defaulting carrier would thereafter be entitled to share equally only in those schedule frequencies subsequently authorized.

This third provision was adjudged adverse to the public interest in that in the event that either party were in fact unable or unwilling to provide authorized service, "the enforcement of this provision of the agreement might result in the exclusion of such party from transatlantic operations for an indefinite time and lead to a monopoly of such transportation by the other party." The division of territory was disapproved on the ground that the question of areas to be served by the parties "should be reserved for future determination in the light of the development of the services of the respective contracting parties," and that the determination of this question in advance by the proposed agreement "might discourage the development of an air transportation system properly adapted to the present and future needs of the foreign and domestic commerce of the United States, of the Postal service and of the national defense." In general, it was found that the proposed agreement "might impair sound economic conditions in . . . [air] transportation, might prevent the coördination of transportation by air carriers, and might prevent competition." [76]

Again, the Board required, as a condition to its approval of the air-express contracts between the air carriers and the Railway Express Agency, the elimination of a provision binding the Agency not to engage in the air-express business through the operation of its own aircraft. Another clause that the Board required to be omitted from the express agreement would have bound the participant carriers not to accept express business

[76] *Ibid.*, p. 4.

from any person other than the Railway Express Agency, thus in effect preventing the participant carriers as well as nonparticipant companies from entering into competition with the Agency. A third provision that was dropped at the suggestion of the Board would have made it difficult for nonparticipant companies to compete with the carriers who were parties to the agreement in the carriage of air express; this clause would have bound the Railway Express Agency not to provide a service to an "outside" carrier similar to that which it rendered to the participant air-transport companies except under certain restrictive conditions.[77]

In addition to its specific condemnation of the proposed limitation of the local West Coast–Hawaii schedules of Pan American in the Pan American–Matson–Inter-Island agreement, the Board has indicated its general disapproval of the agreed limitation of the volume of competitive services in its decision approving a resolution of the International Air Transport Association providing for regional traffic conferences:

There may be some who will assume that the conferences are to have authority to determine and allocate schedule frequencies and seating capacities among carriers, but this is not our interpretation . . . nor our understanding of the intention of the parties to the resolution. In oral argument the Board was advised that generally it was not the intention of the parties to take any such action in the traffic conferences. We accept this statement, but we take this opportunity to indicate that we would expect to find the gravest difficulties if we were asked to approve any specific agreement reached under this traffic conference machinery which undertook to allocate or limit schedule frequencies or capacity.[78]

In view of the special circumstances surrounding each of these instances, it cannot be definitely concluded that *all* agreed restrictions of the schedules and capacity of competing air services are regarded by the Board as contrary to the public interest. For in the first case, the schedule limitation involved was

[77] *Annual Report* of the Civil Aeronautics Board, 1943, pp. 20–21.
[78] IATA Traffic Conference Resoltion, 6 C.A.B. 639, 640–641 (1946).

designed not to allocate the local traffic between Pan American and the proposed jointly owned new carrier, but substantially to exclude the former company from the local market. Hence, the limitation itself could have been regarded by the Board as similar to those undertakings which restrict potential competition by binding the parties not to serve a certain route or general class of traffic. In the second decision, the Board was concerned primarily with preventing limitation of the expansion of United States-flag carriers in international service by action designed to protect the markets of their foreign competitors; it was generally assumed that the competitive position and financial status of the United States airlines would be better in the absence of all restrictions on the allocation of traffic among the carriers than under such a regime of allocation as would probably be imposed either by an international trade association or by an international regulatory commission (or at least by a commission of the type which had at that time been proposed for the regulation of international air transport). Thus this decision cannot be accepted as evidence that the Board would regard any allocation of schedules or capacity by intercarrier agreement as contrary to public policy where such allocation was expected to protect the financial welfare of carriers subject to its jurisdiction and hence, from the Board's point of view, to be conducive to "sound economic conditions" in United States air transportation.

Similarly, the unusual circumstances conditioning the Board's opinion in the IATA Traffic Conference Resolution case as well as its subsequent decisions dealing with action taken by the North Atlantic Traffic Conference created by the resolution cast doubt on the general significance of the principles which in those decisions apparently governed the Board's action on intercarrier agreements with respect to rates. For example, the fact that the Board approved the establishment of machinery whereby international air-transport rates were to "become the subject of agreements between the members of IATA," [79] and subsequently gave its approval to the participation of United States carriers in agreed rates for the transatlan-

[79] *Ibid.*, p. 641.

tic services,[80] might seem to imply that the Board does not regard the conference method of rate making as in itself contrary to the objectives of the Civil Aeronautics Act. Such an interpretation might be strengthened by reference to the Board's contentions, in support of the former action, (1) that this rate-making procedure had received Congressional approbation in other agencies of transport, and (2) that only "theoretical considerations" could be adduced to show that such a procedure would be per se incompatible with the policy of "controlled competition" embodied in the Act.[81]

However, it should be noted that the Board found neither that the conference method would *not* be adverse to the public interest, nor that it *would* be consistent with the Act's policy of "controlled competition"; but, reserving judgment on these points, initially limited its authorization to an experimental trial period of one year. Although the approval of the conference machinery has been subsequently extended on three occasions, it is still at least nominally on a conditional and temporary basis.[82] Furthermore, the Board's temporary authorization was conditioned by a recital of its "understanding" of how the conferences would operate, a recital which was evidently intended to instruct the carriers as to what course should be followed to retain the Board's approval; it is here indicated that the Board expects the rates made by the Conferences to be "reasonable," "economically sound," and "properly related to the reasonably attainable costs of the air carriers." The Board here stated:

The right of independent action of any carrier, once it has observed the conference procedures, must be scrupulously preserved . . . Our approval of the resolution therefore assumes that after conference procedures have been complied with an open rate may, and indeed should, exist if the rate proposals advanced at any conference are

[80] Orders Serial No. 5196. In the Matter of Resolutions, 1–14, second North Atlantic Traffic Conference, International Air Transport Association, September 24, 1946.

[81] IATA Traffic Conference Resolution, pp. 643–44.

[82] See Orders Serial No. E–269 (January 31, 1947), E–1227 (February 20, 1948), and E–3888 (February 9, 1950).

unreasonable or economically unsound and are not properly related to the reasonably attainable costs of the air carriers . . . It is further understood that it is not intended that a rate established by a conference agreement thereafter can be changed only by unanimous action. Such a requirement would enable a single air carrier to freeze the rate structure, and would create an intolerable situation . . . Finally, in giving our temporary approval to the resolution we have emphasized the fact that all rate agreements reached by a conference involving United States air carriers must be approved by the Board pursuant to Section 412 of the Civil Aeronautics Act.[83]

Of still greater importance, however, in evaluating the Board's position is the fact that approval of the resolution was regarded as (1) the only means whereby the Board could obtain any substantial degree of control over international air-transport rates charged by United States-flag carriers, and (2) the only alternative to the unilateral fixing of rates by the governments of foreign nations served by these carriers, as the governments of France and the United Kingdom were doing at the time of the decision.

Hence on the basis of these decisions it cannot be said that, in the absence of the extraordinary considerations which influenced the Board's position, the Board would regard concerted rate making as in general consistent with the public interest, even though the conferences making these rates complied with the specific requirements laid down by the Board as its "understanding" of how the IATA Conferences were to function and the rates fixed by them were "properly related to the reasonably attainable costs of the carriers."

As for the precise nature of the criterion that might be applied by the Board in testing the propriety of the relation of agreed rates to the "reasonably attainable costs of the carriers," decisions hitherto rendered afford little light. The phrase "reasonably attainable" suggests that the Board might not be satisfied with a rate based on "historical" costs, and might insist that the possibility of decreasing unit costs by promotional rate making be taken into consideration. Although the Board's disapproval of the first rate proposal of the North

[83] IATA Traffic Conference Resolution, p. 645.

Atlantic Traffic Conference was explicitly based on a contention that the agreed rates were not shown to be reasonably related to costs,[84] and the second rate proposal of this body was approved because there was found to exist "no unreasonable relationship between the probable attainable operating costs of air carriers" and the rates established therein,[85] neither of these decisions gives any clear idea of the precise cost criterion employed. There is a suggestion in the IATA Traffic Conference Resolution case that "the gearing of rates . . . to the costs of the most efficient operator" would yield results acceptable to the Board;[86] however, it may well be that this concern with the costs of the "most efficient" may be explained in terms of the Board's desire that United States-flag carriers should not be deprived of their presumed competitive advantages by the action of an international trade association. It is significant in this connection that in rejecting the first transatlantic agreed rates the Board stressed the fact that the disapproved resolutions would have greatly increased Pan American's rates, as being "particularly serious" and constituting a special circumstance under which "the public interest does not permit approval of an agreement which lacks an economic basis."[87]

Other actions taken by the Board in connection with agreements designed to affect the rate level are equally barren of precise rate criteria, but also suggest that the Board will require a showing of some relation between rates and operating costs. Thus the Board required, as a condition for its approval of the air-express agreements between the carriers and the Railway Express Agency, the abrogation of clauses (up to that time ineffective in the actual determination of rates) fixing a minimum for air-express rates in terms of the prevailing level of the railway-express charge.[88] More recently, the Board has approved an agreed rise of 10 percent in passenger fares

---

[84] Resolutions of North Atlantic Traffic Conference Relating to Rates and General Conditions of Carriage, 6 C.A.B. 845, 848–849 (1946).

[85] Order No. 5196, p. 4.

[86] IATA Traffic Conference Resolution, p. 644.

[87] Resolutions of North Atlantic Traffic Conference Relating to Rates and General Conditions of Carriage, p. 850.

[88] *Annual Report* of the Civil Aeronautics Board, 1943, pp. 20–21.

charged by the major domestic air carriers, largely on the ground that this action appeared "reasonably likely to bring about a more nearly normal relationship between non-mail expenses and non-mail revenues." [89] Here the required relation between rates and costs is stated in terms of total revenues and total expenses; commercial rates are to be such as to provide revenues bearing a normal relation to expenses allocable to this type of service.

In its decision fixing a general minimum for air-cargo rates, the Board included a discussion of the "more basic principles in a program of sound rate making" which reaffirms its position that "the rate levels [should] have a reasonable relationship to attainable cost levels." [90] Here it is asserted that the *general* "tests of reasonableness" of rate-cost relations "must include recognition of variations in the ability of traffic to carry a full share of costs at different stages in the development of that traffic, the effect of low rates in generating new traffic and the resultant effect of increased volume on reductions in unit costs." [91] Although this discussion is oriented primarily toward outlining the principles that should govern minimum rather than maximum rate regulation, this statement again suggests that the Board in determining whether or not carrier-made rates were too high might consider not only their relation to historical costs but also whether or not they were developing the maximum level of traffic that might profitably be carried. It is, however, highly improbable that the regulatory fixing of rates which do not cover historical costs would be permitted by the courts. Finally, it should be noted that the history of direct passenger-rate regulation by the Board in 1949 and 1950 shows a complete subordination of cost criteria to the general aim of maximizing carrier net revenue.

To return to the position of the Board regarding rate making by agreement: It has been said that the peculiar circumstances surrounding the IATA decisions makes the general applicability

---

[89] Order No. E–389, March 21, 1947.

[90] Air Freight Rate Investigation, Orders Serial No. E–1415, April 21, 1948, pp. 6–7

[91] *Ibid.*, p. 7.

of the principles governing them highly doubtful. Because of these circumstances, the Board's action on detailed agreements formulated by the IATA Traffic Conferences will not be considered here. However, the Board has also sanctioned in the domestic field the existence of an organization within the Air Transport Association that is similar in function to the IATA Traffic Conferences. This organization, known as the Air Traffic Conference, is the instrumentality through which the scheduled air carriers take coöperative action on traffic matters, including tariffs and rates. The Tariff and Rates Division of the ATC, which was set up to handle the publication of the consolidated tariff containing rates charged by the members of the Conference, also provides a formal means whereby all other members are informed in advance of a rate change proposed by any participant carrier.[92] Furthermore, the resolution governing the operation of the Tariff and Rates Division contains a provision requiring each participant carrier to notify the Tariff Agent (i.e., the Executive Secretary of the ATC) and the other carriers party to the resolution at least fifteen days in advance of filing with a regulatory body any new tariff or revision of any old tariff; an exception to this requirement is provided for carriers desiring to "meet competition," who are allowed to file new rates on only five days' notice. It is also agreed that no participant will file any rate change to be effective within less than ten days after filing, unless compelled to do so by a regulatory body or authorized to do so by a majority vote of the Tariff and Rates Committee of the ATC.[93]

In addition, the Tariff and Rates Committee of the ATC provides a formal vehicle for the prior discussion of proposed rate changes by representatives of all the member carriers. This type of discussion is explicitly recognized as one of the func-

---

[92] In the resolution (adopted by the ATC) governing the operation of the Tariff and Rates Division, it is provided that the Division shall inform all members participating in the tariff involved of any "desired changes in any fare, charge, rule or regulation in any tariff published by it."

ATC Trade Practice Manual, reissued August 1, 1945, and subsequently revised, p. 88. The discussion and references in this study pertain to the Manual as revised up to and including February 9, 1951.

[93] *Ibid.*, p. 93.

tions of this Committee, as well as of the Conference itself, in the resolution governing the operation of the Tariff and Rates Division. It is here agreed that "to the extent feasible, at meetings of the Conference or of Committees of the Conference, members of the Conference shall discuss contemplated revisions in their tariffs and contemplated new tariffs, in order that where changes are made which are of concern to more than one member those affected may be fully advised in advance." [94] The resolution discussed above has received the formal approval of the Board. However, the Board has disapproved in the agreement providing for a consolidated joint cargo tariff a clause compelling carriers to notify the Tariff Agent of contemplated rate changes. It has also refused to approve intercarrier discussions of contemplated revisions in local freight tariffs.[95] Similar action will probably be taken with respect to the agreement governing the passenger-fare tariff. In addition, the Board's approval of the resolution has been made "subject to the condition that any holder of a certificate of public convenience and necessity issued by the Board authorizing transportation of passengers by aircraft be authorized to participate in the consolidated local and joint tariff established by that agreement as a matter of right." [96]

The activities of the Air Traffic Conference and of its Tariff and Rates Division, as indicated in the resolution discussed above (and apparently as understood by the Board [97]), do not include the actual making of rates by concerted action of the member carriers. Moreover, the only important carrier-initiated concerted rate action that has received the Board's formal approval is the 10-percent increase in commercial rates agreed upon by the major airlines in March 1947 — an agreement arrived at under extraordinary circumstances and intended to be in effect for only ninety days (with respect to services using

---

[94] *Ibid.,* p. 93–A.

[95] Air Freight Tariff Agreement Case, Orders Serial No. E–5641, August 23, 1951.

[96] Orders Serial No. E–3725, December 19, 1949.

[97] On this point, Board member Lee in his dissenting opinion in the IATA Traffic Conference Resolution case, p. 648, stated: "The existence of the Air Traffic Conference of the domestic air carriers likewise constitutes no precedent [for the approval of the proposed international conferences]. The domestic conference has not in fact fixed rates for the industry."

Constellation or DC-6 aircraft, the duration of the agreement was to be 120 days).

The extraordinary circumstances which were cited by the Board in its order approving the 10-percent rate increase consisted in a rapid rise in air-carrier operating costs per unit of service sold and by a "substantially constant" revenue for each such unit, a situation that had resulted in an unreasonably low ratio of passenger revenues to the cost of rendering the service, and had made "an immediate increase in such revenues . . . desirable in the interest of sound economic conditions in air transportation." Many of the major scheduled airlines had already petitioned the Board for higher mail payments, and the Board had instituted an investigation of the commercial rates of the carriers to discover whether it "should determine and prescribe general levels of rates . . . for the transportation of passengers and property designed to effect an over-all increase in non-mail revenues of the respondents." The Board authorized the rate increase on the ground that it seemed likely that it would provide a means for putting commercial revenues into a more "normal" relation with commercial costs, an aim which would otherwise probably have to be accomplished either by increased mail payments or by a formal order raising commercial rates, since the former method would "constitute an additional burden on the Government" and the latter would be less expeditious than approval of the agreement. A third possibility for increasing airline revenues — individual carrier action to raise rates — was declared infeasible "in view of the competitive situation." [98]

Another general rate action undertaken simultaneously by the domestic carriers with the approval of the Board, but not the subject of a formal intercarrier agreement, was the suspension of all discounts on passenger fares and all special passenger fares on July 1, 1942. Here again, extraordinary circumstances affecting (or expected to affect) the revenues of all the carriers motivated the rate change, namely, the "substantial curtailment in the number of aircraft and operations of the domestic air carriers following our entry into the war, the inauguration of a large volume of contract operations, and the establishment of a

[98] Order No. E–389.

system of priority ratings for passengers and property movement." [99] Similarly, the rate rise apparently agreed upon as a result of a carrier conference in August 1948 informally approved — indeed, sponsored — by the Board, was designed to meet a situation of general unprofitability among the certified carriers. The only other approved concerted rate-fixing actions initiated by the carriers, which provided for uniform charter rates for the United States Government and for other users, were of limited duration.[100]

Thus, although the Board has in certain exceptional instances approved concerted rate action by the domestic carriers, it cannot be said that it has sanctioned the conference method of rate making in the domestic field. It has definitely outlawed compulsory advance notice of freight rate changes and has limited its approval of intercarrier discussions of prospective freight tariff changes to those involving rules, regulations, practices, services and joint rates. Similar action seems likely in the field of passenger rates. Thus, the Board has not yet authorized the general abandonment of rate competition in domestic scheduled-air-transport markets.[101]

It should be noted, however, that in one instance the Board has given specific approval to an intercarrier agreement designed to limit rate competition by restricting the granting of free or reduced-rate transportation to certain specified categories of passengers. (This resolution also provides that no participant carrier shall honor a pass issued by another air carrier.) In finding this agreement not adverse to the public interest, the Board merely referred to the "abuses" that had characterized the issuance of passes by transport companies in the past, and

---

[99] *Annual Report* of the Civil Aeronautics Board, 1943, p. 15.

[100] Uniform charter rates for a temporary period were agreed upon for service performed for the United States Government and for other persons by resolutions of the Air Traffic Conference effective May 22, 1941 and June 26, 1941 respectively. These resolutions were approved by the Board by Orders Serial No. 1578 and 1579, March 2, 1942. The resolutions ceased to be effective January 1, 1943.

[101] The term "competition" as used here and in the following discussion denotes an activity rather than a relation between firms. It is independent profit-maximizing activity considered from the point of view of its repercussions on the revenues of other economic units.

pointed out that compliance with the agreement might reasonably be expected to prevent "lengthy and expensive litigation."[102]

In addition, certain other existing intercarrier agreements not disapproved by the Board might be regarded as restrictions on "disguised" rate competition; e.g., (1) an ATC resolution limiting the period for which credit may be extended in an ordinary ticket sale,[103] (2) a resolution prohibiting the carriers in certain circumstances from paying for passengers' meals on trains,[104] (3) a resolution preventing delivery of tickets to passengers at the expense of the air carriers at points other than the carriers' offices, except by mail or by "sales representatives on their normal solicitation calls," and prohibiting the employment of personnel for the purpose of delivering tickets to passengers,[105] and (4) a resolution binding members not to accept collect telegrams or long-distance telephone calls in connection with reservations except in certain specified instances.[106] However, it seems on the whole more convenient to classify these agreements as restrictions on service competition, since they do not in fact affect the actual payment made by the passenger to the airline company.

Certain other ATC resolutions not disapproved by the Board might also operate to limit competition in service to a minor degree; these include agreements (1) limiting the amount of delivery and communication costs borne by a carrier in connection with mishandled baggage to a maximum of five dollars;[107] (2) limiting the refund of overcharges to the carrier issuing the original flight ticket;[108] (3) binding the "delivering" carrier not to bear any expenses incurred in forwarding delayed passengers who have missed their connections;[109] and (4) providing that any carrier making any new or renewing any existing

---

[102] Airline Pass Agreement, 1 C.A.A. 677, 681 (1940).
[103] Trade Practice Manual, p. 97.
[104] *Ibid.*, p. 77.
[105] *Ibid.*, p. 116.
[106] *Ibid.*, p. 82.
[107] *Ibid.*, p. 115.
[108] *Ibid.*, p. 101.
[109] *Ibid.*, p. 78.

arrangements for ground transportation of air passengers at or to or from any airport shall consult and coöperate with other members, if any, that use this airport "(*a*) in determining the [ground-transportation] services . . . required . . . and the person or persons best qualified to provide them reliably, efficiently and economically, and (*b*) in negotiating and concluding joint or uniform arrangements for the provision of such services"; and also providing that the participant carriers shall "consult and coöperate with other members [of the ATC] (*a*) in determining the manner in which, and the means by which, the objectives of this resolution [i.e., "the provision of transportation services between airports and the areas served thereby, which will best serve the needs of, and conform to the standards demanded by, airline passengers"] can best be accomplished, and (*b*) to the extent determined by the members to be feasible, in negotiating and concluding joint or uniform arrangements for the provision of such services, on a nation-wide, regional, or other basis, at airports served by one or more members." [110]

As of February 9, 1951, none of these agreements relating to service competition had been formally approved as most recently amended. The last resolution, which had not been formally acted upon by the Board, might possibly result in an important restriction of competition in terminal services at some future time; however, it should be noted that any agreements arrived at as a result of the consultation between the carriers provided for in the resolution will themselves be subject to the jurisdiction of the Board. Moreover, it is obvious that the present aim and probable immediate result of the consultation and coöperation provided for will be the improvement through joint action of ground transportation at airports. Thus the agreement is in this respect analogous to those concerned with such matters as procedures for interline reservations, publication of the consolidated tariff, and the like; it provides a means for the accomplishment of improvements in the product offered by each of the participant carriers that could be achieved only through coöperative action. Participation in this type of agreement — particularly those that are

[110] *Ibid.*, p. 71–B.

industry-wide rather than involving only a few carriers — constitutes in effect a necessary condition to the provision of a superior type of air-transport service. Consequently, a refusal to allow any carrier so to participate would be equivalent to excluding it from the production of such a service. The Board has developed a policy of requiring such industry-wide agreements to be nonexclusive — that is, open upon reasonable terms to all certificated air carriers. In a recent opinion dealing with a modification of the agreements covering interline ticketing and baggage arrangements, the Board made its approval subject to a condition that specific Board sanction be obtained for any refusal to allow participation by a certificated air carrier, and explained its position as follows:

The Board has previously established, in its consideration of industry-wide agreements, the principle that coöperative arrangements embracing a large group of certificated carriers should permit future participation of other certificated carriers upon an equitable basis. This principle is clearly in accord with the interpretation of the antitrust laws by the courts and seems to us to constitute sound public policy. We see no reason to depart therefrom in our consideration of the industry-wide agreements providing for uniform interline ticketing and baggage arrangements. Indeed, there is more reason to insist upon such principle in this case than in others involving multilateral contracts. Such arrangements are basic to the institution and maintenance of reasonable through services in air transportation between connecting air carriers.[111]

Another agreement that might conceivably operate to restrict competition in service, but again only to a very limited extent, is an ATC resolution formally approved by the Board providing that "members flying the same type of equipment (including engines) between the same pair of points, over the same course, shall publish the same scheduled time in schedules for public use." [112] At first sight, this agreement appears drastically to limit carrier action in what would seem to be a major dimension of service competition, namely, speed of service. In

[111] Orders Serial No. E–4764, October 23, 1950, p. 5.
[112] Trade Practice Manual, p. 86–B.

fact, however, there is very little possibility for variation by carrier initiative of the time elapsed between two points *under the conditions enumerated in the resolution*. Given compliance with the safety regulations, any such variation would be much smaller in extent than the variations normally resulting from changing wind and weather conditions. Therefore the publication of a shorter scheduled time by a particular air carrier would be merely misleading to the public, and the above resolution might better be classified as a restriction on advertising activity rather than on service.

In addition to the agreements discussed above limiting competition in rates and service, the Board has permitted the domestic carriers to enter into several undertakings that directly restrict competition in "selling" activities — advertising and solicitation of traffic. As to advertising, the Board has not disapproved Air Traffic Conference resolutions (1) limiting the type of publicity that may be employed by Conference members in telephone directories and binding each member to "conduct its advertising program with a view to maintaining the highest ethical competitive standards," such standards including the avoidance of reflecting "discredit, either implied or stated, upon the interests or services of another member";[113] (2) restricting publicity regarding new safety devices and navigational aids;[114] (3) directing that the Advertising Committee from time to time issue recommendations that members refrain from advertising in designated publications, it being provided that "no such recommendation shall be made by the Advertising Committee unless [it] . . . shall determine that advertising in such designated publications would, in its opinion, not have sufficient advertising value";[115] and (4) requiring all members to give at least thirty days' prior notice to the Executive Secretary before participating in any show or exhibit (except window displays), except where notice has been received of the intention of another member to participate in the show or exhibit; the Executive Secretary is directed to transmit

[113] *Ibid.*, p. 29.
[114] *Ibid.*, p. 31.
[115] *Ibid.*, p. 33.

notice given by any member to all other members of the Conference.[116] All but the last named of these resolutions have been formally approved by the Board.

With regard to solicitation of traffic, the Board has not disapproved resolutions (1) providing uniform maxima for commissions to sales agents; (2) requiring approval by the Conference's Agency Committee for the locations of sales agencies; and (3) requiring this Committee's approval for persons who may be appointed as sales agents by the members.[117]

In connection with the remuneration of agents, the General Agency Resolution contains several provisions designed to prevent circumvention of the uniform-payments provision; certain separate resolutions with the same broad objective have also been adopted.[118]

In the light of the Board's actions (and failures to act) on the ATC resolutions explicitly limiting the competitive action of the carriers, it can be said that it has not found that all agreements limiting competition in rates, services, and "selling," or in any one of these categories, are *ipso facto* adverse to the public interest as defined in the Act.

As to rate competition, the Board's approval of the agreement on free and reduced-rate air transportation was clearly influenced by the provisions of the Civil Aeronautics Act relating to the observance of tariffs and to the issuance of passes. Section 403(b) of the Act generally requires the carriers to observe in practice the rates and charges specified in their current tariffs, it being provided that the issuance of passes to certain enumerated types of passenger shall not be prohibited by this requirement. The categories of passengers exempted from the provisions of the agreement appear to be closely similar to those enumerated in the Act. Although the Board explicitly refused to find that the categories of passengers exempted from the agreed prohibition of issuance of passes are the same as those enumerated in the Act, and although the law does not actually prohibit the issuance of passes to categories of pas-

---

[116] *Ibid.*, p. 30.
[117] *Ibid.*, pp. 36–46.
[118] *Ibid.*, p. 83, for example.

sengers not enumerated in the Act, it is clearly implied in the Act that the issuance of passes to persons not enumerated *may* be found to be contrary to the general observance-of-tariffs requirement; thus the agreement might readily be construed as carrying into effect without the necessity for regulatory action a limitation on competition in rates substantially the same as one that was contemplated in the Act itself.

At least three of the restrictions on service competition may be justified by the improvement of service through coöperative action. It has already been pointed out that the intention and at least the immediate effect of the resolution on ground transportation will probably be an improvement in the product offered to the public by each participant carrier. Similarly, the resolutions regarding the refund of overcharges and the handling of passengers who miss their connections probably result in better service through avoiding confusion by fixing a standard procedure. In these instances, the service advantages to be gained from uniform practices may very well outweigh any benefit to the public that might accrue from competition along these lines.

In addition, at least one of the agreements regarding service and most of those relating to "selling activities" might be justified as aiding the traveling public in making a rational choice among airlines or between airline service and any other possible purchase. Among these are the resolutions on (1) the publication of scheduled times; (2) permissible types of telephone-directory advertising and avoidance of direct or implied reflection of discredit on other carriers; (3) participation in shows and exhibits; (4) publicity on new safety devices and navigational aids; and (5) the payment of uniform commissions to sales agents, and related devices tending to promote impartiality on the part of such agents.

The remaining resolution on "selling" activities, namely, that covering advertising in certain designated publications, cannot be justified in this way. Since it would presumably be of no effect whatever except in instances where certain carriers had found it individually profitable to advertise in certain publications, but as profitable (or more profitable) not to advertise in them provided the other carriers also refrained from doing so, there is nothing qualitatively to distinguish the concerted action contemplated in this resolution from any other agreed restriction on "nonprice" competition designed to maintain the *status quo,* i.e., to prevent experimentation in product variation along certain specified lines.[119] Of course, in the event that the carriers were motivated by "uneconomic" rivalry, so that even a mistaken selling expense undertaken by one carrier would be duplicated by others in the field, the resolution could be readily justified. Similarly, there seems to be no particular justification for the remaining agreements limiting service competition. In these cases, the result accomplished by the resolution seems to be merely to protect the carriers from the risks involved in certain types of variation of service.

To sum up: It must be admitted that the available evidence is insufficient to define completely the Board's attitude toward agreements dealing with either rates or volume of service rendered. However, it seems reasonable to conclude that both rate making and variations in volume of service constitute approved dimensions of competitive activity, restrictions on which will be tolerated only under certain special circumstances, the most important being the existence of financial difficulties generally among the carriers. In the second place, the Board has approved several intercarrier agreements limiting some minor aspects of competition in service and in selling, not all of which can be justified by collaborative improvement of the product sold or of the promotion of a more informed judgment on the part of consumers. Some of these agreements seem to be aimed at and to result solely in the protection of carrier revenues from the risks involved in certain types of product variation, for the carriers thereby bind themselves to "nonaggressive" competitive policies in specified channels. On the other hand, the Board has consistently refused to approve agreements under which any carrier obtains protection of its market by binding other participants to refrain from serving a particular area

---

[119] It should be noted that the distinction between "selling activities" and variation in the type of service offered is made only for the purpose of convenient classification, and is not intended to have any analytical significance.

or broad class of traffic, and has held that such undertakings would be contrary to Section 2(d) of the Act.

In view of the Board's usual interpretation of the meaning of this provision — that is, of the nature of the competition required by the Act — these holdings with respect to intercarrier agreements appear almost perfectly consistent and appropriate. It will be recalled that the term "competition" as used by the Board is essentially equivalent to the existence of genuinely substitutable airline services in a given market, that the advantage expected to be obtained from this "competition" is its effectiveness as a stimulus to the development of new techniques of service and operation, and that the Act has been interpreted as requiring the authorization of all such competition (genuinely substitutable services) as is consistent with the maintenance of profitable operation at substantially the current level by carriers rendering existing services. In the Board's sense, then, "competition" does not necessarily imply "aggressiveness" of selling activity or of price policy on the part of the competing carriers, so that the existence of associations limiting competitive efforts along these lines would not have any direct bearing on the maintenance of "competition."

Although the Board's permission of certain agreements limiting "service" competition might appear inconsistent with the Board's general policy, it is clear that "service" competition is a category that includes a very broad sector of competitive activity; so that it may be that the lines of endeavor in which the Board wishes to preserve competition do not include such relatively minor channels as the extension of credit to ticket purchasers, but only such activities as, say, speed and comfort of service through the use of improved equipment. On the other hand, agreements barring service by the participant or other carriers of certain routes or classes of traffic, in so far as they are of any practical effect (that is, in so far as they prevent the inauguration of operations that would have been approved by the Board), constitute obstacles to the accomplishment of the Act's purpose as usually interpreted; they prevent the institution of substitutable services that would have been consistent with "sound economic conditions" among United States air carriers. The same opposition to any action that might prevent the Board from authorizing new competitive operations in any market was exemplified in the first transatlantic-route case, where the Board refused to allocate all the available foreign landing rights to Pan American Airways, on the ground that such a move would exclude potential competition;[120] this position may also have played a part in influencing the stand taken by the Board with regard to proposals for the allocation of foreign air-transport routes by an international regulatory authority.

The Board's condemnation of agreements limiting the capacity for carriage offered by each participant carrier is also entirely consistent with its usual competitive policy. For if genuine substitutability among various services is to have any practical meaning, if, in particular, it is to provide any incentive for the improvement of techniques of operation or service, then the actual substitution of the preferred service by the consuming public must not be hindered by restrictions on the amount of this service that may be supplied. In view of the Board's usual subordination of the competitive to the protective principle, it is of course to be expected that agreed limitations on volume of service, like agreed rates, will be approved if found to be necessary for the preservation of "sound economic conditions" among the carriers subject to the Board's jurisdiction.

A similar consistency is illustrated in the Board's requirement of nonexclusivity in industry-wide agreements effecting improved services. This requirement represents a limitation on private-profit maximization through exclusion of new competition. That the nonexclusivity principle is restricted to *certificated* air carriers is a logical reflection of the major policy of limited entry embodied in the Civil Aeronautics Act. What is in fact accomplished by this requirement is a prohibition of private exclusion more restrictive than the broad exclusion policy inherent in the Act itself.

Here it may well be asked what purpose is in fact served by

---

[120] Pan American Airways Company (of Delaware) — Certificate of Public Convenience and Necessity, 1 C.A.A. 118, 131–132 (1939).

the availability of genuinely substitutable services, or the preservation of the actual possibility of substitution, if the carriers furnishing these services pursue "nonaggressive" price and "selling" policies, and in this sense do not in fact "compete." There would indeed be very little to be said for the "competition" championed by the Board were *all* the channels of competitive effort open to the carriers subjected to mutually protective "self-regulation." Under such circumstances, the distribution of traffic among competing carriers largely would not be susceptible of variation as a result of the activities of the companies; spontaneous changes in the tastes of consumers would provide the only occasion for an adjustment in the volume of traffic served by each. However, the fact seems to be that the Board distinguishes between channels of competitive effort, regarding, for example, certain types of "selling" competition as dimensions that may permissibly be curtailed or extinguished by intercarrier agreement, while favoring aggressive independent action by the carriers along other lines, so long as this action does not threaten "sound economic conditions" among the carriers. Furthermore, it may be conjectured that these favored lines of endeavor would include major alterations in techniques of service and operation, since, as has been noted, the Board has indicated that improvements in such techniques are the principal benefit to be expected from "competition." If this hypothesis is correct, then it would follow that intercarrier agreements restricting innovations in major operating and service techniques would be approved by the Board only where necessary to preserve "sound economic conditions"; so far, no such agreement has been formally passed upon.

Again, however, it may be asked why the availability of substitutable services performed by an independent rival is regarded as necessary to provide a stimulus to the efforts of an airline management to maximize profits through variations in technique. For it would seem that the same opportunities for profit would be open to it along these lines regardless of the state of its competitive relations with other air carriers, and it would be no less to its advantage to avail itself of the best of these opportunities even were its firm in a position of virtually isolated selling with respect to all other firms in the economy. This is of course true; and yet it is also true that the existence of a close competitor can reasonably be expected to stimulate profit-maximizing efforts on the part of the individual firm. The more closely the product of the competitor is substitutable for that of the firm in question, the more likely are the independent maximizing efforts of the former to make inroads on the latter's sales; therefore, the presence of a close competitor in the field ordinarily means that the firm's market is at all times subject to invasion. Under such circumstances, the firm's management is evidently less likely to overlook available means of strengthening its competitive position than it would be in a more sheltered situation, for the possibility of loss of revenue acts as a safeguard against lapsing into the comfortable routine of a sufficiently profitable, protected market.

It is probably impossible to arrive at any incontrovertible conclusions on the extent to which this presumptive case for competition has been justified in practice, because in any given instance the actual course of events cannot be measured against what would have happened if there had been no competition. Gill and Bates have declared that there is no support in the record for this presumption.[121] However, their own careful sifting of the facts has provided a strong case for competition in general, and their refusal to admit that there is therefore any prima facie case for competition in particular seems to be largely based on a consideration of instances in which certain factors affecting the operations of the newly added competitor made it impossible for the full advantages of effective competition to be realized. The authors themselves have summarized their conclusions as follows:

In summary, it may be concluded that although in general competition has been an important force in the maintenance of a high quality, low-price airline service, the type of additional competition which has been certified, especially during the postwar expansion of

<hr>

[121] F. W. Gill and G. L. Bates, *Airline Competition* (Boston: Division of Research, Graduate School of Business Administration, Harvard University, 1949), p. 615.

the domestic air transportation system, has not in a great many instances contributed significantly to either objective. In some of these
cases, competition has not only failed to bring about this desired
improvement in the price or over-all quality of service, but this failure has also . . . been the major reason why some carriers have been
unsuccessful in their competitive efforts to achieve in whole or in
part their goal of self-sufficiency . . .

The detailed analyses on which the above conclusions are based
led to the logical query as to why competition had diverse effects,
sometimes beneficial, sometimes detrimental. In answer to this question, it was found that competition is but one of the basic determinants of the quality of service which a given airline produces in a
particular market. Among the other determinants there are three
which have been outstanding in their influence on the service produced. These can be briefly summarized as follows: passenger traffic
potential, operational factors, and route structure including franchise
limitations . . .

In the many cases previously referred to, in which competition
failed to bring about higher standards of service, any or all of these
other determinants usually outweighed competitive considerations.
The weight given to all these determinants of airline service including competition varies as among airline managements and even
within a single management group. The results are predictable within
such limits, especially with the backlog of experience which has been
accumulated under all kinds of conditions. It remains, then for these
factors to be considered by the carrier and the Civil Aeronautics
Board in decisions affecting future modifications of the domestic
route map.[122]

From this it would appear that the major lesson to be derived
from this study is not that there is no basis for the presumption,
but that in any particular case this presumption should be subjected to possible rebuttal by a detailed consideration of the
economic characteristics of the system of the applicant for new
service.

The incentive provided by competition would, of course, be
greatly weakened were the Board itself to restrict, or to sanction the restriction of, all airline competitive action in accordance with the principle employed in the decisions regarding

[122] *Ibid.*, pp. 628–630.

entry and variations in the physical character of the service. (Similarly, the incentives provided by close competition, like the general discipline provided in most fields of economic endeavor by the fear of loss, are also greatly weakened by the "need-rate" subsidization policy. This point is taken up in the following chapter.) As has been noted, most of the "self-regulation" of carrier activity brought about by intercarrier agreements has involved the exclusion of certain undesirable dimensions of competitive effort rather than restriction of independent action along approved lines, and certain proposals involving the latter type of restriction have been disapproved. In the rate dimension, however, the Board has approved concerted action where this has seemed necessary to prevent general unprofitability among the regulated firms. From this it may be inferred that limitations on competition in approved dimensions (which would be generally inadmissible) are nevertheless acceptable where required to preserve "sound economic conditions" in the regulated field, i.e., where a number of carriers subject to its jurisdiction would otherwise be faced with losses. In fact, not only has the Board sanctioned concerted carrier action on rates in this situation; it has in one notable instance intervened to fix a mandatory limit on rate competition where a certain class of carrier was believed to be threatened with bankruptcy and no carrier-initiated agreement was forthcoming to prevent it.

The language used in this decision leaves no doubt that the main reason for the Board's action was the fact that the noncertificated cargo carriers were faced with financial loss. Thus, in a preliminary section of the decision entitled "The Need for Regulation," primary emphasis is placed on the fact that air-cargo rates recently established by the carriers were "so low as to endanger the sound development of air freight and to undermine the financial condition of the carriers"; it is pointed out that the generally low rate level "would eventually lead to the financial inability of the noncertificated carriers to remain in operation"; and it is concluded that "the destructive aspects inherent in the present and proposed tariffs dictate that some effective regulatory action be taken." [123]

[123] Air Freight Rate Investigation, p. 5.

It is also argued that the freight rates at issue are generally "below cost"; however, the cost standard employed by the Board is the average ton-mile cost actually incurred by the threatened class of carrier in 1947. The use of this cost figure as a basis for a general minimum rate floor is defended on the ground that it represents "a practical minimum for the costs of an all-cargo service" — which in turn is taken to be a reasonable approximation to attainable cost levels for cargo service by all types of carrier when the volume of air freight has reached full development. By the employment of this cost standard, the Board was enabled to reject the "no-cost" and "marginal-cost" standards advocated by the certificated carriers, without committing itself to the concept of "fully allocated cost" advocated by the noncertificated companies. The first two concepts were rejected on the ground that they might be expected to result in rates which, although justifiable for small amounts of air freight accommodated on flights already scheduled for other purposes, would have to be raised when the development of traffic volume necessitated the initiation of all-freight schedules. The "fully allocated cost" concept was rejected because its application "would probably unjustifiably restrict the development of freight volume and unwarrantably deny the public . . . the benefits in reduced unit costs which such volume increases would bring." [124]

Little fault can be found with the reasoning of the Board in rejecting these three cost concepts as bases for a general rate floor. However, in connection with the standard actually used by the Board, two important points should be noted. First, there is no explicit consideration of the possibility that unit costs of the all-cargo services might be lowered with fuller utilization of available capacity, although the considerable spread between average cost per available ton-mile of capacity (11 cents) and average cost per ton-mile on the basis of experienced load factors (16 cents) might suggest that either promotional rates, enabling fuller loading of available planes, or curtailment of available capacity, enabling concentration of loads in fewer

[124] *Ibid.*, p. 10.

planes, could bring about considerable economies. In view of possible practical obstacles to improvements in load factors, and since, as the Board noted, prices of productive factors used by the air carriers had continued to rise since the period for which cost data were used, it cannot be ascertained whether or to what extent the 16-cent floor exceeds "attainable" cost levels when such load-factor improvements are taken into account. The significant point is that these possibilities were not even considered.

Second, the fact that these possibilities were not considered, although they would seem to be eminently relevant to the Board's concept of "reasonably attainable costs," suggests that the cost standard actually employed was chosen because it was believed to be high enough to keep the noncertificated carriers financially solvent rather than because of any intrinsic economic merits. For the purpose of rescuing the cargo carriers, the floor decided upon was certainly liberally low, and the Board was careful to leave the way open for individual exemptions from the order that could be specifically justified;[125] nevertheless, it seems justifiable to conclude that the principal aim and guiding consideration in this decision was the protection of the cargo carriers from bankruptcy.

Even this action does not, of course, represent a clear extension of the protective principle embodied in the entry and variation-of-service cases to the rate dimension of competition. So far, both direct intervention by the Board for protective purposes and approved concerted action by the carriers have been limited to instances where a number of carriers are threatened with loss. It remains to be seen what the Board will do if only one carrier is so threatened by the rate reductions of a competitor. (Competitive repercussions have so far been relatively unimportant factors in the passenger-rate decisions of the Civil Aeronautics Board; however, the asserted improbability that a proposed rate would cover the costs of two competitive carriers was one factor that led to the disallowance of a proposed effective fare reduction between the United States and Hawaiian

---

[125] *Ibid.,* p. 25.

points.[126]) But it is evident that a logical extension of the principles generally employed by the Board would require that it intervene in such an instance to prevent the bankruptcy of an air carrier subject to its jurisdiction, regardless of the cost level "reasonably attainable" by it or by its competitor. We conclude, then, that the protection that must logically be afforded by the Board to the regulated companies must necessarily weaken the incentive provided by the existence of close competition, and in this sense operate to prevent the "maximum development of air transport" that is expected to result from such competition.

Whether or not the decisions of the Board with respect to rate agreements within the IATA machinery may be taken as indicative of a generally favorable disposition toward nonaggressive price policies on the part of carriers under its jurisdiction, it seems probable that the Board's approval of the participation of air carriers in such organizations as the IATA Traffic Conferences and the Air Traffic Conference in itself affects the price-output policies of the carriers by strengthening the tendency toward nonaggressiveness which would seem to be inherent in the fewness of firms that characterizes the typical air-transport market. For it would appear that taking part in such organizations would tend to make the policy determiners within each firm more acutely aware at once of the effect of their own decisions on the fortunes of their rivals and of the influence on their own revenues of the policies adopted by the latter, and thus to insure that the policies followed by each carrier would reflect fully the anticipated repercussions of induced (or retaliatory) price cutting.

It is here that the Board's decisions come to have a bearing on the degree of oligopolistic interdependence reflected in the price-output policies of the regulated firms.

It is evident that the regulatory action of the Board can have no direct effect on the hypotheses governing the actions of the regulated firms; these are subject only to indirect influence through decisions such as those concerned with trade associa-

---

[126] The Hawaiian Common Fares Case, Orders Serial No. E–3625, November 29, 1949.

tions. It is also evident that the practical significance of these hypotheses consists entirely in their actual effectiveness in the determination of price-output policy. Therefore their significance in a regulated industry depends upon the degree to which that policy is allowed to be determined by the managements of the regulated firms rather than the regulatory authority itself; there would be little use in investigating the opinions of airline managements regarding competitive reactions if rates and capacity were determined entirely by the Civil Aeronautics Board.

In fact, however, the initiative in the determination of prices and capacity rests to a very large extent in the hands of airline managements. As regards prices, the Board is indeed empowered by law to set aside such rates as it considers unreasonable, and to prescribe reasonable rates; nevertheless, the carriers retain the initiative in rate making, and until very recently their decisions were revised by the Board only in exceptional circumstances. Apart from certain actions undertaken to reduce the over-all rate level when carrier earnings were exceedingly large because of wartime conditions, and the general freight-rate floor already discussed, the Board's regulation of commercial rates has been mainly designed to insure that such rates shall be such as to maximize the net revenues of the carriers by which they are charged, rather than to bring about conformity to either historical or attainable costs.[127]

In general, the downward revision of a carrier decision on commercial rates, since it requires a finding of "unreasonableness," would seem to involve a showing that the rates in question were greatly in excess of the statistically demonstrable cost of carriage. Any such revision of the rate level *on the initiative of the regulatory body* without such a showing would be unprecedented in the field of transport regulation in this country, and it seems reasonable to suppose that it would be very difficult to obtain judicial sanction for such a decision. For example, let it be assumed that the price-output policy of a particular airline has been determined in the first instance by

[127] See L. S. Keyes "Passenger Fare Policies of the Civil Aeronautics Board" 18 *Journal of Air Law and Commerce* 46 (1951).

reference to a demand curve that reflects some degree of oligopolistic interdependence among the firms, and that the airline is operating at higher prices and smaller capacity than would be indicated by conditions of maximum efficiency. Unless this firm were also earning excess returns, any attempt on the part of the regulatory authority to correct this situation by fixing lower rates would be unprecedented and probably impossible.

As to capacity for carriage, again the initiative is almost entirely with the airline firms, except as regards service found to be necessary for the transportation of mail. Subject to the approval of the Board, the Postmaster General may require the addition of such schedules as are needed for the mail service, and every certificated carrier is obligated under the Act to provide sufficient service to accommodate the mails.[128] Although the Board has power to require the furnishing of "adequate" service, this phrase is usually construed to mean a minimum of performance, and probably could not be relied on to sanction more than a very small degree of initiative on the part of the Board in the adjustment of the quantity of service.[129] Furthermore, the Board cannot determine the amount of service by stipulation in certificates of convenience and necessity.[130] The Board may exert a limited influence on the capacity for carriage offered through its discretion as to what operations to include in computing the amount of the subsidy; in practice,

[128] Section 405(*e*) of the Civil Aeronautics Act provides in part: "The Postmaster General may designate any . . . schedule for the transportation of mail between the points between which the air carrier is authorized by its certificate to transport mail, and may, by order, require the air carrier to establish additional schedules for the transportation of mail between such points." Section 401(*m*) of this Act provides in part: "Whenever so authorized by its certificate, any air carrier shall provide necessary and adequate facilities and service for the transportation of mail, and shall transport mail whenever required by the Postmaster General."

[129] On this point see Transcontinental and Western Air, Inc., *et al.*, Additional North-South California Services, Supplemental Opinion, 4 C.A.B. 373, 374–375 (1948).

[130] Civil Aeronautics Act, Section 401(*f*): "No term, condition, or limitation of a certificate shall restrict the right of an air carrier to add to or change schedules, equipment, accommodations, and facilities for performing the authorized transportation and service as the development of the business and the demands of the public shall require."

however, all operations that are fairly well patronized by the public at the usual commercial rate level have been found eligible for subsidization.[131]

Thus it would appear that both the rate level and the output of airline firms are largely determined by their managements, and the power of the regulatory authority to alter these decisions in the direction of the economic optimum is limited. In this situation, the degree of oligopolistic interdependence reflected in these decisions is of great practical significance. For if, as seems highly probable, the price-output policies of individual firms are fixed on a nonaggressive basis, and these policies prevent lower production costs which would be otherwise attainable, then the rate and entry policies followed by the Board might be expected to lead to results somewhat similar to the equilibrium situation in the Chamberlinian "small group" with free entry.[132]

Furthermore, it will be seen that the Board's power to achieve the economic optimum with respect to the number of firms in any market and the distribution of output among them is limited by its restricted power over rates charged and capacity supplied; in a situation where equilibrium has been attained with too many firms, the Board would probably find it impossible to lower prices and redistribute output in accordance with maximum efficiency.

The ability of the Board to achieve the economic optimum is also limited by the fact that it can only approve or disapprove entry proposals advanced by individual carriers. This condition obviously restricts the action of the Board in connection both with the determination of the investment and the number of firms in any market and with the choice of a carrier to provide service that may be found to be required. In partic-

---

[131] Only schedules that have failed to meet this condition have been disallowed for inclusion in the computation of the mail payment. See, for example, Braniff Airways, Inc., Mail Rates, 1 C.A.A. 353, 358–359 (1939).

[132] E. H. Chamberlin, *The Theory of Monopolistic Competition*, pp. 104–105. The difference between the equilibrium result in the Chamberlinian "small group" with free entry and the equilibrium result to be expected from limited regulation with nonaggressive policies on the part of the regulated firms is discussed in Chapter VII.

ular, the Board cannot order the performance of operation over a new route by any carrier. Moreover, although the Act empowers it to amend existing certificates by including therein new terminal and intermediate points, this provision has been rather narrowly interpreted by the Board itself,[133] and, in view of the very restrictive judicial construction of a somewhat similar provision of the Interstate Commerce Act,[134] it could be argued that this narrow interpretation is the only one that would be acceptable to the courts.

It is of course true that the Board, particularly in the international route cases and to some extent in the recent "area" proceedings, has in fact exercised a considerable degree of initiative in determining the route pattern. In these cases, the applications submitted by the carriers were, in accordance with suggestions made by the Board, of a less specific character than those usually submitted, and therefore permitted a much greater scope for regulatory influence that is ordinarily possible. However, even in these cases the discretion of the Board could be exercised only within an area determined by the prior initiative of the carriers themselves.

The general significance of the limited nature of the Board's regulatory powers will be more fully dealt with in the following chapters.

[133] Section 401(*h*) of the Civil Aeronautics Act provides that the Board "upon petition or complaint or upon its own initiative, after notice and hearing, may alter, amend, modify, or suspend any such certificate [of public convenience and necessity], in whole or in part, if the public convenience and necessity so require." For the Board's own interpretation of this provision, see Panagra Terminal Investigation, 4 C.A.B. 670 (1944).

[134] See I.C.C. v. Oregon-Washington R. Co., 288 U.S. 14 (1933).

PART III

CONCLUSIONS

CHAPTER VII

SUMMARY AND EVALUATION OF REGULATORY POLICY

SUMMARY OF REGULATORY POLICY

IN REGULATING the competitive relations among air carriers subject to its jurisdiction, the Civil Aeronautics Board has not set up any particular value of the Triffinian coefficients as an ideal condition to be aimed at, nor has it directly attempted to bring about an "economic optimum" in terms of total investment in the production of any particular product or in terms of distribution of investment among firms. The initiative in determining the quantity and type of service offered in any air-transport market, including the inauguration of services by new firms (both old and new business enterprises), has remained in general with the carriers themselves, the power of the Board having been exercised to prevent the initiation of any new services or any alterations in existing relations that were expected to affect the revenues of carriers already serving the field in such a way as to make unprofitable the maintenance of their total output at substantially the existing level.

Thus in so far as the action of the Board has been a determining influence in the competitive relations among carriers as affected by entry, this influence has been exerted solely in providing protection for the revenues of carriers already serving the markets in question. This objective has been implemented (*a*) through denial of certification to proposed services, and (*b*) through the imposition of restrictions in the certificates governing such services. The "presumption" in favor of parallel services, and the Board's general predilection in favor of genuinely substitutable services in all markets, has never been allowed to overrule the protective principle adopted by the

Board, but has been significant only in ruling out more restrictive competitive limitations, such as the principle that no competitive operation should be authorized where the carrier already in the field is serving it in a manner that occasions no active complaint on the part of the consumers. In defining the sphere of air-carrier operations to which the control of entry is applied, the Board has logically attempted to include all types of operation that involve potential significant diversion of present traffic from certificated carriers. It has in one notable instance failed to effectuate this policy, but this unintentional aberration has been subsequently corrected.

On the basis of available data, it is not possible to measure in each particular case the extent to which the Board's anticipations as to the economic effects of authorized operations have been realized in practice. However, the steady decline in the average plane-mile mail payment up to the end of the war seems to indicate at least that in general the Board's expectations regarding competitive inroads on revenues were not so unduly optimistic as to prevent rapid progress toward commercial self-sufficiency.

It is true that the feeder lines have turned out to require an unexpectedly large and continuing contribution by the Government; but, as has been noted, this type of operation was always regarded as experimental. Furthermore, the competitive issue in these cases was of minor significance. The extent to which the postwar financial difficulties of the certificated trunk lines can be attributed to error on the part of the Board is problematical. It may be noted, however, that the position of these carriers has improved notably, without any drastic reversals of Board action, and that internal economies by some of these carriers were apparently very effective in bringing this improvement about.

Gill and Bates have attempted to determine to what degree these financial difficulties were due to "excessive competition." They have shown that some of the smaller trunk lines were adversely affected by Board-authorized extensions of their systems into markets in which they could not effectively compete.[1]

[1] F. W. Gill and G. L. Bates, *Airline Competition*, pp. 620–622.

This result, however, may have been due to some extent to transitional difficulties that may disappear once these carriers have become established in these markets. It is not convincingly shown that the Board's authorizations were responsible for the hard times experienced by other trunk lines. The difficulties of three of the Big Four are attributed in part to "excessive competition" in their major markets on the ground that each of these three could probably have operated more profitably in these markets at higher rates and with poorer standards of service in the absence of competition.[2] But it is not clear how any one of these carriers could have been relieved from the pressures of "excessive competition" without depriving some other carrier (or carriers) of its (or their) most heavily traveled routes.

Neither the predilection in favor of substitutable services nor the principle of protection has been justified by the Board in terms of the promotion of a static economic optimum. The former has been defended on the basis of the promotion of improvements in technology and service supposed to be stimulated by the existence of competition; this stimulus in turn has been held to be required by the Act's direction to the Board to promote the maximum development of the industry, and, secondarily, by the declaration in favor of competition in Section 2(d). The Board has defended the latter by reference to its duty to promote "sound economic conditions" in air transport, a phrase that it has interpreted as meaning the promotion of the financial self-sufficiency of the carriers under its jurisdiction without any substantial intermediate curtailment of their operations.

The same limiting principle has been employed by the Board in its decisions on the alteration of existing competitive relations through (a) the alteration of the physical characteristics of a service competitive with another airline operation; and (b) the extension of the route systems of particular carriers through (i) the award of new routes and (ii) the acquisition of routes already operated by another carrier. The requirement of "sound economic conditions" has also been given a broader application

[2] *Ibid.*, pp. 618–620.

in connection with the choice of carriers to operate new routes. The Board has held that both this requirement and the maintenance of competition as directed in Section 2(*d*) justify the award of new routes to relatively small and weak carriers where considerations of maximum through service and minimum cost would have indicated the choice of larger and stronger carriers, in order to improve the financial status of the former. Although the limiting principle, like the broader application of the "sound-economic-conditions" requirement, has tended to favor the weak carriers as compared with the strong, the Board has in no case adopted the equalization of size, competitive strength, or over-all profitability of the carriers as an ultimate aim, and has expressly disavowed such equalization as a regulatory objective.

The Board's exit policy, as indicated in its decisions regarding mergers of lines rendering competitive services, is similar to but not entirely symmetrical with its entry policy. The elimination of a firm from a market, even where it had in the past been operating at the required degree of self-sufficiency and presented no threat to the profitable maintenance of the operations of other firms in the same market, has on occasion been approved by the Board. Although in no case has the Board disapproved a proposed transaction *solely* because of the anticipated elimination of a firm from any market, statements made in connection with approved transactions, as well as the position taken by the Board in a case where the elimination of a firm was one of the considerations entering into the disapproval of a proposed transaction, give reason to suppose that the elimination of a firm would bring about the disapproval of a proposal if it would result in the suppression of *all* genuinely substitutable services in any market (provided, of course, that the competitive services were capable of maintenance at the approved degree of profitability).

In passing upon agreements between the carriers, the Board has consistently refused to authorize any undertaking that would have restricted the routes or general type of traffic served by any participant or nonparticipant company. Such agreements, since they might involve a more restrictive limitation on competitive service than that accepted by the Board, are manifestly contrary to its general policy outlined above. The same principle is embodied in the Board's requirement of nonexclusivity in industry-wide agreements effecting improved service.

Although the evidence regarding the Board's opinion on agreements restricting the quantity of service offered by particular carriers is not sufficient to form a basis for a definite conclusion on this point, it can be said that in the foreign field, at least, it has opposed this type of undertaking as in itself contrary to public policy. A general opposition to such a limitation could be interpreted as a consistent outgrowth of the Board's general policy in favor of competition, since the availability of substitutable services would afford little stimulus to management if the possibility of substitution of preferred services by airline users were hampered by agreed restrictions on the quantity of such services that could be offered. Nevertheless, in view of the Board's usual subordination of the competitive to the protective principle, it is to be expected that such restrictions will be approved if they are found to be necessary to preserve "sound economic conditions" among the carriers subject to the Board's jurisdiction.

With regard to concerted carrier actions designed to limit competition in certain specific dimensions (competition being here defined as a process rather than a relation, i.e., independent profit-maximizing activity considered from the point of view of its effect on the revenues of competitive firms), it is first of all evident that such undertakings are not regarded as *ipso facto* undesirable, which is to say that the Board does not consider that public policy demands that the carriers be free to act in all available dimensions of competitive effort. A broadly similar view is now and has always been generally adopted in practice with respect to the competitive activities of all firms, regardless of the type of commodity produced; the law of contracts, laws requiring the correct labeling of products, the Federal Trade Commission Act, and many other statutes embodying long-accepted principles of public policy represent legal limitations on the dimensions of profit-maximizing activity.

Secondly, it is apparently the case that the Board has not

adopted the view that competition in rates is in itself an undesirable dimension of competitive activity in the air-transport field. The position adopted by the Board may be contrasted with that apparently accepted by the Interstate Commerce Commission, which has favored competition in service but has regarded rate competition with suspicion or indifference. It is true that in the international field the Board has given tentative approval to rate making by conferences of the competitive carriers, a procedure which may in fact amount to the abandonment of competition in the rate dimension (i.e., the independent maximization of profits by the participant carriers by individual rate fixing). The conference method of rate making would *necessarily* involve the abandonment of rate competition only if there were no possibility of independent pricing by individual participants. In this connection, it is significant that, in approving the IATA Traffic Conference Resolution, the Board indicated its understanding that "the right of independent action of any carrier, once it has observed the conference procedures, must be scrupulously preserved." [3] In fact, however, the "right" of individual carriers to pursue independent policies may have no practical significance, since it is to be expected that each participant will feel itself strongly obligated to conform to the decisions of the group, and that nonconformity might result in direct retaliation by the other members of the Conference or their governments. The general significance of even this tentative approval of conference rate making is, however, open to question because of the special circumstances that conditioned the Board's decision in this instance, especially the facts that (1) the agreement procedure was regarded as the only avenue through which effective regulatory control of the rates charged by United States-flag international operators could be achieved, and (2) the alternative to acquiescence to the conference method was conceived to be unilateral control of rates charged by these carriers by the governments of foreign countries served by them. In the domestic field, the Board has disapproved compulsory prior notification and discussion of changes in freight rates other than joint rates and probably

[3] IATA Traffic Conference Resolution, 6 C.A.B. 639, 645 (1946).

will do the same with respect to passenger rates. Here it has not approved conference rate making as such, and has approved major concerted rate actions by the carriers only where this was deemed essential for their financial welfare. Similarly, the only instance in which the Board has itself intervened to limit rate competition was one in which an entire class of carriers — the noncertificated freight lines — were thought to be threatened with bankruptcy. From this it may be tentatively concluded that the Board considers that public policy demands the maintenance of competition in rates where it does not bring about results contrary to "sound economic conditions" among the carriers in general or a class of carriers; it remains to be seen what the Board's position will be with regard to rate competition that threatens the financial welfare of only one or a few isolated carriers. It may be noted, however, that a logical extension of the principle involved in the cases dealing with entry and with variations in the physical character of the service would require not only approval of carrier action to restrict competition in such a situation, but direct restrictive intervention by the Board itself were no such carrier action forthcoming.

The agreed restriction of independent carrier action in a particular subdivision of the rate dimension, i.e., the granting of free or reduced-rate transportation, has indeed been explicitly approved by the Board. In this instance, the limitation designated by the agreement was substantially similar to one that might plausibly be read into the Civil Aeronautics Act itself, and was justified by the Board on the basis of the "abuses" attending the unlimited furnishing of free and reduced-rate service by surface carriers.

The Board has also permitted the carriers to enter into agreements limiting competition in the "service" and "selling" dimensions, most of which may be justified in terms of product improvements that could have been accomplished only through coöperative action, or of the promotion of rational choice on the part of consumers. There are, however, certain agreements not disallowed by the Board that cannot be so justified, and appear to represent merely devices designed to protect the carriers from the risks involved in certain minor subdivisions of competitive activity. It can only be conjectured that the types of product variation involved were regarded by the Board as of such minor significance that their suppression by agreement could not be regarded as contrary to public policy.

Since the Board has explained its predilection in favor of competitive services by reference to the stimulus that is supposed to be afforded to improvements in techniques of operation and service, it seems probable that any agreement limiting the independent action of carriers in the adoption of major changes in such techniques would be disapproved, at least unless the agreed restriction were deemed necessary to preserve "sound economic conditions" in air transport. In view of the position taken by the Board with respect to the alteration of existing competitive relations by such changes in the physical characteristics of the service as are directly subject to its jurisdiction (e.g., the inauguration of nonstop service between centers previously served via one or more intermediate points) and by the extension of the route systems of particular carriers, and in view of its approval of concerted rate making where this was thought to be required for the financial welfare of the carriers, it seems probable that any type of restrictive agreement, even though it limited independent action by the carriers in an "approved" dimension of competitive effort, would be authorized if it were regarded as essential to the preservation of the financial welfare of any or all of the carriers. Indeed, the Board's conception of "sound economic conditions" would seem logically to require not only the approval of any carrier action deemed necessary to protect the financial position of a regulated company, but, if no such action were forthcoming on the part of the carriers, the intervention of the Board on its own initiative, through its rate-fixing or other powers, to accomplish this objective.

Finally, it appears that the Board's policy of protection of the financial status of particular carriers is not necessarily or ultimately an outgrowth of the subsidization program. Even a policy of subsidization based on meeting the financial needs of particular carriers would not in every case require, in order to get the most for the Government's money, the prohibition of new competition resulting in an increased "need" for the carrier rendering an existing service. The policy that *does* always require such a prohibition is that of the maintenance and continuous promotion of the profitability of particular air carriers. If it is postulated that the subsidy "liability" of the Government will cease only when each of the mail carriers is operating at a level of commercial self-sufficiency, then it is true that this promotional policy would coincide with the requirements of long-run Government economy, *defined as the extinction of all obligation to the mail carriers,* as long as any gap exists between total costs and commercial revenues. Nevertheless, it is not necessary to invoke Government economy as an explanatory principle even in connection with the mail carriers; and the use of protective regulation in the interest of nonmail carriers would not, of course, be subject to explanation on this ground. Moreover, the need-rate subsidization program itself does not require progressive self-sufficiency; the Board's adoption of this principle itself represents a not unreasonable interpretation of the Act's mandate to promote "sound economic conditions." It is in fact by direct reference to this mandate that the Board has justified its economic regulatory policy. Thus it is to be expected that the Board will continue to act upon the same essential principles if all the carriers subject to its jurisdiction attain unquestionable commercial self-sufficiency, and even if the "need-rate" subsidy policy should be stricken from the Act.

This is not, of course, to say that the need-rate program of subsidization would itself have been consistent with the achievement of optimum economic performance in the subsidized field. Where the Government's commitment to each carrier is measured by the amount necessary to support its operations at a predetermined level of investment, an arbitrary limitation is placed on the distribution of Government payments along firms. The Government is thus not free to choose that distribution of output among firms that would be required by the attainment of maximum output at the going rate of subsidy, since the payment to existing firms cannot be reduced to reflect any large reduction in their output that might be dictated by considerations of maximum operating efficiency. Where this limitation is operative — that is, where the cost to the Government of any given output is actually increased by the necessity of supporting any firm at a predetermined level of operations — the return in terms of service that can be obtained per unit of expenditure is smaller than that which could be obtained if there were no occasion for such support. Thus even if the Board had followed a policy of permitting new competition wherever it would have resulted in the provision of a larger total output at the accepted subsidy rate than could have been provided by the expansion of an existing firm, and had thus achieved the best results possible within the framework of the need-rate program, these results probably would not in many cases have been as good as those that would have been possible without this limitation on the distribution of Government payments.

This limitation would, of course, represent merely a necessary evil — or an instrumental good — if the support of particular carriers were a legitimate aim of the subsidization program. But it is at once evident that such support cannot conceivably represent an *ultimate* expression of the national interest in this field. Moreover, as is brought out in the following chapter, such support not only is not required by any defensible independent definition of the national interest, but is in conflict with the achievement of any such independent aim.

In so far as the intent of Congress can be discovered by examining the background of the Civil Aeronautics Act and the statements of its leading Congressional advocates, it is possible to say that the administration of the Act by the Board appears to be perfectly consistent with that intent. The final abandonment of the system of competitive bidding for mail routes, the special importance attached to the certification requirement for all new scheduled air services and the arguments adduced in its support, and the relative insignificance of the other regulatory features of the Act, all point to the conclusion that the framers of the Act desired to provide protection for the financial status of the scheduled air-transport companies. It may also be inferred from the arguments used in favor of the certification requirement that it was not advocated primarily as a necessary adjunct to the subsidization policy either to conserve government funds through the prevention of competitive inroads on the revenues of subsidized carriers, or to provide a means of allocation of the subsidy, but as a measure to promote the financial welfare of the carriers for reasons independent of governmental economy. Thus the Board's usual appeal to the "sound-economic-conditions" principle rather than considerations of governmental economy in support of its protective policy seems to conform entirely to the views of Congress.

Although it is impossible on the basis of the record to determine what type or degree of "competition" the Board was directed by the Congressional proponents of the Act to promote — whether or not, for example, they had in mind the gentlemanly emulation between essentially noncompetitive carriers extolled by the Federal Aviation Commission — this competition was certainly to be of a species consistent with the protection of the finances of particular carriers. In this respect, the competition in fact fostered by the Board measures up precisely to the Congressional standard. It does not, of course, conform to the competitive ideal of the Federal Aviation Commission. In defining competition in effect as the availability of genuinely substitutable services, the Board has definitely rejected the position taken by the Commission on this point; the Board's doctrine of a presumption in favor of parallel services is the direct opposite of the Commission's view.

EVALUATION OF REGULATORY POLICY

As was pointed out in Chapter II, the appropriate standard for economic performance to be used in the evaluation of both uncontrolled markets and public policy with regard to regulated markets is what has been termed the unconditional economic optimum, defined for any given product as that investment at which those who pay for the product are obtaining the maximum output for which they are willing to pay the necessary cost (i.e., average transfer cost) and at which no factor unit could increase its productivity by transferring either into or out of the use in question. Accordingly, it is this standard that will be used here in the evaluation of the regulatory policy of the Civil Aeronautics Board (which, as has been noted, appears to be precisely the policy that was intended by its framers to be embodied in the Civil Aeronautics Act). Given the proposition that the Government is interested in obtaining the maximum output that can be obtained at the accepted rate of subsidy, the optimum from the point of view of the Government as subsidizer is identical with that for other demanders of the service. As in the case of these other consumers, the Government's aim of getting the most for its money is here subjected to the limitation that it pay the full cost for the service obtained, that is, that the burden is not shifted by the artificial expansion of commercial demand or retention of factors within the subsidized market by arbitrary limitations on substitute services.

It should be emphasized at the outset that the powers of the Board are quite inadequate for the achievement of the optimum condition through regulatory action and that neither the framers of the Act nor its administrators have conceived this result as an aim of regulation. The question, then, is not whether or to what extent the Board has been successful in bringing about the optimum condition, but rather whether the regulation administered by the Board, directed as it is to the attainment of quite different ends, tends to influence the functioning of the affected markets toward or away from the economic optimum.

Concerning the major influence of regulation on the affected air-transport markets — that is, the influence exerted in implementation of the aim of promoting "sound economic conditions" in the air-transport business — it may be said that this influence has clearly represented an obstruction to the achievement of optimum investment and the most efficient distribution of output among firms.

In connection with the discussion of the Board's entry policy in Part II, it has been pointed out that the principle of protection of the revenues of existing firms would tend to prevent the achievement of the unconditional optimum for investment and of the most efficient distribution of output among firms even if the Board had otherwise unlimited power to set rates and output for each of the regulated carriers in every market. The same argument obviously applies to the protective principle as employed in the regulation of the alteration of existing competitive relations. It has also been suggested that the Board's concern with promoting the profitability of relatively small and weak carriers, which has resulted in some cases in the award of routes to such carriers where considerations of maximum through service and minimum cost of operation would have indicated another choice, and which, like the protective principle, may be explained in terms of the Board's (and Congress') concept of "sound economic conditions" in the air-transport field, presents an obstacle to the accomplishment of maximum efficiency; this would also be true were the Board's powers over rates and investment otherwise unlimited.

Similarly, such unlimited powers would not remove the inevitable regulatory bias in favor of established carriers in the award of new services similar to those already operated by them. In this connection, it has been suggested that although the objectives of protecting or promoting the profitability of existing carriers have probably tended somewhat to weight the available evidence in favor of those companies against "newcomers," a more important factor has been the advantage given to the established companies by the very nature of administrative predetermination of the choice of carrier, which must necessarily give more weight to considerations of cost and service clearly demonstrable in advance than to those which can be proved only by future experience. This inherent tendency of regulation to favor established enterprises is obviously also a direct impediment to the achievement of optimum economic performance in so far as it excludes from the market new firms that would prove to be more efficient than existing enterprises in the production of products already available, or would make available new services capable of the required degree of self-support.

Thus it appears not only that the major influence of the Board's regulation of competitive relations among air carriers has not been directed toward the achievement of an economic optimum in terms of total investment in any sector of the air-transport market or of the distribution of output among firms, but that it is essentially in conflict with this aim, since the persistence of the protective principle would interfere with the accomplishment of the optimum even if the Board had complete power to determine price and output for every carrier. As has been noted, the optimum from the point of view of the Government as subsidizer is the same as that for other consumers. Thus, although the protective program tends toward and may actually result in the extinction of the Government's liability to the carriers, this program itself prevents the obtainment of the best economic results per unit of Government expenditure.

Furthermore, the Board's predilection in favor of genuinely competitive services (where consistent with the major principle) is in itself a hindrance to the achievement of optimum economic performance in so far as it results in the certification of new firms for the rendering of additional services that might be more efficiently produced by firms already serving the markets concerned. The Board's position has not been based on a contention that competition as such would insure the achievement of the economic optimum (conditional or unconditional) in the affected markets. In favoring the establishment of competition, the Board has not relied on any agreement that competition, pure or impure, must result in optimum investment or in the best possible distribution of output among firms. The Board has founded its policy upon firmer ground, namely, the belief that the existence of close competition stimulates progress in techniques of operation and service, i.e., that it brings about a more active experimentation by management in certain types of product variation and production methods than would otherwise occur.

In view of the fact that no state of competitive relations can be relied upon to achieve the (conditional or unconditional) economic optimum in any field in the absence of perfect freedom of factor movement in and out of this field, it is entirely suitable that the Board has not attempted to justify its policy in these terms. It is also entirely suitable that the Board has not prescribed any particular degree of competitiveness (e.g., homogeneous competition) as an ideal by which to judge proposed relations, since neither the economic optimum (conditional or unconditional) nor the Board's own concept of the benefits to be derived from competition requires or implies the existence of any such particular value for the coefficients involved. The working concept of competition (as relation) used by the Board is substantially the same as that indicated by Triffinian theory. For the Board, competition exists between air carriers when they are rendering services that are substitutable for each other to a significant degree.

Moreover, a good prima facie case can be made for the Board's view with respect to the stimulative value of close competition; since the existence of competition ordinarily means that a firm's revenues are at all times subject to curtailment as a result of the independent profit-maximizing activities of its rival or rivals, the policy determiners within a firm subject to competition are less likely to overlook any available means of strengthening its competitive position than they would be in a more sheltered situation. It is entirely possible that the long-range economic value of this stimulus might outweigh any immediate loss resulting from a departure from the distribution of output among firms indicated by the static optimum in order to institute close competition. However, it is to be noted that this stimulus would apply to all dimensions of economic effort — for example, to "selling" activities, to efforts to gain a more favorable strategic position with respect to the routing of traffic, and to attempts to fend off invasion of the market by means of legal devices or restrictive intercarrier agreements, as well as to advances in techniques of operation and service. For example, the competition experienced by the railroads from other agencies of transport in recent years stimulated not only improvements in techniques of rail service and operation and the reduction of some rail rates, but also vigorous and successful efforts through lobbying and publicity to obtain legislation that would protect rail revenues from competitive inroads, and attempts to gain protection by nonregulatory means such as the elimination of competitors by cutthroat competition, acquisition of competitive firms, and the conclusion of restrictive agreements with those firms.

More important than this, since the force of this stimulus is in direct proportion to the possible magnitude of competitive inroads as conceived by the policy determiners, it is in inverse proportion to the degree of protection of revenues assured to them by regulatory or other means. Thus the stimulus would be rendered totally ineffective by an absolute guarantee that the revenues of any firm could not be reduced as a result of the activities of a competitor, and would be greatly weakened if each firm were assured that a legal authority would always intervene to prevent its going bankrupt as a result of competitive inroads on its market, or to limit rigidly its gains at the expense of another regulated firm. Therefore it is clear that the logical extension of the Board's protective policy (as evidenced in connection with entry cases and with those having to do with competitive avenues directly under regulatory control) to include all competitive inroads by any type of firm activity would largely vitiate the intended effect of the Board's policy of fostering competition. Since the Board does not have direct control over all the activities of the carriers (e.g., its approval is not required for the adoption of new types of equipment), there is indeed no assurance of immediate protection of carrier revenues; nevertheless, it is probable that the power of the Board over commercial rates could be successfully used to accomplish effective and fairly prompt protection in most cases. In this event, the competitive stimulus would have little force; "competition" between air carriers would approximate the gentlemanly emulation envisaged by the Federal Aviation Commission. There appears to be an ultimate opposition between the Board's policy of protection and the full realization of the "benefits of competition" for the "maximum development" of air transportation.

The same opposition exists, of course, between the "need-rate" subsidization program and the realization of the benefits of competition. Where a company is assured that the Government will always provide sufficient revenues to keep it out of bankruptcy, it is obviously unreasonable to expect it to be fully sensitive to normal business incentives.

An entirely different principle is involved in the Board's sanction of the complete abandonment of certain lines of competitive effort, as opposed to the limitation of competitive activity in accordance with the policy of protection. As has been noted, the former has been brought about not by direct action originating in the Board, but by permission for "self-regulation" in the form of agreements formulated by the carriers themselves. There are a few such agreements the approval of which seems to be explicable only if it was intended to protect the carriers from the risks involved in certain minor phases of product variation (i.e., as an extension of the protective principle to include whole categories of economic activity apparently regarded as of relatively little significance for the "maximum development" of air transport). Most of them, however, may be justified on the basis of facilitating rational choice on the part of consumers or bringing about improved service. Independent determination of policy by each carrier along the lines dealt with in this class of approved agreements would tend to interfere with rational consumer choice or to detract from the quality of the service offered.

As to the first of these objectives, it may be said that the restriction of economic activity in accordance with this aim is defensible on grounds of both accepted general policy and economic theory. It has been pointed out above that a legal limitation on the dimensions of competitive effort is now and has always been generally practiced with respect to all firms, regardless of the type of commodity produced; it is further evident that misrepresentation of products to consumers has been one of the accepted grounds for restriction of particular activities. From the point of view of economic performance, any activity that prevents or hinders the rational evaluation of products in terms of other available channels of income use obviously impedes the optimum distribution of consumer purchases and of productive resources.

The case for the second type of competitive limitation is not quite so clear. Any administrative determination of what constitutes better "quality" of service must necessarily be open to the charge that it might conflict with the decision of the free market; for example, an elaborate and expensive product might be considered by the administrators to be of better "quality" than a more simple, but less expensive, type of commodity which would actually be preferred by consumers. Nevertheless, in the particular cases at issue here, there is no question of sacrificing economy to obtain "quality" — quite the contrary, in fact; furthermore, it would not be feasible to offer a choice to consumers between the service as conditioned by the agreements and the service as not so conditioned, and either approval or disapproval of the agreements would constitute an administrative determination of the type of service offered. The decisions, then, must be judged on the basis of the probable nature of consumer choice, and by this criterion they appear to be on firm ground. An important procompetitive policy followed by the Board in its regulation of intercarrier agreements is its requirement that industry-wide agreements resulting in an improved product be open to all certificated carriers on reasonable terms. This policy in effect rules out the exclusion of competitors from such agreements as an avenue of private-profit maximization; its limitation to *certificated* carriers is a logical reflection of the broad exclusion policy inherent in the Civil Aeronautics Act.

In approving intercarrier agreements ruling out competition along certain lines, the Board has rightly considered that such agreements do not amount to a total abandonment of competition between the participant carriers. Similarly, the Board has regarded the existence of a trade association dealing with "traffic" problems as entirely consistent with the maintenance of competition between air carriers. Both of these positions seem to be well taken. In the first place, neither the agreements nor the association destroys the competitive relations existing between firms in the air-transport business. Although the association does provide a means for discussion by representatives of competitive carriers of future actions with respect to price-output policy, it obviously does not amount to an annulment of the economic identities of the participant firms. Since it is not a pool (i.e., an organization of companies whereby the independent profit-maximizing activities of the companies concerned are abandoned in favor of unified policy determination to maximize over-all returns in each market served by these companies), it does not render the competitive relations between the services offered by participant carriers merely nominal through annihilating their separate economic existences as firms. In the second place, neither the association nor the agreements substitute concerted action for independent policy determination along all lines of economic endeavor; this substitution would indeed be consistent with the preservation of the economic identities of the firms but would reduce the independent activities of each of them to attempts to obtain policy decisions within the association which would approximate as nearly as possible the decisions that would be made by the individual firm were it to act without outside direction. The effect of the agreements in force is evidently much less restrictive; even the concerted rate making that obtains with provisional approval by the Board in the international markets for air transport merely limits independent activities on the part of the participant carriers in a single dimension of economic effort. Thus neither competition as relation between carriers nor competition as process is inconsistent with the existence of the association or the agreements.

However, it seems highly probable that the very existence of the Traffic Conferences tends to reinforce the tendency toward nonaggressiveness in price-output policy which would seem to be inherent in the fewness of significant competitors (and the quantitative significance of their competitiveness) that characterizes the typical market served by air-transport companies. As has been pointed out in the preceding chapter, it would appear that taking part in such a conference would tend to make the policy determiners within each firm more acutely aware at once of the effect of their own decisions on the fortunes of their rivals and of the influence on their own revenues of the policies adopted by the latter, and thus to insure that the policies followed by each carrier would reflect fully the anticipated repercussions of induced price cutting. Lower per-unit costs conceivably might be made possible by the relative expansion in firm output attending a price policy based on the assumption that all other prices would remain the same. To the extent that the nonaggressiveness in price policy promoted by the existence of the association prevents the attainment of these costs, the Board's sanction of the Traffic Conference tends to impede the attainment of the static optimum. Nevertheless, some such organization would seem to be essential for the achievement of such improvements in product as are made possible by the agreements respecting joint rates, interchange of passengers, and the like; moreover, given the existence of such an organization, it would probably be idle for the Board to prohibit prior discussion of proposed rate changes as one of its functions. Hence the nonaggressiveness in price policy resulting from participation in the organization appears to be inevitable if the "quality" of the air-transport product is to be maintained.

There is, however, another aspect of the regulatory system that tends to promote nonaggressiveness and that is not an inevitable consequence of the maintenance of the quality of the transport product, namely, the inherent tendency of regulation to favor existing carriers as opposed to newcomers in the award of new routes. This tendency, which until the postwar period resulted in the limitation of long-haul air transport between major centers to those carriers which were already operating similar services at the time regulation was instituted, probably promotes nonaggressiveness because of the greater likelihood that existing carriers will respect whatever live-and-let-live arrangements, tacit or otherwise, may have arisen among the carriers already operating in the market entered. The stimulus to promotional rate making resulting from the illegitimate passenger operations of the irregular carriers after World War II reinforces this conclusion.

The practical importance of this nonaggressiveness arises from the facts that (1) the initiative in rate making and determining capacity for carriage rests very largely with the carriers themselves, and (2) the power of the Board to alter these decisions in a promotional direction is extremely limited and (so far, at least) only rarely exercised. It is also probable that participation in such an organization promotes nonaggressiveness in other competitive dimensions — in particular, in those dimensions where the profits to be reaped by a change in policy depend to a large extent on the absence of similar action, or on a time lag before the adoption of similar action, by the competitors of the firm in question. To the extent that this is true, the very existence of the Conference might be expected to restrict competitive effort in certain types of "selling" activity as well as of variations in the type of service offered, and thus possibly to hinder somewhat the achievement of "maximum development" of air transport in the Board's sense.

In view of the large degree of initiative possessed by the carriers themselves in determining the distribution of output among firms in air-transport markets, the net effect of the present regulatory system on this distribution cannot be discovered merely on the basis of the policies followed by the Board, but must necessarily depend in part upon the nature of the decisions made by the carriers as well. An evaluation of the present regulatory system in terms of economic performance must take into consideration the influence of the initiative allowed to the carrier under this system as well as the direct and indirect influence of the decisions of the regulatory authority.

Given the nature of the typical air-transport market, in which the position of the individual firm is that of a significant competitor of one or a few other firms whose individual policies are also of importance for the revenues of the firm in question, and given also the existence of a trade association including representatives of all the scheduled-air-transport firms present in each market, it would seem to be inevitable that, in determining price as well as the particular nature of the product to be offered, the policy makers should take into account the probable repercussions on their own sales of induced reactions by their competitors — in short, that the policy of individual firms should be "nonaggressiveness." Taken together with the Board's entry policy, the net effect of the present regulatory system might be expected to be an equilibrium situation somewhat similar to that described in the Chamberlinian case of the "small group" with free entry in that the price-output policies of individual firms would have been determined by reference to a demand curve taking into account the induced reactions of competitors, and any existing "excess returns" (i.e., returns in excess of *replacement cost*) would have been eliminated by the addition of new competitors.

However, since the Board does not have power to add firms on its own initiative, the achievement of this result will of course depend on whether or not carrier proposals make possible the addition of the required number of firms. Furthermore, the demand and cost situation in the market (including such considerations as factor indivisibilities) might well be such as to make impossible the profitable maintenance of operations by new firms at precisely the level required for the elimination of excess returns of existing firms without any further inroads on their revenues; thus excess returns might persist in some or in all of the regulated markets. There are, moreover, important differences between the equilibrium situation to be expected from the present regulatory system and the Chamberlinian case.

In the first place, the identity of the firms occupying the market, and the distribution of sales among these firms, are determined under the present system by their priority of appearance; since regulatory control is designed to protect the revenues of each existing firm from competitive inroads to the extent necessary to maintain a normal return on all the resources it employs, there is no possibility of either the displacement of an existing firm by new competition or the redistribution of output among the firms in such a way as to force a substantial curtailment of the operations of any existing firm. (Although the Board's power over entry does not include authority to determine the capacity for carriage offered by the entrant, so that it might not through its entry power alone be able to give the desired degree of protection to the existing firms, yet its rate powers are probably sufficient to accomplish this objective should the need arise.)

Secondly, it should be emphasized that the difference between the two equilibria is not merely one of distribution of the output of a given product among firms. Wherever the air-transport firms serving a given market sell services that are not perfectly substitutable in the judgment of consumers, there will be a difference in the relative amounts of various services which are produced as compared with the product pattern that would exist without regulatory control, owing to the influence of time priority under the present regulatory system.

A further difference between the controlled and uncontrolled markets, which results directly from the protective principle but applies to the processes by which the equilibria are achieved rather than to the nature of the equilibria as such, is the absence under regulation of certain economic wastes that might occur because of the immobilization of resources in firms whose output had to be curtailed because of competitive inroads on demand. The quantitative importance of this factor in the air-transport business, however, is probably very small; employment in a particular air-transport firm does not involve any great degree of absolute immobilization of factors, and the costs of transfer to alternative uses for the factors not entirely immobilized appear to be relatively slight in most cases.

Finally, although it can be said that output per firm is probably smaller and the number of firms larger in any given market than would have been the case *if the existing firms had pursued aggressive price policies,* it cannot be said that the number of firms is larger than would have been the case *in the absence of regulation,* even though aggressive price policies had been adopted by all the firms. The protective principle might well result in some markets in the existence of fewer firms than would have survived in any case without the intervention of regulatory authority. The significance of the probable non-aggressiveness of carrier policy under regulation is to superimpose on the protective principle yet another obstacle to the adjustment of factors and consumer spending in accordance with the economic optimum; factors that might have been employed most productively in existing firms may be denied this opportunity because of the nature of the policies adopted by those firms.

The approach to the problem of new competition that has been suggested in the Southern Service to the West case[4] may result in a gradual correction of the tendency toward too many firms (in the sense indicated above) that is inherent in a situation of nonaggressiveness combined with entry control as developed by the Board. The suggested policy envisages the expansion of existing firms where excess returns develop, and a lowering of their rates as demand increases. However, such a policy is evidently no substitute for an unbiased appraisal of all available possibilities for the distribution of output among old and new firms, and logically carried out would presumably result in a tendency to overexpansion on the part of the former. More important than this, it is evident that the new policy does not change the underlying principle of protection.

It is the protection of existing firms that constitutes the essential difference between "regulated competition," as exemplified in the scheduled-air-transport business in this country, and "unregulated competition," as exemplified in industry in general. That aspect of the regulation of the scheduled-air-transport field which is designed to rule out certain avenues of competitive effort — accomplished, as has been noted, through the approval of agreements initiated by the carriers themselves — is to a large extent paralleled in all fields of economic activity, and finds a particularly close analogue in the regulation carried on by the Federal Trade Commission through the so-called Trade Practice Conference. The principle of nonexclusivity applied to industry-wide agreements participation in which is necessary to the provision of a superior product also conforms closely to precedent developed in the regulation of general industry under the antitrust laws. The significance of this type of regulation will be more fully dealt with in the following section. The specific powers over air transport granted to the Civil Aeronautics Board were apparently aimed at, and are probably adequate for, the achievement of the protection of particular firms; they were not aimed at, nor are they adequate for, the achievement of maximum efficiency in terms of economic performance.

[4] Orders Serial No. E–5090, January 30, 1951.

Possible Regulatory Policies for the Future

It has been shown (1) that the present system of regulation of air transport is based on principles differing from those which would be necessary for the achievement of a static economic optimum, (2) that these principles would interfere with the achievement of such an optimum even if the Board's powers over the air-transport business were otherwise unlimited, (3) that they interfere, and are basically in contradiction, with the full attainment of the "benefits of competition" expected by the Board to result from the availability to the public of genuinely substitutable air-transport services, and (4) that the present system tends toward an equilibrium situation that departs from the static optimum (conditional or unconditional). Such a showing is, however, insufficient basis for a recommendation that the present system be abandoned, for it might well be that any other possible policy would be still more unsatisfactory from the point of view of economic performance.

There will be discussed three possible governmental policies toward air transport which immediately suggest themselves as offering certain advantages over the present system: (1) a policy that would empower and direct the Board to channel resources into and within the air-transport business in accordance with the unconditional economic optimum; (2) a policy that would remove the regulatory obstacles to the achievement of the optimum and of the dynamic benefits of competition by abolishing all the present specific regulation of the air-transport business; and (3) a policy that would remove the regulatory obstacles to the achievement of the optimum and of the dynamic benefits of competition by abandoning those particular aspects of the present system which present such obstacles while retaining specific regulation designed to promote these aims. These possibilities will be discussed with only incidental reference to the special problems raised by the present subsidization program. These problems, as well as the general question of the proper scope and method of subsidization, will be discussed in the following chapter.

(1) To empower the Board to alter total investment and the distribution of output among firms in any air-transport market in accordance with the unconditional optimum would require a radical extension of its authority as compared with its present scope. For example, it would be necessary to authorize the Board (*a*) to order the expansion or contraction of capacity for carriage maintained by any firm without reference to the effect of this action on the rate of return on the existing investment in that firm; (*b*) to order the extension, abandonment, or alteration of the routes served by any carrier without reference to the certificated rights of the carrier or to the desires of the carrier's policy makers regarding the routes to be served; (*c*) to order changes in the detailed nature of the service offered on any route, including type of equipment, timing of schedules, and the like; (*d*) to order consolidation or dissolution of present carrier route systems on its own initiative.

It is clear that such broad powers could not be exercised within the framework of private ownership of the air carriers. Not only would the authority of the Board necessarily penetrate to the most detailed aspects of operations policy (logically including even the hiring and dismissal of particular personnel), but the required total disregard of returns on existing investment would certainly bring about results that would be regarded as unconstitutional violations of property rights; moreover, it would most probably be constitutionally impossible to require any sizeable extension of any route system not proposed by the carrier itself, or to abrogate any certificated rights on purely economic grounds.[5] Indeed, since the Board's actions in pursuit of the economic optimum would necessarily be based on estimated demands, and since even the behavior of costs would be in many cases impossible to estimate accurately in advance, a certain risk of loss through error would be unavoidable; it would be manifestly unjust to compel private owners to bear such losses, as well as those resulting from the deliberate in-

---

[5] Under the present law, a certificate may be revoked only after it has been shown that the carrier holding it has intentionally failed to comply with (1) any provision of Title IV of the Civil Aeronautics Act, (2) any rule, order, or regulation issued by the Board under this Title, or (3) any term, condition, or limitation of the certificate. Civil Aeronautics Act, Section 402(*h*).

tent of the Board, since they would be incurred through policies in the making of which these owners had had no voice.

The actual administration of this policy would obviously involve problems of an entirely different order from those confronting the traditional regulatory agency. The difficulties to be expected in anticipating demands and costs have been discussed in Chapter III; it was there pointed out that the relatively rapid and unpredictable changes in the basic data of consumer tastes and available techniques of operation and service in the air-transport business would serve further to complicate the task of administration. This is not to say that the policy itself should be ruled out because of the magnitude of the technical difficulties involved, but it is evident that the administrative task would be one of constant experimentation and readjustment rather than a mere once-for-all revision of the present industrial setup in accordance with a fixed set of norms. At any point in time, therefore, it could not be expected that the adjustment of investment to demand would conform to the economic optimum defined in terms of the basic conditions prevailing at that point.

In the discussion of policy guides in Part I of this study, it has been suggested that the departure from the economic optimum required to justify intervention (with the objective of achieving the optimum) in firms producing commodities subject to close competition or frequent and large changes in demand and cost conditions would have to be large compared with that required with firms not so situated, because of the great difficulties involved in the deliberate accomplishment of this objective in these circumstances. It has also been suggested that the removal of the profit incentive to innovation might be expected to result in a slowing down of the rate of "economic progress" in the regulated field, and that this undesirable effect would be of greater quantitative significance in fields in which possibilities for innovations are more likely to occur; thus a relatively large departure from the optimum under conditions of free-market determination of factor returns would be necessary to justify broad intervention in such fields. Although it is admittedly exceedingly difficult to distinguish this last type of field in practice, it would seem that the air-transport business would have to be included within it, as well as within the two former categories.

Furthermore, particular care would have to be exercised in order that the original objective of the policy should not be sacrificed to obtain the surface appearance of conformity to a static optimum. For example, the manipulation of rates to provide a "fair return" to the resources invested in any or all of the air-transport markets, as a substitute for a required readjustment in the quantity or type of these resources, would have to be carefully avoided, as would the establishment of a fixed scale of relations between rates charged for various services by some such popularly accepted standard as relative length of haul. Such manipulations of rates would probably shield the administrative authority from a good deal of public criticism; but it would also deprive this authority of its major guide in the adjustment of investment.

Despite the fact that the ultimate policy-making functions would be centralized in the general administrative agency, so that the question of distribution of output among firms would not arise, the basic problems involved in this distribution would of course persist. These problems include the distribution of output among various types of service and the determination of the most efficient type of productive organization from a cost point of view. It is probable that certain savings (e.g., through the consolidation of terminal facilities, synchronization of schedules, and the like) could be accomplished more expeditiously under centralized control of the airline system than under the present system of competition; however, the coöperative measures being undertaken now through the Air Transport Association show that such economies can be accomplished without complete centralization of policy-making functions.

The chief advantages of such a system as compared with the present regime may now be summarized. The first (and probably the most important) of these advantages would be the destruction of the obstacle to optimum economic performance represented by the present policy of promoting "sound economic conditions" in air transport. Under this policy, there would be no need to preserve or to enhance the revenues accruing to resources used in the production of particular products or directed by particular management units. Secondly, certain economies could probably be accomplished more expeditiously than through the present system of coöperation between competing carriers. Thirdly, obstacles to the accomplishment of optimum economic performance arising directly from profit-maximizing policies of individual firms would be done away with. Since policy determination would be centralized and specifically directed to the achievement of the economic optimum, the obstacle that might be presented by nonaggressive policies made by individual firms would disappear. There would presumably be no separate problem of channeling economic activity in the air-transport field into those lines which are promotive of rather than contrary to the achievement of the optimum; for example, the Government-directed management would refrain as a matter of course from misleading advertising and agreements restricting the flow of resources into particular air-transport markets.

Finally, the adoption of this course would put an end to the division of responsibility for the profitable operation of the airline firms that has grown out of the present regime of protective regulation. The Civil Aeronautics Act places the Board in the position of protector and promoter of the financial welfare of the certificated air carriers; therefore, it may be interpreted as making that agency ultimately responsible for profitable operation of the airlines at any given level of Government support. This interpretation, taken together with the fact that the law leaves with the carriers the power to make almost all important economic decisions, has resulted in unfortunate confusion, especially in connection with the losses recently incurred by the airline companies.[6] This division of

---

[6] For example, the President of the United Air Lines was able plausibly to make the following statement: "During the past 18 months, the domestic air transport companies have suffered a loss of $36,000,000. The Civil Aeronautics Act has a declaration of policy from which I quote: 'Assures the highest degree of safety in and fosters sound economic conditions. . . .' Sound economic conditions do not produce such tremendous financial losses. That, in itself, would

responsibility arises not only where, as in the airline field, the regulators administer direct support as well as economic controls; it occurs wherever the regulators are given a protective as well as a policing duty. For example, with regard to the economic effects of regulation in the railroad field, K. T. Healy has remarked:

It might be said that the most harmful single thing which has resulted from regulation has been the growth of an attitude among many managements and financiers that their properties are somehow due this "fair return," regardless of almost anything that may happen, and that if they do not get it a gross injustice has been done them. In turn this leads to a failure on their part to do the constructive thing for themselves by way of "sharpening their pencils" and improving their costs, rates, and services to meet new conditions. Any aggressive business in other fields expects to do that, rather than to fall back on the fact that its plant represents a certain investment value and should therefore automatically earn certain profits.[7]

And again:

It is true, of course, that regulatory control does require the railroads to present their story in public and formally defend their proposals before a tribunal. To that extent the regulatory procedure is a bother to management, as well as, in a sense, an affront to its prestige. But what is far more significant is the tendency for managements to use the Commission as somebody to blame for all that has gone wrong or all which they do that is distasteful. In the course of table talk the Commission has had more than a little responsibility heaped on its shoulders for things with which it has never had the remotest connection. To serve as a butt for reproof may be one of the functions that the Commission has to accept in the line of duty, but it has the unfortunate effect, as far as progress in the railroad industry is concerned, of confusing the issue of where responsibility lies and who must lead toward the improvements of the future.[8]

---

reflect against the Civil Aeronautics Board." W. A. Patterson, "Stewardship of the Airlines by the Civil Aeronautics Board," 15 *Journal of Air Law and Commerce* 390, 393 (1948).

[7] Kent T. Healy, *The Economics of Transportation in America* (Copyright 1940, by the Ronald Press Company, New York), p. 519.

[8] *Ibid.*, p. 542.

The problem at issue here is not the question of whether the Government is or is not obligated to make up any deficits that the carriers incur. If the Government is so obligated (as it ultimately appears to be under the "need-rate" subsidy program), then it is evident that, whatever the predetermined rate of mail pay, the ultimate economic responsibility lies with the Board; it is also evident that the Board should be given power adequate to discharge this responsibility. Thus, unless the "need-rate" subsidy program is abandoned, the assumption of complete managerial power by the Board is manifestly the just and logical type of economic control to be adopted by the Government. The logical development of comprehensive control out of "need-rate" subsidization is indicated by the fact that, apparently as a result of the postwar experience with overexpansion on the part of the carriers, the Board is now asking for legislation giving it unprecedented powers over airline management. The requested powers include authority to compel an air carrier to initiate service to new points, to restrict frequency of service, and to control the types of equipment utilized.[9] With such a subsidy program, the superior advantages of this type of control are overwhelmingly evident.

However, as will be argued in the following chapter, it appears that the "need-rate" subsidy program should be abandoned on grounds independent of its implications for the economic control of the industry. Even though some continued subsidization of the airline industry should prove desirable, a more rational policy of administration of subsidy would not require complete governmental economic control. Therefore, the disadvantages of this control, and the available alternatives, should be carefully weighed in considering what may be the most desirable economic policy.

It should also be noted that, as a practical matter, it is doubtful whether assumption of complete managerial control by the Government would put an end to protective legal restrictions as related to the airline field. Exceedingly drastic

---

[9] Statement of Delos W. Rentzel, Chairman, Civil Aeronautics Board, Before the Interstate and Foreign Commerce Committee of the United States Senate, March 15, 1951, pp. 18 and 22 of mimeographed copy.

restrictions have in fact been placed on competing forms of transportation in some countries where Government-owned railroads have suffered decreases in revenues as a result of outside competition. Similar motives might result in the administration of Government management so as to protect particular existing components of the airline system.

There is obviously no way to assess precisely the relative weight of these advantages and disadvantages. On balance, given the difficulty of estimating the concrete nature of the optimum and the practical obstacles in the way of its (even momentary) accomplishment, it would still seem to be possible that the results of this policy would more nearly approach the ideal than those of the present regulatory system.

Nevertheless, there are certain practical obstacles in the way of putting this policy into effect which would indicate that, even if its advantages should be found greatly to outweigh its shortcomings in actual importance, there would be a much greater possibility of achieving reform through the advocacy of some alternative program, even though it should be intrinsically less desirable. Most important of all, it is highly unlikely that Government ownership of the airlines would be accepted by Congress now or in the foreseeable future. Again, the successful administration of this policy would involve the development of management techniques that are entirely different from the regulatory procedures now followed by United States Government agencies concerned with transportation problems; it is therefore to be expected that a period of years would be required for the effective development of these techniques.

(2) As has been indicated, the chief advantage of the removal of all specific regulatory control of the air-transport industry would be the avoidance of the obstacle to factor adjustment presented by the protective principle which is the distinctive characteristic of the present system. An additional result of such a policy, arising directly from the abandonment of regulatory protection, would be the imparting of a much greater force to that competitive stimulus counted upon by the Board to promote the "maximum development" of air transport.

In addition, responsibility for profitable operation of the airlines would be placed unequivocally on the shoulders of private managements.

However, no such program — and no program of the type considered below (the retention of controls for the purpose of channeling competitive endeavor) — could possibly work in conjunction with a "need-rate" subsidy, which, as has been argued, justifies and demands managerial control by the Government. For both of these regulatory programs involve a reliance on normal economic competitive incentives and market direction of investment that would not be reasonable given such a subsidization policy.

It has been noted above that the competition experienced by railroad firms in recent years stimulated profit-maximizing activity by these companies not only along the lines of promotional rates and improved service, but also via such avenues as lobbying for regulatory protection, acquisition of competitive firms, cutthroat competition designed to drive competitors from the field, and the conclusion of restrictive agreements with the new competitors. A similar development might be expected in the air-transport field as a result of the abandonment of protection of particular carriers from inroads on their revenues arising from competition by new or established air-transport firms; at the same time the specific machinery whereby certain types of competitive effort might be subject to regulatory control would have disappeared. Under these circumstances, it is impossible to predict even approximately what the net effect of such a policy would be in terms of economic performance.

It is of course true that were the specific regulatory controls relating to air transport entirely abandoned, the general regulation (including the antitrust laws and the Federal Trade Commission Act) applicable to all industry would still govern the activities of airline companies. Thus the effect of the policy under consideration here would depend to some extent on the manner and effectiveness with which these laws were enforced in the air-transport field. However, because of the vagaries of judicial and administrative interpretations of these laws, and because of the sporadic character of their enforcement, it cannot be predicted with any degree of certainty what their practical influence would be.

It should be noted that there is at least one aspect of the specific regulation of the air-transport industry the abandonment of which would be both undesirable and impossible, namely, the fixing and enforcement of safety standards. Although this aspect of regulation is usually characterized as "technical" rather than "economic," it is obviously both; from the economic point of view, it is a limitation on one dimension of the competitive activities of airline firms.

Since the directions to be taken by the competitive efforts of airline firms in the absence of specific regulatory control cannot be foreseen, it is impossible to enumerate the probable disadvantages of this policy in terms of economic performance. However, it seems reasonable to suppose that at least some of the profit-maximizing activity of the carriers would be directed into channels tending to restrict rather than to promote the achievement of the economic optimum. It can also be said that the tendency toward nonaggressiveness in price policy which has been noted in connection with the present system would persist, though it would probably be somewhat weakened because of the greater ease with which "newcomers" could enter the business. In this respect, the policy under consideration here is superior to the present system but at a disadvantage as compared with Government ownership.

(3) The third possible policy to be considered — abandonment of those aspects of the present regulatory system which tend to obstruct the achievement of the economic optimum, and retention of specific regulation designed to promote it — would possess all the advantages of the second possibility, and would at the same time provide safeguards against diversion of the economic efforts of the airline firms into channels tending away from the economic optimum. Furthermore, it would avoid the major disadvantages of Government ownership and is much more acceptable as a practical program, because it does not represent a drastic break with traditional general economic policy in this country and would not require the development of

techniques of administration entirely different from those already employed in transportation regulation.

This policy would require the abandonment of certification for new routes in accordance with the protective principle that has been the major criterion used by the Board; it would also require the abandonment of the use of this principle in passing upon variations in the physical characteristics of the service, on mergers and similar transactions, on intercarrier agreements, and on rate relations. Similarly, the regulatory supervision of the choice of carriers for new routes in accordance with the objective of promoting the financial welfare of small and weak carriers for its own sake would have to be abandoned.

The primary aim of regulation under this policy would be to direct the competitive activities of the airlines into channels promotive of the achievement of the optimum adjustment of factors; and this aim would be in part accomplished by giving the regulatory agency specific powers to prevent carrier activities tending to impede this adjustment. Although the precise scope of authority that would have to be granted to the agency cannot be defined in detail, since the possible forms of restrictive competitive activity are too many and too varied, it is feasible to indicate certain corollary objectives of this regulation and certain powers that would be necessary to accomplish them.

In the first place, the primary objective of regulation proposed here obviously requires that carrier activities which tend to prevent rational choice on the part of buyers (i.e., a genuine evaluation of the service offered in terms of other channels of income use) be prohibited. Specific powers necessary to accomplish this would include (*a*) the power to prevent misleading advertising, (*b*) the power to require that all agents selling air transportation furnish prospective buyers with full information regarding all available services to the desired destination, and (*c*) the power to require or to provide directly adequate publicity with respect to rates and services offered by all carriers.

In the second place, the primary objective implies that carrier activities tending directly to impede the adjustment of factor supply by restricting opportunities for profitable employment which would otherwise be available should also be prohibited.

Such activities would include all types of intercarrier arrangements aimed at mutual protection from possible competitive inroads on revenues or other risks of loss by restricting the direction of investment, e.g., agreements dividing markets, or binding the parties not to undertake certain types of product variation or experimentation with new techniques of service and operation, as well as those imposing restrictions on rate policy. They would also include such restrictions on new competition as the reservation to members of an existing group of the right to participate in product-improving intercarrier arrangements; as has been noted, this type of exclusion has been prohibited by the Board with respect to certificated carriers. Specific powers necessary to accomplish this aim would therefore include authority to pass on intercarrier agreements, which the Board already has.

Although the powers mentioned above are, and are intended to be, merely illustrative of the type of authority that should be granted to the regulatory agency, it seems clear that the requirement of certification of new services would not have to be retained, nor would the requirement for regulatory approval of certain types of variation in the physical characteristics of the service. With regard to the certification requirement, it may be said that, because of the inevitable preference given to established carriers by the very nature of regulatory control of entry, its abandonment would serve to further the primary aim of this policy. It should also be noted that the effectiveness of restrictive intercarrier agreements, and hence the incentive to conclude them, would probably be weakened by the abandonment of the certification requirement, as would the tendency toward nonaggressiveness in price-output policy, because of the greater possibility that carriers not participating in these agreements, or in tacit live-and-let-live arrangements, might invade the protected markets or pursue more aggressive policies. There seems also to be no apparent reason for the retention of the specific rate powers now possessed by the Board, except to the extent necessary to prevent deliberate elimination or exclusion of competitors by temporary below-cost rate cutting.

This policy could not by any means guarantee the achievement of the economic optimum. In the first place, no amount of honesty or educational effort on the part of the carriers or their agents could assure perfect rationality of choice by buyers. In the second place, prohibition of carrier activities such as are deliberately restrictive of factor adjustment will not bring about perfect freedom of opportunity for factor owners; there will remain, for example, the possibility, albeit reduced, of that non-aggressiveness in price-output policy which may divert factor units that might most productively be employed in the "non-aggressive" firm into other enterprises; there will also remain many other adventitious obstacles to the geographical and occupational mobility of factors. Thirdly, there may well arise in many air-transportation markets demand and cost conditions such that n firms could be supported at a level of returns to factors in excess of replacement cost but $n + 1$ firms could not be supported at a level of returns large enough to equal total transfer cost.

It is impossible to assess accurately the quantitative importance of those obstacles to the attainment of even the conditional optimum for economic performance in the event that the policy under discussion here were adopted. However, it seems probable that they would be of minor significance in the air-transport field, especially if additional governmental action were undertaken to promote consumer knowledge of the exact nature of the products available for purchase (not only, of course, in the air-transport field itself) and to remove obstacles (such as restrictive practices of trade-unions) to the interoccupational mobility of factors that do not arise from policies of the regulated firms.

With regard to maladjustments that may be caused by the third factor mentioned above, it will be recalled that the only *stable* equilibrium situation possible in such circumstances is one in which the (conditional) optimum had been arrived at through the subordination of short-run profit maximization to long-range maintenance of the (sufficiently but not excessively) profitable existence of the firm. It may further be said that this stable equilibrium will be more likely to occur in practice the more likely it is that potential competition may become actual. Because of the relative ease of entry into the air-transport field, it would appear that the potential competition would be a very powerful incentive to the existing firms to bring about this equilibrium in most air-transport markets.

In view of the above considerations, there seems to be a good chance that, were the suggested governmental policies adopted, the conditional optimum would tend to be achieved in most air-transport markets. How closely this conditional optimum would approximate the unconditional would depend in any market on the actual conditions of factor supply. Here again, there seems to be no prima facie reason to suppose that any great divergence would occur; nevertheless, further investigation might conceivably reveal divergences in some or perhaps in many air-transport markets that might warrant intervention to achieve the unconditional optimum.

Because of the facts (1) that the obstacles to the achievement of the conditional optimum that are irremediable short of Government ownership appear to be of relatively minor importance in the air-transport field, (2) that there seems to be no reason to expect a large departure from the unconditional optimum once the conditional optimum has been attained, and (3) that the air-transport business is one in which a relatively large departure from the unconditional optimum would be required to justify Government intervention directly aimed at its achievement, a good case can be made for the view that the policy here under discussion would result in better economic performance than either of the other two policies considered or the policy now in effect. As compared with the present system, it would remove the obstacle to the adjustment of the distribution of factor supply and consumer purchases presented by the protective principle, and would also strengthen the competitive stimulus to progress in air transport. The desirable aspects of the present system — i.e., probable greater stability in rates and avoidance of economic wastes — appear to be of relatively small importance. Again, the policy under consideration here would appear to be more conducive to experimentation with new types of service and techniques than Government ownership, and would avoid the danger involved in the probable propensity of the administrators under this system to achieve the appearance of conformity to a static optimum by rate manipulation; in addition, it seems far more likely to be accepted by the public and by Congress and to be properly administered. It has all the advantages of the complete abandonment of specific regulation without its probable disadvantages.

Perhaps the greatest advantage of this policy, however, is that it would make possible a realistic evaluation of the operation of the free-market determination of factor returns in the air-transport field, and thus furnish a sound basis for future policy decisions. The quantitative importance of the "irremediable" obstacles to the conditional optimum enumerated above, of the divergence of this equilibrium from the unconditional optimum, of the economic wastes that might result from uncontrolled adjustment of investment in air-transport markets, and the possible undesirable effects that might arise from rate instability in uncontrolled markets, are not now known and cannot be known until the policy under consideration here has been tried out in practice. Since this is true, a necessary adjunct of this policy is the undertaking of an investigation of its practical effects, with the objective of evaluating them in terms of the unconditional optimum and making recommendations for further governmental action should this appear to be necessary. This investigation would, of course, have to be continuous, since the underlying demand and technological factors conditioning the performance of the market are subject to constant change. Such an investigation could provide a foundation for the determination of future policy based on adequate knowledge and acceptable economic norms, rather than partisan misinterpretation of past experience or spurious economic reasoning.

In summary, then, it has been found that, given the abandonment of the need-rate subsidy program, the most desirable economic policy toward air transport would seem to be the abandonment of protective regulation with the retention of those forms of regulation designed to channel private economic effort away from undesirable avenues of profit maximization. This would be true even though a general policy of subsidization were continued, for such a policy does not in itself involve the vitiation of market-regulatory forces and incentives, even in the event that the form of subsidization should continue to be direct payments to carriers. In the following chapter, the problem of subsidization is treated in more detail: it is there argued that the "need-rate" principle should be abandoned on grounds independent of its implications for economic control. If this is true, then the way is open for the adoption of a regulatory program of the type recommended here.

The abandonment of the "need-rate" program may, of course, involve varying degrees of hardship on the part of carriers some or all of whose routes or services cannot be sustained by commercial revenues and legitimate postal demand at the level of Government support that may prove to be required by the national interest, and on the part of the businesses and communities served by them. Similarly, the abandonment of protective regulation will probably involve comparable readjustments in the quantity and geographical distribution of airline service. Although these factors make it desirable that the transition to the new regime be made gradually and with due regard for the affected interests, they should not be allowed permanently to deflect the course of policy. There is, of course, no justification for a Federal promotional or regulatory program designed to serve local or special interests at the expense of national objectives.

CHAPTER VIII

THE PROBLEM OF SUBSIDIZATION

As WAS POINTED OUT in Chapter III, the subsidization policy adopted by Congress in 1938 was not oriented by any independent consideration of the amount and type of commercial air transport required by the national interest, but appears rather to have been specifically adapted to helping the then mail carriers out of their financial difficulties, and to protecting them from similar difficulties in the future. This lack of any guide for the direct subsidization program other than the financial exigencies of particular carriers has persisted until the present day, despite the fact that the nation's air policy has been the object of investigations by two *ad hoc* official bodies: the President's Air Policy Commission, appointed by the President on July 18, 1947, which submitted its report on January 1, 1948,[1] and the Congressional Aviation Policy Board, established by law on July 30, 1947, which submitted its report on March 1, 1948.[2]

One consequence of this lack of orientation has already been suggested, namely, the absence of any specific statutory guide by which the Board could determine what new routes would be subsidized; in this connection, it has been maintained that the criterion actually employed by the Board represents the most logical possible extension of the guide *in effect* endorsed by Congress.

In the present chapter, there will be considered some additional results of this lack of orientation which seem to be undesirable from the point of view of the public interest. It will be argued that a proper program of subsidization can be devised only on the basis of a clear definition of the needs of the na-

---

[1] *Survival in the Air Age: A Report by the President's Air Policy Commission* (Washington: Government Printing Office, 1948).

[2] *National Aviation Policy: Report of the Congressional Aviation Policy Board,* Senate Report No. 949, 80th Congress, 2nd Session (1948).

tional defense, the postal service, and the commerce of the United States with respect to commercial air transport, and that such definition should therefore be undertaken by Congress. In this connection, it will be noted that the proper methods of subsidization can be determined only by reference to their efficiency in bringing about the aims so defined, and argued (1) that, regardless of the particular methods adopted, the best possible implementation of the subsidization policy necessitates maximum efficiency in the performance of the subsidized service; (2) that the regulatory policy implied by this aim is the same that would be required for optimum economic performance in the air-transport field if there were no subsidization; and (3) that the only administrative exclusion of firms from any particular market that a proper subsidization policy might involve would be a temporary limitation of the number of participant firms where the method of subsidization is such that its cost increases with the number of firms aided at any particular time.

If this argument is valid, then it evidently demonstrates the desirability of permanently abandoning the "need-rate" subsidization policy; first, because this policy by its very nature involves the determination of the extent and direction[3] of Government support not on a basis of a clear definition of national need but on the basis of decisions of private management largely outside the scope of governmental control, and second, because the program necessarily involves the weakening of normal business incentives on the part of the subsidized carriers — a factor which is inconsistent with maximum efficiency in the performance of the subsidized service. In connection with the first point, it hardly need be noted that the permanent and sustained financial welfare of a particular group of airline firms can by no stretch of the imagination be deemed to constitute a valid *ultimate* definition of national need from any point of view.

---

[3] The term "direction" as used here includes such qualitative aspects of air-transport investment as size and type of transport equipment. Geographical "direction" of the supported service is subject to greater direct control, but is still of course dependent on carrier initiative.

The first and most obvious defect of any subsidization program not based on a clear definition of the amount and type of investment required by national policy is that such a program cannot be relied upon to fulfill these requirements. If it did in fact happen to do so, it would be only by coincidence.

This point can be best illustrated in relation to the needs of the national defense, which is the factor affording the least questionable rationale for public subsidy of commercial air transport. In this connection, it can be argued with some force that the commercial air-transport investment at the beginning of World War II fell far short of the amount that would have been desirable from a defense point of view. Both the number of planes available as a "reserve fleet" for military transport use and the personnel that could be diverted from "essential" civilian services were certainly exceedingly small by comparison with the numbers urgently needed at that time and with the numbers ultimately obtained during the period of wartime preparation for war provided by the grace of God. A similar argument can be made regarding the capacity for aircraft production supported by the subsidized industry, and regarding the rate of progress in techniques of air transport that could be financed under the subsidization program.

With respect to future defense needs, it may be contended that the subsidization program is resulting in too much investment in certain types of air transport and not enough in others. Since there is now in being a Military Air Transport Service which could provide a nucleus from which wartime transport services could grow, at least one justification for the maintenance of large commercial companies capable of managing far-flung scheduled services has apparently vanished. Indeed, since at present it appears that subsidization of commercial air transport is neither an adequate nor an economical means of assuring the availability of the personnel, aircraft-production capacity, or rate of technological progress required by the national defense, the only present justification for such a subsidy from a defense point of view may be that subsidization is required to maintain an adequate "reserve fleet" for wartime transport use. This argument is in fact the only one adduced even by implication by the President's Air Policy Commission to justify the commercial air-transport subsidization program on the basis of the national defense, and the same seems to be true of the Congressional Board. With respect to commercial air transport, the Commission proposed, among other things, (1) that the air-mail payments to the certificated carriers be increased with the objective of bailing these carriers out of their financial difficulties, (2) that decisions on new routes be deferred until a more "clear-cut" route plan should be developed by the Civil Aeronautics Board, (3) that certification of new carriers in the field of air cargo be regarded with disfavor by the Board (although this recommendation is not explicitly stated, it is unmistakably implied by the Commission's statements with regard to the cargo carriers), and (4) that economic regulation be extended to contract carriers in order to deal effectively with the "often intense" competition between the carriers and the certificated companies. These major recommendations are apparently based on an uncritical acceptance of the alleged necessity of keeping the certificated carriers "strong and healthy," by which the Commission means underwriting through financial aid and protective regulation the long-run profitability of these particular companies.

In justification of this position, the Commission merely states that "the air lines have a fleet of aircraft of great value to the military services as a reserve in time of war," and that "as a potential military auxiliary, the air lines must be kept strong and healthy." [4] No attempt is made to relate the subsidization policy directly to any definite estimate of the size or character of the reserve fleet expected to be required for war purposes, or to determine whether the support of particular companies on a cost-plus basis is a necessary or desirable method of assuring the availability of such a reserve. It should of course be recognized that the major concern of the Commission was direct military aviation requirements; for this reason it was perhaps justified in not undertaking an exhaustive reconsideration of civil air-transport policy. In addition, the Commission was ac-

[4] *Survival in the Air Age,* p. 99.

tually unable to obtain from military authorities a firm estimate of the reserve fleet required for the national defense.

In the report of the Congressional Board, there seems to be a similar major reliance on the "reserve-fleet" argument as a basis for subsidization of commercial air transport, and a similar absence of any definite idea of the required size and character of the "reserve fleet." Thus, in its declaration of its "Concept of National Aviation Policy," the Board's report states: "The domestic and foreign air commerce of the United States should be fostered and promoted by whatever means appear most practical until it reaches such stature in passenger and cargo capacity as to constitute in crisis an adequate logistical air arm of the National Defense Establishment." [5] On the necessary size of such a "logistical air arm," the Board has this to say: "The availability to the military air services of commercial transport-type aircraft in as large numbers as possible to serve as auxiliary military air lift is essential . . . The Government is vitally concerned in the existence of such aircraft in large numbers." [6] And again: "National security requires a financially sound, operationally efficient, and technically modern air-transport industry. It envisions a large, civil air fleet operated in foreign and domestic air commerce with safety and certainty . . . Since it is economically impracticable to maintain an air force which will provide absolute security, as many transport aircraft as possible should be operated in commercial service and available to provide a reasonable reserve." [7]

From this point of view, it might well be argued that the present program is devoting too much money to the development of capacity for luxury passenger service and too little to the development of capacity for cargo transport, a type of capacity which might reasonably be expected to be required on a large scale by the military in time of war.

Furthermore, it may very well be that the subsidization of commercial air transport to provide a reserve of equipment to

[5] *National Aviation Policy*, p. 5.
[6] *Ibid.*, p. 13.
[7] *Ibid.*, p. 15.

be available in military emergency is not a desirable course because of (*a*) the increased reliance of the civilian economy on air-transport services which inevitably grows out of such a program, resulting in a proportionate increase in the disruption of this economy should the reserve be called into active service, and (*b*) the impact of the subsidized transport services on the capacity that can be profitably maintained by substitute transport agencies which would be called on in the event of mobilization to accommodate the traffic theretofore handled by the reserve air-transport capacity. This point has been emphasized in a transportation study recently published by the Brookings Institution.[8]

Finally, it may be noted that until very recently there has been available to the public and its legislative representatives no definite statement on the part of military authorities with respect to their views on a proper civil air-transport policy. In 1949, the Senate Committee on Interstate and Foreign Commerce requested the military authorities to present their views on this subject. The Under Secretary of Defense then informed the Committee that a study was being initiated to determine the armed services' "present definition of the 'present and future needs of the national defense' as that phrase is used in the Civil Aeronautics Act of 1938," and asked the Committee to postpone the appearance of a witness representing the military until this study had been completed.[9] When this statement was at last forthcoming, it indicated that the military regarded the "existence of airlift in the commercial airlines" as "a national defense asset" — on a par with "the health of our citizens," "technological progress" in general, the nation's heavy industry, all other forms of transport, etc.[10] It was further stated that the Department of Defense could not itself "determine whether Federal expenditures in support of particular promo-

---

[8] C. L. Dearing and Wilfred Owen, *National Transportation Policy* (Washington: The Brookings Institution, 1949), pp. 144–149.

[9] Letter from Under Secretary of Defense Early to the Chairman of the Senate Committee on Interstate and Foreign Commerce, June 6, 1949.

[10] Statement of Honorable Stephen Early, Deputy Secretary of Defense, before the Senate Committee on Interstate and Foreign Commerce, January 30, 1950 (pp. 6 and 8–9 of mimeographed copy).

tional programs in this field are excessive," and that, in particular, "the payment of subsidies for the continued existence of airlines on the account of national defense is too intangible for us to be able to calculate." [11] Although it was pointed out that "a calculation of the present airlift capacity of the MATS organization and a calculation of available civilian airlift indicates that a very real deficit exists between our present peacetime capacity and the airlift we would require in wartime," [12] it was also emphasized that (*proportionately* smaller) deficits exist in other transport media,[13] and — most significantly — that

the estimated deficit in airlift between present capabilities and mobilization requirement does not create a shortage which is so serious that it requires the use of Department of Defense funds under presently limited budgets. If additional funds could be made available the interests of National Security would best be served by their application to combat minimums and hence, no Department of Defense funds can be diverted to a development of this kind [i.e., specifically, prototype transport-aircraft development] at the expense of prime military procurement" (emphasis supplied).[14]

This last statement forcibly raises the question whether the interests of the national defense would in fact be furthered by the diversion of funds now used to promote civil air transport to, say, the procurement of combat aircraft, research on guided missiles, provision for direct defense or minimization of damage from atomic-bomb attacks, expansion of the military intelligence program, etc.

The merits of these questions cannot of course be determined here, and are in fact irrelevant to the point at issue. They are suggested only to indicate possible ways in which the results of the present subsidization program *might* deviate from those required by the national defense, and the same sort of deviation

[11] *Ibid.*, p. 6.
[12] *Ibid.*, p. 3.
[13] *Ibid.*, p. 4.
[14] Statement of Honorable W. Stuart Symington, Secretary of the Air Force, before the Senate Committee on Interstate and Foreign Commerce, January 30, 1950, p. 2 of mimeographed copy.

would be possible with respect to the investment required by any other aspect of national policy.

However, the other aspects mentioned in the Act, i.e., the needs of the postal service and of the nation's commerce, do not provide any easily discernible rationale for subsidization. Since the present "needs" of commerce are presumably reflected in current market demand, it appears that subsidization from this point of view could be justified only if it could be reasonably expected that the program would result, ultimately, in expediting reductions in cost or improvements in service whose value to commercial users would be sufficient to cover the cost of the program to the Government. Such an expectation might arise if, for example, the investment that could be maintained without subsidy was so small as to be inadequate as a "pilot" or testing ground for technical and service improvements, so that the satisfaction of potential commercial demands for air transport would be made impossible or postponed for a long period.

It is in this sense that an "infant-industry" type of argument might be said to be applicable to air transportation. It hardly need be noted that this argument cannot be used to justify promotion of any particular economic activity merely because it is "young" relative to its competitors; some additional consideration of national benefits must be adduced to render the argument cogent in any given instance. It is quite possible that the above type of argument would have been valid in past years; in this connection, it seems very likely that the investment which could have been maintained without subsidization in the thirties would have been small. Whatever may have been the case in the past, it seems improbable that such a justification could be made at present.

It is sometimes urged that subsidization (and also some forms of protective regulation) can be justified by the necessity for providing commercial transport service to communities or classes of traffic unable otherwise to support them. Unless, however, there is some national end which will be served by the furnishing of such service, and moreover, unless the national interest could not be better served by some alternative expenditure of the necessary funds, this argument cannot be used to justify a *Federal* subsidy. Furthermore, it is evidently unjust to burden an independently profitable market with the support of unprofitable services in other fields, as would be the case where the revenues of carriers serving the former are preserved or enhanced by regulatory restrictions on these routes to enable them to serve the latter.

In the absence of direct evidence to the contrary, it may be reasonably assumed that the needs of the postal service are satisfied when the current demand for air-mail transportation by the Post Office, defined by reference to the amount and type of mail service which in the opinion of Congress should be offered to the public, is met. In this connection, it is evident that the determination of the mail service to be offered to the public should not be confused by introducing such considerations as the effect on the finances of particular firms of expanding or contracting this service. (Such considerations have been prominent in some discussions of the proposal for "all-up" first-class intercity mail service.) Therefore, the needs of the Post Office cannot be said to justify Government promotion of air transport beyond the requirements of current demand; the payments made by the Government to fill postal needs should be limited to the amount necessary to obtain the service currently required (without, of course, throwing an unwarranted burden on other classes of traffic).

This brings us to the second major disadvantage arising from the failure of Congress to define national needs with respect to air transport: in the absence of any independent definition of the amount and type of *air-mail* service desired, both the extent of the subsidy and the extent to which commercial air transport could be supported without subsidy are impossible to determine.

The amount of subsidy included in the mail payments may be defined as the amount by which these payments exceed what would be necessary to obtain, without preferential treatment of the Post Office as compared with commercial users of air transport, the quantity and character of transportation required for the provision of the desired amount and type of air-mail service. Therefore, to discover the proper amount that should be subtracted from total mail payments to arrive at the subsidy, it is necessary to know (*a*) the desired amount and type of airmail service, as well as (*b*) the payments that would have been just sufficient to obtain this service without burdening other users of air transport. It is obviously impossible to make a proper calculation of the subsidy merely by conventional methods of cost allocation for all the routes and schedules operated by the mail carriers, not only because such a method ignores the possibility that on at least some of these routes and schedules the necessary cost to the Post Office might have been higher had the nonmail commercial traffic been charged rates adequate to cover fully allocated cost, and not only because there is no consideration of the possibility that on some routes and schedules the Post Office might have obtained the required service more cheaply through other means than those actually used (e.g., an all-mail service using small planes), but first and foremost because the routes and schedules on which mail payments are made have not been determined primarily by the needs of the postal service.

Furthermore, without any means of determining the payments that would in fact have to be made to obtain the desired amount and type of mail service, it is impossible to discover what quantity and type of air-transport investment could be supported without subsidization, and therefore also impossible to discover to what extent subsidization is necessary to assure the amount and type of service that any aspect of national policy may be found to require.

The third major disadvantage arising from the failure of Congress to define the national need for air transportation is the absence of any reasonable basis for limiting the obligation of the Government to subsidized carriers when these companies incur losses at the going rate of subsidy. For example, the scheduled carriers incurred large deficits in the postwar period, and it is generally agreed that the main reason for these deficits was overexpansion relative to current demand.[15] Heated con-

---

[15] See, for example, "The Airline Squeeze," *Fortune*, XXXV, No. 5 (May 1947), p. 117.

troversy has centered around the question of who is responsible for this overexpansion, the Board or the carriers; however, the important problem at issue is not who is to blame in this particular instance but to what extent the Government should, in general, be called upon to provide revenues for the carriers. The losses incurred by the scheduled airlines in this period have had at least one fortunate result: they serve to emphasize the essentially questionable basis of the "need-rate" subsidization program, and may therefore aid in bringing about a reconsideration of the basic problems involved in the formulation of a rational civil air-transport policy. As long as the liability of the Government to the carriers determined on a "need" basis was largely within the limits foreseen by the Board, and as long as this liability continued proportionally to decrease because of the growing self-sufficiency of the carriers, the meaning and implications of the support program could be readily ignored. It had always been true that the amount and type of service supplied had been very largely determined by the carriers themselves, and that the Government had simply furnished the funds necessary to support this service. The postwar situation in which the rates of mail pay previously determined by the Board proved wholly inadequate to support the capacity supplied may serve to bring public attention to bear in particular on the question of just what the taxpayer is obligated to pay to the carriers and why.

In this connection, it should be noted that the companies could always overexpand relative to any possible rate of subsidy, and that the Board is quite powerless to prevent such overexpansion by the provision of too much carrying capacity on authorized routes. It is therefore quite unreasonable to attempt to determine the proper obligation of the Government on the basis of carrier "need," because on this basis there would be in principle no limit to its obligations. The extent to which the Government should support the expansion of investment by any carrier can be determined only by reference to the public need for such investment.

Thus a program of subsidization which (*a*) can be expected to produce results in accordance with the nation's needs, (*b*) makes possible a precise calculation of the amount of the subsidy, the extent to which commercial air transport could be supported without subsidy, and hence the extent to which subsidization may be required, and (c) provides a reasonable limit for the obligations of the Government to any particular firm, can be developed only on the basis of a clear definition of the amount and type of commercial air transport required by the national defense, the postal service, and the commerce of the United States. Such a definition should be provided by Congress.

If subsidization of commercial air transport is found to be necessary, the form that this subsidization should take should be that best adapted to the achievement of the level and type of commercial air transport required by national policy. Thus the proper method of subsidy cannot be determined until the aims of the program have been defined. However, whatever the objectives sought, and whatever the method adopted, the fact of subsidization can never be used to justify the protection of the revenues of particular firms, and the regulatory program which will most effectively implement the aims of subsidization is the same as that required for optimum economic performance if there were no subsidization.

For regardless of the aim and method of subsidization, it is always to the interest of the Government that the subsidized activity be carried out with maximum efficiency — i.e., that the maximum amount of service be provided whose necessary cost can be met by the revenues available to this activity — and the protection of particular carriers is, as has been shown, an obstacle to the achievement of maximum efficiency. Whether subsidization takes the form of relieving the carriers of a part of their necessary costs or of supplementing their revenues, it is evidently to the interest of the Government that the necessary costs of the desired service be kept at a minimum, and that the amount of service supported by current demand be at the maximum consistent with the preservation of free choice on the part of consumers. Although the protection of the subsidized activity from unsubsidized competition might result in an increase in the cost to the Government of maintaining the former, such protection is in general unjustified since it merely shifts a part of the burden of subsidization from the Government to the users who are deprived of their preferred service (and consequently prevents any precise calculation of the total cost of the subsidization program).

Certain forms of subsidization do, however, justify a limitation on the number of firms participating in the subsidized activity itself at any given time, and since this involves the temporary exclusion of some firms, in this sense the revenues of participant firms are necessarily accorded a certain measure of protection. Where the method of subsidization is such that its cost to the Government does not increase with the number of firms benefited, there is no reason for the administrative exclusion of any firms from the subsidized activity. An example of such a method would be the financing of research and development of more efficient commercial aircraft, a line of action which was recommended by the President's Air Policy Commission as the best way to assure the development of an adequate reserve cargo fleet.[16]

Where, however, the cost of subsidization varies directly with the number of firms benefited at any given time, there must be some form of administrative determination of the number of participant firms and hence an administrative choice of the particular firms to be aided at any given time in order to limit the Government's commitments to the amount appropriated for this period of time. An example of such a method of subsidization would be direct payments to carriers — which might be found to be the means best adapted to promoting United States-flag commercial services in the foreign field beyond current demand (perhaps for reasons of national prestige) where other forms of promotion, whose benefits accrued to foreign as well as United States-flag carriers, might bring about inappropriate results in that the maintenance of the desired amount of United States-flag service would not be assured. Here the number of firms and the particular firms to receive aid should be chosen on the basis of minimum cost to the Government for performing the desired service. Such a choice could best be

[16] *Survival in the Air Age,* p. 115.

made by a periodic process of competitive bidding, each firm being given the opportunity to specify the lowest payment it would accept for performing all of any part of the desired service. It should be emphasized that the justified exclusion of particular firms from the subsidized market is merely a temporary one, and that maximum efficiency requires that no firms be excluded from the process of competitive bidding.

Moreover, the justified exclusion is only that which necessarily results from the limitation of the subsidy to particular firms; there is therefore no reason for any *further* administrative restriction of the activities of any firms. It may be probably taken for granted that (under a system of subsidy awards providing for frequent competitive bidding open to all comers) no unsubsidized carrier could enter into homogeneous competition with the subsidized carriers during the period for which the award held good; it may also be expected that heterogeneous competition during this relatively short period would be foreseen by the carriers and reflected in the amounts of the bids. If unforeseen heterogeneous competition should materialize during this period on a scale sufficient to endanger the maintenance of the subsidized service, it might become necessary to increase subsidy payments above the bid rate for the remainder of the period — but such a situation should be dealt with by an emergency appropriation rather than by regulatory exclusion. The amount by which the necessary subsidy is made larger by the existence of heterogeneous competition, foreseen or unforeseen, is a legitimate addition to the cost of the subsidization program, and should not be avoided by shifting the burden to potential users of unsubsidized services.

The steps that should be taken to put the nation's civil air-transport policy on a sound basis may now be briefly summarized:

(1) A careful definition of the national interest as related to air transport should be developed; there should be included here an estimate of the amount of Government support justified by the national defense and by other national objectives that may be found relevant (considered, of course, in the light of

alternative governmental expenditures and of the possible desirability of reducing the tax burden or the Government debt). Neither the objectives nor the potential expenditures would probably be exclusively in the form of absolutes, but rather in the form of a schedule of possible results and possible costs. For example, if the maintenance of a reserve cargo fleet were deemed desirable, there would be no minimum figure which public policy would demand regardless of cost, but possibly a series of potential fleets which it would be desirable to maintain at varying total cost figures.

(2) The best possible estimate should be developed of the amount and type of air-transport investment that could be sustained without subsidy. In this connection, the formulation of a demand schedule for various air-mail services by the Post Office Department, subject to the disapproval of Congress, would be a necessary step, accompanied by as precise as possible a calculation of the minimum payment required to obtain air-mail service on each particular route (without burdening other traffic), and the subtraction from this total of such minimum costs as exceed the value of the service as determined with reference to this demand schedule, to obtain an estimate of the amount and distribution of legitimate compensatory mail revenues. Such an estimated picture of the potential self-sustaining air-transport system is essential (*a*) to afford a standard by which the need for a support program may be determined and (*b*) to obtain an idea of the extent to which the abandonment of the "need-rate" program may cause temporary hardship, whether or not a continued support program of some other type proves desirable.

(3) If continued Government support of civil air transport appears desirable in the light of the above estimate, a program of administration should be developed designed to achieve with maximum efficiency the objectives of the support policy. It is possible that this step might involve no more (and no less) than the continuation on a modified or expanded basis of programs now in being — e.g., an improved over-all system of aids to air navigation, intensification of aeronautical research, etc. In the

foreign field, it might well involve continuation of direct payments to carriers, but certainly on a modified basis and without regulatory exclusion of unsubsidized carriers.

(4) The "need-rate" program of subsidization and the system of protective regulation now in effect should be abandoned. These steps are desirable regardless of the decisions reached with respect to the continued support of air transport, but should await the completion of the above studies in order that the possible temporary hardships that might be involved could be evaluated, and the merits of cushioning the shock by transitional measures might be weighed. It would, however, be desirable to announce at once that these steps would be taken in the near future, to put the possibly affected parties on notice of the contemplated policy changes and thus to minimize the hardships attendant upon contrary expectations. The type of economic regulatory program that should replace the present one has been suggested in Chapter VII.

APPENDIX

A Further Consideration of the Concept of Optimum Investment

In the discussion in the text of equilibrium output under pure competition, reference was made to a point of view suggested by "welfare" economics, according to which pure competition (defined in terms of infinite elasticity of the firm sales curve) must always result in optimum output of every commodity, and monopoly (defined in such a way as to include any departure from pure competition) in an equilibrium output at variance with the optimum. The following discussion will analyze briefly the line of argument on which this position might be based; in addition, the concept of optimum output embodied in this argument will be compared with that employed in the present text, and certain considerations favoring the adoption of the latter rather than the former as a working goal will be pointed out.

In particular, it will be argued that optimum investment as defined adequately in terms of the "welfare" approach is a concept the application of which involves much greater practical difficulties than are suggested by the typical exposition of the "welfare" viewpoint; indeed, that a consistent application of this optimum concept would involve making most policy decisions by means of working criteria which are to all intents and purposes incapable of being concretely defined by any practicable means. In this connection, it will be shown that an adequate formulation of the optimum concept of the "welfare" economists results in criticisms of the unregulated-market equilibrium which may apply to pure competition as well as to departures from it, and that the approval which might be accorded to the former type of market on the basis of "welfare" analysis would be made possible only by an indefensible concentration of attention on the equilibrium conditions from the point of view of the competitive firm rather than from the point of view of the industry (i.e., on the distribution of output among *firms* rather than among *products*). The term "product" is here used in the strict sense which implies perfect substitutability. It is thus *necessarily* identified neither with the firm nor with the "industry" as this latter term is loosely used (i.e., to cover a nonhomogeneous group of products). However, the "product" may be regarded as coextensive with the purely competitive industry, since perfect substitutability is postulated in this context.

The concept of optimum output espoused by "welfare" economists is frequently defined as meaning that level of output which can be sold at a price equal to its marginal cost, and it is on this definition of the optimum that an unqualified approval of pure competitive equilibrium might be based. Since under pure competition each firm maximizes profit by the equation of marginal cost to price (price being equal to marginal revenue), equilibrium output must be, according to the above definition, at the optimum level; and conversely, since under monopoly the firm cannot maximize profit by the equation of marginal cost to price (price being unequal to marginal revenue), equilibrium output cannot be at the optimum level.

Let us first examine the origins and sphere of applicability of the formulation of the "welfare" optimum in terms of the equality of price and marginal cost.

This definition of the optimum is derived directly as a corollary to the so-called marginal conditions of maximum welfare, a set of propositions defining (in part) the conditions under which no reallocation of units of factors or products among producing or consuming units in the economy would be possible that would make any individual in the economic system better off (i.e., put him in a preferred position) without at the same time making some other individual worse off (i.e., putting him in a less preferred position). With respect to any reallocation, the possibility of compensating any individual(s) made worse off out of the gains of any individual(s) made better off is taken into consideration; hence maximum welfare may also be defined as a position in which no reallocation would be possible for which the resulting gains (measured by the taxes that could be levied on those benefited and leave them exactly as well off as they were before the reallocation) would more than offset the resulting losses (measured by the payments or "bounties" that would have to be given to those made less well off to make them exactly as well off as they were before).

As applied to the determination of output of various products, the criterion of maximum welfare defined above is expressed in a recent work on "welfare" economics by the following marginal condition: "The marginal rate of substitution between any pair of products for any person consuming both must be the same as the marginal rate of transformation (for the community) between them."[1] The marginal rate of transformation (for the community) of any economic good X for any other such good Y denotes the amount of Y that would have to be sacrificed by the community in order to supply one additional unit of X. Similarly, the marginal rate of substitution (for any consumer) of any economic good X for any other such good Y denotes the amount of Y that this consumer would be willing to give up in order to obtain one more unit of X. It follows that if the marginal rate of substitution for any consumer of X for Y were not equal to the marginal rate of transformation of X for Y, it would be possible to make this consumer better off without making any other person in the community worse off. So far, there can be no doubt of the validity of this analysis; it is in its translation into observable market data that difficulties begin to arise.

In order that this condition shall be one of maximum rather than minimum welfare, it is of course necessary that the marginal rates of substitution shall at this point of equality be decreasing at a faster rate than the marginal rate of transformation (for the community). This requirement is one of the "second-order" conditions necessarily supplementing the marginal conditions of maximum welfare. In addition, it should be noted at this point that the marginal and second-order condi-

---

[1] M. W. Reder, *Studies in the Theory of Welfare Economics* (New York: Columbia University Press, 1947), p. 35.

tions are not intended to be sufficient in themselves to define a position of maximum welfare, since they apply only to relative outputs of a given set of products, and to the allocation of a given set of factor units; a complete definition of the conditions of maximum welfare requires that the "total" conditions also be taken into consideration; as Reder says,

> even if the second-order maximum conditions are also satisfied, the satisfaction of the marginal conditions is not sufficient to guarantee maximum welfare. For there is yet another set of conditions which must be satisfied in order that welfare be a maximum. Professor Hicks calls these conditions, the total conditions; they state, inter alia, that if welfare is to be a maximum, it must be impossible to increase welfare by producing a product not otherwise produced (or produced by only one firm); or by using a factor not otherwise used (or used by only one firm). Where welfare can be increased by such operations, the optimum position obviously is not determined uniquely by the marginal conditions; i.e., there is more than one maximum position and one of the maxima lies where the output (input) of a product (factor) by a firm and/or consumption of a product by a consumer is zero.[2]

It is immediately evident that a large number of very important economic decisions fall outside the competence of the marginal and second-order conditions, and into the category of choices between "relative maxima." Not only all decisions as to whether a product should or should not be produced, but also all those involving a choice between two outputs of the same commodity for which the marginal and second-order conditions are fulfilled, must be included in this category. This point is further elaborated below.

If (1) the marginal rate of substitution between any two commodities for any and all consumers of both may be taken to be equal to the ratio between their demand prices, and *if* (2) the marginal rate of transformation (for the community) between any two commodities may be taken to be equal to the ratio between their marginal costs, then it is clear that the above condition of maximum welfare would be fulfilled if the

---

[2] *Ibid.,* pp. 37–38.

output of every product were such that its demand price were equal to its marginal cost.

Condition (1) will be satisfied *provided* (*a*) that for any and all consumers of any product X demand price may be taken as equivalent to the marginal rate of substitution of this product for any other product, say A, selected as numeraire (i.e., that demand price is equal to the amount of A that would be given up by any consumer in order to obtain an additional unit of X), and (*b*) that every consumer seeks to maximize his own satisfaction (i.e., to satisfy his preferences to the fullest degree possible). In this case, it is evident that for any consumer the marginal rate of substitution between any product X and any other product Y must be equal to the ratio between their demand prices; for the marginal rate of substitution between X and Y must be equal for any consumer to the ratio between the marginal rate of substitution of X for A and the marginal rate of substitution of Y for A, otherwise the individual would seek to achieve a preferred position by demanding more of one product and less of the other (i.e., seeking to substitute the numeraire for the less preferred product and the more preferred product for the numeraire).

Condition (2) will be satisfied *provided* (*a*) that for the economic units with respect to which marginal cost is calculated marginal cost may be taken to equal marginal cost from the point of view of the community, and (*b*) that each product is being produced with maximum technical efficiency. From the point of view of any economic unit, the marginal cost of any product X may be defined as that amount of the numeraire A which must be sacrificed by that unit in order to produce an additional unit of X. If each product is being produced with maximum efficiency, then the ratio between the marginal costs of any two products X and Y from the point of view of the community must be equal to their marginal rate of transformation from the same point of view. This is true because maximum efficiency in production requires that the amount of X or Y produced per unit of A expended must be maximum; and this requirement implies that it must not be possible to produce more of Y per unit A by producing a unit of X and transforming it into Y. If, then (under the assumption of maximum efficiency) the marginal rate of transformation between any two products from the point of view of the community is equal to the ratio between their marginal costs from the same point of view, it is evident that this marginal rate of transformation will be equal to the ratio between the marginal costs of the products for any economic unit with respect to which the marginal costs of these products are equal to their marginal costs from the point of view of the community.

The argument in support of the definition of the "welfare" optimum as requiring the equation of demand price to marginal cost may also be expressed more directly in terms of the general maximum-welfare condition, as follows: If for any given output demand price may be taken to be equal to the tax that could be levied on each consumer of this product as a condition to supplying him with an additional unit of the product (i.e., the amount of tax that would leave him just as well off as he would have been had he not been supplied with this additional unit), and if the marginal cost of any given output may be taken to be equal to the payment necessary to compensate all members of the community made worse off by the sacrifice of the alternative product required to supply an additional unit of the product in question, then the production of any amount of product up to the point where demand price is just equal to marginal cost will increase welfare, since up to that point the algebraic sum of the compensating taxes and bounties involved in any increment of output would be positive (that is, the additional compensatory tax that could be levied on consumers supplied with an increment of output would be more than sufficient to cover the additional bounty necessary to compensate those made worse off as a result of supplying this increment).[3]

From this formulation of the optimum, practical recommendations are derived which afford dramatic contrasts with the actual workings of private enterprise. Thus, it is found to be desirable to operate all sorts of enterprises at substantial defi-

[3] *Ibid.*, p. 50.

cits, and to provide the services of railways, utilities, and the like to the public almost without charge.[4] In such instances it becomes strikingly evident that the equation of price to marginal cost is, as it stands, completely inadequate as a criterion for the determination of investment, since approval on this basis could be given to a virtually unlimited number of large projects whose total cost in terms of sacrificed alternatives would not be justified in terms of the total benefits received from them. It is, then, in general not enough to say without qualification that "that output should be produced which can be sold at a price which just covers its marginal cost." This point is, of course, recognized by the "welfare" economists themselves. In fact, it is generally recognized by these economists that only in certain limited circumstances may the price = marginal cost rule be employed as the *sole* working criterion of optimum output;[5] in all other cases, it is admitted that this rule must be supplemented by a broader investment criterion which takes explicitly into account not only those costs which are incurred as a result of the last unit of output, but all costs which are attributable to any amount of the output taken as a whole.

Indeed, the circumstances within which the price = marginal cost rule is an adequate working criterion for optimum output

[4] See, for example, Harold Hotelling, "The General Welfare in Relation to Problems of Taxation and of Railway and Utility Rates," *Econometrica*, VI, No. 3 (July 1938), pp. 260–261: "The efficient way to operate a bridge — and the same applies to a railroad or factory, if we neglect the small cost of an additional unit of product or of transportation — is to make it free to the public, so long at least as the use of it does not increase to a state of overcrowding. A free bridge costs no more to construct than a toll bridge, and costs less to operate; but society, which must pay the cost in some way or other, gets far more benefit from the bridge if it is free, since in this case it will be more used. Charging a toll, however small, causes some people to waste time and money in going around by longer but cheaper ways, and prevents others from crossing. . . . The *distribution* of wealth among members of the community is affected by the mode of payment adopted for the bridge, but not the total wealth, except that it is diminished by bridge tolls and other similar forms of excise."

[5] As has been suggested above, the applicability of the price = marginal cost rule even in these limited circumstances is conditional upon certain assumptions whose validity may by no means be taken for granted in any particular situation. This point is further elaborated at a later stage in this discussion.

are precisely those within which its application results in the recommendation of a *unique* level of output that *cannot* fail to conform to the broader "welfare" rule, which may be stated as follows: only those investments should be undertaken for which the resulting total benefit to the community (measured by the sum of the compensating taxes that could be levied on all those benefited and leave them just as well off as they were before) exceeds the resulting total sacrifice incurred by the community (measured by the sum of the payments that would have to be made to all those injured and leave them just as well off as they were before). Thus, the price = marginal cost rule, even if we accept the initial assumptions which are necessary for its validity, can *never* be regarded as an adequate *theoretical* expression of the criterion for optimum output; it must in general be qualified not only by the requirement that the average-revenue curve cut the marginal-cost curve from above at their point of equality, but also by the requirement that at this point the total compensatory tax shall exceed (or at least equal) the total compensatory bounties associated with this output. The requirement that the average-revenue curve shall cut the marginal-cost curve from above may, with the qualifications that have been indicated in the above discussion of the translation of the marginal conditions of maximum welfare into observable market data, be regarded as equivalent to the "second-order" condition which provides that the marginal rate of substitution for any consumer be decreasing at a faster rate than the marginal rate of transformation for the community. It does not in itself suffice to insure that total compensatory tax exceeds total compensatory bounties; its function is to insure that, *provided* total compensatory tax exceeds total compensatory bounties, the point of equality between price and marginal cost represents a maximum rather than a minimum value for this excess; in a situation where total compensatory tax was exceeded by total compensatory bounties, it would insure that *this* excess was a *minimum*.

Under the same assumptions that were found necessary to the formulation of the marginal maximum-"welfare" condition in terms of the equality of price and marginal cost, this broader criterion may be expressed as being equivalent to a requirement that the integral of the average-revenue curve (on our assumption equal to the total compensatory tax that could be levied on the consumers of any given output, or to the total revenue that could be obtained from its sale at perfectly discriminatory prices) shall exceed (or at least equal) the integral of the marginal-cost curve (on our assumption equal to the total compensatory bounties that would have to be paid to all those injured by the nonproduction of the sacrificed alternative product to leave them as well off as before). On the basis of our assumptions with regard to the marginal-cost and average-revenue curves, which require that these curves shall be *at any point* equal, respectively, to the marginal compensatory bounty (tax) payable to (by) those injured (benefited) by the production of the corresponding output, both of these curves have uniquely determined integrals, equal respectively to the total compensatory bounties and total compensatory tax payable to (by) those injured (benefited) by the production of the corresponding output. This is true because for the first unit of output it is necessary in both cases that the marginal be equal to the total quantity; thus not only the shape but the absolute level of the total curve may be determined by reference to the appropriate marginal curve. It will also be noted that the total-cost curve which is appropriate here is that which excludes not only true rents from the point of view of the product in question, but also any excess payments to factors that arise from an increase in the price of the alternative product as factor units are drawn from this use into the use in question, since neither of these types of excess payment enters at any point into marginal compensatory bounties necessary to compensate additional factor units.

Under what conditions, then, would it be impossible for the price-marginal cost rule to produce results in conflict with this broader criterion? It is evident that the rule *could* produce such results only if at least one point in the range of output under consideration marginal cost has exceeded demand price. Thus it may be said that in circumstances where it is known that at no point in the range of output under consideration does marginal cost exceed demand price, the price $=$ marginal cost rule may, *for this range of output,* be taken as an adequate working criterion for output determination. An example of such a circumstance would be the determination of the number of passengers to be served on a particular train trip, all other decisions pertinent to the trip (including the number of cars to be run) having already been made. In this case, total cost would be almost parallel to the x-axis (i.e., rising at a very slow rate), marginal cost would be parallel to the x-axis (at a level not far above it), and the welfare-maximizing output would be that at which all passengers would be carried who would be willing to pay the small amount of additional cost that could be avoided if they were not carried. Similarly, the determination of the number of persons to be allowed to cross a bridge that has already been built would provide such an example; in this instance, total cost might well be perfectly constant, marginal cost coincident with the x-axis, and the welfare-maximizing output that at which all persons cross the bridge who do not require to be paid to take the trouble. This is not, of course, to say that the rule *will* result in an output in conflict with the broader principle for any range of output within which marginal cost has at any point exceeded demand price, but only that for any such range of output it is necessary to consider, in the actual determination of optimum investment, not only demand price and marginal cost in the neighborhood of the point where they are equal, but also (1) the total cost associated with any given level of output and (2) the total discriminatory revenue that could be obtained from its sale.

The true practical limitations of the price $=$ marginal cost rule in output determination now become evident; it becomes clear that these limits are not adequately expressed either (1) by saying that the rule must be supplemented in making decisions whether or not to produce any particular product or (2) by saying that it must be supplemented in making decisions whether or not to undertake any "large indivisible lump" of investment.

The inadequacy of the former expression may be shown by a consideration of the treatment that might be given on this basis to the problem of output determination in the railway field. To deal with this problem, it might be thought to be sufficient to say that that amount of transportation should be supplied which can be sold at a price just equal to its marginal cost, provided only that the railway could at *some* level of output be supported by perfectly discriminatory pricing, or, *a fortiori,* if it could be supported at some level of output without discrimination. (The latter condition may be accepted as a more than adequate demonstration that the former would be true, since perfectly discriminatory revenue must be at least equal to and most probably will be larger than nondiscriminatory revenue.) It will be seen that the application of this treatment will necessarily result in an output consistent with the broader "welfare" criterion only if for the whole range of output between that level at which it is known that the railway can be supported by discriminatory (or nondiscriminatory) pricing and the level at which demand price is just equal to marginal cost the marginal-cost curve lies below the demand curve. Since for any significant range of increase in railway output it can be expected that the marginal-cost curve will be characterized by a series of "peaks" (reflecting, for example, the filling to capacity of one passenger car and the addition of a second), and that for any of these "peaks" demand price may well be insufficient to cover marginal cost (that is, the marginal passenger may not move at a price high enough to cover the added cost attributable to him), it is evident that the range of output for which the price = marginal cost rule may be safely applied without further investigation will be narrow indeed, and that the application of the above treatment might well result in enormous extravagances of unjustified investment.

We proceed, then, to consider the second formulation of the limitations of the price = marginal cost rule, which would meet the objections to the first formulation in so far as they are based on the fact that it ignores "large" increments of investment incurred at discrete intervals in the expansion of output of a product whose production at *some* level of output may be regarded as justified. In the first place, there arises the question of how "large" an investment "lump" has to be before it gives rise to the need for a working criterion supplemental to the price = marginal cost rule. The correct answer to this crucial question can only be given in terms of our own formulation of the rule's limitations — that is, the "lump" must be only large enough to give rise to a cost increment in excess of demand price — and this fact in itself indicates the essentially vague and thus unsatisfactory character of the second formulation in terms of an indeterminate "largeness."

In the second place, the behavior of the marginal-cost curve cannot be entirely explained in terms of factor "lumpiness"; that is, it is not possible to assume that the marginal cost of any product will be constant merely because there are "no significant factor indivisibilities." If this *could* be assumed, then it would follow that for any product the production of which involved no such indivisibilities the price = marginal cost rule (as modified, of course, by the requirement that the average-revenue curve shall cut the marginal-cost curve from above) could be applied without further investigation; it could be said that for any such product that output should be produced for which demand price was just equal to marginal cost, for with constant marginal cost it would obviously be the case that at no level of output less than that for which demand price was just equal to marginal cost would marginal cost be in excess of demand price. However, since there are other causes besides factor indivisibilities that may result in nonconstant marginal costs for any given product, it is not possible to assume that the absence of such indivisibilities will result in constant marginal costs.

Consider, for example, the question of the determination of output for a product in the production of which there are no significant factor indivisibilities, but the "envelope" curve describing the long-run minimum average cost for the firm is nevertheless U-shaped.[6] It is obviously not enough to say that the product in question should be produced up to the point where demand price is just equal to marginal cost, even though

---

[6] As Professor Chamberlin has shown, there is no necessity to postulate factor indivisibilities in order to arrive at a U-shaped long-run cost curve for the individual firm. E. H. Chamberlin, "Proportionality, Divisibility and Economies of Scale," *Quarterly Journal of Economics*, LXII, No. 2 (February 1948), pp. 229–262.

there are no indivisibilities, since it cannot be assumed that the marginal-cost curve lies below the demand curve throughout its range; thus the application of the unmodified rule might well result in a decision in conflict with the broader "welfare" criterion, *even though it had been ascertained by some means that some output of this product could be sold under perfect discrimination for a total revenue in excess of (or just equal to) its total cost.* Such a situation would arise, for example, where demand is known to be sufficient to support one firm producing this product at a total discriminatory revenue equal to or in excess of total cost, but the maximum output for which demand price is just equal to marginal cost falls within a range for which production could be most efficiently carried on by two firms.

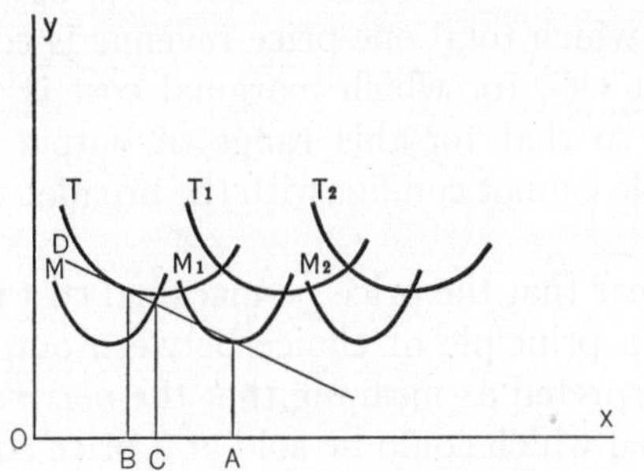

This situation is diagrammatically represented in Fig. 4, where x = output and y = price or cost. Line D represents market demand. Curves T, T_1, and T_2 represent long-run average transfer cost with one, two, and three firms, respectively. Curves M, M_1, and M_2 represent long-run marginal transfer cost with one, two, and three firms respectively. Long-run average transfer cost for the product on the assumption of a variable number of firms is represented for any given output by the fixed-number-of-firms average-cost curve $(T, T_1, \ldots, T_n)$ which is for this output at the lowest level. Long-run marginal transfer cost for the product on the same assumption is represented for any given output by the fixed-number-of-firms marginal-cost curve $(M, M_1, \ldots, M_n)$, which is for this output at the lowest level. At output OA, which is the maximum for which demand price is equal to marginal cost, it might well be that the integral of the demand curve would be smaller than total cost, even though output *OB* of this product could be sold for a total *nondiscriminatory* revenue equal to its total cost. It will be noted that the price = marginal cost rule would also be satisfied at output *OC*, and that for *this* output its application could not, under the cost and demand conditions here represented, result in an output in conflict with the broader criterion. This condition is brought about by the fact that the envelope curve T showing long-run average cost for one firm has been drawn as "smooth" rather than "scalloped," indicating that no significant indivisibilities are present which would result in "scallops." Under this assumption, it may be postulated that the firm marginal-cost curve proceeds smoothly upward between output *OB*, for which total one-price revenue is equal to total cost, and output *OC*, for which marginal cost is just equal to demand price, so that for this range of output the price = marginal cost rule cannot conflict with the broader welfare criterion.

However, it is quite clear that the price = marginal cost rule does not in itself afford a principle of choice between outputs *OC* and *OA;* if it is interpreted as meaning that the *maximum* output should be produced which could be sold at a price equal to marginal cost, it would result in the production of *OA*, where the total condition might well be violated.

A similar situation may also exist in the case of the determination of railway output discussed above. Here, it might well be the case that the addition of a new investment increment would be preceded by a gradual rise in marginal cost reflecting more intensive "utilization" of the former "fixed" elements, so that there would be in the course of output expansion not one but many points where the average-revenue curve cuts the marginal-cost curve from above. Again, the essential point is that the price = marginal cost rule does not in itself afford any principle of choice between these several outputs, and requires as a practical matter to be supplemented by a knowledge for all of these alternative outputs of the actual discriminatory revenue as well as the total cost involved in their sale. We are not, of course, here concerned with the type of problem referred to above, where all decisions relating to the supply of railway services with the single exception of how many persons should be allowed to make a particular train trip were assumed to have been made. On that assumption, it could be justifiably postulated that there would be very little variation in total cost associated with the number of persons accommodated, and that marginal cost would remain constant near zero regardless of how many or how few made the trip. We are here dealing with the over-all determination of the output of railway services, where the only decision which may be regarded as having been made is that *some* such service shall be made available. In this case, the only part of cost which may be regarded as constant is that associated with the furnishing of the "some" amount of service which has been found (by some means) to be desirable; and it is evident that any significant expansion of output will be accompanied by increases in total cost both large and small, that the marginal-cost curve will rise at discrete intervals, but probably follow a generally decreasing course for a relatively large range of output, and that there may be not one but many separate levels of output at which the average-revenue curve will cut the marginal-cost curve from above.

It would seem, on the basis of the above analysis, that the practical significance of the price = marginal cost rule in the actual determination of optimum distribution of output among products would be relatively small. First of all, it is not possible in most cases to determine by means of this rule whether or not any product should be produced at all; the mere fact that some output of this product could be sold at a price equal to its marginal cost necessarily means that this output should be produced *only* where (as in the case of constant or steadily increasing costs beginning at output just in excess of zero) it is known that for *all* outputs up to this level demand price is in excess of marginal cost.

Second, it is in most cases not possible to determine by means of this rule what level of output of any given product should be produced provided only that it is desirable to produce *some* of this product; since any significant amount of expansion in the output of any product will normally involve successive rises and falls in the long-run marginal-cost curve, as successive increments of investment are utilized beyond the point of maximum technical efficiency and new increments are added, or as successive firms expand beyond the minimum point on the envelope curve and new ones are added, there may be expected to be not one but more than one point beyond that level of output which has been found (by some means) to be desirable which will satisfy the requirement that price shall be equal to marginal cost; it cannot be assumed that the maximum concept for which the rule applies will be an "optimum" one merely because *some* output of the product in question can be sold at a total discriminatory revenue in excess of total cost; and the choice between these various output levels consistent with the rule must be made on the basis of an actual knowledge of the total discriminatory revenue and total cost associated with their sale. (More precisely, it is necessary to know only the total cost and total discriminatory revenue associated with the range of output between that level of output for which it is (by some means) known that total discriminatory revenue is equal to or in excess of total cost and the various levels of output which satisfy the price = marginal cost rule.)

Finally, it is clear that the practical limitations of the rule in the determination of optimum output of a product for which it has been decided that some output is desirable cannot be adequately expressed in terms of "large lumps" of investment or of "factor indivisibilities"; in so far as the successive rises and falls in marginal cost are due to the "overutilization" of indivisible investment units and the addition of new units, the "lumps" must be only "large" enough to give rise to marginal costs at some point in excess of demand price; in so far as they are due to the "overexpansion" of individual firms and the addition of new firms, they need not reflect "lumpiness" or "indivisibility" at all.

It appears, then, that even if we accept the validity of the price = marginal cost rule as an accurate translation into observable market data of the marginal condition of maximum welfare that governs the determination of optimum outputs of various products, the decisions that can be made on the basis of this rule alone are of minor practical significance; and that most important investment decisions would have to be made by means of an actual comparison between total discriminatory revenue and total cost. Before going on to examine in more detail the assumptions on which the validity of the price = marginal cost rule must be based, we shall take up the question whether or not the rule, on the assumption that it is valid, may legitimately be used as a basis for unqualified approval of the equilibrium output of an industry producing under conditions of pure competition. If this proposition were found to be true, then it might be said that in at least one sense the "welfare" analysis had provided us with a readily usable policy guide, namely, that a purely competitive industry should be let alone.

Unfortunately, however, it appears that the distinction between pure competition (defined as a condition under which the sales curve of the firm is infinitely elastic) and monopoly (defined so as to include all departures from pure competition) affords no easy means for judging whether a given market will perform in an optimum manner from the "welfare" point of view; that departures from the "welfare" optimum may occur under pure competition as well as monopoly; and that the approval which might be given to pure competition on the basis of "welfare" analysis would arise from concentration of attention on the conditions of equilibrium from the point of view of the firm rather than from that of the industry (i.e., on the distribution of output among firms rather than among products). The ensuing discussion of the assumptions underlying the validity of the price = marginal cost rule will serve to throw further doubt on the significance of the monopoly-competition distinction as a basis for judgment of economic performance, since it is only within the framework of these assumptions that this distinction has even the limited validity which, we shall find, can be assigned to it from a "welfare" point of view.

An assertion that under conditions of pure competition output is always at the optimum level might be based on the fact that under these conditions the maximization of profit by individual firms involves the production by each of a quantity of product whose marginal cost is equal to its demand price. Since we are considering here the level of output actually produced by functioning competitive firms and industries, it is assured that both for the firm and for the industry the equilibrium level of output conforms to the condition that total cost shall not exceed total compensatory tax (which will, of course, never be less than total revenue). However, although this proposition must always be true of the competitive firm, it is by no means always true of the competitive industry. The general condition of equilibrium for competitive industrial output is not that demand price shall equal marginal cost to the industry, but that demand price shall equal supply price, which is always equal to average cost to the industry, including rent. The latter is in turn equal to industrial marginal cost, excluding rent, only in circumstances where there are no economies or diseconomies of large-scale industry. Thus it is only in such circumstances that the competitive equilibrium output of any product conforms to the price = marginal cost rule, and any unqualified approval of pure competitive output on "welfare" grounds must rest on a concentration of attention on the firm rather than the industrial equilibrium output.

It is furthermore evident that it is *industrial* rather than *firm* equilibrium which should hold the center of the stage, since it is the allocation of resources among various products, rather than among various firms, that is the central problem involved in the determination of optimum output. Equality between price and marginal cost from the point of view of the *competitive* firm obviously provides no basis for the judgment of the output of any particular product, since for the competitive firm price will be equal to marginal cost regardless of how much or how little of the product is produced.

In this connection, it is interesting to note that if we concentrate our attention on the distribution of output among firms, we find not only that competitive output is always at the "welfare"-maximizing level, but also that (with industrial equilibrium) its production is always a matter of indifference from the "welfare" point of view — i.e., that its contribution to "welfare" is maximized at zero. This is true because from the point of view of the competitive firm demand is infinitely elastic, and consequently the total discriminatory revenue available for any output is always just equal to the total (non-discriminatory) revenue. Since, at equilibrium, total revenue is in turn just equal to total cost, the net contribution to "welfare" is zero, and the existence of any competitive firm is a matter of indifference.

Similar conclusions result if we inquire whether or not conditions of pure competition insure (*a*) that any product will be produced the total cost of which can at any level of output be covered by perfectly discriminatory pricing or (*b*) that any firm will be established which could by perfectly discriminatory pricing cover its total costs. It is obvious that under pure competition only those products will be produced, and only those firms established, whose total cost can be covered by total revenue at some one price, since no discrimination is ever possible with pure competition. (It is, therefore, quite wrong to suppose that failure to produce any product which could be financed by perfect discrimination but not by uniform pricing is in any way attributable to the absence of pure competition. Such products would, in fact, be much more likely to be produced under conditions of monopoly, where some discrimination may be feasible.) These conclusions can be avoided only by concentrating attention on the competitive *firm;* from this point of view, it can be said that any firm will be established whose total costs can be covered by the total discriminatory revenue available from its output, because given the perfectly elastic demand curve there can be no difference at any output between the total one-price revenue and the total discriminatory revenue.

We turn now to a more detailed consideration of the validity of the price $=$ marginal cost rule as a practical index for the maximization of welfare. This validity, as has been suggested, rests on two assumptions: (*a*) that demand price for any output is for each consumer of this output equal to the amount of the numeraire that he would be willing to sacrifice in order to be supplied with the last additional unit of this product (that is, to the tax that could be levied on each consumer supplied with any unit of this output and leave him just as well off as if he had not been supplied with it); and (*b*) that marginal cost from the point of view of the economic unit under consideration is for any output equal to marginal cost from the point of view of the community (that is, to the bounties that would have to be paid to all members of the community injured by the nonproduction of the sacrificed alternative output and leave them just as well off as if it had been produced).

The problem is here considerably simplified by ignoring benefits and injuries to persons other than the producers and consumers of the products whose output is affected. If these are taken into consideration, the translation of the "welfare" criterion into observable market data becomes even more difficult.

Since the price = marginal cost rule and the broader rule as well do not deal specifically with benefits to factor owners derived from the output in question, but only with the compensatory tax available from the *consumers* of this output, it might be thought that only *consumer* benefits are taken into consideration on the "credit" side, whereas on the "debit," or cost, side, injuries to producers as well are included. This, however, is not the case. The compensatory tax available from the consumers of the given output, which is equal to the total discriminatory revenue available from its sale, represents the total benefit available for distribution among the consumers and producers of this output, and its actual distribution is irrelevant to the problem under consideration. The "net benefit" to producers *and* consumers of this output is equal to the excess of this total over the total benefit available to producers and consumers of the sacrificed alternative product; if in the use in question perfect discrimination were actually practiced, this "net benefit" would accrue entirely to the factor owners; if, on the other hand, the incomes received by the factor owners in this use were precisely equal to the total benefit available in the alternative use, the "net benefit" would accrue entirely to the consumers.

(*a*) Although it is logically conceivable that the demand price for any given output of some product might represent the marginal compensatory tax that could be levied on each consumer of this output and leave him just as well off as he was before, it appears that this proposition can by no means be taken for granted in any particular case.

The relation between demand price and marginal compensatory tax (= marginal discriminatory revenue) in fact depends upon the particular structure of demand in the market under consideration. Where demand is infinitely elastic, demand price of course coincides for every output with marginal discriminatory revenue (and also with marginal revenue), just as total (one-price) revenue coincides with total discriminatory revenue for every output; however, this case is of trivial practical significance; since (except as a fiction in the mind of a pure competitor) it is inconceivable that the demand for any product should be infinitely elastic throughout, and highly improbable that it should be infinitely elastic over any significant range of output.

In the ordinary case of the demand curve that slopes downward to the right, the relation between demand price and marginal discriminatory revenue depends on the nature of the indivual demands that are summed up in the market demand curve. In general, demand price may for any range of output be taken to be equal to marginal discriminatory revenue *only if within this range the amount of the additional purchases induced by any lowering of price is unaffected by other transactions made at higher prices,* for only in this case could a perfectly discriminating monopolist in fact make the additional sales indicated by the demand curve for any given demand price (that is, only in this event does the area under the demand curve indicate total discriminatory revenue).

In the absence of concrete evidence to the contrary, it would seem reasonable to presume that in any particular market this condition would not be fulfilled, since at least some of the additional purchases that the demand curve indicates would be called forth at a lower price may ordinarily be expected to be those of purchasers who are also ready to make some (smaller) purchase at a higher price; and the additional purchases attributable to such buyers would not be as large as would be indicated by the demand curve if they had in fact to buy a portion of their total purchase at a higher price. Indeed, in some markets it is possible that any transaction at any given price would rule out any purchases of additional amounts at any lower price; this would be true, for example, where all the individual demands making up the market demand curve were of unit elasticity.[7] In such a market, the total compensatory tax available for any output would be equal to the total (one-price) revenue available for that output; the marginal compensatory tax would be equal to marginal revenue; and average revenue would hence exceed marginal compensatory tax by an amount equal to the excess of average over marginal revenue.

It is thus evident that marginal compensatory tax may vary, according to the structure of demand, between a maximum value equal to demand price and a minimum equal to marginal revenue; therefore it is certainly not defensible to assume in any given market that demand price is actually equal to marginal compensatory tax. Thus the practical implementation of the principle supposed to be embodied in the price = marginal cost rule becomes enormously more difficult; it becomes necessary either to estimate a priori the value of the marginal compensatory tax for any given output, or to try to determine it experimentally, a procedure which will in most cases not be feasible because of the practical impossibility of perfect discrimination.

(*b*) Similarly, although it is logically conceivable that marginal cost for any given output of some product might represent its marginal cost from the point of view of the community (i.e., the bounties that would have to be paid to the consumers and consumers of the sacrificed alternative product to leave them as well off as they were before), it appears that this proposition can by no means be taken for granted in any particular case.

From the point of view of any given product, marginal cost may be defined as the outlay necessary to attract the factors that must be employed to produce the marginal unit of output. In general, this outlay will for each factor unit be equal to the income that it could obtain in the next best alternative employ-

---

[7] See Oskar Morgenstern, "Demand Theory Reconsidered," *Quarterly Journal of Economics*, LXII, No. 2 (February 1948), pp. 170–171.

ment, an amount which will in turn be equal to its marginal revenue product in this alternative employment (that is, to the market value of the product attributable to this factor unit in this alternative employment as measured by the difference between the market values of the total outputs (total revenues) with and without the employment of this factor unit). If, then, the difference between the total revenues received from the sale of the alternative product with and without the employment of this factor unit may be taken to be equal to the bounties that would have to be paid to the producers and consumers of the sacrificed alternative output to make them as well off as before, marginal cost may for the product in question be taken to equal marginal cost from the point of view of the community.

This proposition and the ensuing analysis hold true in all cases where the maximizing unit is coextensive with the product — that is, where there is only one firm producing the commodity. If there is more than one firm producing the commodity, the marginal revenue product of the factor to the firm will exceed its marginal revenue product from the point of view of the commodity, since the addition (subtraction) of the factor to (from) this firm will decrease (increase) the value of the output of the other firm or firms producing the same commodity. Thus under pure competition the marginal revenue product of the factor to the firm (which determines factor income) exceeds its marginal revenue product from the point of view of the industry to the extent that average revenue to the industry exceeds marginal revenue to the industry. If the alternative employment from which a factor unit is drawn is a purely competitive industry, the outlay necessary to attract it will represent the sum of the bounties necessary to compensate both producers and consumers of the sacrificed alternative product *if the average revenue curve for this product may be taken to be the derivative of the total compensatory tax curve* — i.e., that curve which represents the maximum tax that could be levied on consumers furnished with various amounts of the product and leave them just as well off as they were without it. The difficulties that arise in this connection have been discussed above.

Since marginal cost from the point of view of the product in question must necessarily be equal to the alternative incomes available to the factor units employed in the production of the marginal unit of output, it may also be taken to be just equal to the amount of the bounties necessary to make these factor units as well off as they would have been had this marginal unit of output not been produced. The question, then, becomes one of whether it would be necessary to pay any bounties to the consumers of the sacrificed alternative output to make *them* as well off as before — that is, whether they are just as well off without purchasing the sacrificed alternative output. It is evident that this would be the case only if the total income saved by them in not purchasing the sacrificed output, an amount equal to the difference between the total revenues ($=$ their total expenditures) received from the sale of the old (larger) and the new (smaller) levels of output, were precisely equal to *the amount of the compensatory tax that could be levied on them in return for being supplied with the amount of output sacrificed.* If the income saved by these consumers were less than the maximum amount that they would pay in order to consume the sacrificed alternative product, then the sacrifice of this product without additional compensation would leave them worse off than before; a bounty equal to the difference between the total income saved and the total compensatory tax would have to be paid to them to make them as well off as before; and the marginal cost of the product under consideration would be less than its marginal cost to the community by an amount equal to this consumers' bounty.

Under what circumstances would it be true that the difference between the total revenues received from the sale of the two levels of output would be equal to the amount of the compensatory tax that could be levied on the consumers of the sacrificed output (an amount equal to the total revenue available from its sale under conditions of perfect discrimination)? (1) If the demand for the alternative product were infinitely elastic, then this would certainly be true, since total revenue is in this case for any given output always equal to total compensatory tax. This case is of minor practical importance. (2) If all the individual demands making up the market demand curve for the alternative product were of unit elasticity, then total revenue would also be equal to total compensatory tax, and the above condition would hold. It appears probable that this case also is of minor practical importance. At any rate, it seems quite clear that it *cannot* be assumed in any particular case that the marginal cost of any product is equal to its marginal cost from the point of view of the community; on the contrary, the latter quantity, like the marginal compensatory tax, is to all intents and purposes not translatable into observable market data.

We conclude, then, (*a*) that conformity with the price = marginal cost rule, even within the limited sphere for which we have found it to be an adequate criterion for the determination of "welfare"-maximizing output (if the assumptions underlying its validity are accepted), can in no case be taken to be sufficient evidence that output is at a "welfare"-maximizing level; and (*b*) that the actual level of output that would maximize "welfare" cannot be determined by any practicable means. Since the broader "welfare" criterion (which must, as we have seen, be used for most important investment decisions) depends for its validity on precisely the same basic assumptions as the price = marginal cost rule, the same conclusions apply with respect to it.

Finally, since the proposition that pure competitive output is always at the "welfare"-maximizing level depends for its validity (even where there are no economies or diseconomies of large-scale industry) on the acceptance of the price = marginal cost rule, our case against this proposition is now complete; both the price = marginal cost rule and the condition of pure competition are found to be entirely unreliable as indicators of "welfare"-maximizing output.

Thus we have found that all three practical guides suggested by the "welfare" analysis for the judgment of economic performance and for the determination of economic policy are defective for the purpose intended, and must logically be replaced by criteria that are in practice incapable of use.

As compared with a consistent and logical formulation of the "welfare" optimum, then, the major advantage that can be claimed for the "unconditional-optimum" concept suggested in this study is this: that it offers a guide for the judgment of economic performance and for the determination of economic policy which involves the allocation of productive resources in accordance with the maximization of productivity in terms of economic "benefits" *in so far as these "benefits" may be determined by the use of observable market data* (and in so far as this allocation can be achieved without recourse to methods of factor distribution other than the inducements provided by relative incomes; this point is taken up at a later stage). It is readily admitted that this concept cannot compete with the "welfare" economists' optimum on the latter's own ground; there seems to be a perfectly defensible sense in which the achievement of our "unconditional optimum" will not bring about the maximization of economic "welfare." However, since market values are in fact the only objective indexes of benefits that are available for use, it may be considered proper to formulate guides for policy based on them even though it is realized that they are only rough approximations of the actual benefits involved. It is submitted that the faults of our concept from the "welfare" point of view are largely the results of the necessary imperfections of the price system as an indicator of relative benefits to consumers, combined with the practical necessity of using this indicator if any workable scheme of resource allocation in accordance with consumer demand is to be devised.

It should be noted that a strong case can be made for the view that even a logically consistent formulation of the "welfare" optimum, if it could be applied in practice, would not result in the maximization of "welfare" unless the marginal utility of income were the same for every member of the community. From this point of view, the formulation of completely valid "welfare" guides would involve not only the modifications of the usual formulations of policy rules that have been indicated in the text, but also in every particular instance the evaluation of "bounties" or "taxes" payable to or paid by any individual producer or consumer in terms of his own particular valuation of income. If this is true, then the complete uselessness of the "welfare" criteria in actual practice becomes more than ever evident.

Thus, whereas the "welfare" analysis consistently employs total discriminatory revenue as a measure of the benefits derived from any given output, our own treatment in general employs total (one-price) revenue in this capacity. In considering the desirability of any given output, the "welfare" analysis involves essentially the comparison of the total discriminatory revenue that could be obtained from the sale of this output with the total discriminatory revenue that could be obtained from the sale of the sacrificed alternative product;[8] our own concept involves the comparison of the total (one-price) revenue that could be obtained from the sale of the output in question (an amount which we term "the maximum that consumers are willing to pay") with the "necessary cost" of this output. The "necessary cost" may be taken to be equal to the total (one-price) revenue obtainable from the sale of the sacrificed alternative product with the following exception: that "necessary cost" as we have calculated it will exceed this revenue by the total amount of any excess of payments to factor units attracted to the use in question over the market value of sacrificed alternative output which arises from an increase in the price of the alternative product as its output is decreased. This type of excess payment is not a true rent, since it does not represent a difference in the payment of any given factor unit in the use

[8] As we have seen, the formulation of the welfare criterion in terms of the excess of total discriminatory revenue over total cost is valid only if total cost represents the total compensatory bounties that would have to be paid to the producers and consumers of the sacrificed alternative product and leave them as well off as before — that is, where the consumers of the alternative product require no compensation in addition to the income that they save by not purchasing the sacrificed product. Since total cost must be equal to the total (one-price) revenue obtainable from the sale of the sacrificed product, and also to the compensation required by the producers of the sacrificed alternative product to make them as well off as before, and since the additional bounties required to compensate consumers must be equal to the difference between the total (one-price) revenue obtainable from the sale of the sacrificed alternative product and the total discriminatory revenue obtainable from its sale, the sum of the compensatory bounties must in any case be equal to the total discriminatory revenue obtainable from the sale of the sacrificed alternative output.

in question over its revenue productivity in the use from which it is drawn.

Our definition of "necessary costs" in such a way as to permit the inclusion of some payments in excess of the market value of the sacrificed output may be defended on the ground that were such payments excluded, even though they are not true rents, the achievement of the "unconditional optimum" would involve a forced distribution of factor units by some means other than the inducements of relative income payments. In this sense, however, our "unconditional optimum" may be said to be "conditional" — it is based on a definition of "necessary costs" that takes as an unalterable condition the distribution of factors among various uses by means of income inducements.

Further, it has been pointed out that our own rule, as opposed to the "welfare" criterion, is based on a definition of economic benefits (i.e., "the maximum that consumers are willing to pay") which applies generally only within the framework of a one-price system. In view of the practical necessity of such a system in most cases, and in view of the net disadvantage to certain classes of consumers that results in most cases from a discriminatory price system, the use of this definition in the actual determination of output can be defended on both practical and theoretical grounds, provided that exceptions are made in cases where (a) discrimination is feasible in practice, so that an objective indication of discriminatory value is in fact available, and (b) where no net disadvantage to any class of consumer is involved in the existence of a discriminatory price system.

It is of course true that the use of potential discriminatory revenue as a measure of consumers' benefits does not logically involve the practice of discriminatory pricing; however, the estimation of discriminatory revenue without discrimination in practice must in fact be rejected as involving the use of unverified and nonobjective criteria. What is being sought is an objective measure; for this purpose, we may reasonably choose one-price valuations partly on the ground (a) that they are in general the only available objective measures, and partly on the ground (*b*) that the discriminatory practice necessarily involved in the actual determination of discriminatory revenue results in general in a net disadvantage to certain classes of consumers as compared with a nondiscriminatory price system. Thus exceptions must be made in cases where (*a*) and (*b*) do not apply, and perhaps also where the *advantages* that may accrue to certain classes of consumers may be found to outweigh the disadvantages to others.

For example, such an exception would clearly be in order in the case of a railway which, although it could at no uniform rate earn a total revenue equal to its total cost (excluding rent), could be supported by a feasible system of discrimination. For in this event, (*a*) there exists an objective indication that the maximum which consumers are willing to pay for the services of the railway is larger than the total necessary cost involved, even though total (one-price) revenue is not; and (*b*) it being assumed that no restriction such as might arise from protective regulation exists that compels any class of consumer to use the railway rather than any alternative means of transport, and that the degree of discrimination is no larger than necessary to maintain the railway at a self-supporting level, it may be said that every class of consumer is better off under a discriminatory price system than it would be were the discrimination not practiced and the railway service not available. A similar argument would apply where the increase in traffic made possible by a discriminatory as compared with a uniform system of pricing would bring about reductions in average cost such that rates to all classes of shippers could be lowered.

Discrimination is sometimes condemned on the ground that it results in a "misallocation of product" among consumers, in that each unit of product sold does not necessarily go to that individual who values it most (is willing to pay the highest price for it). However, it is only in the event that this consumer could, in the absence of discrimination, be supplied with this unit of product at a price which he would be willing to pay that he can be said to be harmed by the existence of discrimination. To the extent that discrimination (*a*) is necessary to finance the production of any good, or (*b*) to bring about a volume of sales that makes possible a reduction of prices charged to all classes of consumers, it cannot be said to result in a net disadvantage to any class of buyer. Although "misallocation" in the above sense still persists, its correction by means of a uniform system of pricing would result in every class of consumer being worse off than with discrimination, that is, (*a*) the product would become unavailable to all or (*b*) the necessary price payable by every buyer would be higher. In either case, all those buyers who were excluded from the market under discrimination would still be excluded in the absence of discrimination, and the exclusion of additional consumers which would result from a uniform price system would represent a net loss to them with no compensating benefit to others.

LIST OF CASES

American Export Airlines, Inc., Trans-Atlantic Service, 2 C.A.B. 16 (1940), 120 ff., 125, 127, 254

American Export Lines, Control of American Export Airlines, 3 C.A.B. 619 (1942), 255

American Overseas Airlines, Inc., *et al.*, South Atlantic Routes, 7 C.A.B. 285 (1946), 173

American President Lines, *et al.*, Petition, 7 C.A.B. 799 (1947), 255

Braniff Airways, Inc., Mail Rates, 1 C.A.A. 353 (1939), 303

Braniff Airways, Inc., *et al.*, Memphis–Oklahoma City–El Paso Service, 6 C.A.B. 169 (1944), 244, 246, 250

Canadian Colonial Airways, Ltd., Permit to foreign air carrier, 3 C.A.B. 50 (1941), 131

Caribbean-Atlantic Airlines, Inc., Puerto Rican Operations, 3 C.A.B. 717 (1942), 131

Clark Common Carrier Application, 1 M.C.C. 445 (1937), 120

Colonial Airlines, Inc., *et al.*, Atlantic Seaboard Operation (Supplemental Opinion), 4 C.A.B. 552 (1944), 117, 118, 121, 122, 126, 128, 171, 173, 248

Colonial Airlines, Inc., *et al.*, Washington-Ottawa-Montreal Service, 6 C.A.B. 481 (1945), 144, 248

Continental Air Lines, Inc., *et al.*, Additional Air Service in Texas, 4 C.A.B. 215 (1943), 144

Continental Air Lines, Inc., *et al.*, Denver–Kansas City Service, 4 C.A.B. 1 (1942), 128, 174, 247 ff., 250

Continental Air Lines, Inc., *et al.*, Mandatory Route, 1 C.A.A. 88 (1939), 173

Continental Air Lines, Inc., Roswell-Hobbs-Carlsbad Operation, 1 C.A.A. 598 (1940), 110

Continental Air Lines, Inc., *et al.*, Texas Air Service (Supplemental Opinion), 4 C.A.B. 478 (1943), 112

Delta Air Corporation, *et al.*, Additional Service to Atlanta and Birmingham, 2 C.A.B. 447 (1941), 171 ff., 173

Eastern Air Lines, Inc., *et al.*, Additional Washington Service, 4 C.A.B. 325 (1943), 114

Eastern Air Lines, Inc., *et al.*, Great Lakes to Florida Service, 6 C.A.B. 429 (1945), 164, 172, 251